OCCUPATIONAL THERAPY AND THE OLDER ADULT

A Clinical Manual

Aspen Series in Occupational Therapy
Rhona Reiss Zukas, MOT, OTR, FAOTA, Series Editor
Assistant Dean
School of Occupational Therapy
Texas Woman's University
Dallas, Texas

Early Occupational Therapy Intervention: Neonates to Three Years
Caryl J. Semmler and Jan G. Hunter

Quick Reference to Occupational Therapy
Kathlyn L. Reed

OCCUPATIONAL THERAPY AND THE OLDER ADULT

A Clinical Manual

Edited by

Jean M. Kiernat, MS, OTR, FAOTA

Long Term Care Consultant
Phoenix, Arizona

Aspen Series in Occupational Therapy
Rhona Reiss Zukas, Series Editor

AN ASPEN PUBLICATION®
Aspen Publishers, Inc.
Gaithersburg, Maryland
1991

Library of Congress Cataloging-in-Publication Data

Occupational therapy and the older adult : a clinical manual /
edited by Jean M. Kiernat.
p. cm. — (Aspen series in occupational therapy)
Includes bibliographical references and index.
ISBN: 0-8342-0239-5
1. Occupational therapy for the aged—Handbooks, manuals, etc.
I. Kiernat, Jean M. II. Series. [DNLM: 1. Occupational Therapy—in old age.
WB 555 01414]
RC953.8.022023 1991
615.8'515084'6—dc20
DNLM/DLC
for Library of Congress
91-17191
CIP

The authors have made every effort to ensure the accuracy of the information herein,
particularly with regard to techniques and procedures. However, appropriate information
sources should be consulted, especially for new or unfamiliar techniques or procedures.
It is the responsibility of every practitioner to evaluate the appropriateness of a
particular opinion in the context of actual clinical situations and with due consideration
to new developments. Authors, editors, and the publisher cannot be held responsible
for any typographical or other errors found in this book.

Editorial Services: Lisa Hajjar

Library of Congress Catalog Card Number: 91-17191
ISBN: 0-8342-0239-5

Printed in the United States of America

1 2 3 4

*To my mother who teaches me much about aging
and to my husband who accompanies me along the aging pathway*

Table of Contents

Contributors

Charlene L. Ager, MA, OTR, FAOTA
Emerita Assistant Professor
Occupational Therapy
Colorado State University
Fort Collins, Colorado

Jeffrey L. Crabtree, BS, OTR
President, ElderServe
Suisun City, California

Richelle N. Cunninghis, MEd, OTR
Executive Director
Geriatric Educational Consultants
Willingboro, New Jersey

Nancy B. Ellis, PhD, OTR, FAOTA
Associate Director for Education
University of Pennsylvania
Philadelphia, Pennsylvania

Cynthia F. Epstein, MA, OTR, FAOTA
Executive Director
Occupational Therapy Consultants, Inc.
Bridgewater, New Jersey

Carolyn Glogoski, MS, OTR
Lecturer
Occupational Therapy and Program in
  Gerontology
San Jose State University
San Jose, California

Betty Risteen Hasselkus, PhD, OTR, FAOTA
Assistant Professor
Occupational Therapy Program
University of Wisconsin-Madison

Cheryl L. Herring, MA, OTR
President
Herring Health Enterprises
Missouri City, Texas

Patricia K. Kasper, BS, OTR
Staff Therapist
Oregon Rehabilitation Center
Sacred Heart General Hospital
Eugene, Oregon

Toni T. Kawamoto, BA, OTR
Occupational Therapist
Rehabilitation Medicine Service
Veterans Affairs Medical Center
Sepulveda, California

Frances A. Kelley, BS, OTR
Former Chief, Occupational Therapy
Rehabilitation Medicine Service
Veterans Affairs Medical Center
Sepulveda, California

Margaret M. Kirchman, PhD, OTR, FAOTA
Emerita Associate Professor
Occupational Therapy and Community Health
  Sciences
University of Illinois at Chicago

Lela A. Llorens, PhD, OTR, FAOTA
Professor, Chair, and Graduate Coordinator
Occupational Therapy
San Jose State University
San Jose, California

Ferol Menks Ludwig, MS, OTR
Occupational Therapist
Nova Care
Phoenix, Arizona

Nancy Luttropp, BS, MSW
Associate Executive Director
A Classic Residence by Hyatt
2960 North Lake Shore Drive
Chicago, Illinois

Charlotte Campbell Maloney, BS, OTR
Staff Therapist
Oregon Rehabilitation Center
Sacred Heart General Hospital
Eugene, Oregon

Guy L. McCormack, MS, OTR
Associate Professor
Occupational Therapy
San Jose State University
San Jose, California

Mary Ann Miller, MOT, OTR
Assistant Director
Occupational Therapy Department
Johnston R. Bowman Health Center for the
  Elderly
Chicago, Illinois

Lory P. Osorio, MPH, OTR
Executive Director
Stuart Circle Center, Inc.
Richmond, Virginia

Cindy Patrice Paulson, MA, OTR, MATh
Private Practice
Auburn, California

Laurence Z. Rubenstein, MD, MPH
Associate Professor of Medicine
UCLA School of Medicine
Director, Geriatric Research, Education &
  Clinical Center (GRECC)
Veterans Affairs Medical Center
Sepulveda, California

Barbara Szekais, MOT, OTR
Occupational Therapist
Rehabilitation Services
Ballard Community Hospital
Seattle, Washington

Barbara Thompson, BS, OTR
Coordinator of Regional A.L.S. Center
Hospice Department
St. Peter's Hospital
Albany, New York

Francesca D. Wolfe, MSW
Chemical Dependency Therapist and Elderly
  Specialist
Tri-City Behavioral Services
Mesa, Arizona

Preface

This book was written to put into practice what we believe to be of most importance in geriatric care. First, assessment and treatment must look at the total person, with consideration given to physical, psychological, social, cultural, and environmental factors. Second, the focus of intervention is always on functional performance, whether one is assisting a client with a stroke, severe dementia, or a terminal illness.

A third requirement for comprehensive geriatric programs is the availability of options through a continuum of care. Intervention must begin early with health promotion for the well elderly. Community-based programs such as day care and home care must be available, and therapists in acute-care rehabilitation must prepare patients for discharge to the next setting.

Long-term care therapists need to maintain a broad vision of service that includes consultation, program development, ensuring meaningful everyday activities for older residents, and assisting terminally ill clients in their final developmental task.

It is my sincere hope that students preparing to serve the aging and clinicians engaged in geriatric practice will find this book both stimulating and motivating.

Part I

Working with Older Adults

Chapter 1

The Rewards and Challenges of Working with Older Adults

Jean M. Kiernat

Working with older adults presents a special set of rewards and challenges that cannot be shared by those therapists who have chosen to work with children or even younger adults. Those who work in gerontology know that older adults are not only our clients or patients. They are also are teachers. They enrich our lives by allowing us to observe and experience the results of a long life filled with struggles, accomplishments, triumphs, and defeats.

Older adults are pioneers in a new population cohort—one that is reaching advanced age in unprecedented numbers. Since 1950, the number of Americans 65 and over has doubled (Horn & Meer, 1987). The 25.5 million Americans over 65 in 1980 are expected to increase to 64 million by 2030 ("The Search," 1990). The sheer numbers require us to pay attention to this age group, to understand them better, to design programs that address their needs, to recognize their strengths, and to assist them in areas where they are functionally challenged.

ELDERS AS TEACHERS

There is a great deal that we do not know about older people, and that is understandable, for these pioneers "occupy a space in the life course that is new territory in human experience. Extended life, better health, and retirement laws have created a new interval between work and death; and the people who occupy it now are pioneers who must explore and define the potential of a new territory for human habitation" (Keith, 1982, p. 1). These new elders are teaching us as we observe them charting new courses for their age group.

They are pushing back the boundaries of where we once thought old age began. No longer is 65 years viewed as anything more than a qualification for Medicare coverage. Older adults are creating new roles for themselves and providing us with new role models for our own future. Through them, we are learning to prepare better for our own old age.

As elders explore new biological and social territory, we observe their physical, emotional, cognitive, and social behaviors. We learn, through them, what it is to experience and cope with major life changes, including retirement, death of a spouse, moving from a familiar setting filled with memories, and chronic conditions that may or may not limit function. As one psychologist-researcher admitted, "I study the topic partly to discover more effective ways of helping old people cope with their problems, but also to load my own armamentarium against that inevitable day" (Horn & Meer, 1987, p. 81).

To those who would say that the old are set in their ways, are rigid, and cannot change, we who have worked with them have learned otherwise. They do prefer to rely on old habits and patterns, but we can now see the adaptive nature of these characteristics.

Memory is enhanced by always keeping items in the same place. The benign forgetfulness of old age is kept at bay. Energy is conserved when performing motor tasks by habit. Habits and patterns provide purpose and orderliness to one's life. One can exert control over "things" at a time when control over one's health and external events may be jeopardized. While in her eighties, Florida Scott-Maxwell (1968) wrote of a day when she felt very depressed:

> The grey sky seems very grey, but I finally soothe myself by small duties, putting away freshly ironed linen, watering plants. Order, cleanliness, seemliness make a structure that is half support, half ritual, and if it does not create, it maintains decency. I make my possessions appear at their best as they are my only companions. (p. 130)

At the same time that habits and patterns are strongly relied upon, we see the tremendous resiliency of older adults. Their ability to change and adapt to enormous stressors is a positive and powerful lesson for us. It is a humbling experience to see a 75-year-old caregiver provide 24-hour care for a very frail spouse, administering medications, providing activities, feeding and dressing, transferring, bathing, and managing medical care and the home simultaneously. If there was any doubt that old people can learn or can change, it is quickly dispelled when observing situations such as this.

We also learn that individual dependence is simply interdependence of generations when viewed over the life course. These older adults in need of services were the generation that built our schools, paved our roads, fought our wars, developed our parks, and provided for us in many, many ways. It is simply our turn to reciprocate, as we hope our children will do for us.

Old people teach us about life as well as about aging. They give us a historical perspective on the human agenda. They had their struggles and successes just as we have ours. Through their reminiscences we learn how they coped with adversity, and it gives us strength to know that we can do the same.

We also learn that they would like us to enjoy their reminiscing. "You don't live 50 years without having some tales to tell," stated a retired physician. "When you see me you may never learn that I once heard Rachmaninoff play the piano, hitched sled rides on the back of horse-drawn sleighs, regularly watched four sets of neighbors go back and forth to their out-door privies from our breakfast room window, or treated tuberculosis before antibiotics" (Bates, 1987, p. 35). And he promises that if you take the time, he might just tell you; he would like to do just that.

Most of all, what we learn in working with older persons is that they are not so different from anyone else (Keith, 1982).

QUALITY OF LIFE

Improving the quality of life for older adults is a truly enriching and rewarding experience. Preventing a life-threatening fall, integrating an isolated elder back into the community after a bout with depression, releasing a nursing home patient from the bondage of restraints—these are the rich rewards awaiting the therapist working in geriatrics. Eric Pfeiffer (1985) echoed our feelings when he responded to the frequently held assumption that working with the elderly is dull or depressing:

> Let me tell you that life at the frontier, which work with the elderly represents, is never dull, and the frontiersman cannot afford depression. However, there is one aspect of work with the elderly that can be described in pathologic terms. Work with the elderly is frankly addicting. Very few people who enter the field of geriatrics and gerontology ever leave it. (p. 74)

REHABILITATION AND GERIATRICS

It is also rewarding for occupational therapists to know that working in geriatric rehabilitation puts one at the very heart and core of geriatric medicine. Rehabilitation provides the guiding philosophy for practice in this specialty area (Williams, 1986), and therapists can teach other professions about the importance of function as a measure of health.

T. Franklin Williams, Director of the National Institute on Aging, advocates that rehabilitation should be the central approach for all older adults with debilitating illness. He dreams that one day every hospital will have a comprehensive geriatric rehabilitation unit for both acute and extended care, that every geriatric patient will receive a consultation by a team that includes a geriatrician, a nurse, a social worker, an occupational therapist, and a physical therapist. Dr. Williams states, "My dream will stay alive until rehabilitation therapy actually is the very core of geriatric medicine. Only in this way can an older person reap the full benefit of a long and functional life" (Williams, 1989, p. 17).

When this philosophy is so strongly promoted by the head of the National Institute on Aging, one cannot help but feel an intense sense of pride at being an occupational therapist in geriatrics. "There is a special satisfaction in being a specialist in geriatric occupational therapy and in bringing to gerontology the rehabilitation philosophy and the focus on function and independent living" (Hasselkus & Kiernat, 1989, p. 79).

THE CHALLENGES

While the rewards are many, working with the older adult is also one of the most challenging of practice areas in occupational therapy. Clearly, an overriding challenge in geriatrics is to confront our attitudes toward older persons as well as our own aging.

Since Robert Butler (1969) coined the term "ageism" to describe the prejudices and stereotypes regarding older people sheerly on the basis of their age, we have become aware that our attitudes toward aging influence our treatment of older persons. Ageism, like racism, is a way of pigeon-holing people and treating them all alike. By doing this, younger persons are shielded from dealing with the fact that they will one day be old themselves and have similar needs.

Ageism is exhibited in the myriad tasteless birthday cards based on the over-the-hill theme. It is prevalent in the many jokes about senility, loss of sexuality, and the general frailties of older adults. Ageism is not restricted to the general public. It is found in medical services, with references to "crocks" (hypochondriacal persons) and "gomers" (get out of my emergency room) and the use of other derogatory labels for older adults.

Nor is rehabilitation exempt from ageism. In a study of age bias among physical therapists, attitudes and expectations clearly affected treatment planning (Barta Kvitek, Shaver, Blood, & Shepard, 1986). One hundred and twenty-seven physical therapists were given a description of a patient for whom they were asked to develop treatment goals. Half of the therapists were told the patient's age was 28, while the other half were told the age was 78. Goal setting for the 28-year-old was far more aggressive than for the 78-year-old, even though the condition was identical. In addition, among the therapists who had the older patient, those with more positive attitudes toward aging set more aggressive goals.

An earlier study by Kosberg and Gorman (1975) looked at the way nursing home personnel viewed the rehabilitation potential of the residents. Little more than half of the therapists had positive perceptions regarding the rehabilitation of residents in their care.

In the same study, residents themselves scored very poorly. Only 8% believed in their own rehabilitation potential. If elderly persons believe that their limitations are not improvable, they will not seek the help they need, nor will they be motivated to participate if a rehabilitation program is prescribed.

We must have expectations for older adults—a belief in their ability to improve—and we must instill in them a belief in their ability to help themselves. American society has looked upon the failure of elderly persons to return to their former levels of function after an illness as acceptable and often even appropriate (Brody & Ruff, 1986). Therapists must counteract such ageist influences.

Geriatric therapists are challenged to maintain optimism, to believe, even in the face of adversity, that they can effect a positive change (Kemp, 1987). Optimism, as defined by Kemp, is more than not being pessimistic. It involves transcending the problems that are present and concentrating on the positive benefits that can be achieved.

When a patient has three or more chronic conditions with acute illness overlays and has recently lost a spouse, it is a true challenge to remain optimistic. But that is exactly what must happen. The therapist must hold on to the belief that improvement is possible, for it is only in this way that the therapist can dispel pessimism and encourage optimism in the patient.

Families must also be included in the rehabilitation programs, and they must share the optimism. Therapists are challenged to help families—and sometimes physicians—understand the benefit of small gains. Even when independence will not be achieved, gains in strength that allow for minimum assist instead of maximum assist transfers save family caregivers much stress and strain. Small gains may mean the difference between an intermediate care placement and personal care that can be provided at home or in less restrictive settings.

A NEW AGEISM

While fighting the remnants of the old ageism, a new stereotype of the elderly is beginning to be seen. It pits the elderly against younger generations and stresses the financial burdens of caring for an older population. The new stereotype depicts the elderly as affluent and selfish—as voting against schools, receiving too many high-cost medical services, and receiving benefits at the expense of children (Sheppard, 1990).

Complaints about the cost of Social Security continue to be aired, yet there is no discussion of the fact that 3.2 million children were receiving Social Security benefits in 1988 due to the retirement, disability, or death of a worker (Sheppard, 1990). It is ironic that the very programs that provided medical care for the elderly and removed many from poverty by increasing their income are now being condemned because of their success.

One must continue to be on the watch for ageist arguments. It is imperative that professionals in aging look in depth at social and political issues that affect their practice and the lives of those whom they serve. Both children and the elderly should have access to programs that optimize function and ensure that basic health and social needs are met.

THE MASTER GENERALIST

The occupational therapist in geriatrics must be very skillful in many areas, because geriatric patients are characterized by multiple problems in multiple areas of life. Physical health problems may be accompanied by mental health problems, and these may be compounded by social issues such as isolation, financial insecurity, and the inability to live independently (Pfeiffer, 1985).

The patient might have diabetes, arthritis, and macular degeneration and then suffer an acute illness. When this happens, it may raise a whole spectrum of concerns: "Is this the beginning of the end?" "Will Mom be able to live alone or does she need to go to a nursing home?" "How will Dad function now that Mom is unable to care for him?"

While illness should not be considered as normal in old age, it does occur with increased frequency (Brummel-Smith, 1986), and a mixture of acute illness and multiple chronic conditions is common. The occupational therapist serving older adults must have advanced knowledge of physical rehabilitation and behavioral health and be a specialist in independent living and the repertoire of community agencies and social support services.

GERIATRIC KNOWLEDGE

Specialized knowledge in geriatrics is imperative because health care of the elderly is different from other age groups and it is often very complicated. The first symptom for a variety of illnesses—from urinary tract infections to congestive heart failure—may be confusion. Depression may be disguised as dementia. Hypothyroidism may present as depression.

The older person exists in a delicate state of balance. Disturbance of homeostasis by any disease process will be "expressed in the most vulnerable, delicately balanced system" (Besdine, 1983, p. 651). The most precarious balance is often reflected in a sudden change in cognition, which must be investigated to uncover the cause.

There are also special conditions seen in the older adult that are not a part of practice with younger age groups. A therapist performing a functional assessment of an older adult who has fallen might find that the family is concerned about some recent confusion. In discussing bathroom activities, the family reluctantly admits that there has also been some recent incontinence. The knowledgeable geriatric therapist will know that normal-pressure hydrocephalus is characterized by this triad of symptoms and would immediately discuss this with the physician. Early diagnosis of this relatively rapidly progressing dementia may allow improvement through a surgical procedure (Kane, Ouslander, & Abrass, 1989).

The way illnesses present in older adults differs from the way they present in younger people. Pain responses may be altered, as may temperature responses. Pharmacokinetics and pharmacodynamics change with physiological aging, and adverse reactions to medications are common (Kane, Ouslander, & Abrass, 1989).

Because of the breadth of knowledge required for geriatrics, occupational therapists who choose this field must be exceptionally well prepared. They must be comfortable in their own field and able to work in a transdisciplinary role with others.

STAYING CURRENT

An exciting challenge is posed by the wealth of research being conducted in the field of aging. New findings often refute earlier claims regarding the inevitability of the decline of specific functions.

For example, the widely held belief that cardiac output declines with age in all older adults is simply not true. Yet all textbooks in aging published before 1984 state that the decline in cardiac output is a normal age change (Williams, 1986). A decline in kidney filtration rate was also assumed to be a normal age change, but Williams has described new findings showing that while the majority of study subjects showed varying degrees of decline, many stayed the same over years and a small percentage actually improved!

What is aging? What is disuse? And what is disease? In many cases, the final verdict is not yet in, but there is an escalation in the new information available in geriatrics. This is a new field, and therapists choosing it are part of a pioneering movement. It is most exciting and challenging!

PRESERVING AUTONOMY

It is an absolute necessity that rehabilitation programs for frail older adults rest upon a foundation of preserving autonomy. It is easy to fall into the pattern of making decisions, assuming responsibility, and taking control when working with the dependent elderly. But paternalistic patterns such as these serve only to further enhance a sense of dependency.

Autonomy has been defined and described in a variety of ways. Collopy (1988) includes the notions of self-determination, freedom, independence, and liberty of choice and action. Zimmerman and Kultgen (1984) define an autonomous person as one who behaves independently and makes considered choices even under substantial duress. All agree that dependence does not preclude autonomy. The individual need not be the master of all circumstances to be self-determining.

Autonomy may be expressed through decision making even when the ability to carry out a decision is limited. In fact, it is precisely when independence is threatened that the need for decisional autonomy is paramount (Collopy, 1988).

Even the most dependent elder can exercise choice in some areas (e.g., by making decisions about what food to eat, which dress to wear, or whether to accept chemotherapy or tube feeding). Making decisions, no matter how limited the scope, gives a sense of control, and a sense of control has a definite and positive role in sustaining life (Lefcourt, 1973) and in maintaining morale (Ryden, 1984).

Choice, control, and responsibility to oneself and others are critical elements of rehabilitation programs. To ignore the challenge of maintaining autonomy is to create dependency.

MANPOWER CHALLENGE

The final challenge in serving the elderly is a challenge to the profession as a whole. The demand for geriatric occupational therapy services will outstrip the number of therapists available in the work force. The shortage has already begun.

In 1982, 19% of occupational therapy personnel worked with the elderly, with 7.8% working in nursing homes (Peterson, 1988). This number did not even meet the demands of the nursing home population at that time.

The growing number of elderly in nursing care facilities and in the community is increasing the demand for occupational therapy services. The supply of therapists is not keeping pace, however, and by the year 2000 a shortfall of 2,300–3,900 therapists is anticipated (Peterson, 1988).

Peterson has pointed to the following disincentives as reasons why relatively few therapists choose to enter the field of aging: lack of good role models, lack of specific required coursework in gerontology, and bad experiences in geriatric fieldwork. There is also a general perception that service in aging is technologically unsophisticated.

Therapists who choose geriatrics for their practice area must address these barriers to entry. They must pass on their excitement and convey to students and fellow therapists the challenges and the rewards of working with older adults. The opportunity to be a pioneer in a new field where occupational therapy plays a central and highly visible role should be too enticing to refuse.

REFERENCES

Barta Kvitek, S., Shaver, B., Blood, H., & Shepard, K. (1986). Age bias: Physical therapists and older patients. *Journal of Gerontology, 41,* 706–709.

Bates, R. (1987). What an older doctor can tell you about elderly patients. *Medical Economics, 64,* 30–35.

Besdine, R.W. (1983). The educational utility of comprehensive functional assessments in the elderly. *Journal of the American Geriatric Society, 31,* 651.

Brody, S.J., & Ruff, G.E. (Eds.). (1986). *Aging and rehabilitation: Advances in the state of the art.* New York: Springer.

Brummel-Smith, K. (1986). Interviewing the older adult. In A.J. Enelow & S.N. Swisher (Eds.), *Interviewing and patient care* (149–162). New York: Oxford University Press.

Butler, R. (1969). The effects of medical and health progress on the social and economic aspects of the life cycle. *Industrial Gerontology, 1,* 1–9.

Collopy, B. (1988). Autonomy in long term care: Some crucial distinctions. *The Gerontologist, 28,* 10–17.

Hasselkus, B., & Kiernat, J. (1989). Not by age alone: Gerontology as a specialty in occupational therapy. *American Journal of Occupational Therapy, 43,* 77–79.

Horn, J.C., & Meer, J. (1987). The vintage years. *Psychology Today, 21,* 76–90.

Kane, R., Ouslander, J., and Abrass, I. (1989). *Essentials of clinical geriatrics.* (2nd ed.). New York: McGraw-Hill.

Keith, J. (1982). *Old people as people: Social and cultural influences on aging and old age.* Boston: Little, Brown.

Kemp, B. (1987). A report on the national conference on rehabilitation in the aging. *Long-term care currents. A Ross Timesaver, 10,* 11–14.

Kosberg, J., & Gorman, J. (1975). Perspectives toward the rehabilitation potential of institutionalized aged. *The Gerontologist, 25,* 398–403.

Lefcourt, H. (1973). The function of the illusion of control and freedom. *American Psychologist, 28,* 417–425.

Peterson, D.A. (1988). Personnel to serve the aging in the field of occupational therapy. Los Angeles: University of Southern California, Andrus Gerontology Center.

Pfeiffer, E. (1985). Some basic principles of working with older patients. *Journal of the American Geriatric Society, 33,* 44–47.

Ryden, M. (1984). Morale and perceived control in institutionalized elderly. *Nursing Research, 33,* 130–136.

Scott-Maxwell, F. (1968). *The measure of my days.* New York: Knopf.

The search for the fountain of youth. (1990, March 5). *Newsweek,* pp. 44–48.

Sheppard, H. (1990). Damaging stereotypes about aging are taking hold: How to counter them. *Perspectives on Aging, 19,* 4–8.

Williams, F.T. (1986). Geriatrics: The fruition of the clinician reconsidered. *The Gerontologist, 26,* 345–349.

Williams, T.F. (1989). Rehabilitation's role in geriatric medicine. *Provider, 15,* 16–17.

Zimmerman, M., & Kultgen, P. (1984). A program for preventive and supportive care for the troubled elderly. In S.F. Spicker & S.R. Ingman (Eds.), *Vitalizing long-term care.* New York: Springer.

Chapter 2

Culturally Diverse Elders

Guy L. McCormack, Lela A. Llorens, and Carolyn Glogoski

Culturally diverse elders are those older persons who belong to a group that has experienced discrimination and subordination within a dominant white society. They are also referred to as *ethnic minority elders*. These older persons bear the burdens of aging and the historical effects of being a member of an ethnic minority group.

Most live in urban areas. Their income and educational levels tend to be lower than those of white Americans. In addition, the health status of ethnic minorities suggests that they are greatly underserved when compared to the white population (U.S. Bureau of the Census, 1980a). Population trends of the culturally diverse elderly show that Black Americans make up the largest ethnic minority elder group (65 and older), followed by Hispanics, Asians, and Native Americans.

HEALTH BELIEFS AND PRACTICES

Ethnic minority elders tend to have different health beliefs and practices than those of nonminorities. Some continue to practice various forms of folk medicine that have been passed down from generation to generation, especially minority elders who have lived in inner city ghettos or have been isolated from the mainstream of Western scientific medicine. Unfortunately, acute illness or chronic progressive disorders may thrust the elderly into the health care system of the larger society (Katz, 1978). In order to meet the needs of these individuals, the therapist must be sensitive to a variety of well-established cultural values, health beliefs, and self-help practices. The therapist can enrich the quality of care that is provided by simply acknowledging the significance of the client's belief system, which is a powerful healer in its own right (Justice, 1987).

The following provides some basic information about health beliefs and practices among selected ethnic minority elderly populations. These characteristics are prevalent but cannot be expected to hold true for all individuals in an ethnic group. The information should be used with the understanding that there are more differences between people of the same ethnic group than there are between people of various ethnic groups.

Black American Elders

Black American elders constitute the largest and in many ways the most underprivileged minority group in the United States (Wylie, 1971). Much has been written about the fact that most Blacks came involuntarily to America as slaves in the early 1600s. Many Black American elders had grandparents who were slaves or were children of slaves. While much of the African cultural background was destroyed during slavery, certain health beliefs have survived. Snow (1983) has written about the health beliefs and practices among lower class Black Americans. According to Snow, illnesses are categorized as "natural" or "unnatural." Natural illnesses are considered to be caused by nature's forces, cold, dirt, improper diet, and divine punishment. Unnatural illnesses are believed to be brought about by witchcraft, voodoo, hoodoo, hexes, or root work. Healers are the only persons who can cure an unnatural illness, because they have to remove the "hex." Cultural healers include priests and priestesses, spiritualists, and the person called "the Old Lady." In African tradition, there is respect for elders, and old age is regarded as a sign of dignity. Also, in the oral tradition of Black Americans, elders were trained to remember family history in great detail so that it could be shared with the children. Therefore, the cultural healers are often grandparents who have retained knowledge of root work and healing remedies (Wylie, 1971).

Black American elders belong to an extended family system that is highly integrated and serves as a survival resource and source of social mobility. Family support is important in the care of the elderly. However, more Black elders may be found living alone than with family members, both in cities and in rural areas (Markides & Mindel, 1987). Kinship links are not easily observed but can be elicited by the therapist after a relationship has been established with the elder.

Black elders span the financial range from total independence to dependence upon public social systems. They expect to be treated with the dignity that befits the years that they have achieved. Experiences with discrimination may temper this expectation but usually will not extinguish it. An elder's cooperation with medical and therapeutic intervention may be in direct relationship to the respect that is accorded her or him by the health professional.

Elder Americans of Latin Origin (Hispanics)

Americans of Latin origin are the fastest growing minority group in the United States. There has been some confusion about how to refer to this group because of its vast ancestry. Some scholars dislike the term *Hispanic* and prefer *Raza-Latina*, which means the Latin race. However, elder Americans of Latin origin include many Indian tribes, Spaniards, Mexicans, Cubans, Puerto Ricans, several nationalities from Central and South America, and Caribbean islanders of Spanish ancestry. The elders in this group take pride in their Spanish ancestry, many are Roman Catholics, and those in the lower socioeconomic income groups live in neighborhoods called *barrios* (Ahumada-Monroy, 1983).

According to Maduro (1983), the term *curanderismo* refers to a traditional healing system used throughout Latin America and imported to the United States in more or less organized forms. According to this belief system, diseases are associated with strong emotional states. A state of imbalance can occur within one's environment, the soul may be separated from the body, individuals can be victimized by malicious forces, and cures require participation of the entire family. The origin of *curanderismo* can be traced to Aztec, Spanish, Greek, and Roman views of health and illness (Martinez, 1977). Many elder Latino patients believe in the importance of balance and harmony and that the body and mind are inseparable. Therefore, they readily accept the existence of psychosomatic disorders. For example, Latino patients commonly believe in a syndrome called *biles*, which is an illness supposedly caused by the experiencing of a strong emotional state such as rage. Another disorder supposedly caused by a strong emotion, in this case fright, is called *susto* (Rubel, 1960). *Susto* can result in strong emotional reactions, and it is believed that the soul detaches from the body. Latino elders may also believe that certain individuals have the power to place a hex on them (*malpuesto*) through witchcraft (Martinez & Martin, 1966).

Elder Latinos may dichotomize illnesses on the basis of hot and cold. For example, fevers, rashes, and nausea are "hot" conditions, whereas "cold" conditions are due to imbalances or exposure to cold drafts. The cold air may be responsible for earaches, rheumatoid arthritis, or muscle spasms (called *pasmo*) (Martinez & Martin, 1966). Imbalances of hot and cold substances in the body, called *calidades*, are treated with foods and medications to offset the excess. Cold foods include fresh vegetables like cilantro, tropical fruits, and milk products. Hot items include spicy foods (e.g., chili peppers), pork, and medications (e.g., penicillin). Latino elders may attempt to regulate or restore the balance of their *calidades* through self-treatment or by seeing a cultural healer called a *curandero* (Maduro, 1983; Martinez, 1977). A *curandero* works closely with the whole family, providing psychological, physiological, social, and spiritual support for syndromes identified within the *curanderismo* belief system.

Kinship networks are highly integrated in the Latino community, and they provide Latino elders with emotional and financial support. A preference for relying on family rather than on formal social systems is characteristic. Older people are accorded respect from youths and children. This respect is reflected in speech, manners, and behavior. Deference is accorded the elders in the cultural group (Markides & Mindel, 1987).

Southeast Asian Elders

Southeast Asians include the Indochinese, Vietnamese, Laotians, H'mong, Mein, and Cambodians (Muecke, 1983). Large numbers of refugees from Southeast Asia were first admitted to the United States in 1975. The first group consisted predominantly of government officials, professionals, and those associated with the military. The "second wave" of refugees arrived in 1979. In general, these refugees were less educated and less literate, came from rural areas, and were less familiar with Western civilization (Montero, 1979). The majority of the refugees from Southeast Asia reside in the Western states, with California, Washington, Oregon, and Colorado absorbing the greatest numbers (U.S. Department of Health and Human Services, 1983).

Southeast Asians are culturally diverse. Their health belief system has been termed "natural medicine," the "Universal Order," and "Sino-Vietnamese medicine" (Tung, 1980). In general, their system is similar to Hippocratic medicine, since it is grounded in a belief in the healing power of nature (Muecke, 1983). There is also a hot-cold theory relating to the four elements: water, fire, air, and earth. In addition, the system acknowledges the bodily humors and accepts the importance of harmonious equilibrium with the universe.

Specific folk illnesses are identified on the basis of excesses or weaknesses of specific bodily systems. For example, organ systems may be underactive, causing a weak kidney, weak heart, weak lung, and so on. Remedies include the use of herbs, acupuncture, and dermal abrasive techniques. These procedures are believed to activate organ systems that will offset or "tonify" the weakened systems. Therefore, elderly Southeast Asians may exhibit cutaneous bursas or hematoma along skin pathways (meridians) associated with certain organs. Dermal abrasive techniques such as coin rubbing are believed to relieve the excessive "air" attributed to certain illnesses.

There is a hot-cold theory among Southeast Asians, but it differs somewhat from the Hispanic theory. Symptoms such as infection, constipation, dark urine, and flatulence are believed to indicate a "hot" imbalance. In contrast, "cold" conditions may be associated with chronic illness, low energy, and eating too many fruits and vegetables. The belief in a hot-cold balance may affect Southeast Asian elders' compliance with Western medical procedures such as drawing blood (venipuncture), because they believe blood volume is a fixed amount and removal of blood upsets the balance (Muecke, 1983; Yeatman & Dang, 1980).

Established Asian Americans

Established Asian Americans include the Japanese, Chinese, and Filipinos. Although each group has its own culture, values, attitudes, traditions, and health beliefs, the established Asians are judged to be extremely successful in their assimilation into North American society. Established Asians immigrated early in the settlement of North America, and they have achieved economic status, have attained high levels of education, and are represented in all walks of life, including the professions.

In general, Asian Americans have been called the "silent minority" (Chang, 1981). Four major values are upheld by Asian Americans: (1) self-control, (2) social reciprocity, (3) filial piety, and (4) shame. *Self-control* refers to the control of emotions and the show of patience and perseverance. *Social reciprocity* refers to the return of favors through compliments or gifts. *Filial piety* describes the strong family bond and the concept that the family comes before the individual. *Shame* refers to the kind of embarrassment felt by Asian Americans when they do not fulfill the obligation to uphold the principles and code of behavior that they value (McCormack, 1987).

Japanese Americans

The majority of Japanese Americans reside on the West Coast and in Hawaii. They tend to be healthy and to have achieved a comfortable socioeconomic status. The stable financial base of this group supports the family and contributes to society. Within Japanese culture, men and elders are accorded high status. Elders receive financial support—in some cases total support. Very few receive public financial assistance. In a study conducted by Marmot and Syme (1976), Japanese Americans who adhered to traditional practices were found to have a lower incidence of coronary heart disease than white Americans. This study reported the importance of family and community ties as a source of wellness.

Kitano (1976) studied the evolution of Japanese Americans according to their generational categories. The first generation (*Issei*) worked diligently to develop the railroads, the fishing industry, farms, and sawmills. A dwindling number of *Issei* are alive today. Many of these Asian elders are cared for by their families or reside in Asian American senior citizen facilities. One study showed that 65% have daily contact with at least one of their children (Osako, 1979). The second generation (*Nisei*) were born before World War II and became extensively acculturated. The third (*Sansei*) and fourth (*Yonsei*) generations continue to achieve high levels of education and to be further assimilated.

The major health belief system for elder Japanese Americans is derived from the Shinto religion, which is characterized by its focus on balance and harmony with nature. Lock (1980) refers to the preservation of harmony and balance as the "soft rule." It is based on the view that spiritual power is more important than individual rights. Lock has observed ritual behavior among Japanese Americans. That is, on the surface they will comply with Western medicine, but they retain folk beliefs in the home. Traditional Japanese Americans also believe that cleansing the body (bathing) maintains balance and that acupuncture, herbal medicine, and massage are principal therapeutic modalities. It has been observed that among Japanese Americans who were interned during World War II, there appears to be a disruption of traditional health beliefs and an almost total acceptance of Western medicine (Morioka-Douglas, 1988).

Chinese Americans

Chinese Americans are sometimes stereotyped as mysterious and quiet. Chinese immigration to the United States began in 1849 with the California Gold Rush. Although many Chinese Americans have made strides educationally and financially, they still experience individual discrimination. Many Chinese American elders reside in Chinatowns or live with large families in small living quarters. Many of the male elders have never married. Historically, some who are now elders were unable to bring their wives to America due to immigration laws and restrictions. These men may be dependent upon the Chinese kinship network for emotional support but may be financially independent. The Chinese family is close knit and children have been expected to care for their elders. This custom is currently being challenged to some extent by younger Chinese Americans, who have been influenced by Western culture, which does not mandate that family members assume the care-taking role.

The health belief system of traditional Chinese American elders is derived from Taoism, Confucianism, and Buddhism, which are called the "great traditions" (Holbrook, 1981). There is the belief in the five elements (wood, water, metal, air, and earth), yin and yang, and chi (qi), or life force energy. Chi energy is a dynamic force that is believed to move around and through soft tissues of the body on a 24-hour cycle via pathways called meridians. This system of medicine dates back more than 3,000 years and continues to be practiced today (Fung, 1961). According to this belief, illness is caused by a blockage of the chi energy, resulting in underactivity or overactivity of certain organ systems. Another source of illness is called "wind" (feng), which is an excess of cold air or a noxious force that enters the body. "Poison" (tu) describes contaminated or impure substances that are ingested and cause endogenous imbalances. Chinese American elders continue to use traditional treatments, including herbal medicine, acupuncture, acupressure, moxibustion, and cupping. The logic behind the use of these treatments is to release the blocked energy (chi) and reestablish the balance between yin and yang (Holbrook, 1981).

Filipino Americans

Filipino Americans began immigration to North America in 1765, during the Spanish colonial period. Statistics suggest that their number may surpass one million, making them the largest Asian minority. As a group, Filipino Americans are considered culturally diverse, because the Philippines is an archipelago of about 7,000 islands. Filipino elders are highly respected in this family-oriented culture. Many elderly Filipinos are devout Catholics and have a fatalistic world view (U.S. Bureau of the Census, 1980b). Their fatalistic view (*bahala na*) is based on the belief that the course of life is determined by God's will and supernatural forces that control the universe. Many Filipinos subscribe to traditional values, such as the avoidance of interpersonal conflict by conceding gracefully while preserving self-esteem and the family's honor.

Elder Filipino Americans, who are called the "old timers," reside mainly in rural communities. However, the wave of recent Filipino immigrants are settling in urban areas.

The health belief system used by traditional elder Filipinos, called *timbany*, is based on the principle of balance. Health results from balance, and illness results from imbalance (Anderson, 1983). The hot-cold dichotomy is also a feature of this belief system. For example, the ingestion of cold foods or drinks in the morning is believed to bring about cramps in the diaphragm (*massiskmura*). A sudden cooling of the body or the entry of cold air ("winds") can upset the balance of the body. Resulting disorders are believed to include respiratory distress, rheumatism, fever, and pneumonia (Anderson, 1983). Overheating the body is also believed to be responsible for fever, pains, and disorientation. Sudden unexpected experiences, such as being startled or awakened from a deep sleep, can cause illness. A culturally bound syndrome called *mali-mali* results in preservation behaviors such as echolalia and command automatism (Hart, 1969). Folk practices are aimed at reestablishing the balances of the body. Flushing is a remedy that induces vomiting, perspiration, or flatus to rid the body of impurities. Heating the body by putting on several blankets or sitting in frequent hot baths is a remedy for an excess of "cold." Supernatural illnesses caused by the evil eye or spells cast by witches are believed to be neutralized by the wearing of amulets, religious articles, and rosaries (Anderson, 1983).

Middle Eastern American Elders

The Middle East, which is here assumed to include all the Arab countries in North Africa, is a vast land mass stretching 3,400 miles from Iran to Morocco and Mauritania. This land mass includes 21 Arab countries, plus Iran, Israel, and Turkey. Middle Easterners vary ethnically yet share similar values, including the need for affiliation and close family ties as well as cultural attitudes toward health and illness (Lipson & Meleis, 1983).

Middle Easterners have developed a respect for Western medicine, since many who live along the Arabian Gulf coast receive government-provided Western medical care paid for out of the money derived from oil exports. Therefore, Middle Eastern elders may demand and expect more care from scientific medicine when they arrive in the United States than other groups.

Although most Middle Easterners acknowledge that disease is transmitted by germs, they also believe in folk illnesses. The evil eye is believed to be a common cause of illness by Arabs and Iranians (Meleis, 1981). It is believed that a positive event, such as the birth of a beautiful child or a job promotion, provokes jealousy and envy on the part of others. Envy empowers an envious person's eyes to inflict harm or illness on the fortunate person or party. Many Middle Easterners burn a seed (*esfand*) and wear turquoise beads or amulets showing a hand with five fingers to encourage God's protection.

Food deprivation or lack of appetite (*masafish nefs*) is thought to bring on illness. In fact, poor appetite alone can be regarded as a disease, while the ingestion of elaborate meals is considered healthy.

Middle Easterners also tend to believe that extreme shifts in temperature or excessive amounts of dampness or dryness can cause illness. There is also a fatalistic viewpoint that illness is predetermined by God's will. Illness may be regarded as God's punishment for sins, since each person's fate is sealed from the moment the soul is created.

Many elder Middle Easterners have high expectations of Western medicine. In their view, the more intrusive the procedure, the better the potential for recovery. Injections are preferred over oral medications, colored pills are thought to be more potent than uncolored ones, and intravenous treatment is preferred over intramuscular injection (Lipson & Meleis, 1983). Middle Eastern elders may also exhibit a need for social affiliation. There appears to be a strong need to maintain an extensive social network to assist with coping and adaptation. Many visitors may come to console the ill, and daily family gatherings are very common. These social gatherings are commonplace in the Middle East. In Kuwait, they are called *dewanias*, and in Saudi Arabia they are called *majles* (Meleis, 1981).

Native American Elders

Before the colonization of North America, Native Americans lived in hundreds of different tribal societies throughout the land. Many Native Americans were later forced to live on reservations, where many of the elders continue to live at the present time. Today, there are 270 Indian tribes residing in 26 states (Farris, 1978). The largest numbers of Native Americans live in California, Arizona,

Oklahoma, New Mexico, and Alaska (Primeaux, 1977). The largest surviving Native American group are the Navajo. They live in Arizona and New Mexico.

The diversity within Native American culture is to some extent a reflection of regional differences. Traditional kinship support systems may be weak due to the influence of Western culture, since many traditional bonds, customs, and rites were destroyed or weakened when tribes attempted to comply with federal and state laws and Christian religious customs. Reawakening of Native American culture and respect for elders is a part of a renaissance that is helping to strengthen Native American communities.

In the early 1800s, the Indian Health Service was able to curb contagious diseases among tribes living near military bases. Today, the Indian Health Service is responsible for providing health services to Native Americans living on reservations. In recent years, large numbers of Native Americans have moved into urban areas, where they have often encountered difficulties adjusting to the health care system (Wilson, 1983).

The health belief system for some Native Americans stems from the notion of harmony with nature and the universe (Boyd, 1974). According to Vogel (1970), Native Americans traditionally believed that illness was due to a discord with the laws of nature. Causes of illness may include sorcery or witchcraft, violations of tribal taboo, and external intrusions, such as snake and insect bites, fractures, and skin abrasions. Another supposed cause of illness is possession by evil spirits. Soul loss is often associated with mental disorders. It is believed that the soul can leave the body during a deep dream state and travel about (Vogel, 1970). Thus the soul can be lost or captured by evil spirits. The symptoms of soul loss may be observed in someone who is very unhappy, is easily frightened, or wanders about without eating. Navajos believe that dreams are a significant medium for communicating with spiritual beings.

Native American healers are believed to be chosen by the divine spirits and gifted with extrasensory perception. According to Bean (1976), there are six types of Native American healers: (1) medicine persons of a positive nature, (2) medicine persons who possess good or evil powers, (3) diviner-diagnosticians, (4) specialist medicine persons, (5) medicine persons who protect souls, and (6) "singers."

IMPLICATIONS FOR INTERVENTION WITH ETHNIC ELDERS

Edinberg (1985) identifies several barriers that impede the use of health care services by ethnic elders. These include a distrust of health care providers and health care systems, a strong sense that the health care system does not fit with cultural traditions, a lack of knowledge about or access to health care services, language barriers, a reliance upon family for care and support, and a possible lack of cross-cultural training and experiences with health care providers. Also, a lack of awareness of ethnic stereotypes may affect a provider's ability to provide appropriate services.

Effective treatment will depend upon the sensitivity of the therapist to the elder's culture, language, and traditions; respect for the elder as an individual; and a recognition of the elder's cultural worth and uniqueness (Bello, 1976).

Participant Involvement

When designing services, programs, and treatment for ethnic elders, it is essential that they be actively involved in the planning. In this way, important information can be received about cultural practices and etiquette. The needs of elders to speak their native language, celebrate holidays, and eat favorite food dishes should be taken into account whenever possible. Inadvertent violation of cultural norms, such as challenging sex roles, interfering with relationships between men and women, and ignoring food preferences, should be avoided (Markides & Mindel, 1987). By incorporating cultural practices, the appeal of treatment and the likelihood of success can be greatly enhanced.

Use of Informed Support System

Longston (1981) suggests a model that uses an informal system of support provided by family, friends, neighbors, or community helpers to facilitate the connection between an ethnic elder and the formal systems of care. This informal system of support, while not a substitute for professional services, can provide essential information about how the elder is actually progressing and in what areas assistance or intervention is required. The therapist can offer support and consultation to members of the informal system in a collegial manner. In some situations, the therapist may coordinate or organize the actions of community helpers. When special needs of the client must be met, such as activities of daily living and personal care, the therapist can train and educate helpers on how to best meet these needs.

Utilization of the informal system can help to overcome distrust and can increase accessibility to health care providers and services. The therapist must adapt to the informal support system of the ethnic elder. Family members and community helpers who are accorded value and treated with respect will be invaluable in providing information about cultural traditions and in overcoming language barriers.

Service Location

In overcoming barriers to the use of health care by ethnic elders, it may be important to locate services in the elders' own community. Locating programs near community institutions such as churches, community centers, and neighborhood organizations may decrease the elders' suspicions and distrust of health care services. Programs and services in familiar locations that are easily accessible may be viewed as more responsive to the elders' needs (Markides & Mindel, 1987). In many instances it may be necessary to bring services to elders by visiting them in their homes. The home visit may introduce a leveling factor into the relationship, improve rapport, and increase understanding of the environment and life variables.

Overcoming Language Barriers

Lack of a common language has been cited by Edinberg (1985) as a frustrating barrier between health care provider and receiver. He indicates that some ethnic elders consider it the responsibility of the provider to offer health services in the elder's native tongue. Bilingual providers and contracts with minority organizations have been suggested as solutions by Cuellar and Weeks (1980). Increasing the numbers of therapists who are bicultural and bilingual could have a very positive effect upon the health care of ethnic elders.

While fluency in the elder's native tongue would be ideal, Edinberg (1985) recommends the use of bilingual interpreters from other community agencies, paid volunteers, or, in some instances, family members. He suggests caution when using family members, since they may be uncomfortable interpreting the intense personal feelings of elders or may distort what has been said due to their own interpretations. When children or grandchildren interpret, a lack of understanding of abstract concepts or in some cases a violation of cultural norms and role expectations can occur. Male interpreters should be used with men and female interpreters with women in the interviewing process (McCormack, 1987). McCormack has suggested that the interpreter sit next to the elder and face the therapist and that the therapist talk to and look in the direction of the elder, not at the interpreter.

Establishing Rapport

Developing a helping relationship with an ethnic elder requires that the therapist carefully consider the elder's interactional style. Several authors (Hall & Whyte, 1960; Sue, 1981) have found that culture affects interactions in numerous ways.

Culture can determine timing, physical distance, physical contact, eye contact, subject matter, place, emotions, and many verbal and nonverbal behaviors.

Generally in establishing a relationship with an ethnic elder, the therapist must plan to spend more time on the first several interviews than usual. Ample time should be alloted so that a relaxed atmosphere can be created and so the therapist can sit and "visit a spell" before getting down to business (Vontress, 1976). It may take time for the elder to determine whether the therapist is going to be respectful and accepting. A formal approach that also reflects sincerity and warmth can be effective in gradually dispelling fears of racial discrimination and rejection. The elder may ask the therapist personal questions, including questions about age, marital status, number of children, place of residence, and where the therapist's family is from (Zuniga-Martinez, 1983). A willingness to answer these questions can be very productive in establishing an atmosphere of mutual trust. This is particularly true in contacts with Mexican American families (Aguilar, 1972).

Formal titles such as "Mr.," "Mrs.," or "Miss" accompanied by the last name should be used, since this is considered an indication of respect by many Black, Hispanic, and Asian American elders (Edinberg, 1985; White, 1977). When conversing with the elder or the interpreter, the use of short, simple sentences in formal English, not slang, can facilitate communication and avoid misunderstandings (McCormack, 1987). Much can be learned by taking the time to listen and observe carefully. Rushing to complete the interview or speaking in a rapid and pressured way indicates that the therapist is in a hurry to get away or does not think the client is important. Taking the appropriate amount of time is frequently difficult to do, since Anglo culture stresses time management as very desirable and time as a precious commodity. Many minority cultures are oriented toward a slower pace.

Silence is used and interpreted differently in different cultures. The use of silence in many Asian cultures is an indication of politeness and respect. Silence following a conversation does not always mean the elder has finished speaking. It may mean that a point has been made and the elder wishes to continue speaking (Sue, 1981). Verbal communication styles can be quite complex. Hispanics may appear to readily agree with perceived authority figures by nodding their heads but may in fact be demonstrating politeness. Black elders may verbalize the opposite of what they feel in order "to play it cool" (Vontress, 1976, p. 133). Asian Americans may also communicate in an indirect manner, verbalizing somatic complaints as a more acceptable means of expressing emotional problems (Sue, 1981).

Nonverbal Communication

Other important aspects of communication include personal space, eye contact, and touch. The health professional should make an effort to sit in a position that is comfortable for conversation when talking with an elder. In some instances it might be necessary, because of deficits in sight and hearing, to move closer than is culturally acceptable. It is best to ask the elder for permission and move slowly. The elder can feel overwhelmed and in some instances threatened, especially if he or she is confined to bed or lacks mobility (Zuniga-Martinez, 1983). In some cultures, the amount of personal space needed by an elder may be less than that to which the therapist is generally accustomed. This can be the case with Hispanics and some Black Americans (Sue, 1981).

The use of eye contact should depend upon the culturally influenced preference of the elder. Generally Anglos rely on reciprocal eye contact to indicate that the person to whom they are speaking is being attentive and that the speaker is understood. Direct eye contact from an ethnic elder may or may not indicate understanding, and lack of eye contact should not be interpreted as boredom or disregard. For Hispanic Americans, Asian Americans, and Native Americans, lack of eye contact can indicate modesty, respect, or deference. Direct eye contact can be interpreted as rude, confrontive, or hostile in the case of Native Americans and some Black Americans (Sue, 1981). However, lack of eye contact on the part of health care providers can be viewed as an insult by some Black Americans (McCormack, 1987). It may be safest in an initial contact to look at the elder's eyes for very brief periods of time and then direct one's gaze in the direction of the client's ear or chin until a preference has been indicated.

Physical contact should be used with care. It is important for the therapist to discover whether physical intimacy is permitted or restrained by the elder's cultural tradition (Brownlee, 1978). Touch by an outsider, particularly a stranger, is not acceptable in many cultures. At times a touch on the shoulder or on the hand may prevail over cultural preferences when expressing warmth, concern, or comfort or dealing with pain (Zuniga-Martinez, 1983).

The information in this chapter regarding culturally diverse elders should not be used as if it provided a recipe or a definitive approach. Rather, the hope is that the reader will be motivated to acquire further knowledge. Contacts with ethnic elders should be humanizing ones. Sensitivity to their cultures, traditions, health practices, and languages will produce better helping relationships, greater understanding and acceptance, and stronger links between cultures. Such sensitivity can also lead to more successful therapeutic experiences for ethnic elders.

REFERENCES

Aguilar, I. (1972). Initial contacts with Mexican-American families. *Social Work, 17*, 66–70.

Ahumada-Monroy, L. (1983). Nursing care of Raza/Latina patients. In M.S. Orque, B. Block, & L. Ahumada-Monroy (Eds.), *Ethnic nursing care* (pp. 115–144). St. Louis: C.V. Mosby.

Anderson, J.N. (1983). Health and illness in Philipino immigrants in cross-cultural medicine. *Western Journal of Medicine, 139*, 811–819.

Bean, L.J. (1976). California Indian shamanism and folk curing. In W.D. Hand (Ed.), *American folk medicine: A symposium* (pp. 109–123). Berkeley, CA: University of California.

Bello, T. (1976). The third dimension: Cultural sensitivity in nursing practice. *Imprint, 23*, 36–38.

Boyd, D. (1974). *Rolling thunder*. New York: Random House.

Brownlee, A. (1978). *Community, culture and care*. St. Louis: C.V. Mosby.

Chang, B. (1981). *Asian-American patient care: In transcultural health care*. Menlo Park, CA: Addison-Wesley.

Cuellar, J.B., & Weeks, J. (1980). *Minority elderly Americans: A prototype for area agencies on aging*. San Diego, CA: Allied Home Health Association.

Edinberg, M.A. (1985). *Mental health practice with the elderly*. Englewood Cliffs, NJ: Prentice-Hall.

Farris, L. (1978). The American Indian. In A. Clark (Ed.), *Culture, childbearing, health professionals* (pp. 20–33). Philadelphia: F.A. Davis.

Fung, Y. (1961). *A short history of Chinese philosophy*. New York: Free Press.

Hall, E.T., & Whyte, W.F. (1960). Intercultural communication. *Human Organization, 19*(1), 5–12.

Hart, D.V. (1969). *Bisayan Filipino and Malayan humoral pathologies: Folk medicine and ethnohistory in Southeast Asia* (Data Paper No. 76, Southeast Asia Program). Ithaca, NY: Cornell University.

Holbrook, B. (1981). *The stone monkey: An alternative Chinese-scientific reality*. New York: William Morrow.

Justice, B. (1987). *Who gets sick: Thinking and health*. Houston, TX: Peak Press.

Katz, S.H. (1978). Anthropological perspectives on aging. *Annals of Applied Anthropological Perspectives and Social Studies, 438*, 1–12.

Kitano, H. (1976). *Japanese Americans: The evaluation of a subculture* (2nd ed.). Englewood Cliffs, NJ: Prentice-Hall.

Lipson, J.G., & Meleis, A.I. (1983). Issues in health care of Middle Eastern patients in cross-cultural medicine. *Western Journal of Medicine, 139*, 50–57.

Lock, M. (1980). *East Asian medicine in urban Japan: Variables of medical experience*. Berkeley, CA: University of California.

Longston, E.J. (1981). Models for linking formal and informal networks: Implications for policies and programs. In E.P. Stanford & S.A. Lockery (Eds.), *Trends and status of minority aging*. San Diego, CA: San Diego State University.

Maduro, R. (1983). Curanderismo and Latino views of disease and caring in cross cultural medicine. *Western Journal of Medicine, 139*, 868–874.

Markides, K., & Mindel, C. (1987). *Aging and ethnicity*. London: Sage.

Marmot, M., & Syme, S.L. (1976). Acculturation and coronary heart disease in Japanese-Americans. *American Journal of Epidemiology, 104*, 225–247.

Martinez, C. (1977). Curanderos: Clinical aspects. *Journal of Operational Psychiatry, 8*(2), 35–38.

Martinez, C., & Martin, H.W. (1966). Folk diseases among urban Mexicans. *Journal of the American Medical Association, 196*, 161–164.

McCormack, G. (1987). Culture and communication in the treatment planning for occupational therapy with minority patients. In F.S. Cromwell (Ed.), *Sociocultural implications in treatment planning in occupational therapy* (pp. 17–36). New York: Haworth Press.

Meleis, A.I. (1981). The Arab American in the health care system. *American Journal of Nursing, 81*, 1180–1183.

Montero, D. (1979). *Vietnamese Americans: Patterns of resettlement and socioeconomic adaptation in the United States.* Boulder, CO: Westview.

Morioka-Douglas, N. (1988). Impact of culture on health care of ethnic elders: Report on the state-of-the-art, Asian/Pacific Island elders. In *Health care for ethnic elders: The cultural context* (Working Paper Series No. 7). Stanford, CA: Stanford Geriatric Education Center, Division of Family Medicine.

Muecke, M.A. (1983). In search of healers: Southeast Asian refugees in the American health care system in cross cultural medicine. *Western Journal of Medicine, 139,* 835–840.

Osako, M.M. (1979). Aging and family among Japanese Americans: The role of ethnic tradition in the adjustment to old age. *The Gerontologist, 19,* 448–455.

Primeaux, M. (1977). American Indian health care practices: A cross-cultural perspective. *Nursing Clinics of North America, 12*(1), 55–65.

Rubel, A.J. (1960). Concepts of disease in Mexican-American culture. *American Anthropology, 62,* 795–814.

Snow, L.F. (1983). Traditional health beliefs and practices among lower class black Americans in cross-cultural medicine. *Western Journal of Medicine, 139,* 828–829.

Sue, D.W. (1981). *Counseling the culturally different: Theory and practice.* New York: Wiley-Interscience.

Tung, T.M. (1980). Indochinese patients: Cultural aspects of the medical and psychiatric care of Indochinese refugees. In *Action for Southeast Asians* (pp. 13–16, 30–35). Washington, DC: Action for Southeast Asians.

U.S. Bureau of the Census. (1980a). *Current population reports: Population characteristics, persons of Spanish origin in the United States* (Series 361, 20 [81-12040]). Washington, DC: Government Printing Office.

U.S. Bureau of the Census. (1980b). *Census of population: Subject reports, Japanese, Chinese and Filipinos in the United States.* Washington, DC: U.S. Superintendent of Documents.

U.S. Department of Health and Human Services. (1983). *Refugee reports: Office of refugee resettlement* (Nos. 4, 16 [81-50169]). Washington, DC: Government Printing Office.

Vogel, V.J. (1970). *American Indian medicine.* New York: Ballantine.

Vontress, C.E. (1976). Counseling middle-aged and aging cultural minorities. *Personnel & Guidance Journal, 55,* 132–135.

White, E.F. (1977). Giving health care to minority patients. *Nursing Clinics of North America, 12*(1), 27–40.

Wilson, U.M. (1983). Nursing care of American Indian patients. In M.S. Orque, B. Block, and L. Ahumada-Monroy (Eds.), *Ethnic nursing care: A multicultural approach* (pp. 272–295). St. Louis: C.V. Mosby.

Wylie, F.M. (1971). Attitudes toward aging and the aged among black Americans: Some historical perspectives. *Aging and Human Development, 2,* 66–70.

Yeatman, G.W., & Dang, V.V. (1980). Cao gio (coin rubbing): Vietnamese attitudes towards health care. *Journal of the American Medical Association, 244,* 2748–2749.

Zuniga-Martinez, M. (1983). Social treatment with minority elderly. In R.L. McNeely & J.L. Colen (Eds.), *Aging in minority groups* (pp. 260–269). Newbury Park, CA: Sage.

Chapter 3

Aging, Functional Change, and Adaptation

Nancy B. Ellis

Work with older adults presents both an opportunity and a challenge to the occupational therapist. Successfully aging individuals in the final three to four decades of life (i.e., 60 years old and above) have developed a repertoire of skills that enable them to meet the demands of daily life and to adapt to changing circumstances, changing social roles, and changing environmental expectations.

It is well established that functional capacities change with increasing age and that, in general, these changes reflect a decrement in the individual's peak functional performance in younger years. These age-related functional changes present a challenge to the aged individual who seeks to maintain a relatively stable, satisfying pattern of day-to-day living. This challenge is increased tenfold by the advent of disease or illness. In working with older individuals, the therapist needs to recognize the fact that the elderly are not a homogeneous group and that there is a great deal of variability in the timing and the magnitude of age-associated changes.

Working with older patients gives the therapist the opportunity to help these individuals identify and use their adaptive skills to accomplish new goals as required by the treatment programs. In treating older patients, the therapist is challenged to integrate knowledge and understanding of age-related functional changes with knowledge and understanding of pathological processes that affect functional capacity and performance.

The therapist who understands the normative functional changes of late adulthood and the challenges these changes present to the aged individual will be better able to work with older persons and enhance their performance in self-care, leisure, and productive pursuits.

Failure to take normative age-related changes into account when treating the older individual will result in difficulties in implementing the treatment program, feelings of frustration and failure for the patient, and a less functional or less satisfactory treatment outcome. For example, in teaching homemaking skills to an older individual who has a hemiparesis, the therapist should take into account the need to provide increased-intensity, glare-free lighting conditions. Similarly the therapist should adjust the pace of the program to accommodate the need for a rest period following treatment activities that require physical exertion.

Early work on age-related changes in function gave rise to the notion of a decline in virtually all physical and mental processes beginning when individuals are in their thirties and progressing irrevocably to physical dependence and dementia at the end of the life span. Thus, health professionals came to expect that all older individuals would be infirm and functionally impaired. The vigorous, self-directed, fully functioning 70- or 80-year-old was considered a remarkable exception, someone who had somehow escaped the aging process.

Current research presents a more optimistic picture. Today, older individuals who maintain the capacity to engage fully in the life style they have chosen are viewed as examples of successful aging rather than as exceptions to the aging process. There are two reasons for this. First newer findings suggest that many of the decrements in function once considered part of the normal aging process and therefore inevitable in fact reflect disease-induced change and involve pathological processes. For example Jarvik's (1988) research into mental functions in late adulthood led her to suggest that learning, memory, and problem-solving abilities should remain intact and stable at least through 75 or 80 years of age and possibly throughout the life course. She asserts that deficits in cognition in older individuals should be viewed as pathological and that such findings merit close study in order to identify etiology and to find effective means of intervention or prevention.

In a similar vein, recent studies of cardiovascular function document changes in the basic mechanisms that mediate cardiac response but indicate that, in the absence of disease and poor health habits (e.g., smoking, excessive alcohol consumption), heart and circulatory function remain wholly adequate to meet the usual demands of daily living through the ninth decade of life (Weisfeldt, Gerstenblith, and Lakatta, 1985).

The second reason for optimism is the upward shift in the periods of life when age-related functional losses are typically expected to occur. Gerontologists once thought that age-related deficits in sensory and somatic functions severe enough to impair day-to-day living were typical of 50- and 60-year-olds. Longitudinal studies indicate otherwise. Functional losses that impair performance do not generally appear until the seventies. In some individuals, functionally significant age-related changes do not occur until the individuals are 80 or even 90 years of age.

One of the principal findings in research on aging is the wide variability in the timing and the degree of age-related changes in older individuals. Despite this variability, it is clear that age-related decrements in function do occur. Not all decrements are preventable, nor are they all manifestations of illness or disease. Andres (1985) suggests that it is counterproductive to juxtapose aging and disease as if they were dichotomous. He points out that the age-related changes that occur at differing rates and at varying times in the course of the life span may be precisely the factors that make a disease process probable or inevitable.

The basic significance of age-related changes for older individuals and therapists working with them lies in the degree of functional loss associated with these changes and the degree to which the loss impedes the older individual's ability to respond adaptively to environmental opportunities and demands. Adaptive capacity is not synonymous with youth. Most aged individuals retain and strengthen their capacity to adapt to changing somatic and sensory functions. The degree of adaptation required can be considerable, and there is some truth in the adage that aging is not a game for sissies.

The remainder of this chapter highlights age-related changes in mental and physical function that have particular relevance to occupational therapists working with older individuals. Throughout this chapter, the term *older individual* refers to those over the age of 70. Specific consideration is given to functional changes that affect the older person's adaptive capabilities; therefore, the content is selective. For a more detailed and comprehensive treatment of age-related changes, readers are referred to Andres, Bierman, and Hazzard (1985), Cohen (1988), Pesmen (1984), and Saxon and Etten (1987).

AGE-RELATED ORGANISMIC CHANGES

There are several generalized somatic changes associated with aging that, by their very nature, have a pervasive effect on the older individual's overall function. Three such age-related changes are considered here. The first change is a loss of elasticity and pliability, the second is a change in the composition of the body as a whole, and the third is a change in the time required to respond to environmental stimuli.

The loss of elasticity and pliability in tissues is related, at least in part, to changes in collagen linkages. The effects of these changes are found in all body systems, including the integumentary, musculoskeletal, cardiovascular, and pulmonary.

As the individual ages, there is a change in the ratio of fat and water content in the body. In young adults, the ratio of body water to body fat is approximately 60:40. In late adulthood, this ratio changes to 50:50 or even 45:55 (Rossman, 1977). The proportional decrease in body water may be reflected in increased viscosity of mucous secretions, decreased saliva production, decreased ocular lubrication, decreased intestinal mobility, and decreased sweat production.

The third age-related change that affects multiple systems is an increase in the time required to respond to a stimulus. Gerontologists have not identified the cause (or causes) of this slowed response time, but they generally attribute it to changes occurring both centrally and peripherally in the nervous system. Slower response time is evident in many different activities. For example, slower performance on speed-dependent tasks, an increase in the time it takes the eyes to accommodate to changes in light conditions, a decrease in heart rate, an increase in the time it takes the cardiovascular system to return to its resting rate following exercise, and an increased transport time for food moving through the digestive track.

These changes occur gradually over a 10- or 20-year period, giving older individuals time to make small adjustments in their daily activities to compensate for the changes without much conscious effort. Therapists, on the other hand, must maintain a conscious awareness of the effects of these systemic changes and take them into account when working with older individuals.

AGE-RELATED SENSORY CHANGE

Vision

Age-related changes in vision usually begin in midlife, when a decrease in the pliability of the lens of the eye results in a diminution of accommodation capacity. Other age-related visual changes usually occur in individuals in their 70s and 80s. The lens becomes more rigid and develops a yellow pigmentation that affects the perception of colors. Blue-green discrimination becomes difficult, and pastel shades of all colors are less easily distinguished. About 95% of individuals over 70 years of age evidence some clouding of the lens indicative of cataract formation. The high incidence of cataracts in the late years raises the issue of whether the process of cataract formation should be considered a normal age-related change or a pathological change.

The pupil becomes smaller and refractive ability diminishes. This change, coupled with the yellowing of the lens, substantively reduces the amount of light reaching the retina. The vitreous humor becomes less clear, which produces a scattering of light rays on the retina, resulting in a blurred visual image. Slower pupil opening and changes in the retina's visual receptors result in a slower adaptation to dark-light transitions. The receptors themselves require almost 50% more light in order to respond to a visual stimulus. All together these changes lead to a decrease in visual acuity. The majority of individuals over 75 years of age evidence these changes.

It is possible to compensate environmentally for many of these changes. Older individuals and therapists working with them can increase illumination, reduce glare, use large, clear visual images, and use higher contrasts between foreground and background materials.

Hearing

Changes in acoustic acuity accompany aging and are most notable for the negative effects on older individuals' ability to understand speech. Typically changes in acuity begin in midlife. However, the decrements are very mild until 60 or 70 years of age, when high frequency loss becomes a significant problem for over a third of older individuals. By the age of 80, two-thirds have significant hearing problems.

Changes that affect hearing occur in outer, middle, and inner ear structures. In the outer ear, cerumen (ear wax) becomes thicker and drier and may accumulate, resulting in a conductive hearing loss. Middle ear structures become stiffer. The membranes and ossicles are less responsive to vibratory stimuli, and there is a consequent decrease in sound transmission to the inner ear. In the cochlea, structural and metabolic changes give rise to a loss of acuity. The deficit is most pronounced in the high-frequency range. This loss, termed *presbycusis*, makes it difficult to distinguish consonants and hence to understand verbal messages. "That's the wrong way" may be interpreted as "That's the long way," or "I'll have more salad" as "I have four ballads."

Therapists can help the individual who has a high-frequency loss by using a low-pitched voice, speaking slowly, and making sure that the speaker's face is in clear view of the listener. They should avoid background noise and can use a pocket communicator to improve volume.

Taste

Taste sensation, an important component in the selection and enjoyment of food, shows only minor changes in late adulthood. The ability to taste salt appears to be moderately diminished, while detection of sweet, sour, and bitter flavors remains relatively unimpaired. It is worth noting, however, that dental disease, poor oral hygiene, and some medicines can alter the ability to taste (Baum, 1985).

Smell

The ability to appreciate flavors and to derive pleasure from eating is mediated, in large measure, by the sense of smell. Odor identification, odor detection, and the appreciation of pleasant smells all diminish with age (Doty & Snow, 1988). In testing over 2,000 older individuals, Doty found that 50% of those 65 to 80 years old evidenced major impairment in odor identification. This figure rises to 75% for those over the age of 80. Doty also notes that there are wide variations in olfactory function among aged individuals and that some 25% do not show any changes in function at all.

The mechanisms responsible for the diminution in sensitivity to smell are currently unknown. However, decreases in olfactory receptors and in the number of fibers in the olfactory nerve have been reported. It is presently unclear whether olfactory changes are primarily age related and therefore to be expected in the later years or whether the decline in odor identification and smell acuity reflects a pathological change and should therefore be considered potentially preventable.

What is evident is that older individuals who have a diminished sense of smell will lack the stimulus afforded by the pleasant odor of food, which may affect their appetite and nutrition. They will also be at risk for succumbing to noxious substances in their environment such as leaking gas or spoiled food. Frequently older individuals are not aware of their altered capacity to smell. Therapists should evaluate the senses of taste and smell when working with older individuals.

Temperature and Pain

During one's 70s, 80s, and 90s, vasomotor responsiveness decreases, subcutaneous fat diminishes and both sweating and shivering are reduced. Together these changes lead to an increased risk of experiencing hypothermia and hyperthermia. Hypothermia can occur in an older individual in even moderately cold indooor temperatures. Readings of 50° to 65°F are sufficient to cause hypothermia in a sedentary older person.

The danger of hyperthermia exists when the external temperature exceeds normal body temperature so that the body actually begins to absorb heat. The older individual's decreased capacity to evaporate moisture through sweating places him or her at greater risk of succumbing to heat stroke (Besdine & Harris, 1985).

There is little research to substantiate the often heard assertion that sensitivity to pain decreases in older individuals. While it is true that acute illness may manifest without any pain (e.g., the silent myocardial infarction), it does not follow that pain, when present, is less well-perceived (Harkins et al., 1986).

Therapists alert to changes in thermoregulatory capacities can help older individuals use strategies for protecting themselves from a drop in body temperature through maintaining adequate room heat, layering indoor and outdoor clothing, and keeping physically active. They can also help older individuals maintain normal body temperature when the heat is oppressive by keeping air circulating to encourage heat loss by convection, increasing intake of cool water and other liquids, and wearing loose, absorbent clothing.

Touch, Position Sense, and Balance

Information on age-related change in sensitivity to touch is sparse and somewhat conflicting. Studies indicate diminution of two point discrimination and a decline in tactile sensitivity in the extremities, more so in the feet than the hands. Increased difficulty identifying stimuli presented homolaterally, as opposed to contralaterally, is reported (Abramson & Lovas, 1988). The need for further research into changes in touch sensation with aging is obvious. Information on position sense and balance in older individuals is equally fragmentary. The primary finding is that postural sway increases with age for both men and women, but is more pronounced in women (Abramson & Lovas, 1988). Current studies document a wide variability in response sensitivity. The evidence for age-related change in these areas of sensation is rudimentary and inconclusive at present.

AGE-RELATED CHANGES IN COGNITIVE FUNCTION

Responsivity

Probably the one fact that everyone accepts about the brain and aging is that adults lose thousands of brain cells each day and that brain cells do not regenerate. The brain reaches its maximum weight at about 20 years of age and shows a progressive loss of weight due to atrophy totaling approximately 100 grams for individuals in their nineties. This cell loss is not evenly distributed in the central nervous system. The cerebral cortex, for example, shows a larger weight loss than the brain stem, and some nuclei show age-related losses whereas others appear to remain stable throughout life. In general, the areas of the brain responsible for producing neurotransmitters do not show any changes until after the age of 70. Current research indicates that loss in brain weight in otherwise healthy older individuals does not lead to a decrement in intellectual function (Cohen, 1988).

The brain seems to have the ability to compensate for decrements in the number of cells through a variety of feedback mechanisms that serve to maintain its functional capacities. A decrease in the number of neurotransmitter cells, for example, triggers feedback loops that both stimulate the remaining cells to increase their production of neurotransmitters and increase the sensitivity of the receptor sites to the neurotransmitter substance (Cohen, 1988). New evidence of plasticity in the aging brain is emerging. Studies of rats placed in an enriched environment showed cortical thickening and an increase in brain weight and enzyme activity. Old as well as young rats showed these changes.

In the older individual, there is a particularly close association and a delicate equilibrium between physical illness, emotional stress, and mental function. Impaired thought processes are not an expected change with age; therefore, a diminution in mental function should alert the therapist to the possibility of an intercurrent illness. The therapist should also be prepared for a transitory decrease in mental function, perhaps for as long as several weeks, in older individuals who have an episode of acute illness.

The question of the relationship between mental function and age generates great interest and concern among gerontologists. Current reports of longitudinal studies by Jarvik (1988), Schaie (1983), and others indicate that there is a measurable, statistically significant age-associated decline in scores on standardized tests such as the Wechsler Adult Intelligence Scale and the Primary Mental Abilities Test. The decline seems to begin between 70 and 80 years of age and continues through each successive decade to the end of life. The decline in each decade is small, but persistent, even when the factor of speed is eliminated.

An important question now being addressed in research on mental function is whether these small overall decrements in test scores that occur for most individuals over the age of 75 have any significance in the individuals' ability to carry out day-to-day activities. Do individuals show changes in learning, in ease of problem solving, or in remembering things that are interesting and salient in their own environment? Current evidence indicates that, despite the measured decline in scores on standardized tests and problem-solving tasks, older individuals retain the capacity to learn, to respond appropriately to challenges, and to adapt to new situations (Poon, 1987). Denny and Pearce (1989) note that older adults typically perform better in solving practical problems than they do when confronted with the types of problem-solving tasks used in traditional testing situations. They further note that while performance on practical problem-solving tasks appears to peak in the middle years, the level of performance of 60- and 70-year-olds is essentially the same as that of 20-year-olds. The degree of function that is retained is more than sufficient to meet the demands of day-to-day living.

Jarvik (1988) suggests that declines in scores on specific subtests of the Wechsler Adult Intelligence Scale (WAIS) may be predictive of mortality and that low scores on other WAIS subtests may be predictive of the subsequent development of dementia. She also notes the wide variability in cognitive performance found among older individuals.

Interestingly, some individuals show no decline in test scores even into their nineties. This is yet another example of the wide variability of response that characterizes older individuals. Jarvik (1988) suggests that the presence of 80- and 90-year-olds who show no decrements in scores on standardized tests of intellectual function opens the possibility that age-related change may not be inevitable and may in fact represent an underlying pathological process of some kind.

Evidence is accumulating that cognitive activity and intellectual performance are the most important factors in maintaining mental health and life satisfaction for older individuals (Cohen, 1988).

Behavior and Personality

Studies of behavior and personality traits provide increasing evidence that older people continue to develop new ways of responding to their environment. Older individuals do not necessarily become more rigid and less open to new experiences with increasing age (Cohen, 1988).

In older individuals, physical illness and psychological stress are factors that frequently precipitate decline in cognitive skills and changes in behavior. A rapid decrease in mental function or a sudden change in customary behavior may presage the onset of an acute illness such as pneumonia or may be one of the sequelae of a systemic infection. Cognitive skills may diminish following a prolonged period of stress. In these instances, improvement in cognitive function usually accompanies resolution of the illness or the stressful situation.

AGE-RELATED CHANGES IN PHYSICAL ACTIVITY

The ability to be mobile, to engage in activity, and to accomplish physical tasks depends upon the combined functions of the cardiovascular, respiratory, and musculoskeletal systems. Age-related changes in these three systems are well documented in the literature; however, the inevitability of some of these changes is currently in question.

Circulation

Structural and functional changes in the heart and blood vessels are seen with increasing age in the absence of any identifiable pathology. Heart valves thicken and become more rigid, the left ventricle hypertrophies, and peripheral blood vessels thicken and lose as much as 50% of their elasticity. With increasing age, the loss of elasticity in the peripheral blood vessels leads to an increase in blood pressure, most notably in systolic pressure, forcing the heart to pump harder (Wenger, 1984).

A pattern of increasing systolic blood pressure up through the 70s is found throughout the Western world. In less developed countries, this relationship between age and increased systolic pressure does not seem to pertain. In these societies, systolic pressure tends to remain stable or even to decline during the second half of the life span. Data from studies in less developed countries raise the question whether an increase in blood pressure is, in fact, a normative age-associated occurrence (Whelton & Klag, 1989).

Structural alterations in the cardiovascular system give rise to changes in the mechanism by which the heart responds to the need for an increase in blood supply during activity. In younger individuals, the need for an increase in blood supply is met primarily through an increase in heart rate. As individuals age, the resting heart rate decreases, as does the ability to increase the heart rate sufficiently to meet metabolic needs. The older individual's cardiovascular system meets the demand for an increased blood supply primarily by increasing the volume of blood pumped with each heartbeat.

Despite these changes, there seems to be no obligatory decline in cardiovascular function when the body is at rest or while engaged in regular day-to-day activities. Overall cardiac output is not affected by age. In the absence of disease, cardiac function in older persons remains adequate to support a level of activity consistent with the patterns of activity established during their middle years (30–40 years of age).

Respiration

Age-related changes in respiration are attributable to the loss of elasticity in lung tissue and to an increase in the rigidity of the chest wall and rib cage. As a consequence, the volume of air that the lung can hold after a normal inspiration (vital capacity), the rate of air flow (forced expiratory volume), and the efficiency of gas exchange are reduced.

Movement

Peak muscle strength is attained about the age of 30. After 30, lean muscle mass decreases and overall strength declines in linear fashion during each successive decade. This loss is so gradual (about 1 percent a year) that it does not present a challenge to the performance of day-to-day activities until the age of 70 or 75. Striated muscle fibers and ligamentous tissues supporting the joints both lose some of their elasticity, becoming more rigid and less pliable with age. What results is loss in joint range of motion as well as slower, less fluid body movements.

Postural Support

Bone density decreases over time. The loss of bone mass begins in the thirties and forties and continues throughout life. Over their lifetime, women lose about 35% of their cortical bone and as much as 50% of their trabecular bone mass, while men lose about 20% and 35% respectively. Cortical bone predominates in the shafts of the long bones, and trabecular bone is found in flat bones such as the vertebrae and the hip girdle. Resorption of trabecular bone begins about a decade earlier than cortical bone loss. This loss of mass in the flat bones is accelerated following menopause (Riggs & Melton, 1986).

Both the degree of bone loss and the rate of resorption are influenced by gender, race, physical activity, calcium absorption, and nutritional status. The age-associated loss of bone density is probably most significant in thin, Caucasian, postmenopausal women. This is primarily because bone density in these women is lower throughout life. Thus, age-associated loss places them at greater risk of fracture and loss of postural stability. Research into the degree to which bone loss can be prevented or bone regained is ongoing. Exercise, calcium intake, and hormone replacement therapy are all under study.

Together, the cardiovascular, pulmonary, and musculoskeletal systems govern the individual's overall capacity to engage in physical activity. It is generally agreed that the absolute energy required to accomplish a specific task is essentially fixed and is the same for all individuals. However, as age increases, an individual's aerobic capacity decreases. The result is that the older individual has to expend a larger percentage of total energy capacity to accomplish a specific task. Activities that an individual accomplished with ease in the middle years may not only seem more difficult at 70 or 80 but may actually be more demanding, because the individual has to use a larger percentage of total aerobic capacity to accomplish the task. Thus the *relative* energy expenditure needed to carry a bag of groceries for a woman aged 70 may be almost twice as great as that required for a woman of 20 (Bruce, 1985).

Even with all these changes interacting, the healthy older person generally has no significant difficulty performing the physical activities he or she is accustomed to doing regularly. Performance of activities becomes difficult for the 70- or 80-year-old who attempts to go beyond current capacity to energize the musculoskeletal system.

What diminishes in the older person is the ability to respond to unusual demands. What constitutes an unusual demand or stress for a particular older individual depends upon the individual's health status and the level of day-to-day activity. A 15-minute walk may be too demanding for a sedentary 75-year-old woman, whereas an 80-year-old woman who routinely walks three miles a day will find the walk challenges her capabilities only if she is required to climb a steep hill along the way. Regardless of differences in aerobic capacity, older individuals will need a longer time to recover from their exertion than would a 30-year-old in comparable health. In the healthy older person, disuse and a sedentary life style, not age per se, are probably the most salient factors in a diminished capacity to engage in physical activity. Current interest in health promotion programs should encourage healthy, but sedentary, older individuals to modify their life styles so as to incorporate an activity program aimed at preventing loss of function through disuse. Therapists using physical activities in rehabilitating older individuals should be cognizant of the demand exercise places on all body systems and the increasing risk of injury that results from age-related changes in skeletal and soft tissues.

AGE-RELATED CHANGES IN DIGESTION AND EXCRETION

Ingestion

Inadequate care, not age, is the primary factor leading to tooth loss and hence difficulty chewing food in the older adult. Up through about 30 years of age, care of the teeth focuses on prevention and treatment of caries. After 30, the primary concern becomes prevention and treatment of gum disease. It is possible to prevent most gum disease. Failure to prevent gingival disease or to treat it once it occurs leads to tooth loss and the edentulous state once considered inevitable for older individuals. For individuals in their 70s and 80s, gum tissue tends to recede, and there may be some bony resorption in the mandible and maxilla. The roots of the teeth may be exposed, giving rise to new dental caries.

Recent studies demonstrate no general decrease in the amount of saliva produced by older individuals. There are, however, reported changes in masticatory function in older individuals. Feldman et al. (1980) indicate that older individuals prepare food less adequately for swallowing and are willing to swallow larger sized particles of food than younger individuals. Thus, the potential for choking and apnea while eating are increased in the older individual.

Absorption

Age-related physiological changes have been identified in the stomach and intestinal tract. There is a decrease in production of hydrochloric acid in the stomach which results in an incomplete breakdown of food and less efficient absorption of nutrients from the intestine (Pesmen, 1984). In some older individuals, achlorhydria reaches a level where vitamin B_{12} is no longer absorbed. This vitamin is essential to DNA synthesis and to amino and fatty acid metabolism. Depletion of B_{12} leads to severe anemia.

Elimination

The transport time required for food to move through the large intestine increases in older individuals. Changes in collagen and elastin structure give rise to a decreased resistance to stretch in the large intestine, which results in a slowing of peristaltic movement. The mucous lining that protects the intestine from mechanical damage gets thinner and more sparse. In otherwise healthy older individuals, these changes do not impede the digestive process. Much has been written about constipation in the older individual. The problem, when it occurs, is essentially related to debility or disease and is not thought to be associated with aging per se.

Excretion

The renal system exhibits marked changes in older individuals. By the age of 80, kidney mass has usually diminished by about 40%. This loss is primarily attributable to nephron (glomeruli) loss. Structural changes in the arterioles also occur due to sclerosis and anastomoses. There is also a decrease in renal blood flow, a loss of elasticity in the urinary tract structures (particularly in the bladder), and a decrease of about 50% in the bladder's capacity to store urine.

Despite these age-related changes, renal function is adequate to maintain a normal volume and composition of blood and urine. As is true with many of the body's other organ systems, the kidney has a reserve capacity that is sufficiently large to maintain adequate filtration or clearance function under normal conditions even in the face of a 40% loss in mass. However, in the case of salt and water deprivation or excess, as may occur during illness, the kidney of an older individual will be less able to compensate, making the older individual more prone to dehydration or edema.

AGE-RELATED CHANGES IN THE BODY'S DEFENSE MECHANISMS

Skin

The skin is the largest organ in the body. It protects the internal organs, prevents dehydration, and helps regulate body temperature. Changes in the skin are readily recognizable in older individuals. Facial wrinkles are the most noticeable, but other effects occur as well, including changes in the texture, color, and growth rate of hair; the texture of finger- and toenails; wound healing; and thermoregulation. There is no evidence that age-related changes in the skin have any significant effect on longevity.

With increased age, the epidermis becomes more permeable and loses moisture. Thus the skin becomes dryer and is increasingly prone to roughness, fissuring, and chapping. Topical creams can help prevent the problems that accompany dryness. Recently Retin-A, an anti-acne cream, has been found to be effective in reducing facial wrinkles.

Immune Response

Clinical data indicate that infectious diseases are more frequent and more serious in older individuals. The general consensus among gerontologists has been that the effectiveness of the immune system decreases as individuals age. Current studies suggest that the immune functions in older individuals may not be as compromised as had been previously thought and that some of the observed changes in immune function may not reflect age-related changes per se (Fiatarone et al., 1989; Goldberg, Schumacher, & Baker, 1989). In general, immunizations should be kept up to date and flu shots taken yearly.

AGE-RELATED CHANGES IN SEXUAL ACTIVITY

Physiological Factors

Age-related changes in the reproductive tract occur in both men and women. In men, the changes include a decrease in sperm production and ejaculatory force, an increase in the time it takes to achieve erection, a lengthening of the refractory period prior to achieving a subsequent erection, and hypertrophy of the prostate gland.

In women, changes include the climacteric and the cessation of menstrual activity; an atrophying, loss of elasticity, and increasing dryness of vaginal tissue; a decrease in the size of the uterus and the ovaries; and a general diminution of muscle tone in genital and breast tissue.

These physical changes in the reproductive systems of men and women may necessitate some adaptation in patterns of sexual intimacy established in earlier years, but they do not preclude sexual activity or enjoyment (Saxon & Etten, 1987; Pesmen, 1984).

Psychological and Behavioral Factors

The major finding in studies of sexuality in older individuals is a decrease in the frequency of sexual intercourse. There are a number of possible reasons for this decrease: the physiological changes noted above, ill health, and a decrease in the availability of sexual partners. Recent research indicates that diminished hormonal levels (i.e., free testosterone) accounts for only part of the variance in sexual activity. Older men who showed no decrease in testosterone levels also reported a decrease in sexual activity. Yet another instance of the variability that characterizes older individuals is reported by Butler and Lewis (1977), who found that 15% of individuals over the age of 60 showed an increase in sexual interest and sexual activity. Although frequency of intercourse generally decreases in older individuals, satisfaction in sexual expression remains high for both men and women (Davidson, 1985).

CONCLUSION

In the past ten years, a great deal has been learned about the older individual and the variability that characterizes the aging process. It is apparent that there are numerous age-related changes in structure and function throughout the body and that virtually all systems change to some extent in later life. It is increasingly apparent that many older persons maintain their ability to function effectively—both physically and intellectually—right up to the time of death. There is much heterogeneity in older individuals' responses to age-associated change. It is probable that some of the changes currently considered primarily or solely age associated will be found to be linked to underlying incipient pathological processes or life-style factors such as diet and exercise.

Current views of age-related change can be summarized as follows:

1. Age-related changes occur throughout the body in the absence of any identified pathology.
2. Age-related changes occur gradually.
3. There is a large degree of heterogeneity among older individuals and a high degree of variability in how age-related changes manifest themselves at different ages.
4. Decrements sufficient to impair day-to-day function do not occur before 70 or 80 years of age in the majority of older individuals.
5. It is possible to delay, ameliorate, and perhaps even prevent a significant number of age-related functional losses.

The therapist's knowledge of age-related changes is critical to the treatment process. It provides the basis for an appropriate treatment program. Research into normative aging continues, and new findings challenge current views almost daily. Therapists in geriatric practice will find it useful, indeed essential, to stay up to date on gerontology and geriatric research. It is important for therapists to establish a linkage with sources of information on aging and age-related changes in order to keep abreast of current developments. Options include online data bases concerning aging, academic institutions with aging and/or geriatric centers, and membership in national or regional gerontology associations. Therapists working with older individuals should not lose sight of the impact that age-related changes can have on the implementation and outcomes of rehabilitation programs. Neither should therapists lose sight of the potential each individual possesses for successful adaptation to aging and the process of change it entails.

REFERENCES

Abramson, M., & Lovas, P.M. (Eds.). (1988). *Aging and sensory change: An annotated bibliography*. Washington, DC: Gerontological Society of America.

Andres, R. (1985). Normal aging versus disease in the elderly. In R. Andres, E.L. Bierman, & W.R. Hazzard (Eds.), *Principles of geriatric medicine* (pp. 38–41). New York: McGraw-Hill.

Andres, R., Bierman, E.L., & Hazzard, W.R. (Eds.). (1985). *Principles of geriatric medicine*. New York: McGraw-Hill.

Baum, B.J. (1985). Alterations in oral function. In R. Andres, E.L. Bierman, & W.R. Hazzard (Eds.), *Principles of geriatric medicine*. New York: McGraw-Hill.

Besdine, R.W., & Harris, T.B. (1985). Alteration in body temperature (hypothermia and hyperthermia). In R. Andres, E.L. Bierman, & W.R. Hazzard (Eds.), *Principles of geriatric medicine* (pp. 209–217). New York: McGraw-Hill.

Bruce, R.A. (1985). Functional aerobic capacity: Exercise and aging. In R. Andres, E.L. Bierman, & W.R. Hazzard (Eds). *Principles of geriatric medicine*. New York: McGraw-Hill.

Butler, R.N., & Lewis, M.I. (1977). *Aging and mental health* (2nd ed.). St. Louis: C.V. Mosby.

Cohen, G.D. (1988). *The brain in human aging*. New York: Springer.

Davidson, J.M. (1985). Sexuality and aging. In R. Andres, E.L. Bierman, & W.R. Hazzard (Eds.), *Principles of geriatric medicine* (pp. 154–161). New York: McGraw-Hill.

Denny, N.W., & Pearce, K.A. (1989). A developmental study of practical problem solving in adults. *Psychiatry and Aging, 4*, 438–442.

Doty, R.L., & Snow, J.B. (1988). Age related alterations in olfactory structure and function. In F.L. Margolis & T.V. Getchell (Eds.), *Molecular neurobiology of the olfactory system: Molecular membranous and cytological studies* (pp. 355–374). New York: Plenum.

Feldman, R.S., Kapur, K.K., Alman, J.E., and Chauncey, H.H. (1980). Aging and mastication: Changes in performance and in swallowing threshold with natural dentition. *Journal of the American Geriatric Society, 28*, 97–103.

Fiatarone, M.A., Morley, J.E., Bloom, E.T., Benton, D., Solomon, G.F., and Makinodar, T. (1989). The effect of exercise on natural killer cell activity in young and old subjects. *Journal of Gerontology: Medical Sciences, 44*(2), M37–45.

Goldberg, T.H., Schumacher, H.R., & Baker D.G. (1989). Interleukin-1 and the immunology of aging. *Center for the Study of Aging Newsletter* (University of Pennsylvania), *2*(2), 5–6.

Harkins, S.W., Price, D.D., and Martelli, M. (1986). Effects of age on pain perception: Thermonociception. *Journal of Gerontology, 41*, 58–63.

Jarvik, L.F. (1988). Aging of the brain: How can we prevent it? *The Gerontologist, 28*, 739–747.

Pesmen, C. (1984). *How a man ages*. New York: Ballantine.

Poon, L.W. (1987). Learning. In G.L. Maddox (Ed.), *The encyclopedia of aging* (pp. 380–381). New York: Springer.

Riggs, B.L., & Melton, L.J. (1986). Medical progress: Involutional osteoporosis. *New England Journal of Medicine, 314*, 1676–1685.

Rossman, I. (1977). Anatomic and body composition changes with aging. In C.E. Finch & L. Hayflick (Eds.), *Handbook of the biology of aging* (pp. 189–221). New York: Van Nostrand Reinhold.

Saxon, S.V., & Etten, M.J. (1987). *Physical change and aging* (2nd ed.). New York: Tiresias Press.

Schaie, K.W. (1983). The Seattle longtitudinal study: A twenty-one year exploration of psychometric intelligence in adulthood. In K.W. Schaie (Ed.), *Longitudinal studies of adult psychological development* (pp. 64–135). New York: Guilford Press.

Weisfeldt, M.L., Gerstenblith, G., & Lakatta, E.G. (1985). Alterations in circulatory function. In R. Andres, E.L. Bierman, & W.R. Hazzard (Eds.), *Principles of geriatric medicine* (pp. 248–279). New York: McGraw-Hill.

Wenger, N.K. (1984). Cardiovascular status: Changes with aging. In T.F. Williams (Ed.), *Rehabilitation in the aging* (pp. 1–12). New York: Raven Press.

Whelton, P.K., and Klag, M.K. (1989). Epidemiology of high blood pressure. In W. Applegate (Ed.), *Clinics in geriatric medicine* (pp. 639–655). Philadelphia: W.B. Saunders.

Chapter 4

Maintaining Fitness in Later Life

Cheryl L. Herring

Health promotion is defined in *Occupational Therapy: Its Definitions and Functions* (American Occupational Therapy Association, 1966) as "the practice of informing, educating, facilitating behavior change . . . so people can assume responsibility for living a life style that is centered on optimal well-being" (p. 204). Prevention of disease and disability includes any activity designed to avert certain diseases or disabling conditions from occurring or worsening. Exercise is one of the self-responsible activities in which an older adult can participate to promote optimum health.

The benefits of exercise are the same for all age groups, and they contribute to both physical and mental well-being. De Vries and Hales (1974), in *Fitness After 50*, describe the physical results from routine exercise. Such exercise

- decreases blood pressure
- develops auxiliary networks of small blood vessels to decrease the load on the arteries
- increases levels of high-density lipoproteins (HDLs), which scientists believe are important in slowing or resisting the buildup of cholesterol in the arteries
- raises the amount of oxygen used per heartbeat, so the heart needs to beat less frequently per minute
- helps heart attack victims return to the same performance levels as healthy sedentary persons
- strengthens the respiratory muscles
- increases endurance
- lessens symptoms of chronic obstructive lung disease
- strengthens elasticity of the chest wall to allow for easier breathing
- increases calories the body uses every day

- consumes excess fatty tissue while building up lean body mass so that essential active tissue is not lost and the body fat percentage remains at the appropriate level
- raises the metabolic rate for more than 6 hours after exercise so that the body continues to use more calories during and after workouts
- decreases appetite for those leading a fairly sedentary life
- increases the supply of glycogen (the fuel for physical activity) in the muscles, which helps sustain activity
- increases oxygen available at the muscles to permit more intense activity
- conditions a muscle to work more before becoming fatigued
- slows the rate at which fatigued muscles select others to complete a task

Exercise also helps a tense body and stressed mind to relax. De Vries and Hales (1974) cite the following benefits to emotional well-being from regular exercise:

- Exercise decreases the activity of the sensory receptors in the muscle that send information to the central nervous system. Tension makes these receptors oversensitive so they bombard the nervous system with electrical impulses
- Exercise lessens the load on the nervous system by slowing the electrical signals from the muscles.
- Exercise helps lessen depression and improve mood.
- Exercise improves the ability to sleep restfully.

EXERCISE PROGRAMS FOR THE WELL ELDERLY

Physical fitness has been defined by many different people in many different ways. Even among the general public, physical fitness may mean one thing to one person and something else to another. Cooper (1982), a leading expert in the field of physical fitness, gives the following example of physical fitness. If individuals are participating in a physical fitness program, they should be able to use their bodies without undue fatigue and with enough energy to participate in leisure time pursuits and to successfully encounter the average physical stresses in emergency situations.

Occupational therapists interested in developing fitness programs for older adults should have special knowledge of the components of fitness. The Cooper Institute of Aerobics and Research divides fitness components into two categories: health-related components and motor-related components.

The health-related components, according to Cooper (1982), are strength, dynamic strength, flexibility, cardiovascular or cardiorespiratory endurance, and body composition. These components are very important, because they add to an individual's ability to be *"fit for life*—a functional, productive human being for everyday *living"* (p. 3).

The motor-related components prepare an individual for success in athletic pursuits or an area of motor performance. These components are coordination, agility, power, balance, speed, and accuracy.

These health- and motor-related components have been combined to form six components that are important for fitness and function for older adults:

1. cardiovascular (cardiorespiratory) endurance
2. flexibility
3. strength
4. dynamic strength
5. balance and coordination
6. body composition

Brief synopses of these six components are presented below.

Cardiovascular Endurance

The heart and lungs respond best to what is known as *aerobic exercise*. Aerobic means "with air" (de Vries & Hales, 1974). Sustained aerobic exercise builds or develops oxygen consumption.

A functional measure of physical fitness is maximal aerobic capacity. The largest amount of oxygen one can consume per minute is called maximal oxygen uptake (VO_2 max). A body's ability to maintain effort over a prolonged period of time is limited by the blood's ability to deliver oxygen to active tissues (Getchell, 1987). A higher oxygen intake indicates the increased ability of the heart to pump blood, the lungs to ventilate larger volumes of air, and the muscle cells to absorb oxygen and eliminate carbon dioxide.

Genetics play a major role in determining the VO_2 max. With exercise, a maximal aerobic capacity can increase 20% to 30%, yet the overall improvement depends on genetic factors, the initial fitness level, and the intensity and duration of the exercise program.

Flexibility

Flexibility is the ability to have full joint range of motion. With normal aging, muscles can lose elasticity, and the tissues around the joints dry and become brittle. Stretching to obtain flexibility nourishes the joint and therefore helps to increase or maintain full joint range. The benefits of stretching include a reduction of muscle tension, increased coordination of movements, saturation of the muscle tissue with O_2, improvement in circulation, increased body awareness, and improved posture.

Strength

The strength component of fitness can be described as the maximal power a person can generate. Later in life, there is a decrease in the size and number of muscle fibers. As strength improves, the older adult will simultaneously strengthen muscles around the joint and improve muscle tone, stamina, and posture. How much muscle strength can increase is dependent upon genetic factors and how much stress the muscle fibers get. A particular necessity for those over 40 is retaining the strength of the abdominal muscles. Strong abdominal muscles are critical in preventing lower back problems.

Calliet and Gross (1987) state that one reason to accept the claim that a stronger "front" makes the best "back" is the "air bag theory." They write that the abdominal wall forms one side of the air bag within the abdominal cavity; the other three sides are the pelvis, the diaphragm, and the spine. The stronger the abdominal muscles, the greater the push against the contents of the abdominal cavity—the intestines, fluid, and air. The larger the push, the more pressure on the curve of the spinal column. Therefore, pressure from the abdominal muscles translates into a straighter spine. Abdominal strengthening is much easier than coping with lower back pain. Strengthening can begin with isometric training (static contraction), followed by isotonic training (dynamic contraction).

Dynamic Strength

Dynamic strength is also known as *muscle endurance*. Endurance is described by de Vries and Hales (1974) as the ability to participate in physical activity and resist muscular fatigue. All body systems, including physiological elements and psychological elements, are interwoven to produce degrees of general endurance. With increased endurance, an individual has more stamina and can participate in daily activities for longer periods of time.

Balance and Coordination

It is generally believed that as a person ages, motor performance decreases. However, if the person is involved in a consistent movement program, muscle control and overall postural balance systems are maintained or even improved. Exercise also assists with body integration, which involves perceiving and regulating the position of various muscles and body parts in relation to each other during static and movement states (Lewis, 1979).

Body Composition

Body composition refers to the percentage of body fat, which may be regulated by weight control. Being overweight is associated with many diseases, ranging from hypertension to gallstones and diabetes.

Experts agree that one of the most common causes of obesity is a lack of physical activity. With exercise, the metabolic rate increases and causes energy loss (burning of calories). To maintain a healthy body composition as one ages, it is necessary to increase energy expenditure (exercise) and decrease food intake (diet).

The best activity for weight reduction is vigorous, endurance-type exercise. Such exercise should be gradually progressive, include proper warm-up, be of high intensity (as tolerated), and be performed for at least 20 minutes three or four times a week. If an individual can combine increased exercise and a balanced diet (and maintain this combination throughout the life span), the effects of the aging process can be slowed.

There are many publications describing weight control through a careful balance of diet and exercise. A nutritionist can be scheduled to speak to an exercise class or, if time does not allow a speaker, nutrition handouts can be given to participants.

THE EXERCISE PROGRAM

There is not one standard exercise program for older adults, just as there is not one specific treatment plan for an individual with diabetes. The leader must take the total group into consideration. The members may be separated by age (e.g., 45–59, 60–74, and 75–90) or mixed.

Objectives for the exercise program need to be specified. Skinner (1987) suggests the following:

- to improve self-care capabilities and general well-being
- to improve cardiovascular condition and general endurance
- to maintain or improve flexibility, coordination, and balance
- to maximize social contact and enjoyment of life

- to improve weight control and nutrition
- to aid digestion and reduce constipation
- to promote relaxation
- to relieve anxiety, insomnia, and depression
- to sustain sexual vigor

The exercise program must be safe, effective, and fun!

PHASES OF AN EXERCISE CLASS

Warm-up

Older adults feel a little more stiff than most younger persons. This stiffness is partly due to the crisscrossing collagen in the muscle fibers adhering together. Loosening these fibers requires body heat. A simple method of initially creating body heat is deep breathing accompanied by isometric tension. The tightening of certain muscle groups occurs as one inhales, holds for a count of five, relaxes and exhales slowly. This breathing can be done while sitting, and the sequence can be repeated 5 to 10 times. The surge of blood through the muscles is accomplished without stress on joints.

Now that the muscles and joints are nourished by increased circulation, a normal stretching and warm-up phase can begin. This phase includes slow, rhythmic, gentle, steady stretches in all planes of motion. These stretches improve flexibility and help maintain the ability to stoop, bend, and reach.

The leader should start with the head and neck and end with the toes. Often the feet are forgotten (or the leader believes they are not important), yet they carry the total body weight. Lack of attention given to the feet is inexcusable. Some participants may be unable to spread their toes or rotate their ankles initially. By the end of an exercise semester, these participants are usually delighted to be able to do such simple movements!

Conditioning Phase

The aerobic conditioning phase for older adults should be of a lower intensity than the conditioning phase for younger individuals because of possible bone, joint, or neuromuscular ailments. When participating in aerobic activity, a large percentage of body muscles are used in gross body activity. The central mechanisms of respiration, circulation, heat dissipation, and the nervous system all are called upon. Aerobic capacity is a measure of cardiorespiratory endurance.

The literature supports several methods of determining training heart rate. For people over 60 or those who have had restrictions or physical limitations, the starting intensity is suggested to be 30% to 40% VO_2 max. VO_2 is the amount of oxygen one can consume per minute. The maximal (max) volume is referred to as *maximal aerobic capacity*. It is suggested that the minimal intensity for a training response in an older man is about 40% VO_2 max. Smith and Gilligan (1983) indicated that this minimal intensity be 40% to 70% VO_2 max. A formula for calculating a training heart rate, presented by Getchell (1987, p. 50), is contained in Exhibit 4-1.

For middle-aged adults, a target rate (70% of heart rate reserve) is approximately 140–170 beats per minute. For older adults, a natural decline of maximal heart rate occurs and a lower training heart rate is adequate. For a 60-year-old, 96–120 beats per minute is a good training heart rate (60% to 75% of heart rate reserve).

As a rule of thumb, individuals should be able to keep a conversation going while exercising at their training heart rate. If they cannot talk, they most likely are working too intensely. For efficiency during an exercise class, 10-second pulse rates may be taken to assess exercise heart rates. A chart can be placed on the wall for quick calculation (see Table 4-1). For example, if 26 beats occur over 10 seconds, the individual can quickly see the exercise heart rate is 156 beats per minute.

To take a pulse, a participant should place the tips of the fingers on his or her chest below and to the side of the left nipple. A pulse may also be taken on the inside of the wrist by placing the tips of two fingers immediately below the base of the thumb. The participant should press lightly and count for 10 seconds. The participant should not stop moving while taking a pulse, because the blood pools in

---

Exhibit 4-1 Formula for Estimating Target Heart Rate

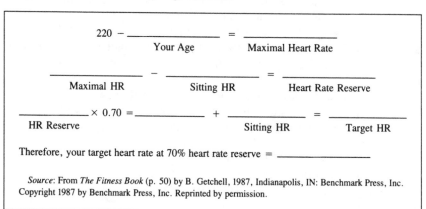

$$220 - \underline{\hspace{3cm}} = \underline{\hspace{3cm}}$$

Your Age   Maximal Heart Rate

$$\underline{\hspace{3cm}} - \underline{\hspace{3cm}} = \underline{\hspace{3cm}}$$

Maximal HR   Sitting HR   Heart Rate Reserve

$$\underline{\hspace{3cm}} \times 0.70 = \underline{\hspace{2cm}} + \underline{\hspace{2cm}} = \underline{\hspace{2cm}}$$

HR Reserve   Sitting HR   Target HR

Therefore, your target heart rate at 70% heart rate reserve = \underline{\hspace{3cm}}

Source: From *The Fitness Book* (p. 50) by B. Getchell, 1987, Indianapolis, IN: Benchmark Press, Inc. Copyright 1987 by Benchmark Press, Inc. Reprinted by permission.

Table 4-1 Chart for Converting 10-Second Pulse Counts into Beats per Minute

10-Second Pulse Counts	Heart Beats per Minute
15	90
16	96
17	102
18	108
19	114
20	120
21	126
22	132
23	138
24	144
25	150
26	156
27	162
28	168
29	174
30	180

Source: From *The Fitness Book* (p. 50) by B. Getchell, 1987, Indianapolis, IN: Benchmark Press, Inc. Copyright 1987 by Benchmark Press, Inc. Reprinted by permission.

---

the legs and chemical buildup in the blood can raise blood pressure and produce a cardiac strain. The participant should be encouraged to keep walking in place or marching. Taking a carotid pulse is not always suggested for older adults, because they may already have a circulatory problem. If while taking a pulse, an older individual presses too hard on the carotid artery, he or she increases the chance of reducing the most immediate blood supply to the brain.

If the exercise leader observes no distress among participants, the standard heart rate may not need to be taken. Loss of sensitivity in the fingers may make it difficult for older adults to locate their pulse. Many individuals may experience irregular heartbeats, which make counting in a 10- to 15-second time frame unfeasible. Ratings of perceived exertion (RPE) can be monitored. As previously stated, if participants cannot talk comfortably while exercising, they are working too hard.

Calliet and Gross (1987) suggest individuals should increase their physical sensitivity to determine whether they are feeling the benefits of a workout. They indicated that if participants are receiving a vigorous workout,

- they will feel it (their hearts beat faster)
- they will hear it (their breathing is quicker)
- they will sense it (their skin feels moist and their skin temperature rises)
- they will begin to feel exhilarated

Individuals must exert themselves but not destroy themselves from overexertion. Calliet and Gross state that individuals can maintain an activity until they are pleasantly fatigued.

What types of activities can be done that are of cardiorespiratory value? The usual recommended activities are walking, swimming, biking, and jogging. In an exercise class for older adults, walking and marching in place and circles or patterns with various arm motions can be used. Large muscle group activities should be stressed. Towels, scarves, wands, bands, or balloons may be included to allow diversity. Dancing can be incorporated as a cardiovascular exercise. Polkas, folk dancing, and square dancing can be fun. If the class must sit for safety purposes, foot and leg motion, combined with upper extremity movements, can raise heart rates.

Balance and coordination activities are incorporated during some of the cardiovascular exercises. If a participant has difficulty with balance, activities should be performed using some type of support (sitting, standing, holding a chair, or lying on the floor or in the water). A useful reference is *Therapeutic Dance/ Movement* (see ''Additional Resources'' at the end of this chapter). The activities suggested by the authors may have to be adapted for a group, yet the book provides suggestions for balance, coordination, strengthening, and stretching activities.

It is suggested that cardiovascular activity be performed 20–30 minutes three times a week. This regimen will result in increased cardiovascular endurance.

Pre–Cool Down

This phase should take approximately 5 minutes. This is the period in which the heart rate is allowed to decline gradually. This prevents dizziness, lightheaded feelings, or loss of consciousness. A slower paced walk or activity is suggested.

Muscle Strengthening

If resistance cannot be used due to very weak muscles, a strengthening program may begin using the resistance of gravity, then gradually adding weight. Participants should achieve complete joint range, if possible, prior to incorporating resistance. Bands, tubing, bags of beans or sand, and dumbbells are a few items that can add resistance. A simple rule of thumb is to start with a light weight that will allow complete joint range and that can be lifted four to eight times. If resistance is too strong, participants may assume inappropriate postures. They may not be aware of their substitution. This is a time for ''hands on'' physical adjustment, particularly for the purposes of injury prevention. Muscle strengthening activities should last approximately 10 minutes.

Cool Down

The purpose of the cool down is to minimize soreness and stiffness and to encourage relaxation. The time period should be approximately 8–10 minutes. Some of the same stretches used in the warm-up cycle may be used. A variety of movements should be incorporated to ensure involvement of all muscle groups (extensors, flexors, rotators).

Intermediate exercise classes should consist of the following phases:

Warm-up	10 minutes
Conditioning	20 minutes
Pre–cool down	5 minutes
Muscle strengthening	10 minutes
Cool down	10 minutes

Following are particular warm-up and cool-down activities that are always enjoyed. These activities include:

- deep breathing
- lateral and forward head rolls
- shoulder rotations
- shoulder flexion
- shoulder extension
- wrist rotation
- finger extension and abduction
- "safe" lower back stretch
- knee extension
- ankle rotation
- foot dorsiflexion

At the end of this chapter, there is a list of resources that can help in developing exercise programs. There is not one specific standardized regimen. The program will depend upon the leader's creativity and the participants' responses.

OTHER CONSIDERATIONS

Assessments and Screenings

The ideal consideration would be for the group leader to do a physical assessment of each participant. However, that is not always possible. The registration form may be the only means of obtaining information about the participant. Each participant must complete a form prior to engaging in the fitness program. The form should contain a health history, the present health status, medications, physical limitations, the physician's name and phone number, and the name and phone number of a contact person in case of emergency. It is strongly suggested that the participant have a recent physical exam or a statement from the physician approving participation in the exercise program.

Individuals 30–39 years of age should have a physical checkup within the three months preceding the exercise program (Cooper, 1982). This physical should include a resting ECG. For persons 40–59 years of age, the same physical exam is recommended, but the ECG should be done while exercising to check heart rate. The pulse rate during this test is expected to approach the level reached during aerobic workouts. For individuals over 59 years old, the same physical exam is recommended. However, it should be done immediately before starting the exercise program.

It is helpful if the therapist is familiar with the participants' attitudes and habits. Keying in on what the participants want to gain physically, functionally, or mentally can provide encouragement.

Presently, there are no documented norms for a functional fitness test for older adults. A committee of the American Alliance for Health, Physical Education, Recreation and Dance (AAHPERD) has developed a physical functional evaluation. The committee is gathering information to establish norms for older adults. For further information and results, write to AAHPERD, 1900 Association Drive, Reston, VA 22091.

Motivating Participants

The most important motivating factor for participants is the instructor. The instructor must be enthusiastic and must display sincere enjoyment in collaborating with older individuals. The instructor's cheerfulness will be contagious. The instructor must be able to laugh at him- or herself because this will allow the participants to do the same. A sense of humor is extremely important.

Another good motivational tip for the leader is to practice a healthy life style. Who wants to be led by someone who walks in eating corn chips and drinking a sugary carbonated beverage?

The leader should compliment and praise students regarding their attendance, attitude, and effort. Charts can be made for attendance, and simple awards can be given at the end of a session. Ribbons and "Olympic" medals are enjoyed at any age.

Educational tips are motivating for the class. The participants appreciate knowing why they are doing an exercise. It is useful for them to know that moving their hands behind the head with shoulders abducted and elbows flexed is the same motion that is used to fix their collars and comb their hair.

Well-chosen music accompanying the exercise is a strong motivator for participants. The music can take their mind off the activity and transfer their thoughts to the rhythm or tune. The right music can encourage the body to move easily and can help with coordination.

Current pop music, country music, jazz, show tunes, and "oldies but goodies" have all been used successfully. The clients can be surveyed for their preferences. If the music selected for an activity does not coordinate with it well, it can be less fun, less motivating, and even stressful.

Searching for the appropriate music and making tapes is extra work for the instructor, but the rewards are observable during the class. The instructor should be sure to practice with the music prior to the exercise session. A change of music once a month is suggested to maintain interest and motivation.

Education of Group

The group should be taught why they are doing specific activities, what the benefits are, and how to maintain safety. This education should occur at each session. It does not matter if some information is repeated. As it is repeated, it becomes more ingrained and more fully incorporated into the participants' daily activities. With older adults, one person may hear the information the first time and another the next time. The therapist may feel uncomfortable repeating, but some participants are newly receiving the information each time.

If some participants are at an advanced fitness level compared to others, the leader must take into account both groups. Personal one-on-one communication with the beginners will make them feel they are participating to their fullest. In other words, even though they fail to reach the levels of activity of the more advanced participants, they should still feel good about what they are doing. They should also be encouraged to stop when they have reached the limits of their endurance and yet still feel good about their participation. Care should be taken to alleviate any type of situation that could cause embarrassment for beginners. They should be stationed within a view of the group leader so he or she can observe their level of involvement and screen for possible fatigue.

If the therapist can have hands-on contact, it is helpful to walk through the group, assist one person to correct posture, raise another's arm a little higher. The therapist can help the participants to appropriately and perceptively feel what the leader is directing them to do.

Safety

In planning an exercise program, safety considerations must be a priority. As in all clinical work, the therapist is liable for his or her actions and the information given to the participants.

Obtaining a doctor's approval, accompanied by a release form, is recommended. Exhibit 4-2 lists important guidelines for a leader of an exercise program to follow.

The leader also needs to be familiar with the common major health problems of the older population and their risk factors while exercising. Common health problems include cardiovascular disease, hypertension, hypercholesterolemia, obesity, osteoarthritis, arthritis, diabetes, osteoporosis, and respiratory disease.

It is the instructor's responsibility to question a participant or contact the physician if there are concerns regarding a participant with one or more of these conditions.

Environment

Check the ambience of the setting and environmental aspects such as space. Other environmental considerations include square footage per participant, room temperature, adequacy of lighting, physical properties, acoustics, and flooring.

Timing

The timing of the program is another consideration. Potential participants should be consulted about their preferences regarding the time of day of the program. Also important is the amount of time for each individual activity. Time should be allowed for a warm-up, conditioning exercises, and cool downs.

Expectations Regarding Levels of Participant Involvement

If one participant is only able to raise a hand and the rest of the group are raising the whole arm, the leader should accept and be happy with the lower degree of movement. In other words, the professional who works with older adults will realize that there may be limits to the participants' physical abilities. Although

Exhibit 4-2 Safety Guidelines for Exercise Programs

Be CPR certified.

Monitor class participants carefully. Make sure they are working at the appropriate level.

Suggest loose, stretchable clothing and support shoes.

Educate participants to flex knees when going to floor or stretching hamstring and to pull stomach muscles in.

Have appropriate warm-up and cool down periods. Let late arrivals know it is important to warm up before they begin exercising with the class.

Encourage the participants to listen to their bodies. Exhaustion after class is a sign of overwork. Remember "perceived exertion."

Teach injury prevention tips during classes. Handouts are always appreciated.

Encourage deep, slow breathing.

Use a variety of movement techniques to avoid fatigue.

Listen to comments from participants.

Continually read updated literature.

Attend continuing education classes regarding exercise.

Make no assumptions; give detailed instructions.

Know what type of medication participants are on and the potential side effects.

Know general first aid and the RICE principle: Rest, Ice, Compress, Elevate.

Have first-aid supplies available.

Encourage thick towels or pads to be used for floor work.

Teach the low back stretch from a chair.

Encourage participants to drink water.

Teach abdominal crunches.

Discourage straight leg bends; they can hurt the back. At least one leg should be slightly bent when bending from the hip.

Never allow deep knee bends.

Eliminate neck extension stretches. There could be a cervical disc problem.

Always move slowly while stretching. Fast movement could cause muscle tears and soreness.

Teach deep breathing techniques.

Let the participants know it is better to gradually build up stamina than to do too much activity initially.

Participants should be able to talk and not be breathless.

Start a session with a safety tip or encouraging word.

exercise programs are designed to raise these limits, it is entirely possible that for some older adults maintenance may become the prime goal rather than increased fitness. Retarding loss of function is a perfectly legitimate goal for an exercise program.

STRESS REDUCTION AND RELAXATION

Up to this point, physical activity and the benefits of physical functioning have been stressed. The exerciser can move easily and for a longer time. However, there are also emotional effects of exercise.

There have been numerous studies to document the relaxing effects of exercise. De Vries and Hales (1974) measured the muscle tension of students before and after a walking program. Exercise was discovered to work better than tranquilizers as a muscle relaxant.

Exercise also has a direct effect on body image, which influences self-esteem. Self-worth influences life style and consequently general health. However, researchers believe the way in which exercise reduces anxiety is not completely understood. The theory has been advanced that reduction of anxiety by exercise has to do with the body's release of endorphins. These hormones dull pain and increase one's sense of well-being (Cooper, 1982).

Exercise is a form of play, and it provides an opportunity to express what is often kept in. Exercise can be a means of self-expression, and it offers a socially acceptable method for adults to alleviate inhibitions and handle tensions and frustrations more successfully. Self-expression can certainly occur if the leader devises a progressive and realistic program that is enjoyable to the participants.

Relaxation Techniques

Exercise programs can incorporate relaxation techniques to enhance the stress reduction benefits of the movement program. The strategy is to identify life stressors, focus on how the body feels under stress, and then find a solution. The stressors may be minor hassles, life-style changes, or feelings of helplessness due to particular situations.

There are specific relaxation techniques that can be incorporated into a daily routine or practiced while in a "hassling" situation—a traffic jam, a busy checkout counter, or a major change, such as the death of a loved one or a loss of income. Simple relaxation techniques include deep breathing, clearing one's mind, autogenics, progressive resistive relaxation, stretching, and visualization.

Deep breathing and stretching were described earlier in this chapter as part of the warm-up phase of exercise. Clearing one's mind is essentially a form of meditation. This purposeful act involves focusing on a single peaceful thought, word, or image, and it helps the individual take a mental and physical retreat from the real world. Five to ten minutes are needed to clear the mind.

Autogenics is a progressive technique in which a person concentrates on a mental suggestion, such as "My mind is at rest" or "My left arm feels heavy."

This technique requires a little more time, practice, and commitment than clearing one's mind. It should be practiced twice a day for approximately 10 minutes at a time.

Progressive resistive relaxation combines tensing a muscle group, becoming aware of the tense feeling, and finally releasing the tensed muscle group. This exercise allows an individual to experience the feeling of released tension. This is an easy technique to include at the end of an exercise class.

Visualization can be considered a mini-mental vacation. Relaxation can be produced by using one's imagination. At the close of an exercise class, the leader can suggest a mental break on a tropical island, feeling warm, calm, and relaxed while listening to the waves and smelling the fresh air.

Massage, a hands-on technique, can also release particular muscle trouble spots. Gentle movement over the spot can relieve tight muscles by speeding blood flow and releasing the tension.

Developing a positive attitude is also an important "technique." It can help an individual accept the challenge of learning new behavior techniques such as exercise and approach everyday stressors with a spirit of adventure.

OTHER CONSIDERATIONS FOR THE THERAPIST

Liabilities

Anyone who teaches an exercise group should have professional liability coverage. As a paid member of AOTA, the therapist has access to private liability insurance. The therapist can also become a member of the International Dance Exercise Association and buy private liability insurance from a broker suggested by the association solely for coverage of exercise groups.

Continuing Education

Advanced educational courses for instructors of exercise classes are strongly recommended. There are day, weekend, and week-long programs offered across the country that focus on planning, development, safety features, and leadership skills.

CONCLUSION

Occupational therapists can be facilitators, coordinators, and educators in the pursuit of health promotion and disease prevention by developing safe and fun fitness programs for older adults (American Occupational Therapy Association, 1988). The benefit to be derived from a fitness program is twofold. The participants feel better about themselves and their health status frequently shows improvement. The therapist or group leader is rewarded by the positive responses from the group as well as by the knowledge that he or she has contributed to the attainment of the goals of health promotion and disease prevention.

REFERENCES

American Occupational Therapy Association. (1966). Occupational therapy: Its definitions and functions. *American Journal of Occupational Therapy, 20*, 204–205.

American Occupational Therapy Association. (1988). *Occupational therapy in the promotion of health and the prevention of disease and disability*. Position paper. Rockville, MD: Author.

Calliet, R., & Gross, L. (1987). *The rejuvenation strategy*. Garden City, NY: Doubleday.

Cooper, K.H. (1982). *The aerobics program for total well-being*. New York: Bantam.

de Vries, H.A., & Hales, D. (1974). *Fitness after 50*. New York: Scribner's.

Getchell, B. (1987). *The fitness book*. Indianapolis, IN: Benchmark Press.

Lewis, S.C. (1979). *The mature years*. Thorofare, NJ: Slack.

Skinner, J.S. (1987). *Exercise testing and exercise prescription for special cases*. Philadelphia: Lea & Febiger.

Smith, E.L., & Gilligan, C. (1983). Physical prescription for the older adult. *Physicians Sports Medicine, 11*, 91.

ADDITIONAL RESOURCES

American Academy of Physical Education Papers
Physical Activity and Aging (1988)
Human Kinetic Books
Champaign, IL 61820

American Alliance for Health, Physical Education, Recreation and Dance
1900 Association Drive
Reston, VA 22091

American College of Sports Medicine
P.O. Box 1440
Indianapolis, IN 46206-1440

Biegel, Leonard
Physical Fitness and the Older Person (1984)
Aspen Publishers, Inc.
Gaithersburg, MD 20878

Caplow-Linder, E., Harpaz, L., & Samberg, S.
Therapeutic Dance/Movement (1979)
Human Sciences Press
New York, NY 10011

Center for the Study of Aging
706 Madison Avenue
Albany, NY 12208

Creative Fitness, Inc.
50+ Workout (1985)
2730 Doehne Road
Harrisburg, PA

Flatten, K., Wilhite, B., & Reyes-Watson, E.
Exercise Activities for the Elderly (1988)
Springer Publishing Company
New York, NY 10012

Institute for Aerobics Research
12330 Preston Road
Dallas, TX 75230

International Dance Exercise Association
6190 Cornerstone Court East, Suite 204
San Diego, CA 92121-3773

National Institute for Fitness & Sport
250 North University Boulevard
Indianapolis, IN 46202

Ostrow, Andrew C.
Physical Activity and the Older Adult (1984)
Princeton Book Company
Princeton, NJ

Shephard, R.J.
Physical Activity and Aging (1987)
Crom Helm Ltd.
Beckenham, Kent BR 3 1AT
England

Chapter 5

Education for Empowerment

Betty Risteen Hasselkus and Jean M. Kiernat

Old age is honored only on the condition that it defends itself, maintains its rights, is subservient to no one, and to its last breath rules over its domain.

Cicero

Long before the advent of nursing homes or senior coalitions, dependency in old age carried a strong negative image. Cicero's statement from the first century B.C. resounds like a battle cry against the stereotypes of old age, calling for vigorous resistance to servility and forceful maintenance of autonomy "to its last breath." Cicero is, in effect, calling for empowerment in old age.

People in the health professions have traditionally considered their primary professional purpose to be the elimination of disease and disability. Occupational therapists have focused on restoring independent function in activities of daily living and promoting a meaningful quality of life. Yet, in recent years, health professionals have themselves come to be regarded as sources of dependence and powerlessness in many arenas of health care (Illich, 1976; Levin, 1977). A renewed valuing of self-help and a wariness regarding prolonged reliance on formal health care systems have evolved (DeJong, 1983; Levin, 1977, 1981).

This renewed recognition of self-care is reflected in the literature on health care and older people (Doress & Siegel, 1987; Hasselkus, 1989; Marshall, 1981). It is argued that a high degree of patient self-care activity is called for in the case of chronic illness. The demedicalization of health, the need to focus on caring rather than curing in long-term care, and the need to help people live *with* illness are issues being explored and incorporated into geriatric health practice. "Aging is a part of the life span and should not be turned into a medical event. We can help ourselves, and one another in maintaining our good health, and in other situations in which we have been taught to turn to professionals for answers" (Doress & Siegel, 1987, p. xxiv).

This chapter explores the concept of a therapeutic relationship that fosters empowerment and self-care through individual and group educational strategies. It is suggested that educational approaches that reflect a partnership between occupational therapists and their older clients can yield a therapeutic process and therapeutic outcomes satisfying to all. Educational programs that illustrate this partnership and empowerment are described as they relate to the practice of occupational therapy in gerontology.

SELF-CARE EMPOWERMENT

"The therapist will be through with her visits next week—that will be her last week. I'll miss the service because then at least it was done and it was done right. . . . There's lots of habits you can get into that are wrong and I wouldn't know, but she *does* know."*

The above statement was made by a 69-year-old woman who was a caregiver for her 71-year-old husband. She and her husband had been coping for 10 years with episodes of acute illness—infection, hospitalizations, and eventual bilateral lower extremity amputations—secondary to her husband's diabetes mellitus. A long-term pattern of active involvement with health professionals in the hospital, outpatient clinic, and home health agency was evident. Despite a decade of experience living with a chronic illness, this caregiver's confidence in her own abilities was shaky at best. It was her perception that the therapist was sure to do it "right" but that she herself might not—in fact, she might not even *recognize* right from wrong.

How different this caregiver's statement was from that of another caregiver who, in describing the termination of a therapist's visits to her husband, stated, "We decided that we could handle that [the therapy] now ourselves. . . . We just felt we were ready to take over." In this instance, the caregiver expressed confidence in her own ability to manage the situation without the health professional, and a sense of having worked together with the therapist to reach this point of expertise was conveyed.

Dependency is the reliance on others for assistance to carry out expected roles and tasks in everyday life. Dependency is one possible functional outcome of the interactions between an older individual and the health professionals in that individual's environment. Dependency was obviously the outcome of the interactions between the first caregiver above and the therapist in her environment, yet it was not the outcome of the second caregiver's interactions with her therapist. One might ask the question, was the helping relationship between the caregiver and the therapist in the first example truly a therapeutic relationship? What therapeutic components were present in the second case example but absent in the first that led to the vastly different view the second client had of her own capabilities?

The environment has basically three primary components: physical, institutional, and interactional. All three components act either to support or not to

---

*Verbatim caregiver quotations are taken from raw data for the study "Family Caregivers for the Elderly at Home: An Ethnography of Meaning and Informal Learning." See Hasselkus & Ray, 1988.

support an individual's independent function within the environment. For example, a ramp is a physical feature that may enable a person to negotiate a building entrance independently. Institutional rules that restrict entering or exiting the building to certain hours of the day curtail independence in the same activity.

The helping relationship between a health professional and an older client is an interactional component of the environment, and, as noted above, this relationship may lead to either dependent or independent function. The use of educational strategies—variously termed *patient education, patient activation,* and *health education*—in professional-client interactions may maximize the potential for independence and self-sufficiency to be an outcome of therapy (Hasselkus, 1986; Pfister-Minogue, 1983; White & Rose, 1988).

Educational strategies in health care have both a philosophical and a programmatic component (Hasselkus, 1986; Squyres, 1980). Effective use of educational activities in the helping relationship is dependent on an egalitarian rather than authoritarian view of health care. Health professionals and clients come together in partnership to share their respective areas of expertise and their personal values in order to facilitate optimum long-term health behaviors. Additionally, planning for educational strategies in therapy programs requires careful balancing of individualized learning needs with programmatic opportunities and constraints (Cross, 1981; Hasselkus, 1983; Okun, 1982; Spencer, 1980). "Recruitment strategies, active learner participation, self-directedness, attention to past life experiences, family involvement, and adapted methods of instruction are all factors to be considered in planning patient education for the older person" (Hasselkus, 1983, p. 68).

THE PHILOSOPHICAL COMPONENT

The Partnership Relationship

The emerging view of health care as a partnership between clients and professionals stems from the impact of the consumer and self-help movements of the 1970s on the formal health care system (DeJong, 1983). As management of long-term chronic health problems replaced the previous medical emphasis on acute care, it became increasingly apparent that patients needed self-sufficiency and the ability to make independent decisions in day-to-day health-related matters. To bring this about, a movement toward a more cooperative approach to health care evolved.

Contributing further to the belief that the client should be an active partner in the health care process was a growing body of research findings that linked health behaviors to people's beliefs and values and the social context (Freidson, 1961; Kleinman, Eisenberg, & Good, 1978; Mechanic, 1977; Shontz, 1972). Illness became redefined as a cultural experience rather than a pathological scientific entity. It was asserted that people ascribe personal meaning to an illness experience and on the basis of that meaning "can open or close options for actively dealing with it or the feelings it evokes" (Mechanic, 1977, p. 81).

The realization that health professionals also ascribe meaning to their clients' illnesses led to descriptions of professional-client interactions as negotiations of two clinical realities—the reality constructed by the patient and the reality constructed by the professional (Freidson, 1961; Kleinman et al., 1978). A "clash of perspectives" results if the two realities represent major discrepancies in values and expectations (Freidson, 1961). Hasselkus and Ray's (1988) findings from a study of family caregiving for community elderly supported the notion of a clash of perspectives between professionals and clients and its effect on health behaviors. Family caregivers' views of the caregiving situation were often at odds with those of the health professionals with whom they interacted. Based on their personal views of the situation, caregivers tended to come up with their own reasons for caregiving problems. In addition, the instructions given to them by formal service providers were almost always critiqued and modified, as in this example: "They told me to let him do some of that washing up and dressing himself, but he's so slow and he gets up so late it'd be forever. He'd never get his breakfast if I waited for him to get washed and everything, and I do a better job, use soap and that."

Many of the long-term family caregivers expressed a sense of special knowledge and expertise about their own caregiving abilities, feeling the need to monitor and supervise the health professionals so that care tasks were done "right." Rarely, a sense of "figuring it out together" (by professional and caregiver) was conveyed by the caregivers. "The nurse and I are watchin' her feet cuz there is a chance that they could start goin' gangrenous any day . . . she got an open area on there that we been bathin' with betadyne" was one rare expression of mutuality and partnership in the data.

Barriers to the Partnership Model

Arnstein (1971) defined a partnership between a professional and a layperson as a relationship of negotiation in which there is a balance of power and in which shared planning and decision making take place. Given the prevailing evidence for a clash of perspectives in health care relationships, it might be argued that a partnership as defined by Arnstein is all but impossible to bring about between a health professional and a patient. Bloom and Speedling (1981) stated, "The patient appears to be inherently dependent within the situation of doctor-patient exchanges" (p. 158). Marshall (1981) concurred that the patient is at a distinct disadvantage in any negotiation because of a lack of expert knowledge and because of traditional patterns of deference to authority.

It might further be argued that partnerships between health professionals and *older* patients are especially difficult to bring about. "With older patients, these differences are only exacerbated because of the lower educational levels of most older people, because of their generally lower-social-class origins, and because of the fact that a very large proportion of them have been downwardly mobile if measured by level of income" (Marshall, 1981, pp. 104–105).

Negative stereotypes of older people held by health professionals is another major barrier to the development of partnerships between professionals and older clients. Health professionals tend to see older people when they are most frail and dependent. Unfortunately, this often leads to an overestimation of debilitation in old age (Baltes, 1988; Timko & Rodin, 1985). The presence of ageism in the health professions (negative beliefs about people based solely on their age; Butler, 1969) has been shown to affect attitudes and communication between health professionals and older patients (Crane, 1975; Greene, Adelman, Charon, & Hoffman, 1986; Kosberg & Gorman, 1975; Miller, Lowenstein, & Winston, 1976). For example, in Kosberg and Gorman's (1975) study of staff attitudes toward rehabilitation, only 55% of the therapists' responses were positive regarding rehabilitation of the older patients.

Ageism also exists among older people in their perceptions of themselves as being too old to learn (Spencer, 1980). The perception of powerlessness by older people is explored by Miller (1983) and Miller and Oertel (1983). They focus on the interplay between society-induced perceptions of incompetence, the sense of helplessness associated with chronic illness, and lowered self-esteem linked to disengagement from previously valued tasks such as work. Timko and Rodin (1985) review research on the self-fulfilling nature of negative stereotypes on dependency behaviors in older people in nursing homes. "Researchers working directly with the institutionalized elderly have suggested that if staff members have stereotypic beliefs about older person's abilities and the aging process, prolonged exposure to such an environment will lead to maladaptive, dependent behaviors on the part of residents" (p. 97).

It is evident from the above discussion that partnerships between health professionals and older patients will not simply fall into place. A partnership must be planned for and nurtured, consciously and deliberately. The obstacles to such a relationship—obstacles due to the older person and the health professional—must be addressed and overcome. Educational strategies that incorporate exchanges of meanings, sharing of expertise, and cooperative planning increase the probability of partnerships and empowerment.

Wilner (1988) has described the empowering outcomes of two self-help groups for older people and their caregivers. "Members who joined with feelings of impotence in dealing with their worlds learned to see the similarity in their experience, to share valuable information, and to practice skills necessary for taking care of themselves and enhancing their life satisfaction'' (p. 161).

So, too, the triumphant statement of a 60-year-old woman regarding the care of her husband following his cerebral vascular accident attests to the empowerment she derived from a helping relationship that overcame the barriers to partnership: "When he was in the hospital, I just dreaded the time I would have to go down to therapy with him because I was worried, all those people sitting there, patients that are waiting their turn, and they're all looking at you it seems like. I'd think, 'Well, what if I really goof it up?' At the time, I thought, 'I'll never learn any of this.' But you *can* teach an old dog new tricks, I'll tell you that. It's surprising."

THE PROGRAMMATIC COMPONENT

Educational Programs in Health Care

The 15 million Americans who currently belong to 500,000 self-help groups (Zimmer, 1987–1988) attest to the fact that older adults recognize a need and gain strength by coming together for education and mutual support. The expectation of such groups is that members will not only receive but will also give help. They will be empowered by giving help to others as they themselves learn (Riessman, Moody, & Worthy, 1982).

The partnership between health professionals and older persons can be fostered through self-help and other group educational programs. The literature has clearly shown that older adults are motivated to continue learning throughout their life spans (Lumsden, 1987–1988). There is a desire to know and understand what they are experiencing currently and what can be expected in the future.

Group programs may be offered at a hospital, a clinic, a community agency, or an institutional setting such as an extended care facility. It is also possible to reach out to seniors by taking programs to places where they tend to congregate. Senior centers, church groups, and voluntary nonprofit groups are usually very eager to obtain speakers who can provide valid information and who represent trusted institutions in the community.

Many hospitals and health facilities support community education as part of their mission. Community service enhances an organization's public image and supports its nonprofit status. Education is also an excellent marketing tool for the sponsoring organization. It is often through educational programs that families become aware of services that can assist them in addressing their own needs.

Model Programs

There are a number of excellent examples of health education programs that can serve as models for therapists who wish to develop new programs.

The Growing Younger program offered by Healthwise, Inc. of Boise, Idaho, is a neighborhood-based health promotion program for people aged 60 and over (Kemper, 1986). The program uses a "Tupperware" approach, with partylike sessions in the homes of older adults. Neighborhood groups, recruited at the parties, agree to meet together once a week to practice skills learned in the program. Physical fitness, nutrition, stress management, and medical self-care are the topics covered in the four 2-hour workshops. Significant behavioral changes were noted by participants, and biometric tests showed significant positive changes following completion of the program (Kemper, 1986). The empowerment of the graduates was evidenced by the wide range of community activities they have undertaken since completing the program.

The Dartmouth Institute for Better Health developed the very successful Self-Care for Senior Citizens Program, which consists of thirteen 2-hour classes (Simmons, Roberts, & Nelson, 1986). This program focuses on medical self-care and tries to get participants to assume responsibility for their own welfare and learn about and use community services and resources to maintain independent living. The workbook for this program, *Medical and Health Guide for People over Fifty,* is listed as a selected resource at the end of this chapter.

A third model program that has effectively empowered older adults to maximize their independence and improve the quality of their lives is the Wallingford Wellness Project (FallCreek & Mettler, 1982). This project began in 1979 with an Administration on Aging grant given jointly to the University of Washington School of Social Work and King County Senior Services and Centers. The manual resulting from this project is also listed in the resource section. One of the authors of this chapter has found it exceptionally helpful in planning program content and activities.

Long-term care facilities have also had exciting new programs that empower residents through special educational efforts. The Stevens Square Home in Minneapolis replaced a medical model with a wellness model and used education as a key component of the new program development (Ryden & Rustad, 1985). Personal growth classes were attended by both residents and staff, who discussed the material together and shared personal issues. Many women in both groups offered comfort, and the giving and receiving promoted a sense of belonging and bonding among residents and staff.

A final example, although there are many more available, is the Living Is for the Elderly (LIFE) program. This unusual program focuses on nursing home rights, and it promotes self-help and political activism for over 100 nursing homes in the Boston area (Kautzer, 1988). Through this program, residents are empowered to advocate on their own behalf in many different settings, including their own facilities, community forums, radio and television talk shows, and even state house hearings!

Program Content

Health and wellness education programs may cover a wide range of topics, but there is a core of content which is common to most of them. Normal age changes, symptoms and management of common illnesses, coping with chronic disease and personal losses, personal growth and development, and knowledge of community services form the basis of many programs.

Normal Aging

Older adults are interested in learning about normal changes that occur with age. For a long time, any physical or cognitive change that happened to older individuals was considered part of the aging process and something to be accepted. Over the years, research has shown that many conditions are not inevitable but rather are disease processes that can be treated or at least improved through treatment. This optimistic message needs to reach older adults.

Chapter 3 in this book is a good basis for preparing presentations on the topic. Since aging research programs are steadily producing new information on age changes, therapists must constantly update their knowledge in this area. Belonging to organizations such as the Gerontological Society of America and reading its journals is one way of accessing some of the latest findings. The Age Page, a continuing series of fact sheets published by the National Institute on Aging, contains current thinking on a variety of aging issues. The address for the Age Page is listed at the end of this chapter.

Perhaps the single most important concern of older adults is loss of memory. The current emphasis on Alzheimer's disease has promoted fear among seniors that any forgetfulness is the first stage of an irreversible dementia. A presentation on aging and memory can reassure older individuals and their families that some benign forgetfulness is normal and that many strategies can be employed to improve memory. Confusion, they need to know, is never normal and must be investigated. *A Memory Retention Course for the Aged* (Garfunkel & Landau, 1981), published by the National Council on the Aging, is a very helpful resource in planning group sessions on this topic.

Other popular age change topics include blood pressure, vision changes, and hearing and aging. In the case of any topic, the information should include the changes that commonly occur as we age, ways to compensate for these changes to maintain maximum function and safety, and changes that are not normal and need to be treated.

Illness and Chronic Conditions

Elderly persons want to understand those illnesses and chronic conditions that they or their friends are experiencing. What is dementia? What treatment is available for osteoporosis? What is a cataract? Can anything be done for incontinence problems? What is the latest treatment for heart attacks? Is there anything new about the medical management of arthritis? What are some of the latest treatments for cancer? These are questions in the minds of many older adults and they need to be answered.

Behavioral health problems also need to be addressed, although older adults are not as psychiatrically oriented as the younger population and may not raise these questions without some prodding. Depression may be best covered as "Beating the Blues." Offering a program on the treatment of "depression" may result in few attendees. "Surviving the Loss of a Spouse," "Your Grown-up Children," and "Time out for Caregivers" are examples of other topics that may be covered through group programs.

Self-Maintenance

Another topic to be considered is staying healthy in the later years. Information (and related activities) on the benefits of exercise, techniques for promoting relaxation and reducing stress, good nutrition, and the importance of meaningful activity can be offered. "Staying Active: Wellness after Sixty" is an excellent 29-minute video that addresses these four issues in a very upbeat manner. The film is available from Spectrum Films, Inc. in Carlsbad, California.

Medication is a topic many older adults are eager to learn about. The popular press has sensitized the public to the problems of polypharmacy, and some older adults may choose noncompliance over taking prescribed medications because of their fear of harmful effects. The side effects of prescribed drugs, cautions regarding the use of over-the-counter medications (OTCs), and systems that help the older adult self-administer medications appropriately should be addressed as part of this topic.

Self-maintenance can also be enhanced by teaching elderly individuals to improve communication with their physicians. Preparing for a visit to the doctor by writing down questions and symptoms ahead of time will avoid the possibility of forgetting any information during the stress of the visit. Role-playing an assertive patient can be fun for a group of older adults, can promote a sense of control, and can lead to their getting the information they need to care for themselves effectively.

Spiritual Growth

Spiritual well-being is an integral part of health and wellness programs. While spiritual growth may not be addressed in many hospital or senior center educational programs, it should be addressed in extended care programs. Spiritual well-being is an affirmation of life in relation to God, self, community, and environment, an affirmation that accepts the past, celebrates the present, and has hope for the future (Ryden & Rustad, 1985). *Reaching in, Reaching up*, a program described by Hately (1987–1988), has been very successful in guiding older adults to a deeper level of personal insight and self-understanding and to higher levels of spiritual awareness.

Resources and Services

A final category of potential topics includes the services and resources available in the community. Older adults and their caregivers may profit from knowing if there are geriatric assessment clinics available, how their services can be accessed, and if they are covered by Medicare.

Daycare for older adults is not well understood by the general public, who often think of it as similar to child care or as a nursing home program. Daycare is a very valuable resource for frail elderly, and it provides an important respite service for the caregiver. Invitations to visit or to volunteer at the day center can be offered to families during the presentation. This provides a valid picture of the service and becomes a great marketing opportunity for the daycare program.

Partial hospitalization programs for behavioral health, in-home functional assessments by occupational therapists, counseling, and many other special services can be described. Knowledge of these services increases the range of resources older adults can use to assist themselves and their family members. Education empowers them by making options available that they can use in their self-maintenance programs.

Guidelines for Program Planning

In presenting educational programs to groups of older adults, there are a number of guidelines worth following. Here are ten helpful hints for consideration:

1. Be sure that what you plan to teach is what the group wants to learn. Unless a particular topic was requested by the group, you should get input from older adults regarding their interests and needs before proceeding. You cannot empower others if you are making decisions for them. You may give them a list of possible topics so that they have some idea of what you are able to cover. They can then choose those topics that are most important to them.
2. Plan to present information for 20 to 30 minutes, and leave considerable time for questions. One of the biggest mistakes you can make is to try to cover too much material in one presentation.
3. Consider the environment. Will everyone be able to see and hear well? Don't shy away from the use of a microphone. It may be the difference

between presenting a successful talk and providing unintelligible noise for some of the audience. Large, bold print should be used on any overhead transparencies or slides. Room lighting should be focused upon your face so that your lips can be read and your gestures and expressions can be seen.

4. Begin your presentation with an overview. Tell the group what you will present and why you feel it is important. The overview provides a frame of reference. If individual words are missed, the context will help supply meaning.

5. Encourage participation. You can get the group involved immediately by asking questions such as "How many of you take more than four medications?" or "Does anyone here know someone who is depressed?"

   Role-playing can also be used to stimulate involvement and provide meaning. If you are discussing hearing loss and you want to encourage people to admit their loss and be assertive, you might present a dilemma for the group. "Imagine that you went to a lecture at the museum and you arrived a few minutes late. The only seat is way down in the front. If you stay in the back you will not be able to hear. What will you do?"

   Involvement and the use of real-life situations will make the talk meaningful. However, be careful that questions from the group do not get too numerous. You can quickly lose control in a presentation if many individuals begin asking about their unique problems. Should this happen, you will need to acknowledge their interest and their verification that this is truly an important topic and direct attention back to the main issues.

6. Use humor. Humor reduces anxieties and allows individuals to focus on the message.

7. Avoid jargon and professional terminology. *Joint protection* and *energy conservation* convey very specific concepts to therapists but the lay group may have no idea what these terms mean.

8. If you are providing handouts, give them out after the talk unless you will be going over them with the group as part of the presentation. Inform the participants during the overview that you will be providing handouts they may take home. Thus they will know they do not have to take notes and can focus upon your discussion.

9. Summarize your major points at the end of the talk. This will help people to remember the key points.

10. Solicit feedback from the group. Have a brief evaluation that allows listeners to rate the presentation. This is also a good opportunity to ask about future topics they would like to hear discussed.

Effective education programs can help older adults maintain their own health, avoid disease and conditions associated with disease, and cope better with daily living challenges. Empowering elderly individuals to assume responsibility and control over their own health status not only assists the individuals but has an economic benefit for society as a whole, since it reduces the costs associated with seeking help too late or becoming unnecessarily dependent.

REFERENCES

Arnstein, S.R. (1971). Eight rungs on the ladder of citizen participation. In E. Cahn & B. Passett (Eds.), *Citizen participation: Effecting community change* (pp. 69–91). New York: Praeger.

Baltes, M.M. (1988). The etiology and maintenance of dependency in the elderly: Three phases of operant research. *Behavior Therapy, 19,* 301–319.

Bloom, S.W., & Speedling, E.J. (1981). Strategies of power and dependence in doctor-patient exchanges. In M.R. Haug (Ed.), *Elderly patients and their doctors* (pp. 157–170). New York: Springer.

Butler, R.N. (1969). Age-ism: Another form of bigotry. *The Gerontologist, 9,* 243–246.

Crane, D. (1975). *The sanctity of social life: Physicians' treatment of critically ill patients.* New York: Russell Sage Foundation.

Cross, K.P. (1981). *Adults as learners.* San Francisco: Jossey-Bass.

DeJong, G. (1983). Defining and implementing the independent living concept. In N.M. Crewe & I.K. Zola (Eds.), *Independent living for physically disabled people* (pp. 4–27). San Francisco: Jossey-Bass.

Doress, P.B., & Siegel, D.L. (1987). The potential of the second half of life. In P.B. Doress & D.L. Siegel (Eds.), *Ourselves growing older: Women aging with knowledge and power* (pp. xxi–xxvi). New York: Simon & Schuster.

FallCreek, S., & Mettler, M. (1982). *Healthy old age: A sourcebook for health promotion with older adults.* Washington, DC: U.S. Department of Health and Human Services, Administration on Aging.

Freidson, E. (1961). *Patients' views of medical practice.* New York: Sage.

Garfunkel, F., & Landau, G. (1981). *A memory retention course for the aged: Guide for leaders.* Washington, DC: National Council on the Aging.

Greene, M.G., Adelman, R., Charon, R., & Hoffman, S. (1986). Ageism in the medical encounter: An exploratory study of the doctor–elderly patient relationship. *Language and Communication, 6,* 113–124.

Hasselkus, B.R. (1983). Patient education and the elderly. *Physical and Occupational Therapy in Geriatrics, 2,*(3), 55–70.

Hasselkus, B.R. (1986). Patient education. In L.J. Davis & M. Kirkland (Eds.), *The role of occupational therapy with the elderly* (pp. 367–372). Rockville, MD: American Occupational Therapy Association.

Hasselkus, B.R. (1989). Occupational and physical therapy in geriatric rehabilitation. *Physical and Occupational Therapy in Geriatrics, 7*(3), 3–20.

Hasselkus, B.R., & Ray, R.O. (1988). Informal learning in family caregiving: A worm's eye view. *Adult Education Quarterly, 39,* 31–40.

Hately, B.J. (1987–1988). Reaching in, reaching up. *Generations, 12,* 42–45.

Illich, I. (1976). *Medical nemesis: The expropriation of health.* New York: Pantheon.

Kautzer, K. (1988). Empowering nursing home residents: A case study of "Living Is for the Elderly," an activist nursing home organization. In S. Reinharz & G. Rowles (Eds.), *Qualitative gerontology* (pp. 163–183). New York: Springer.

Kemper, D. (1986). The healthwise program: Growing younger. In K. Dychtwald (Ed.), *Wellness and health promotion for the elderly* (pp. 263–273). Gaithersburg, MD: Aspen Publishers.

Kleinman, A., Eisenberg, L., & Good, B. (1978). Culture, illness and care: Clinical lessons from anthropologic and cross-cultural research. *Annals of Internal Medicine, 88,* 251–258.

Kosberg, J.I., & Gorman, J.F. (1975). Perceptions toward the rehabilitation potential of institutionalized aged. *The Gerontologist, 15,* 398–403.

Levin, L.S. (1977). Forces and issues in the revival of interest in self-care: Impetus for redirection in health. *Health Education Monographs, 5,* 115–120.

Levin, L.S. (1981). Self-care in health: Potentials and pitfalls. *World Health Forum, 3,* 177–184.

Lumsden, D.B. (1987–1988). How adults learn. *Generations, 12,* 10–15.

Marshall, V.W. (1981). Physician characteristics and relationships with older patients. In M.R. Haug (Ed.), *Elderly patients and their doctors* (pp. 94–118). New York: Springer.

Mechanic, D. (1977). Illness behavior, social adaptation, and the management of illness. *Journal of Nervous & Mental Disease, 165,* 79–87.

Miller, D.B., Lowenstein, R., & Winston, R. (1976). Physicians' attitudes toward the ill aged and nursing homes. *Journal of the American Geriatrics Society, 24,* 498–505.

Miller, J.F. (1983). Patient power resources. In J.F. Miller (Ed.), *Coping with chronic illness: Overcoming powerlessness* (pp. 3–13). Philadelphia: F.A. Davis.

Miller, J.F., & Oertel, C.B. (1983). Powerlessness in the elderly: Preventing hopelessness. In J.F. Miller (Ed.), *Coping with chronic illness: Overcoming powerlessness* (pp. 109–131). Philadelphia: F.A. Davis.

Okun, M.A. (Ed.). (1982). *New directions for continuing education: Programs for older adults* (No. 14). San Francisco: Jossey-Bass.

Pfister-Minogue, K. (1983). Enabling strategies. In J.F. Miller (Ed.), *Coping with chronic illness: Overcoming powerlessness* (pp. 235–256). Philadelphia: F.A. Davis.

Riessman, F., Moody, H.R., & Worthy, E.H. (1982). *Self-help and the elderly: Considerations for practice and policy.* Washington, DC: National Council on the Aging.

Ryden, M., & Rustad, R. (1985). Wellness model replaces medical model. *Journal of Long-Term Care Administration, 13,* 115–119.

Shontz, F.C. (1972). The personal meaning of illness. *Advances in Psychosomatic Medicine, 8,* 63–85.

Simmons, J., Roberts, E., & Nelson, E. (1986). The Dartmouth self-care for senior citizens program: Tools, strategies, and methods. In K. Dychtwald (Ed.), *Wellness and health promotion for the elderly* (pp. 235–246). Gaithersburg, MD: Aspen Publishers.

Spencer, B. (1980). Overcoming the age bias in continuing education. In G.G. Darkenwald & G.A. Larson (Eds.), *New directions in continuing education: Reaching hard-to-reach adults* (No. 8, pp. 71–86). San Francisco: Jossey-Bass.

Squyres, W.D. (Ed.). (1980). *Patient education: An inquiry into the state of the art.* New York: Springer.

Timko, C., & Rodin, J. (1985). Staff-patient relationships in nursing homes: Sources of conflict and rehabilitation potential. *Rehabilitation Psychology, 30,* 93–108.

White, G.G., & Rose, C. (1988). Empowering the older adult learner: Community education as a delivery system. *Lifelong Learning: An Omnibus of Practice and Research, 11*(7), 20–22, 30.

Wilner, M.A. (1988). The transition to self-care: A field study of support groups for the elderly and their caregivers. In S. Reinharz & G. Rowles (Eds.), *Qualitative gerontology* (pp. 147–162). New York: Springer.

Zimmer, A.H. (1987–1988). Self-help programs and late life learning. *Generations, 12,* 19–21.

SELECTED RESOURCES FOR EDUCATIONAL PROGRAMS

Age Page
Newsletter published by the National Institute of Aging Information Center, 2209 Distribution Center, Silver Spring, MD 20910.

Comfort Zones: A Practical Guide for Retirement Planning and *The Unfinished Business of Living: Helping Aging Parents Help Themselves*
These two books are available from Crisp Publications, 95 First Street, Los Altos, CA 94022.

Fitness for Life: Exercises for People over 50, Life after Work: Planning It, Living It, Loving It, and *Medical Health Guide for People over Fifty*
These three books are available from the American Association of Retired Persons, 1909 K Street, NW, Washington, DC 20049.

Growing Younger
This workbook is available from Healthwise, Inc., PO Box 1989, Boise, ID 83701.

Healthy Life for Seniors. Because an Apple a Day Isn't Enough
This workbook is available from the American Institute for Preventative Medicine, 19111 West 10 Mile Road, Suite 101, Southfield, MI 48075.

A Healthy Old Age: A Sourcebook for Health Promotion with Older Adults
This source book was developed by the U.S. Department of Health and Human Services, Administration on Aging. It is available from the U.S. Superintendent of Documents Office, Washington, DC 20402.

Making Life More Livable: Simple Adaptations for the Homes of Blind and Visually Impaired Older People
This book is published by the American Foundation for the Blind, Inc., 15 West 16th Street, New York, NY 10011.

Part II

Treatment in the
Acute Care Setting

Chapter 6

Assessment of the
Geriatric Patient

Frances A. Kelley, Toni T. Kawamoto, and Laurence Z. Rubenstein

Geriatric assessment is a multidimensional, usually interdisciplinary, diagnostic process intended to evaluate an elderly person's medical, psychological, and functional capabilities and problems with the intention of arriving at a comprehensive plan for therapy and long-term follow-up. Assessment has assumed a critical role in geriatric care because of the complexity of health problems of frail elderly patients, because of the vast number of unmet needs facing the rapidly growing older population, and because assessment has been increasingly associated with improvements in care outcomes (Rubenstein, Campbell, & Kane, 1987). Occupational therapy has always played a crucial role in the geriatric assessment process. This chapter will provide an overview of geriatric assessment, its components and effectiveness, and the role of occupational therapy in the assessment process.

CONCEPTS OF GERIATRIC ASSESSMENT

The concepts of geriatric assessment began to solidify by the 1930s among pioneers of British geriatric medicine such as Drs. Marjory Warren, Lionel Cosin, and Ferguson Anderson. These early geriatricians noted a disturbingly high rate of long-term institutionalization among disabled elderly patients, most of whom had neither been evaluated carefully from a medical or psychosocial standpoint nor been given a trial of rehabilitation. They also found a high prevalence of readily identifiable remediable problems among both institutionalized and noninstitutionalized patients, and they showed that most of these patients could experience improvement when provided with appropriate therapy and rehabilitation. This early work led to two basic and still valid principles of geriatric medicine: (1) Many elderly patients, particularly those who are frail and have complex problems, need a more broadly based and interdisciplinary diagnosis and therapeutic approach than do younger patients, and (2) elderly patients should not be admitted to a long-term care facility without a careful medical and psychosocial assessment and, in most cases, a trial of rehabilitation.

In the United States, geriatric assessment concepts and programs have been growing in the last two decades, particularly in the past 5–10 years. Geared to local needs and conditions, these programs and processes vary in many of their structural and functional components. Geriatric assessment programs are often located in acute care hospitals (with assessments performed on special geriatric units or through a consultant team approach), chronic care or rehabilitation hospitals, hospital outpatient departments, free-standing offices or clinics, and nursing homes; assessments can also be performed as part of comprehensive home care programs. Some programs are carefully targeted at the most frail elderly population, while others are open to virtually everyone over a certain age of eligibility. Despite the diversity, most of these programs share several characteristics: performance of multidimensional diagnostic assessment, use of a multidisciplinary team approach, provision of limited treatment or case management, and use of a broad-based referral and follow-up network.

Serious and scientific efforts by researchers to scrutinize geriatric assessment, to view it as sufficiently concrete to produce valid and reproducible results, and to measure its benefits have been evolving since the concept of geriatric assessment emerged in England. These evaluative efforts gained momentum in the United States and culminated in the 1980s in a series of carefully executed randomized clinical trials. The National Institute on Aging, in conjunction with other federal agencies and private foundations, convened the Consensus Development Conference on Geriatric Assessment Methods for Clinical Decision-making in 1987. The statement from this panel, chaired by David Solomon (1988b), concluded that comprehensive geriatric assessment contributes significantly to improving important health outcomes when coupled with ongoing implementation of resulting care plans.

Comprehensive geriatric assessment includes evaluation of several clinical domains, including physical health, mental health, socioeconomic resources, functional status, and environmental conditions. The resources and strengths of the individual in each domain are identified, the need for services is outlined, and a care plan is developed. Some aspects of the assessment may be provided by self-rating scales done by the patient or caregivers, which frequently offer a different perspective than assessments done by members of the health care team. Questionnaires or self-reports are commonly used in assessment with surprising accuracy, although the most accurate assessment is probably obtained by observation of the patient's actual performance in the home or a simulated home environment (Solomon, 1988b). Although there is a reasonably good correlation between a patient's self-assessed functioning and professionally observed or family member judgment, some studies have observed a significant tendency for patients to overstate their abilities and for families to overstate their disabilities, which must be kept in mind (Rubenstein, Schairer, Wieland, & Kane, 1984).

STRUCTURE AND LOCATION OF ASSESSMENT PROGRAMS

Comprehensive geriatric assessment may be initiated by referral from any of a number of sources, most commonly relatives and community service agencies. Less common sources are the clients themselves, friends, and physicians. Assessment involves clinicians from the many health care professions who are necessarily involved in good geriatric care. The core team consists of at least a physician, a nurse, and a social worker, each with special expertise in caring for older people. Following initial screening and findings, a more detailed, in-depth assessment is done. This assessment often requires the participation of professionals from other disciplines, including audiology, clergy, clinical psychology, dentistry, nutrition, occupational therapy, optometry, pharmacy, physical therapy, podiatry, and speech pathology. Support from other medical disciplines, such as neurology, ophthalmology, orthopedics, rheumatology, physiatry, psychiatry, surgery, and urology, is commonly needed as well. Reassessment and modification of the care plan are essential in the dynamic ongoing process of comprehensive geriatric assessment.

Professionals and society in general are becoming increasingly aware that elderly people are susceptible to iatrogenesis, are at high risk for premature or inappropriate institutionalization, and are often given less careful attention due to various forms of ageism. Interdisciplinary comprehensive geriatric assessment and geriatric assessment programs are therefore viewed as increasingly important (Wetle & Besdine, 1982). It is predicted that the field of geriatrics will become more complex, with assessment packages for particular clinical situations being developed and better methods for the prevention and management of health problems of the elderly being sought (Solomon, 1988a).

The goals of comprehensive geriatric assessment are to (1) improve diagnostic accuracy, (2) guide the selection of interventions to restore or preserve health, (3) recommend an optimal environment for care, (4) predict outcomes, and (5) monitor clinical change over time. To accomplish these goals, assessment methods need to identify potentially remediable problems, predict patient outcomes, carefully consider the patient's values, and detect small changes in function. Randomized controlled trials, described in the next section, have shown that most of these goals—and ultimately health care outcomes—can be affected favorably by comprehensive geriatric assessment.

Persons most likely to benefit from comprehensive geriatric assessment are older persons who are frail and have an identifiable functional disability. Efforts are also being made to develop focused geriatric assessments to evaluate physical fitness, monitor health promotion and disease prevention for well older persons, and guide the humane care of irreversibly disabled and terminally ill older persons (Rubenstein, Campbell, & Kane, 1987; Solomon, 1988a).

As regards medical rehabilitation, it was recognized that there is a crucial need for rehabilitation clinicians to demonstrate the effectiveness and cost-benefit efficiency of their treatment interventions and to identify treatment outcomes (Granger, Hamilton, Keith, Zielezny, & Sherwin, 1986). The American Congress of Rehabilitation Medicine/American Academy of Physical Medicine and Rehabilitation (ACRM/AAPMR) authorized the Task Force to Develop a Uniform National Data System for Medical Rehabilitation in March 1984. An attempt is being made to standardize measurements and treatment outcomes utilizing the Functional Independence Measure (FIM). Functional assessments used in medical rehabilitation focus on disease consequences as well as the disease. Patients' remaining capabilities and assets, as well as their deficits and limitations, are identified. Use of the functional approach will likely result in more systematic and comprehensive care and will address the functional consequences of long-term illness. Factors that determine the extent of functional limitations in task performance include the relevant diagnosis; the anatomical, physiological, psychosocial, and mental deficits; the capacity to perform social roles; the family and social support systems; and the environment. The principal evaluators will be nurses, physical and occupational therapists, social workers, and physicians.

IMPACT OF GERIATRIC ASSESSMENT PROGRAMS

A growing body of research data, including many randomized controlled trials, show that the frail elderly population can benefit from assessment programs. These have been recently reviewed (Rubenstein, Campbell, & Kane, 1987; Rubenstein & Wieland, 1989; Wieland, 1989). Of the more than 80 published studies, 17 used control groups of one form or another, and 10 were true randomized controlled trials. Although results from the studies do vary, several patterns emerge.

First, diagnostic accuracy and other process-of-care measures are greatly enhanced by comprehensive assessment. Second, one or more health care outcomes are usually improved, although the specific benefits and their magnitude vary from program to program. Third, the programs showing the most benefit tend to accept patients of greater levels of frailty and disability and to have higher levels of clinical control and follow-up capability than programs showing less benefit. The most widely documented benefits from geriatric assessment programs (GAPs) are listed below:

- improved diagnostic accuracy
- improved discharge location (placement)
- improved functional status
- improved affect or cognition
- decreased use of medications
- decreased use of nursing homes
- increased use of home health services
- decreased use of hospital services
- decreased medical care costs
- prolonged survival

Improved diagnostic accuracy is the most widely attested effect of GAPs (accuracy is indicated by substantial numbers of problems uncovered). Average frequency of new diagnoses found ranged from almost one to more than four per patient following the assessment process. It is likely that this improved diagnostic accuracy and understanding are the keys to the improvement of other outcomes.

Improved placement location has been demonstrated, beginning with T.F. Williams' classic study in New York (Williams, Hill, Fairbank, & Knox, 1973) and including three recent controlled trials (Hendricksen, Lund, & Stromgard, 1984; Kennie, Reid, Richardson, Kiamari, & Kelt, 1988; Rubenstein, Josephson, Wieland, et al., 1987). Several studies have described the functional status of patients before and after care in a GAP, and most show general improvement in status. Similarly, aspects of psychological function have been examined in several studies, and significant findings have been shown in both cognitive and affective function, all in the positive direction. Although not all studies documented significant functional improvement, most did show some improved parameters, and none documented significant deterioration.

Given the high prevalence of polypharmacy in frail elderly people, the impact on prescription drug use has often been examined. In most studies looking at this indicator, drug regimens were generally made more appropriate, usually by decreasing the number of prescribed drugs.

Use of health care services and costs were examined in several controlled studies employing one-year follow-up or more. A reduction in nursing home days was shown in four controlled studies (Lefton, Bonstelle, & Frengley, 1983; Reid & Kennie, 1989; Rubenstein, Josephson, English, et al., 1984; Schuman et al., 1978). A reduction in the number of hospital days was shown in four controlled studies (Hendricksen et al., 1984; Rubenstein, Josephson, English et al., 1984; Tulloch & Moore, 1979; Williams, 1987). Four studies showed an increase in the use of community care services (Hendricksen et al., 1984; Hogan, Fox, Badley, & Mann, 1987; Tulloch & Moore, 1979; Vetter, Jones, & Victor, 1984), an increase that was at least partly responsible for the reduction in hospital and nursing home use. A reduction in the use of institutional services, even when accompanied by a greater use of community services, led to lower annualized health care costs in the studies that performed careful cost analyses (Hendricksen et al., 1984; Rubenstein, Josephson, English, et al., 1984; Williams, 1987).

Perhaps most striking is the positive impact of GAPs on survival, now reported in several controlled studies (Collard, Bachman, & Beatrice, 1985; Hendricksen et al., 1984; Hogan et al., 1987; Reid & Kennie, 1989; Rubenstein, Josephson, English, et al., 1984; Vetter et al., 1984). Although a few studies, mostly small ones, failed to show a significant impact on survival, none showed any adverse effects. Taken as a whole, the contribution of GAPs toward preventing avoidable deaths has been dramatic.

Even though studies offer evidence that GAPs can lead to long-term financial savings in patient care by reducing days in acute hospitals and nursing homes, there is not an adequate mechanism for reimbursement. Inpatient programs with a greater variety and intensity of services also have greater costs. Geriatric assessment done on an outpatient basis is less costly and works well for those patients who are relatively independent, who do not need inpatient testing, and who can attend outpatient therapy programs. Further development of cheaper ambulatory facilities for geriatric assessment, though it will have less impact, will likely occur. Another important issue involves identifying patients expected to benefit most to ensure maximal use of scarce resources (Rubenstein, Campbell, & Kane, 1987; Solomon, Judd, Sier, Rubenstein, & Morley, 1988).

OCCUPATIONAL THERAPY IN THE ASSESSMENT PROCESS

Occupational therapy assessment is defined as "the process of determining the need for, nature of, and estimated time of treatment; determining the needed coordination with other persons involved; and documenting these activities" (Gwin, Hertfelder, & Schafer, 1988, p. 799). Included in the assessment process are (1) screening, (2) patient-related consultation, (3) evaluation, and (4) reassessment.

The process of the occupational therapy evaluation or assessment has been described by Smith and Tiffany (1988) as collecting and organizing data, setting treatment objectives, and performing continual reassessments. It may involve record reviews, observation, interviews, and the administration of data collection procedures. These procedures include but are not limited to the use of standardized tests, performance checklists, and activities and tasks designed to evaluate specific performance abilities. Specific categories of occupational therapy evaluation and treatment include (1) independent living/daily living skills and performance, including physical daily living skills, psychological and emotional daily living skills, work, and play; (2) sensorimotor components, including neuromuscular and sensory integrative skills; (3) cognitive components; (4) psychosocial components, including self-management and dyadic and group management; (5) therapeutic adaptations, including orthotics, prosthetics, and assistive or adaptive equipment; and (6) prevention, including energy conservation, joint protection and body mechanics, positioning, and coordination of daily living activities.

The initial occupational therapy assessment is usually general rather than complete and specific because of time limitations or the condition of the patient. The initial treatment plan is usually based on the most obvious concerns. A complete evaluation may be included in the overall treatment plan during the treatment process. The broad skills in rehabilitation, aging, mental health, cognitive levels, and sensory integration needed by the geriatric occupational therapist to interpret data and select pertinent and appropriate assessment methods are increasingly recognized as "advanced generalist" abilities (Rogers, 1987).

The occupational therapist is sensitive to the importance of detecting and distinguishing depression, dementia, delirium, and anxiety and recognizes that these problems affect performance and function from mild to severe degrees. Proper identification of any problem is necessary for planning and carrying out efficient, effective treatment (Roth, 1988). The difficult-to-measure specific indications of the level of quality of life, such as lack of control, feelings of helplessness, and lack of the opportunities that give meaning and structure to an individual's time, are clearly addressed in occupational therapy treatment. Rogers (1986) points out that data obtained by taking a history have value in showing what the person does routinely and what the habits of daily living are. Focal points of occupational therapy intervention include distinctions between what the person does, can do, should be doing, and has the potential to do. Essential to capturing the person's cooperation is the recognition and inclusion of perceived needs in treatment objectives. Perceived needs are needs the person regards as crucial, and they represent personal interests, values, and conscious desires. They may not be real or vital needs, but their inclusion in the treatment regimen will most likely result in a more successful outcome and will certainly result in a more enthusiastic client (Hasselkus, 1986).

Referral to occupational therapy most frequently comes from the diagnosing physician, who may be a physiatrist, geriatrician, rheumatologist, neurologist, other specialist, or general practitioner. The referral usually states the diagnosis, identifies problem areas, and requests an occupational therapy evaluation or assessment; it may also request specific treatment. The duration of the occupational therapist's initial evaluation may depend on the patient's tolerance and ability to respond or on the time constraints of the therapist's schedule. The purpose of the initial evaluation is to establish rapport between the therapist and the patient, identify basic problem areas and their extent, get a sense of the needs and desires of the patient and the family or caregiver, and determine the need for additional specific or in-depth evaluation. The evaluation process might include a review of the patient's medical record; an interview, including self-report or proxy report questions; a demonstration of basic ADL skills; and a gross assessment of sensation and cognition. At this time, the patient can be informed about how often, for what length of time, and for what purpose occupational therapy will be scheduled. Feedback to the physician and others involved in the patient's treatment program is documented in the patient's medical record and discussed in the interdisciplinary team meeting. In-depth reassessments and resulting modifications of the treatment process are ongoing.

Standardized evaluations of daily living activities are available, such as the Katz ADL scale, Lawton and Brody Philadelphia Geriatric Center ADL and Instrumental ADL (IADL) scales, and the Functional Independence Measure (FIM) developed by Granger. The Katz and the Lawton and Brody scales have been popular instruments for use in research efforts because of the ease in weighting values, the ease of administering by self or proxy, the apparent reliability of the information, and the inclusion of IADL with the basic ADL. The FIM requires demonstration and extends to areas of cognitive, emotional, and social function. The computer feedback offered by the FIM identifies dependency levels to enable selection of the most appropriate discharge arrangement and allows an assessment of rehabilitation potential. Similar assessment packages designed to control costs and improve accountability are likely to emerge.

Occupational therapists in geriatric practice sensitive to the effects of psychological, psychosocial, and cognitive function utilize instruments such as the Kohlman Evaluation of Living Skills (KELS), the Allen Cognitive Levels (ACL) evaluation, and the Assessment of Occupational Functioning to assess judgment, decision making, expectation of self-care level as related to cognitive level, and level of quality of life. Use of the Activities Configuration and of depression scales supports occupational therapy treatment direction or the need for referral to other disciplines. The Interest Check List is sometimes interpreted to indicate depression, indecisiveness, social isolation, and memory problems.

Table 6-1 summarizes ADL and IADL scales that were found in the medical and gerontological literature as well as the occupational therapy literature. Kane and Kane (1981), Branch and Meyers (1987), Asher (1989), and Gwin, Hertfelder, and Schafer (1988), reinforced by the practical use by occupational therapists at the Sepulveda Veterans Affairs Medical Center (SVAMC), were the major sources for this list. The list is meant not to be exhaustive but to be a starting point and a source for acquiring evaluation instruments. Careful scrutiny of an ADL or IADL scale by the user is suggested.

The scales listed in Table 6-1 are organized into four main categories, utilizing the American Occupational Therapy Association's (1988) "Uniform Terminology for Reporting Occupational Therapy Services" as a guide. The categories are (1) independent living/daily living skills, which include physical daily living

Table 6-1 Tests Used in Evaluation

*Designates occupational therapy test.

Test	Purpose	Format	Reliability	Validity	Source
Independent Living/Daily Living Skills					
Physical Daily Living Skills					
Barthel Index	Feeding Grooming Transfer Toileting Bathing Walking/locomotion Continence	Performance	X	X	Mahoney & Barthel (1965); Wylie (1967); Kane & Kane (1981)
Basic Living Skills Battery*	Living arrangements Employment Money handling Transportation Communication Recreation Interpersonal relationships Personal care and hygiene Sexual knowledge Personal feeling scale Mental status	Self-report & performance			Teresa Skolaski-Pellitteri Mental Health Ctr. of Dane County, 31 South Henry, Madison, WI 53707
Comprehensive Evaluation of Basic Living Skills (CEBL)*	Meal preparation Use of public transport Telephone Languages Time Math Money skills	Performance		X	Asher (1989); Casanova & Ferber (1976)

Instrument	Description	Method			Reference
Congruence Model of Person-Environment Interaction	Assesses the match between environmental characteristics and individual needs	Interview and observation	X	X	Asher (1989); Kahana (1975)
Functional Assessment Scale (FAS)*	Self-care function/dysfunction in institutionalized patients; Outcome performance only "Total care" to "prepared to live independently"	Checklist by therapist or observer/proxy; Performance	X	X	Asher (1989); Geri-Rehab, Inc., Box 170, Hibbler Rd., Lebanon, NJ 08833 (1983)
Functional Independence Measure (FIM)	Measures disability; Indicates outcome of care; Self-care; Sphincter control; Mobility/transfers; Locomotion; Communication; Social cognition	Performance	X	X	Granger et al. (1986)
Independent Living Behavior Checklist	Mobility; Self-care; Home maintenance; Safety; Food; Social and communication skills; Functional academic skills	Performance (343 items, 6 categories)	X	X	West Virginia Rehab. Research & Training Ctr., West Virginia University, 509 Allen Hall, Morgantown, WV 26506 (1979)
Katz ADL (original)	Eating; Bathing; Dressing; Transfers; Continence; Toileting	Performance (subsequently self-report)	X	X	Katz et al. (1963); Kane & Kane (1981)

continues

Table 6-1 continued

Test	Purpose	Format	Reliability	Validity	Source
Kenny Self-Care Evaluation	Bed activities Transfers Locomotion Continence Dressing Feeding	Performance	X	X	Schoening & Iversen (1968); Kane & Kane (1981)
Klein-Bell Activities of Daily Living Scale	Dressing Elimination Mobility Bathing hygiene Eating Emergency telephone communication	Performance (170 items, 6 areas)	X	X	Klein & Bell (1982)
Kohlman Evaluation of Living Skills*	Self-care Safety and health Money management Transportation and phone Work and leisure	Performance (18 items, 5 categories; 15–20 minutes)	Research in progress		Kels Research, Box 33503, Seattle, WA 98133
Modified ADL Scales	Eating Ambulation Bathing Dressing Transfers Personal Grooming Continence Toileting	Self-report, proxy, performance	X	X	Branch & Meyers (1987); Kane & Kane (1981); Katz et al. (1963)
Nurse's Observation Scale for Inpatient Evaluation (Nosie)	Basic ADL Confirm or correlate with changes on OT assessments	Observation by ward staff			Gwin et al. (1988); Honigfield et al. (1965)

Instrument	Items	Method			Reference
Older Americans Resources and Services Instrument (OARS)	Telephone Shopping Transportation Meal preparation Housework Medication Finance Eating Dressing Grooming Walking Transfers Bathing Continence Toileting	Self-report	X	X	Duke University, Center for the Study of Aging and Human Development, Durham, NC 27710 (1978); Kane & Kane (1981)
Pace II	Telephone Finance Shopping Housekeeping Meal preparation	Self-report, proxy		X	U.S. DHEW (1978); Kane & Kane (1981)
Parachek Geriatric Rating Scale*	Physical capabilities Self-care skills Social interaction skills	Performance (10 items, 3 categories)		X	Miller & Parachek (1974)
Philadelphia Geriatric Center (PGC) Scale	Telephone Shopping Food preparation Housekeeping Laundry Use of public transport Medications Finances	Self-report, proxy	X	X	Lawton (1975); Kane & Kane (1981)

continues

Table 6-1 continued

Test	Purpose	Format	Reliability	Validity	Source
Quick Neurological Screening Test (QNST)	Maturity of motor development Skill in controlling large and small muscles Motor planning and sequencing Sense of rate and rhythm Spatial organization Visual and auditory perceptual skills Balance and cerebellar-vestibular function Disorders of attention	Performance	X	X	Asher (1989); Mitchell (1983)
Range of Motion	Motions of shoulders Elbows Wrists Fingers Thumbs Hips Knees Ankles	Performance	X		Granger (1974); Kane & Kane (1981)
Scorable Self-Care Evaluation*	Personal care Housekeeping chores Work and leisure Financial management	Performance (18 subtasks, 4 subscales)	X	X	Slack, Inc., 6900 Grove Rd., Thorofare, NJ 08086 (1984)

Instrument	Description	Method			Reference
Sickness Impact Profile (SIP)	Sleeping Eating Working Home management Recreation Ambulation Mobility Body care Social interaction Alertness behavior Emotional behavior Communication	Self-report	X	X	Bergner et al. (1981)
Stockton Geriatric Rating Scale	Physical disability Apathy Communication failure Socially irritating behavior	Observation-based rating scale (33 items, 4 factors)	X	X	Asher (1989); Meer & Baker (1966); Plutchik, Conte, & Lieberman (1971)
Psychological, Emotional, and Psychosocial Daily Living Skills					
Activities Configuration*	Daily activities performed Feelings about performing the activities	Self-report and performance	Research in progress		Spahn (1969); Watanabe (1968); Tina Barth, Health Related Consulting Services, New York, NY
Assessment of Occupational Functioning*	Screens occupational functioning based on model of human occupation	Interview (self-report)	X	X	Asher (1989); Watts et al. (1986)
Geriatric Depression Scale	Tool used to identify depression in the elderly	Self-report (30 items)	X	X	Yesavage et al. (1982–83)
Internal/External Scale	Measures belief in internal vs. external control over the consequences of personal action	Self-report (23 question pairs)	X	X	Rotter (1966)

continues

Table 6-1 continued

Test	Purpose	Format	Reliability	Validity	Source
Beck Depression Index	Measures depression	Interview (21 sets of 4–5 graded statements, each set showing increased depression; subject chooses response)	X	X	Beck et al. (1961) *Archives of General Psychiatry*
Life Satisfaction Indexes: Life Satisfaction Rating and Life Satisfaction Indexes A & Z	Assesses life satisfaction, present & overall	Self-report	X	X	Asher (1989); Neugarten, Havighurst, & Tobin (1961)
Mosey Evaluations*	Survey of task skills Group interaction Child care survey Work survey Recreation survey	Performance			Gwin et al. (1988); Mosey (1973)
Philadelphia Geriatric Center Morale Scale	Agitation Attitude toward own aging and lonely dissatisfaction	Interview (17-item scale, 3 dimensions)	X	X	Asher (1989); Philadelphia Geriatric Ctr., 5301 Old York Rd., Philadelphia, PA 19141
Purpose-in-Life Test	Measures degree to which individuals experience purpose and meaning in their lives	Self-report (20 items)	X	X	Psychometric Affiliates, Box 807, Murfreesboro, TN 37133
Self-Esteem Scale	Measures degree of positive and negative attitudes toward one's abilities and accomplishments	Self-rating (10 items)	X	X	Asher (1989); Robinson & Shaver (1973); Rosenberg (1965)
Social Readjustment Rating Scale	Stress prediction	Self-report (43 stress-related items)			Girdano & Everly (1979); Gwin et al. (1988)

Instrument	Description	Method			References
(Holmes & Rahe Stress or RAHE Scales); Recent Versions: Life Events Inventory, Life Change Events Scale					
Zung Self-Rating Depression Scale (SDS)	Measures depression	Self-report or interview (20 statements related as they apply to subject)	X	X	Zung (1965)
Play, Leisure, and Work					
Activity Index: Activity Patterns and Leisure Concepts among the Elderly*	Measures activity, leisure, and the meaning of leisure	Interview (61 questions)	X	X	Asher (1989); Nystrom (1974)
Adult Activity Inventory	Assesses adjustment of older adults by measuring participation in activity	Self-report or interview	X	X	Asher (1989); Cavan et al. (1979); Matsutsuyu (1969)
Interest Checklist*	Identifies interest patterns and characteristics	Self-report (80 items)	X	X	Asher (1989); Gwin et al. (1988); Matsutsuyu (1969)
Leisure Activities Blank	Looks at past leisure activities and tries to predict future satisfaction with these activities	Self-report (121 activities)	X	X	Asher (1989); Gwin et al. (1988); Morgan & Godbey (1978)
Needs Satisfaction of Activity Interview*	Assesses the satisfaction needs that the elderly gain from activities in their environment	Interview	X	X	Asher (1989); Tickle & Yerxa (1981)

continues

Table 6-1 continued

Test	Purpose	Format	Reliability	Validity	Source
Occupational Behavior and Life Satisfaction*	Assesses the meaning and significance of activity among the elderly	Self-report	X	X	Gregory (1983)
Self-Assessment of Leisure Interests*	Designed for arthritics to identify interest in leisure activities appropriate to this population	Self-report (71 activities)		X	Asher (1989); Kautzmann (1984)
Significance of Leisure Activities	Identifies what meaning leisure has by evaluating favorite leisure activities and leisure life styles	Interview	X	X	Asher (1989); Havighurst (1979)
Sensorimotor Components					
Flower-House-Self	Unilateral neglect Body visualization 3 pace concepts	Performance			Gwin et al. (1988); Siev & Fershat (1976)
Jebsen Hand Function Test	Major aspects of hand function often used in activities of daily living	Performance			Gwin et al. (1988); Jebsen et al. (1969)
Minnesota Rate of Manipulation Test	Measures arm-hand dexterity	Performance	X	X	American Guidance Service, Inc., Circle Pines, MN 55014
Object Manipulation Speed Test*	Measures psychomotility (may be reflective of sensory integrative status)	Performance	Some norms established; data being collected		Gwin et al. (1988)
Cognitive Component					
Allen Cognitive Level Test*	Assesses cognitive disability	Demonstration, instruction, performance	X	X	Allen (1985); Asher (1989); Gwin et al. (1988)

Instrument	Description	Method			References
Bay Area Functional Performance Evaluation*	Assesses cognitive, affective, and performance skills in selected daily living tasks	Performance	X	X	Asher (1989); Bloomer & Williams (1982); Houston, Williams, et al. (1989)
Mental Status Questionnaire (MSQ)	Taps awareness of current events and memory for more distant events	Interview (10 questions)	X	X	Kahn et al. (1960)
Mini-Mental State (MMS)	Measures cognitive performance	Performance	X	X	Folstein et al. (1975)
Person Drawing (Draw-A-Person; D-A-P)	Projective	Performance			Gwin et al. (1988); Western Psychological Services (1991-92)
Short Portable Mental Status Questionnaire	Measures intellectual impairment in elderly persons	Performance (10 items)	X	X	Gwin et al. (1988); Pfeiffer (1975)
Role Component					
Moorhead Occupational History Review*	Function in occupational, school, family, student, homemaker roles General use of time	Interview			Asher (1989); Moorhead (1969)
Occupational History/ Occupational Role History*	Identifies occupational roles and habits	Interview (self-report)	X	X	Asher (1989); Gwin et al. (1988); Florey & Michelman (1982)
Occupational Questionnaire*	Identifies how time is used in daily activities and how it relates to values, interests, and personal causation	Self-report	X	X	Asher (1989); Smith, Kielhofner, & Watts (1986)
Role Checklist*	Assesses productive roles in adult life by indicating perceptions of past, present, and future roles	Self-report	X	X	Asher (1989); Gwin et al. (1988); Oakley, Kielhofner, Barris, & Reichler (1986)

skills, psychological, emotional, and psychosocial daily living skills, and play, leisure, and work; (2) sensorimotor components; (3) cognitive components; and (4) role components.

The informal evaluations and interpretations frequently used by occupational therapists may lack stability and may not produce the information intended and needed. The absence of evaluation instruments designed for occupational therapy treatment and based on occupational therapy frames of reference has been noted. A need for occupational therapy assessments with empirically demonstrated reliability and validity is recognized, particularly in settings where research is stressed. As this need is remedied, a review of acquired knowledge and familiarity with specific frames of reference may be vital (Watts, Kielhofner, Bauer, Gregory, & Valentine, 1986).

FUTURE DIRECTIONS

Present and future needs for geriatric occupational therapists and advanced generalists include (1) the need to educate and train occupational therapy personnel in the selection and application of methods for the evaluation of elderly people; (2) the need to develop a reference pertinent to the selection, use, and interpretation of evaluations designed for occupational therapy treatment as well as those appropriate for use by occupational therapists in the assessment of older persons; (3) the need to establish empirically the reliability and validity of evaluations designed for occupational therapy treatment through research and cooperative studies; and (4) the need to further explore areas of occupational therapy treatment that require evaluation procedures.

Valid, accurate evaluation is the first step in providing the best possible service for older persons. With the demand for faster inpatient progress, predictable outcomes, and predictable treatment durations, evaluations that the therapist can rely on to point out the real problems and support treatment predictions are necessary. Finding the best methods and acquiring expertise in their use is not a simple task. Networking, exploring the literature, and pursuing continuing education constitute a beginning. With more than 30% of the registered occupational therapists working primarily with persons over age 65, there is a growing need for the training of occupational therapy personnel in the use of evaluation instruments to identify direct care needs so they can plan the best possible treatment programs for the sick, disabled, frail, and well elderly (Davis, 1986).

REFERENCES

Allen, C.K. (1985). *Occupational therapy for psychiatric diseases: Measures and management of cognitive disabilities.* Boston: Little, Brown & Company.

American Occupational Therapy Association. (1988). Uniform terminology for reporting occupational therapy services. In H. Hopkins & H. Smith (Eds.), *Willard and Spackman's occupational therapy* (pp. 799–806), 7th ed. Philadelphia: Lippincott.

Asher, I.E. (1989). *An annotated index of occupational therapy evaluation tools.* Rockville, MD: American Occupational Therapy Association.

Beck, A.T., Ward, D.H., Mendelson, M., Mock, J., & Erbaugh, J. (1961). An inventory for measuring depression. *Archives of General Psychiatry, 4,* 53–63.

Bergner, M., Bobbitt, R.A., Carter, W.B., & Gilson, B.S. (1981). The sickness impact profile: Development and final revision of a health status measure. *Medical Care, 8,* August 19, 787–805.

Bloomer, J., & Williams, S.K. (1982). The Bay Area functional performance evaluation. In B. Hemphill (Ed.), *The evaluation process in psychiatric occupational therapy* (pp. 255–308). Thorofare, NJ: Charles B. Slack.

Branch, L.G., & Meyers, A.R. (1987). Assessing physical function in the elderly. *Clinics in Geriatric Medicine, 3,* 29–51.

Casanova, J.S., & Ferber, J. (1976). Comprehensive evaluation of basic living skills. *American Journal of Occupational Therapy, 10,* 101–105.

Cavan, R.S., Burgess, W.W., Havighurst, R.J., & Goldhammer, H. (1979). *Personal adjustments in old age.* New York: Arno.

Collard, A.F., Bachman, S.F., & Beatrice, D.S. (1985). Acute care delivery for the geriatric patient: An innovative approach. *Quality Review Bulletin, 11*(6), 180–185.

Davis, L.J. (1986). Introduction. In L. Davis & M. Kirkland (Eds.), *The role of occupational therapy with the elderly* (pp. 1–9). Rockville, MD: American Occupational Therapy Association.

Florey, L., & Michelman, S.M. (1982). The occupational role in history: A screening tool for psychiatric occupational therapy. *American Journal of Occupational Therapy, 36*(5), 301–308.

Folstein, M.F., Folstein, S.E., & McHugh, P.R. (1975). Mini-mental state: A practical method for grading the cognitive state of patients for the clinician. *Journal of Psychiatric Research, 12,* 189–198.

Girdano, D., & Everly, G. (1979). *Controlling stress and tension: A holistic approach.* Englewood Cliffs, NJ: Prentice-Hall.

Granger, C.V. (1974). Medical rehabilitation research and training center No. 7. *Annual progress report.* Boston: Tufts University School of Medicine.

Granger, C.V., Hamilton, B.B., Keith, R.A., Zielezny, M., & Sherwin, F.S. (1986). Advances in functional assessment for medical rehabilitation. *Topics in Geriatric Rehabilitation, 1*(3), 59–74.

Gregory, M.D. (1983). Occupational behavior and life satisfaction among retirees. *American Journal of Occupational Therapy, 37*(8), 548–553.

Gwin, C.H., Hertfelder, S.D., & Schafer, M.K. (Eds.). (1988). *Mental health information packet.* Rockville, MD: American Occupational Therapy Association.

Hasselkus, B.R. (1986). Roles and functions of occupational therapy in gerontic practice. In L. Davis & M. Kirkland (Eds.), *The role of occupational therapy with the elderly.* Rockville, MD: American Occupational Therapy Association.

Havighurst, R.J. (1979). The nature and values of meaningful free-time activity. In R.W. Kleemeier (Ed.), *Aging and leisure.* New York: Arno.

Hendricksen, C., Lund, E., & Stromgard, E. (1984). Consequences of assessment and intervention among elderly people: Three year randomized controlled trial. *British Medical Journal, 289,* 1522–1524.

Hogan, D.B., Fox, R.A., Badley, B.W., & Mann, O.E. (1987). Role of a geriatric consultation service in management of patients in an acute care hospital. *Canadian Medical Association Journal, 136*, 713–717.

Honigfeld, G.F., & Klett, C.J. (1965). Nurses' observation scale for inpatient evaluation: A new scale for measuring improvement in chronic schizophrenia. *Journal of Clinical Psychology, 21*, 65–71.

Houston, D., Williams, S.L., Bloomer, J., & Mann, W.C. (1989). The Bay Area functional performance evaluation: Development and standardization. *American Journal of Occupational Therapy, 43*(3), 170.

Jebsen, R.H., Taylor, N., Trieschmann, R.B., Trotter, M.J., & Howard, L.A. (1969). An objective and standard test of hand function. *Archives of Physical Medicine and Rehabilitation, 50*(6), 311–319.

Kahana, E. (1975). A congruence model of person-environment interaction. In P.G. Windley, T.O. Byerts, & F.G. Ernst (Eds.), *Theory development in environment and aging*. Washington, DC: Gerontological Society of America.

Kahn, R.L., Goldfarb, A.I., Pollack, M., & Gerber, I.E. (1960). The relationship of mental and physical states in institutionalized aged persons. *American Journal of Psychiatry, 117*, 120–124.

Kane, R.A., & Kane, R. (1981). *Assessing the elderly*. Lexington, MA: Lexington Books.

Katz, S., Ford, A.B., Moskowitz, R.W., Jackson, B.A., & Jaffe, M.W. (1963). Studies of illness in the aged. The Index of ADL: A standardized measure of biological and psychosocial function. *Journal of the American Medical Association, 185*, 94ff.

Kautzmann, L. (1984). Identifying leisure interests: A self-assessment approach for adults with arthritis. *Occupational Therapy in Health Care, 1*(2), 45–52.

Kennie, B.C., Reid, J., Richardson, I.R., Kiamari, A.A., & Kelt, C. (1988). Effectiveness of geriatric rehabilitative care after fracture of the proximal femur in elderly women: A randomized clinical trial. *British Medical Journal, 297*, 1083–1085.

Klein, R.H., & Bell, B. (1982). Self-care skills: Behavioral measurement with the Klein-Bell ADL scale. *Archives of Physical Medicine and Rehabilitation, 63*, 335–338.

Lawton, M.P. (1975). The Philadelphia geriatric morale scale: A revision. *Journal of Gerontology, 30*, 85–89.

Lefton, E., Bonstelle, S., & Frengley, J.D. (1983). Success with an inpatient geriatric unit: A controlled study. *Journal of the American Geriatrics Society, 31*, 149–155.

Mahoney, F.I., & Barthel, D.W. (1965). Functional evaluation: The Barthel index. *Maryland State Medical Journal, 14*, 61–65.

Matsutsuyu, J.S. (1969). The interest checklist. *American Journal of Occupational Therapy, 23*, 323–328.

Meer, B., & Baker, J.A. (1966). The Stockton geriatric rating scale. *Journal of Gerontology, 21*, 392–403.

Miller, E.R., & Parachek, J.F. (1974). Validation and standardization of a goal-oriented, quick screening geriatric scale. *Journal of the American Geriatrics Society, 22*, 278–281.

Mitchell, J.V. (Ed.). (1983). *Tests in print III*. Lincoln, NE: Buros Institute of Mental Measurement, University of Nebraska Press.

Moorhead, L. (1969). The occupational history. *American Journal of Occupational Therapy, 23*(4), 329–334.

Morgan, A., & Godbey, G. (1978). The effect of entering an age-segregated environment upon the leisure activity pattern of older adults. *Journal of Leisure Research, 10*, 77–190.

Mosey, A. (1973). *Activities therapy*. New York: Raven Press.

Neugarten, B.L., Havighurst, R.J., & Tobin, S.S. (1961). The measurement of life satisfaction. *Journal of Gerontology, 166*, 134–143.

Nystrom, E.P. (1974). Activity patterns and leisure concepts among the elderly. *American Journal of Occupational Therapy, 28*(6), 337–345.

Oakley, F., Kielhofner, G., Barris, R., & Reichler, R.K. (1986). The role checklist: Development and empirical assessment of reliability. *Occupational Therapy Journal of Research, 6*(3), 157–169.

Pfeiffer, E. (1975). A short portable mental status questionnaire for the assessment of organic brain deficiency in elderly patients. *Journal of the American Geriatrics Society, 23*(10), 433–441.

Plutchik, R., Conte, H., & Lieberman, M. (1971). Development of a scale (GIES) for assessment of cognitive and perceptual functioning in geriatric patients. *Journal of the American Geriatrics Society, 19*, 614–623.

Reid, J., & Kennie, D.C. (1989). Geriatric rehabilitative care after fractures of the proximal femur: One year follow-up of a randomized clinical trial. *British Medical Journal, 299*, 25–26.

Robinson, J., & Shaver, P. (1973). *Measures of social psychological attitudes.* Ann Arbor, MI: Institute of Social Research.

Rogers, J.C. (1986). Roles and functions of occupational therapy in gerontic practice. In L. Davis & M. Kirkland (Eds.), *The role of occupational therapy with the elderly* (pp. 117–121). Rockville, MD: American Occupational Therapy Association.

————. (1987). Gerontic occupational therapy. In B. Brooks, L. Davis, M. Kirkland, & E. Nystrom (Eds.), *ROTE II: Role of occupational therapy with the elderly* (pp. 3–8). Rockville, MD: American Occupational Therapy Association.

Rosenberg, M. (1965). *Society and the adolescent self-image.* Princeton, NJ: Princeton University Press.

Roth, E.J. (1988). Principles and practices of rehabilitation management. *Topics in Rehabilitation Management, 3*, 27–59.

Rotter, J.B. (1966). Generalized expectancies for internal versus external control of reinforcement. *Psychological Monographs, 80*, 1–28.

Rubenstein, L.Z., Campbell, L.J., & Kane, R.L. (Eds.). (1987). *Geriatric assessment.* Philadelphia: Saunders.

Rubenstein, L.Z., Josephson, K.R., English, P.A., Wieland, G.D., Sayre, J.A., & Kane, R.L. (1984). Effectiveness of a geriatric evaluation unit: A randomized clinical trial. *New England Journal of Medicine, 311*, 1664–1670.

Rubenstein, L.Z., Josephson, K.R., Wieland, G.D., Pietruszka, F., Tretton, C., Strome, S., Cole, K.D., & Campbell, L.J. (1987). Geriatric assessment on a subacute hospital ward. *Clinics in Geriatric Medicine, 3*(1), 131–144.

Rubenstein, L.Z., Schairer, C., Wieland, G.D., & Kane, R.A. (1984). Systematic biases in functional status assessment of elderly adults: Effects of different data sources. *Journal of Gerontology, 39*, 686–691.

Rubenstein, L.Z., & Wieland, G.D. (1989). Comprehensive geriatric assessment. *Annual Review of Gerontology & Geriatrics, 9*, 145–192.

Schoening, H.A., and Iversen, I.A. (1968). Numerical scoring of self-care status: A study of the Kenny self-care evaluation. *Archives of Physical Medicine and Rehabilitation, 46*, 689–697.

Schuman, J.E., Beattie, E.J., Gibson, J.E., Merry, G.M., Campbell, W.D., Kraus, A.S., & Steed, D.A. (1978). The impact of a new geriatric program in a hospital for the chronically ill. *Canadian Medical Association Journal, 118*, 639–645.

Siev, E., & Fershat, B. (1976). *Perceptual dysfunction in the adult stroke patient.* Thorofare, NJ: Charles B. Slack.

Smith, H.D., & Tiffany, E.G. (1988). Assessment and evaluation: An overview. In H. Hopkins & H. Smith (Eds.), *Willard and Spackman's occupational therapy,* 7th ed. (pp. 211–215). Philadelphia: Lippincott.

Smith, N.R., Kielhofner, G., & Watts, J.H. (1986). The relationship between volition, activity patterns, and life satisfaction in the elderly. *American Journal of Occupational Therapy, 40*(4), 278–283.

Solomon, D. (1988a). Geriatric assessment: Methods for clinical decision making. *Journal of the American Medical Association, 259,* 2450–2452.

Solomon, D. (1988b). National Institutes of Health consensus, development conference statement: Geriatric assessment methods for clinical decision making. *Journal of the American Geriatrics Society, 36,* 342–347.

Solomon, D.H., Judd, H.L., Sier, H.C., Rubenstein, L.Z., & Morley, J.E. (1988). New issues in geriatric care. *Annals of Internal Medicine, 108,* 718–732.

Spahn, R. (1969). The patient gets busy: Change or progress? *Evaluation procedures in occupational therapy.* Illinois Council on Practice, Region IV, The American Occupational Therapy Association.

Tickle, L.S., & Yerxa, E.J. (1981). Need satisfaction of older persons living in the community and in institutions. Part 2, Role of activity. *American Journal of Occupational Therapy, 35,* 650–655.

Tulloch, A.H., & Moore, V. (1979). A randomized controlled trial of geriatric screening and surveillance in general practice. *Journal of the Royal College of General Practitioners, 29,* 733–742.

U.S. Department of Health, Education and Welfare (HEW). (1978). *Working document on patient care management.* Washington, D.C.: Government Printing Office.

Vetter, N.J., Jones, D.A., & Victor, C.R. (1984). Effects of health visitors working with elderly patients in general practice: A randomized controlled trial. *British Medical Journal, 288,* 369–372.

Watanabe, S. (1968). Social adaptation: Making it. AOTA Regional Institute on the Evaluation Process. Final Report, Rehabilitation Services Administration, 123-T-68.

Watts, J.H., Kielhofner, G., Bauer, D.F. Gregory, M.D., & Valentine, D.B. (1986). The assessment of occupational functioning: A screening tool for use in long-term care. *American Journal of Occupational Therapy, 40,* 231–240.

Western Psychological Services. (1991-92). *Catalogue.* Los Angeles: Manson Western Corporation.

Wetle, T.T., & Besdine, R.W. (1982). Ethical issues. In J.W. Rowe & R.W. Besdine (Eds.), *Health and disease in old age,* 1st ed. (pp. 425–430). Boston: Little, Brown & Co.

Wieland, D. (1989). Geriatric assessment: A guide and review of the literature. In J.C. Brocklehurst & T.F. Williams (Eds.), Multidisciplinary health assessment of the elderly patient. [Special gerontology supplement], *Danish Medical Bulletin, 7,* 7–24.

Williams, M.E. (1987). Outpatient geriatric evaluation. *Clinics in Geriatric Medicine, 3,* 175–183.

Williams, T.F., Hill, J.G., Fairbank, M.E., & Knox, K.G. (1973). Appropriate placement of the chronically ill and aged: A successful approach by evaluation. *Journal of the American Medical Association, 266,* 1332–1335.

Wylie, C.M. (1967). Gauging the response of stroke patients to rehabilitation. *Journal of the American Geriatrics Society, 15,* 797–805.

Yesavage, J.A., Brink, T.L., Rose, T.L., Lum, D., Huang, V., Adey, M., & Leirer, V.D. (1982-83). Development and validation of a geriatric depression scale: A preliminary report. *Journal of Psychiatry Research, 17*(1), 37–39.

Zung, W.W. (1965). A self-rating depression scale. *Archives of General Psychiatry, 12,* 63–70.

Chapter 7

Geriatric Rehabilitation Programs

Mary Ann Miller and Margaret M. Kirchman

Geriatric rehabilitation is a relatively new term in geriatric medicine. The term emphasizes certain approaches to rehabilitation care and treatment that specifically consider the needs of the elderly patient.

Occupational therapists in geriatric rehabilitation must have good knowledge of the aging process in addition to superior rehabilitation skills. These two bases of knowledge—physical rehabilitation and gerontology—are requirements for planning a successful geriatric rehabilitation program.

This chapter will contain guidelines for developing a geriatric rehabilitation program and a specific interdisciplinary model for effective treatment planning with this age group. Specific treatment techniques and considerations for common neurological, orthopedic, pulmonary, and cardiac conditions will be presented.

REHABILITATION SETTINGS

Rehabilitation of the older adult may occur at the acute care, intensive rehabilitation, or extended care level. The structure and focus of services vary given the patient's medical status and needs. Early prerehabilitation intervention begins at the acute care level. It is well documented that immobility, including bedrest, has negative effects on cardiovascular and pulmonary function, on musculoskeletal structures, and on other systems as well (Williams, 1988). The elderly patient who enters a hospital-based rehabilitation program is medically stable and in need of an intensive rehabilitation program. A comprehensive rehabilitation program addressing the needs of the older adult has proven to achieve greater functional outcomes than usual rehabilitation services (Williams, 1988). The older adult who is deconditioned after surgery will benefit from a short-term rehabilitation program on an extended care level designed to return the individual to community living.

INTERDISCIPLINARY TEAM

One component of a successful geriatric rehabilitation program is establishing a team to identify strategies for patient and family problems. A comprehensive program will include intensive, skilled rehabilitation nursing, physical and occupational therapy treatment, speech pathology and audiology services, and prosthetic and orthotic services. Other team members include psychologists, social workers, chaplains, dietitians, therapeutic recreational specialists, and physicians.

An interdisciplinary team is an important part of any rehabilitation program, and each profession has its own specialized area of knowledge. However, in a geriatric program, a blending of roles occurs to meet the needs of older patients. Consistent, repetitive approaches are required for the attainment of established treatment goals and functional outcomes.

The interdisciplinary team collaborates with the patient and support system to design and implement treatment plans and achieve mutually acceptable functional goals that maximize the patient's performance. Given the complexity and chronicity of the patient's problems, the geriatric rehabilitation program has a multitude of tasks to perform.

Each task requires different techniques to achieve a functional outcome. The patient is entering a new situation and may feel overwhelmed. The success of the rehabilitation process is contingent on the collaborative efforts of the team members in regard to the older adult's role and on their cooperative efforts in regard to the treatment program.

Although communication occurs between disciplines, a concrete, constructive base of communication is necessary in order to develop joint strategies for dealing with patient and family problems. Medicare and other regulatory organizations look for evidence of methods used by a facility to promote a team approach to patient treatment and care.

One interdisciplinary method of ensuring consistent communication among the core disciplines is weekly miniteam meetings. The object of the meetings is to provide continuity in care; promote ongoing communication between the occupational therapist, physical therapist, and nurse for weekly treatment planning; and ensure collaboration in treatment implementation and carry-over of functional performance from patient admission to discharge.

During each team meeting, the members share data and perspectives in defining problems as well as formulating goals that affect the achievement of functional skills. Treatment times are determined by considering the needs of the patient, who is a member of the team and participates in the decision-making process. One goal of the team meetings is to increase the client's responsibility for the rehabilitation program. The team discusses what the family needs to know before the patient returns home, and it coordinates the times for family teaching.

It is important to remember that the purpose of the miniteam is to develop a holistic approach to older adult treatment and care. The medical chart and the patient care plan are utilized to document the goals and strategies identified by the team. Table 7-1 shows common interdisciplinary goals that relate to occupational therapy.

One method of monitoring the weekly miniteam meetings is through a chart audit that tracks written documentation of the meetings. Additionally, a component of peer review may target interdisciplinary communication as essential for comprehensive treatment planning. Exhibit 7-1 is an example of a peer review work sheet that includes an interdisciplinary component.

PATIENT AND FAMILY ORIENTATION

Many older adults who enter a rehabilitation facility feel a sense of loss. Although the rehabilitation program is anticipated as a positive experience, significant life changes imprint their psychological and physical effects on individuals who undergo them. Other older adults may not be aware of the benefits to be gained from transferring to a facility for rehabilitation services and may need more support and information about the rehabilitation program. In general, perceived control during a change in environments reduces the stress of a new experience and place (Averill, 1973; Beaver, 1979; Killian, 1970; Tobin & Lieberman, 1976).

One basic need is to attain a sense of belonging through association, through being accepted, and through face-to-face relationships (Fried, 1966; Hasselkus,

Table 7-1 Common Miniteam Goals

Goal	Strategy
Improve transfers	Provide consistent cues during transfer
Improve body scheme and increase body awareness	Position self on affected side
Improve endurance and energy conservation awareness	Schedule rest periods
Improve safety	Elicit patient's awareness of foot rest and cue to lock brakes
Upgrade standing balance and tolerance	Have patient stand while performing oral/facial hygiene
Upgrade sitting balance and tolerance	Have patient sit unsupported on bed for breakfast meal

Source: Courtesy of the Occupational Therapy Department, Johnston R. Bowman Health Center for the Elderly, Chicago, Illinois.

Exhibit 7-1 Peer Review Work Sheet

Week of: _____

Reviewer: _____

Reviewee: _____

1. Documentation Reviewed: YES _____ NO _____ (Explain)

	CONS	FREQ	OCC	RARE	N/A	COMMENTS
Number of Patients Reviewed/Caseload: ___/___						
2. STGs and LTGs						
a. Are deficits realistically addressed?						
b. Are goals measurable, functional, with realistic time frames?						
c. Do goals reflect expected discharge status?						
d. Do goals include interdisciplinary emphasis?						
3. TX Cards						
a. Information is clear.						
b. Cards are complete.						
c. Precautions are noted.						
d. Activities are appropriate.						
e. Strategies included for designated interdisciplinary approach.						
f. Cards are updated to reflect changes.						

4. Interdisciplinary Communication							
a. ID 1–2 goals with Nursing and PT.							
b. Discuss support systems and expected D/C environment with SW.							
c. Collaborate with TR re: leisure skills; deficits which may interfere.							
d. ID communication level with SP, including strategies for intervention in all language-based functions.							
e. Discuss treatment approach, trans, positioning, body scheme, and equipment needs with PT.							
5. Patient/Family Education Addressed							

Source: Courtesy of the Occupational Therapy Department, Johnston R. Bowman Health Center for the Elderly, Chicago, Illinois.

1978). One method of achieving a sense of belonging when an older adult is transferred to a rehabilitation setting is to design a patient-family group.

The older adult needs to be aware of the benefits that can be derived from a rehabilitation program (Crabtree, 1988). The possibilities for improvement of function and personal involvement in achieving this goal are explored in a patient-family orientation group. The knowledge gained during this initial support group may create a change in the attitude of the older patient. Rather than deciding to disengage from activities and significant roles, the older person steadily engages in the rehabilitation process, ultimately becoming a participant in practical life tasks and previous roles. The family acquires information on how the rehabilitation process may reduce the patient's limitations and enhance the quality of life.

Several topics may be pursued in group discussions. The group leader may describe a routine day in the rehabilitation program. The group participants express what rehabilitation means to them. The patient and family are introduced to the rehabilitation process, including evaluation, treatment, patient care conferences, and discharge planning. The group leader identifies members of the rehabilitation team and their roles in the rehabilitation process and also describes the patient and family's vital role in the process. The information shared in the group may include descriptions of additional services available, such as parking, haircutting, and volunteer and religious services. The patient-family orientation group may also review the patient bill of rights. This reinforces the patient's role as active participant in the decision-making process.

SENSORY CHANGES

Sensory changes require careful consideration in an older adult's rehabilitation program. Knowledge of biological changes and the way an older adult compensates for these losses will enable the occupational therapist to achieve better evaluation and treatment outcomes. General guidelines to follow prior to evaluation and treatment are listed in Exhibit 7-2.

The evaluation process should be limited according to the patient's endurance, frustration tolerance, and attention span. The testing of cognitive and perceptual skills or other areas may yield better results if the fatigue factor is eliminated by administering the test earlier in the day. It is important to give clear, concise directions in order for the elderly patient to understand. The therapist must make sure the patient is comfortable prior to administering a lengthy evaluation.

NEUROLOGICAL REHABILITATION

Stroke and Parkinson's disease are two common neurological conditions that significantly impact the older adult's motor function. Stroke is the most common

Exhibit 7-2 Compensating for Sensory Loss

Eliminate interfering background stimulation/noise during the evaluation and treatment process.

Check to see if the patient's hearing aid is working and adjust volume. The application of the hearing aid is a necessary part of activities of daily living.

Obtain eye contact to facilitate active listening.

Check whether patient's eyeglasses are clean. The application of visual aids is included in activities of daily living retraining.

Plan treatment activities to alternate periods of close work with activities less visually demanding.

Utilize touch to reinforce attention to the task.

Make certain that table top glare is eliminated and that light is adequate in the treatment area.

Determine that materials used in testing or treatment are large, legible, and well contrasted.

Source: Courtesy of the Occupational Therapy Department, Johnston R. Bowman Health Center for the Elderly, Chicago, Illinois.

---

neurological condition in the older age group (Roth, 1988), and Parkinson's disease is a degenerative disease that is prevalent among older adults (S. Lewis, 1979).

Stroke Rehabilitation

The motor deficits resulting from a stroke vary in severity and duration. Gains in motor function may be compounded by preexisting conditions. Although the primary admitting diagnosis is cerebral vascular accident (CVA), many associated illnesses may become obvious when the elderly patient's medical history is examined. The various concurrent conditions affecting the cardiovascular and musculoskeletal systems are considered when evaluating an elderly stroke patient and formulating a treatment approach. Table 7-2 gives examples of basic treatment techniques to facilitate normal motor response and considerations related to the geriatric patient.

In addition, it is important to recognize that the patient may experience cognitive, behavioral, and affective changes after a stroke. These changes have implications for the learning process. The older adult's poor judgment, decreased problem-solving ability, impaired sequencing skills, emotional lability, and tendency toward denial present obstacles to rehabilitation. The occupational

Table 7-2 Treatment Considerations and Concurrent Problems

Treatment Technique	Concurrent Illness	Consideration
Weight bearing (WB) or developmental posture	Bursitis, osteoarthritis, and rheumatoid arthritis	Restrict WB on painful joints or modify WB position
Progressive resistive activities and exercise	Osteoporosis	Prevent overload of osteoporotic bone
Rhythmical stabilization	Hypertension and heart disease	Prevent Valsalva's maneuver
Anterior/posterior pelvic tilts	Osteoarthritis and rheumatoid arthritis	Facilitate movement within available range

Source: Courtesy of the Occupational Therapy Department, Johnston R. Bowman Health Center for the Elderly, Chicago, Illinois.

---

therapist, in collaboration with other disciplines, develops special approaches and techniques to address these critical areas (Foley, Shahrokhi, & Robinson, 1990; Hibbard, Grober, Gordon, Aletta, & Freeman, 1990).

The presence of multiple diagnoses influences the occupational therapist's treatment choices and challenges the therapist's analytical skills from the initial treatment planning to the development of a home program.

The musculoskeletal changes related to pathology, along with spasticity or other typical hemiplegic shoulder problems, may create pain during joint movement (Gibson & Caplan, 1984). Prior to the occupational therapy treatment, the nurse may (with a doctor's order) premedicate the patient as a routine pain management strategy.

The therapist who is working with a patient with a painful shoulder may initiate therapy using an indirect approach rather than beginning with the painful shoulder. For example, while the patient is supine on a mat, the therapist may facilitate trunk rotation and indirectly provide sensory input and modified weight bearing on the affected shoulder. Therapeutic activities may be introduced in this position and may effectively decrease pain experienced with movement (Nelson & Peterson, 1989).

Hypertension should not be a barrier to utilizing various treatment approaches in stroke rehabilitation (Zankel, 1971). A patient entering an intensive rehabilitation program with a history of cardiovascular problems requires close monitoring during challenging physical activities. The patient's blood pressure and pulse are monitored before, during, and after an intensive treatment session.

Parkinson's Disease

Parkinson's disease is a degenerative neurological disease seen in older adults. The symptoms include bradykinesia, resting tremor, postural reflex impairment, and rigidity. In addition, some patients experience aches and pains due to tremors and rigidity as well as changes in breathing pattern as a result of an imbalance in the muscle groups involved. Swallowing problems and excessive sweating may be due to neurological changes (Duvoisin, 1984).

Given the degenerative course of the disease, the older adult with Parkinson's disease is often readmitted when functional capacities change or drug management fails. A common method of improving drug effectiveness is by subjecting the patient to a drug holiday. When medication is introduced and adjusted to achieve the correct therapeutic dose, the patient's functional abilities will fluctuate until the symptoms are controlled by the appropriate dosage. A side effect of levodopa is low blood pressure. The patient's blood pressure may be normal during sitting activities but may drop when standing activities are attempted. The occupational therapist teaches the patient how to move to avoid falls caused by dizziness related to autonomic dysfunction. It is important to monitor the blood pressure in various positions and to collaborate with other disciplines when orthostatic hypotension is present.

A proprioceptive neuromuscular facilitation (PNF) approach to augmenting motor function in Parkinson's disease patients has been presented in other publications (Melnick, 1985; Scott, 1983). Table 7-3 contains a list of problems and PNF techniques to facilitate function.

The PNF techniques are utilized in preparation for functional activities. The treatment focus with the Parkinson's patient must initially be the vital and related functions that may be impaired. Both rigidity and bradykinesia affect the muscles of respiration (Scott, Caird, & Williams, 1985). The PNF techniques may impact endurance by improving respiration and reducing rigidity. According to Melnick (1985), the occupational therapist must be cautious when engaging a patient in resistive activities so as to prevent further rigidity. Lakke, De Jong, Kappyan, and Van Weerden (1980) indicated that patients with Parkinson's disease show signifi-

---

Table 7-3 PNF Techniques for Parkinson's Disease

Problem	Treatment
Reduced respiration	Slow reversals to facilitate diaphragmatic breathing
Decreased stability	Rhythmic stabilization to the trunk
Decreased initiation	Rhythmic initiation
Reduced trunk rotation	Slow reversal holds with diagonal trunk patterns in sitting position
Decreased upper extremity range of motion	Bilateral asymmetrical patterns to reduce proximal rigidity

Source: Courtesy of the Occupational Therapy Department, Johnston R. Bowman Health Center for the Elderly, Chicago, Illinois.

cant limitations of axillary movements in a supine position. Therefore, activities to facilitate movement yield the best results in a sitting position. PNF techniques, as well as a range of motion program, prior to activities of daily living (ADL) will promote the movement necessary for ADL performance.

SELF-MANAGEMENT

The most effective treatment approach for enhancing motor function is instructing the older patient in self-management. The older adult is provided with a motor management program that takes into account his or her special needs. A person with a CVA is instructed on how to utilize the involved upper extremity in everyday activities. The older adult with Parkinson's disease requires a unique approach to motor management. Gauthier, Dalziel, and Gauthier (1987) recommended incorporating auditory and visual cues to facilitate initiation and speed of movement. A mirror may be used for visual feedback, and music may be utilized for auditory cues.

It is important to provide the older adult with relevant information regarding the link between functional problems and treatment techniques used in muscle reeducation. Self-ranging instructions begin as soon as possible to reinforce the patient's responsibility as an active participant in the rehabilitation process. Begin with small increments and provide visual information to reinforce learning when applicable. The range of motion exercises may be performed prior to ADL in the morning and before bedtime. Other areas of instruction in upper extremity self-management may include massage, positioning, and inhibition as well as relaxation techniques. An effective home program will include activities that the older person participated in throughout his or her rehabilitation program.

Given the complexity of the functional deficits occurring with a CVA and with Parkinson's disease, the family has a vital role in facilitating function. Family members must be given the opportunity to demonstrate involvement in the rehabilitation process. They may be instructed in range of motion activities to assist in the recovery of the hemiplegic arm or to provide help when rigidity hampers functional activities. Providing aid also gives them an opportunity to maintain physical contact and reinforce the caring relationship between them and the patient. For many elderly, life is significantly enhanced by their families.

The adult children must be allowed to interact and observe their parent in therapeutic activities in which the parent demonstrates functional capacities. The coaching and guidance given the adult children during the parent's rehabilitation program may help to ensure they have a positive attitude regarding the parent's functional abilities.

As reported earlier, social and introspective issues must be considered throughout the rehabilitation process. Emotional and family needs may directly affect the patient's stress level. Motivation to improve and maintain motor function may be present, but the individual may be overwhelmed by emotional stresses related to psychosocial needs. Reminiscence and life review serve a vital psychological function for the older person in coping with stress. Incorporating these psychosocial approaches into daily treatment sessions effectively raises the older person's self-esteem and has a positive influence on the rehabilitation outcome (C.N. Lewis, 1979).

ORAL MOTOR FUNCTION

Strokes and degenerative neurological disorders are pathological causes of oral motor dysfunction in the elderly. Elliot (1988) reported that between 46% and 60% of older adults in nursing homes demonstrate a swallowing disorder. Several occupational therapy treatment interventions may be utilized to facilitate normal motor response. These techniques are listed in Table 7-4. The presence of natural

Table 7-4 Common Oral Motor Deficits and Treatment Techniques

Oral Motor Deficits	Treatment Techniques
Decreased lip closure	Icing orbicularis oris muscles
	PNF facilitation techniques
	Lip exercises
	Facial hygiene for sensory stimulation
Decreased lingual movement	PNF facilitation techniques
	Oral hygiene for sensory stimulation
	Lingual exercise and activities (removing peanut butter from around mouth)
Decreased lingual coordination	Positioning food on tongue to facilitate motility
Decreased mandibular function	PNF techniques to head and neck
	Mandibular exercises
Reduced or absent swallow reflex	Thermal stimulation
Decreased pharyngeal peristaltic movement	Alternating solid and liquid foods
	Allowing 2 or 3 swallows to clear food
Decreased laryngeal adduction	Facilitating co-contraction through weight-bearing position (prone on elbows or quadruped position)
	PNF techniques to head and neck
	Instructing patient in supraglottic swallow

Source: Courtesy of the Occupational Therapy Department, Johnston R. Bowman Health Center for the Elderly, Chicago, Illinois.

or artificial dentition is important in mastication of food. Tooth loss or poorly fitting dentures usually results in lower performance in mastication (Chauncey, Feldman, & Wayler, 1983). Therefore, diet selection is determined by the elderly patient's oral motor and dental status.

Oral motor function is sometimes a neglected aspect of geriatric occupational therapy assessment and treatment. The ability to feed oneself is one of the primary aspects of self-care. Before beginning a feeding/swallowing program with an elderly patient, several factors must be considered. It is important to have knowledge of the aging process as it impacts oral motor function as well as knowledge of the anatomy and physiology of the feeding/swallowing process. Lastly, it is important to understand how various diagnoses may affect the feeding/swallowing process.

A comprehensive feeding/swallowing program for an elderly patient includes consultation and collaboration with other disciplines. The speech pathologist may be faciliating oral motor function to improve verbal communication. The principal methods the speech pathologist uses to augment oral motor function may reinforce the occupational therapist's efforts. The occupational therapist communicates with the dietitian regarding the nutritional status of the patient, diet recommendations, and intake requirements. The primary nurse follows through with feeding/swallowing recommendations and monitors the patient's medical status.

ORTHOPEDIC REHABILITATION

Among the elderly, the reasons for orthopedic hip surgery include traumatic injury, severe osteoarthritis, and rheumatoid arthritis. The older adult patient after hip surgery will be less mobile than a younger counterpart. Contributing factors include "postfall syndrome," age-related changes, and architectural barriers (Kauffman, 1990; Felsenthal & Stein, 1988). A supportive effort is necessary to promote efficient recovery of functional abilities needed for independent living. The occupational therapist works closely with other health professionals. Communication with the physician is essential in identifying weight-bearing status and hip precautions. Collaboration with the nurse ensures carry-over in adaptive device training. Discussion with the physical therapist prior to introducing homemaking activities is critical in augmenting gait training and identifying specific handling techniques or cues used to facilitate learning mobility skills. Coordination with the social worker is a prerequisite for quality discharge planning that includes family training, equipment requirements, and home services. The occupational therapist, along with other professionals, obtains information regarding the person's previous activities so that function may be restored to prior levels.

The most common traumatic injury resulting in hip surgery in the older adult population is a femoral fracture (B.C. Lewis, 1985). A significant number of hip fractures are due to falls. The high frequency of falls among older adults is related to changes in posture and balance (Hasselkus, 1974; Ross, 1977). In the case of osteoporotic bones, less force is required to create a fracture. Indeed, everyday activities can result in a fracture (Saudek, 1985). The elected surgical procedure is usually internal fixation or joint replacement (Barnes & Dunovan, 1987; Saudek, 1985).

Total hip replacement is the most frequently performed arthroplasty. The surgical procedure involves removal of the proximal femur, insertion of a metal ball, and replacement of the acetabulum with a prosthetic socket (Harris, 1984). In the older adult population, osteoarthritis is prevalent and usually affects the weight-bearing joints (Mankin, 1986). The deterioration of the cartilage and bone produces pain and limitation in movement. The course of rheumatoid arthritis differs from other rehabilitation conditions in that the older adult with rheumatoid arthritis may have longstanding medical conditions (Kulp, O'Leary, Wegener, Fang, & Brunner, 1988). Inflammation, pain, stiffness, and joint damage are characteristic of the disease. In cases of osteoarthritis and rheumatoid arthritis, when nonsurgical relief of pain fails and function diminishes, the physician may recommend surgical intervention to improve function.

The type of surgical procedure and other factors are considered when determining weight-bearing status and hip precautions. Appropriate weight-bearing and joint protection techniques are incorporated in transfer training, activities of daily living, and homemaking tasks.

OCCUPATIONAL THERAPY TREATMENT

An older adult who has fallen and sustained a hip fracture may be fearful of falling again. Postural insecurity may become obvious during transfer training and activities of daily living performed while standing. An element of security with movement may be acquired by performing activities in a supine position. Total patterns of movement are possible at this level. Postural and righting reactions may be facilitated during bedside activities (Knott & Voss, 1968). When the person is ready to perform bed mobility activities, such as rolling from side to side and assuming a sitting position, a leg lifter may be used to assist in the placement of the affected lower extremity during transitional movements.

The term *postfall syndrome* has been used to describe the dysmobility an older adult experiences as a result of fear of falling (Kauffman, 1990). The patient who is experiencing fear and anxiety during transfer retraining needs to begin functional transfers at his or her comfort level. Using a sliding board may provide the patient with added surface contact, giving a greater sense of stability with movement. Transfers may begin with a sliding board, but the patient may progress to a stand pivot transfer. As the patient progresses to a stand pivot transfer, joint compression provides increased proprioceptive input to the trunk and lower extremity. The patient continues to implement proper weight bearing and joint protection to prevent stress and guard against injury during transfer training. Toilet and tub transfer retraining may include recommendations for raised toilet seat, grab bars, and tub bench as well as a handheld shower attachment.

Proper positioning is of utmost importance in preventing contractures and pressure areas from occurring. Hip rotation can be controlled by either a towel or blanket roll on the lateral side to prevent external rotation (Melvin, 1977). An abduction splint or pillow between the legs can be used for prevention of hip adduction and internal rotation. When side lying in bed, a pillow is positioned between the lower extremities to maintain proper alignment. Wheelchair positioning may include an abduction splint as well as an elevated leg rest when edema is present in the lower extremity.

Activities of daily living and homemaking activities, coupled with functional mobility, are the focus of treatment. As the older adult progresses in gait training in physical therapy, standing balance and tolerance activities are emphasized in occupational therapy. Homemaking activities begin as soon as possible to promote appropriate use of ambulation devices during these activities. Exhibit 7-3 is a sample treatment card designed for orthopedic patients.

During homemaking and self-care activities, the patient with a total hip replacement will follow full hip precautions, whereas the patient with an internal fixation device may have to follow only weight-bearing precautions. The therapist will introduce equipment and devices necessary for transferring objects to and from the kitchen area.

According to Someya, Miaki, Assai, Tachino, and Nara (1988), rheumatoid arthritis patients have multiple joint problems, often making it difficult to use ambulation devices for gait training after a hip replacement. The occupational therapist may design a hand splint to address this problem. Additionally, the ambulation device handles may be built up to minimize stress to hand joints.

In cases of total hip replacement, the surgery is generally planned, and therefore preoperational training is possible. During preoperational training, the occupational therapist may introduce the older adult to adaptive devices that are used in activities of daily living, explain hip precautions, and provide position recommendations. Postsurgical occupational therapy intervention requires a continuation of patient education regarding the new hip. Figure 7-1 is an example of the kind of patient education material that might be helpful for an older adult with a total hip replacement.

ENDURANCE ACTIVITY

Many factors influence the older adult's activity tolerance. The evidence of cardiopulmonary changes in the elderly is documented in the occupational therapy

Exhibit 7-3 Treatment Card for Orthopedic Patients

Patient's Name _____
Room Number _____
Physician _____
Diagnosis _____

Precautions: [box]

Factors That Interfere with Functional
Independence:
Weight Bearing _____
Mobility _____
Transfers _____
Joint Limitations ┘
Impaired Sensation
Impaired Judgment
Impaired Vis. Perc. _____

Prescribed Diet: [box]

Special Equipment,
Recommendations, and Dressing
Techniques on back.

ADL Checkout/Homemaking Needs Survey

	DEP	MAX	MOD	MIN	SUP	IND
1. Make Bed						
2. Laundry						
3. Plan Meals						
4. Grocery Shopping						
5. Prepare Meals						
6. Clean Dishes						
7. Housekeeping						
8. Home Maintenance						
9. Money Management						
10. Communication						
11. UE Dressing						
12. LE Dressing						
13. Grooming—O/F Hygiene						
14. UE Bathing						
15. LE Bathing						
Home Safety Booklet						
Hip Precautions Booklet						

Source: Courtesy of the Occupational Therapy Department, Johnston R. Bowman Health Center for the Elderly, Chicago, Illinois.

CARING FOR YOUR NEW HIP

□ Your artificial hip will, in time, give you renewed comfort and ease of motion. However, the muscles and ligaments that hold your leg bone in the hip socket need time to heal after surgery. You should avoid bending in ways which put stress on these muscles and ligaments. Too much stress will cause your hip to dislocate—the stem will pop out of the socket.

□ You should observe the following precautions until your physician says you may stop. Generally, you should avoid the following positions:

DON'T BEND OVER AT THE HIP.

DON'T CROSS YOUR LEGS OR ANKLES.

AVOID:

Bending while sitting.   Bending while standing.

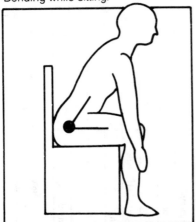
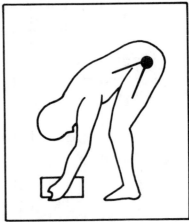

Crossed legs.   Crossed ankles.

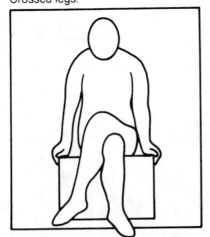
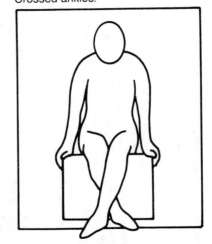

Figure 7-1 An example of education materials for patients who have undergone a total hip replacement. *Source:* Courtesy of the Occupational Therapy Department, Johnston R. Bowman Health Center for the Elderly, Chicago, Illinois.

literature (Davis, 1986; C.N. Lewis, 1979; Menks, 1986). Normal age-related changes will not produce significant limitations in endurance needed to carry out various daily activities. However, the combination of normal changes, cardiac or pulmonary disease, and immobility due to bed rest does produce a significant reduction in the older person's endurance (Blessey, 1986; Irwin, 1986; Patrick, 1986). An occupational therapy cardiopulmonary program designed for the older adult requires special attention to patient education, monitoring vital signs, and activity intensity.

One of the most effective components of cardiopulmonary programs is education. An endurance program to improve the pulmonary system may vary somewhat in content information from a cardiac program, but the overall focus is the same—to make the patient aware of how to improve functional abilities given the problems associated with the disease (Green, 1984). Patient education expectations are identified in Exhibit 7-4.

The ultimate goal of patient education is improving patient self-management. Education assists older adults to live their preferred life style as much as possible despite the limitations imposed by the cardiac or pulmonary disease. An abun-

---

Exhibit 7-4 The Goals of Cardiopulmonary Patient Education

The Patient Will:

- understand basic information about the cardiopulmonary system as it relates to the patient's diagnosis.
- understand how therapeutic activities improve the cardiopulmonary system.
- distinguish between normal and abnormal cardiopulmonary responses to activities.
- assess pulse rate, respiratory rate, and/or blood pressure as they relate to the patient's diagnosis.
- demonstrate ways of incorporating energy conservation and work simplification techniques into self-care and homemaking activities.
- demonstrate proper body mechanics and describe their effects on cardiopulmonary function.
- describe how to become aware of stress and ways to experience relaxation.
- discuss how cold and heat stress affect cardiopulmonary systems and methods for avoiding them.
- describe environmental irritants that have an adverse effect on the pulmonary system.
- understand how environmental adaptation will improve space efficiency and reduce the energy required to complete a task.

Source: Courtesy of the Occupational Therapy Department, Johnston R. Bowman Health Center for the Elderly, Chicago, Illinois.

dance of information may be acquired from the American Heart and Lung Association.

A cardiopulmonary program that upgrades activity tolerance must be individualized to take account of the severity of the disease as well as other complications. General guidelines can be used based on an understanding of cardiac and pulmonary rehabilitation and age-related changes in the elderly. Exhibit 7-5 identifies guidelines for the therapist to follow when working with an elderly person.

These guidelines are based on research and literature addressing cardiopulmonary rehabilitation with the elderly (Frontera & Evans, 1986; Irwin, 1986; Patrick,

---

Exhibit 7-5 Therapist Guidelines for Building Endurance

Assess pre-hospital activity level, including types of activities performed in a normal, routine day.

Discuss medication effects upon blood pressure, heart rate, and respiration with the nurse.

Discuss patient's baseline blood pressure and heart rate with the nurse.

Ensure that the patient wears comfortable clothing during physical activity.

Monitor and record blood pressure, heart rate, respiratory rate before (at rest), during, and after activities.

Discontinue activity if the heart rate decreases and contact the nurse for supportive medical intervention.

Discontinue activity if severe elevation or decrease in blood pressure occurs.

Discontinue activity if breathlessness occurs. Respiratory rate normally increases with physical activities but shortness of breath is a sign of cardiac stress.

Start activity slowly and include a warm-up and cool down phase.

Measure endurance through an increase of repetitions, duration, and intensity of activity. Since less activity is required to produce maximal cardiac output, consider the need for few repetitions, shorter duration, and less intensity.

Plan longer rest periods to allow the heart to return to the baseline status.

Instruct the patient to report any discomfort during the treatment session, such as pain, palpitations, cramping, or dizziness. Observe the patient's overall appearance and behavior for effort symptoms.

Instruct the patient to report fatigue, and utilize the activity for instructing the patient in pacing.

Recognize the importance of positioning for energy output and enhanced task accomplishment.

Source: Courtesy of the Occupational Therapy Department, Johnston R. Bowman Health Center for the Elderly, Chicago, Illinois.

Exhibit 7-6 Occupational Therapy Treatment Card

JRB O.T. TREATMENT PLAN CARD

Dx: _____   Diet: _____   Transfers: _____   Date: _____

Precautions: _____   Baseline B/P: _____   HR: _____

Behavioral Considerations: _____

Approach/Special Handling: _____

X = Goal of Treatment
Circle = ® = Right Side   Ⓛ = Left Side

Specific Activities
(Set-up/Equip./Techniq./Cues/Position)

1. Cognitive   Increase:
   Memory
   Orientation
   Problem Solving
   Following Directions
   Attention to/Initiation of Task
   Safety Awareness

2. Perceptual   Increase:
   Bilateral Integration
   Spatial Relations
   Motor Planning
   Awareness/Use   R L
   Sequencing

continues

Exhibit 7-6 continued

Patient Name: _____   Rm.: _____   Dr.: _____   OT/PT _____

3. Sensation   Increase:

    Tactile Desensitivity   [ ][ ]   R L

    Compensation   R L

Specific Activities
(Set-up/Equip./Techniq./Cues/Position)

X = Goal of Treatment

Circle = ℝ = Right Side   Ⓛ = Left Side

4. Motor Skills   Increase:

    Range of Motion   R L

    Strength   R L

    Isolated Movement   R L

    Arm Placement   R L

    Grasp/Release   R L

    Gross Coordination   R L

    Fine Coordination   R L

    Edema Control   R L

    Trunk Rotation   R L

Specific Activities
(Set-up/Equip./Techniq./Cues/Position)

5. Mobility   Upgrade:

   Bed Mobility

   Sitting Balance/Tolerance

   W/C Mobility

   Transfers

   Standing Balance/Tolerance

   Endurance

   Transitional Movements

6. Self-Care   Upgrade:

   Feeding/Oral Motor

   O/F Hygiene

   Bathing

   Toileting

   Dressing

   Homemaking

7. Equipment: (Splints, Slings, Lapboard, etc.)

*REMEMBER TO UPDATE WEEKLY

Source: Courtesy of the Occupational Therapy Department, Johnston R. Bowman Health Center for the Elderly, Chicago, Illinois.

1986; Wenger, 1984; Zadai, 1986). The effectiveness of a cardiopulmonary rehabilitation program is demonstrated through gradual increases in activity tolerance.

When formulating a treatment plan to improve endurance for older adults with pulmonary problems, additional communication is needed with the nurse regarding the use of oxygen therapy during physical activities. Exhibit 7-6 is an occupational therapy treatment card designed for the purpose of recording special needs of the older adult. The therapist may record blood pressure, heart rate, special handling, and other considerations. The older adult with chronic obstructive pulmonary disease will require instruction in diaphragmatic, pursed lip breathing during activities of daily living as well as endurance activities. An activity or exercise program for the home will include these recommendations.

CONCLUSION

This chapter covers a variety of rehabilitation programs and stresses the importance of creating an interdisciplinary team. The patient's orientation, as well as orientation of the family, provides the foundation for a successful program. Specific neurological, orthopedic, and cardiopulmonary programs for older adults are especially effective when age-related changes and other critical factors are taken into account.

REFERENCES

Averill, J. (1973). Personality control, aversive stimuli and its relationship to stress. *Psychological Bulletin, 80*, 286–303.

Barnes, B., & Dunovan, K. (1987). Functional outcome after hip fracture. *Physical Therapy, 67*, 1675–1679.

Beaver, M.L. (1979). The decision-making process and its relationship to relocation adjustment in older people. *The Gerontologist, 19*, 567–574.

Blessey, R.L. (1986). Energy cost in the physically impaired geriatric population. *Topics in Geriatric Rehabilitation, 2*(1), 33–43.

Chauncey, H.H., Feldman, R.S., & Wayler, A.H. (1983). Oral aspects of aging. *American Family Physician, 28*, 147–152.

Crabtree, J.L. (1988). Rehabilitation advocacy: A new role for therapists working with the elderly. *Physical & Occupational Therapy in Geriatrics, 6*(2), 3–11.

Davis, L. (1986). Physical pathology and aging. In L. Davis & M. Kirkland (Eds.), *Role of occupational therapy with the elderly* (pp. 93–102). Rockville, MD: American Occupational Therapy Association.

Duvoisin, R.C. (1984). *Parkinson's disease: A guide for patient and family* (2nd ed.). New York: Raven Press.

Elliot, J.L. (1988). Swallowing disorders in the elderly: A guide to diagnosis and treatment. *Geriatrics, 43*, 95–113.

Felsenthal, G., & Stein, B.D. (1988). Rehabilitation of dysmobility in the elderly: A case study of the patient with a hip fracture. In S.J. Brody & L.G. Pawlson (Eds.), *Aging and rehabilitation II: The state of the practice* (pp. 110–129). New York: Springer.

Foley, M.A., Shahrokhi K., & Robinson, K.M. (1990). A behavioral neuropsychologic approach: Strategies for the difficult geriatric patient. *Topics in Geriatric Rehabilitation, 5*, 32–42.

Fried, M. (1966). Grieving for a lost home: Psychological cases of relocation. In J.Q. Wilson (Ed.), *Urban renewal: The record and the controversy* (pp. 359–379). Cambridge, MA: MIT Press.

Frontera, W.R., & Evans, W.J. (1986). Exercise performance and endurance training in the elderly. *Topics in Geriatric Rehabilitation, 2*(1), 17–31.

Gauthier, L., Dalziel, S., & Gauthier, S. (1987). The benefits of group occupational therapy for patients with Parkinson's disease. *American Journal of Occupational Therapy, 41*, 360–365.

Gibson, C.J., & Caplan, B.M. (1984). Rehabilitation of the patient with a stroke. In T.F. Williams (Ed.), *Rehabilitation in the aging* (pp. 145–160). New York: Raven Press.

Green, M. (1984). Patient education. In C.W. Bell (Ed.), *Home care and rehabilitation in respiratory medicine* (pp. 51–68). Philadelphia: Lippincott.

Harris, C.M. (1984) Joint replacement in the elderly. In T.F. Williams (Ed.), *Rehabilitation in the aging* (pp. 199–228). New York: Raven Press.

Hasselkus, B.R. (1974). Aging and the human nervous system. *American Journal of Occupational Therapy, 28*, 16–21.

Hasselkus, B.R. (1978). Relocation stress and the elderly. *American Journal of Occupational Therapy, 32*, 631–636.

Hibbard, M.R., Grober, S.E., Gordon, W.A., Aletta, E.G., & Freeman, A. (1990). Cognitive therapy and the treatment of post stroke depression. *Topics in Geriatric Rehabilitation, 5*(3), 43–55.

Irwin, S.C. (1986). Cardiac rehabilitation for the geriatric patient. *Topics in Geriatric Rehabilitation, 2*(1), 44–54.

Kauffman, T. (1990). Impact of aging: Related musculoskeletal and postural changes on falls. *Topics in Geriatric Rehabilitation, 5*(2), 34–43.

Killian, E. (1970). Effects of geriatric transfers on mortality rates. *Social Work, 15*, 19–26.

Knott, M., & Voss, D. (1968). *Proprioceptive neuromuscular facilitation: Patterns and techniques* (2nd ed.). New York: Harper & Row.

Kulp, C.S., O'Leary, A.A., Wegener, R.T., Fang, W.L., & Brunner, C.M. (1988). Inpatient arthritis rehabilitation programs in the U.S.: Results from a national survey. *Archives of Physical Medicine & Rehabilitation, 69*(10), 873.

Lakke, J.P., De Jong, P.J., Kappyan, E.H., & Van Weerden, T.W. (1980). Observations and postural behavior: Axial rotation in Parkinson's patients after L-dopa treatment. In U.K. Rinne, M. Klinger, & G. Stomm (Eds.), *Parkinson's disease: Current progress, problems, and management* (pp. 187–196). New York: Elsevier North-Holland Biomedical Press.

Lewis, B.C. (1985). Clinical implications of musculoskeletal changes with age. In B.C. Lewis (Ed.), *Aging: The health care challenge* (pp. 17–140). Philadelphia: F.A. Davis.

Lewis, C.N. (1979). Reminiscing serves a vital purpose. *Geriatric Care, 11*(2), 1.

Lewis, S. (1979). *The mature years: A geriatric occupational therapy text.* Thorofare, NJ: Slack.

Mankin, H.J. (1986). Normal and pathological aging of the joint structures. In R.W. Moskowitz & M.R. Haug (Eds.), *Arthritis and the elderly* (pp. 18–33). New York: Springer.

Melnick, M.E. (1985). Basal ganglia disorders: Metabolic, hereditary, and genetic disorders in adults. In D.A. Umphery (Ed.), *Neurological rehabilitation* (Vol. 3) (pp. 416–441). St. Louis: C.V. Mosby.

Melvin, J.L. (1977). *Rheumatic disease: Occupational therapy and rehabilitation.* Philadelphia: F.A. Davis.

Menks, F. (1986). Anatomical and physiological changes in later adulthood. In L. Davis & M. Kirkland (Eds.), *Role of occupational therapy with the elderly* (pp. 41–48). Rockville, MD: American Occupational Therapy Association.

Nelson, S.L., & Peterson, C.Q. (1989). Enhancing therapeutic exercise through purposeful activity: A theoretic analysis. *Topics in Geriatric Rehabilitation, 4*(4), 12–22.

Patrick, D.F. (1986). Pulmonary rehabilitation of the geriatric patient. *Topics in Geriatric Rehabilitation, 2*(1), 55–69.

Ross, M.D. (1977). Effects of aging on the otoconia. In S.S. Han & D.H. Coons (Eds.), *Special senses in aging: A current biological assessment* (pp. 163–177). Ann Arbor, MI: Institute of Gerontology at the University of Michigan.

Roth, E.J. (1988). The elderly stroke patient: Principles and practice of rehabilitation management. *Topics in Geriatric Rehabilitation, 3*(4), 26–61.

Saudek, C.E. (1985). The hip. In J.A. Gould III & G.J. Davies (Eds.), *Orthopaedic and sports physical therapy* (Vol. 2) (pp. 365–407). St. Louis: C.V. Mosby.

Scott, A.D. (1983). Degenerative disease. In C.A. Trombly (Ed.), *Occupational therapy for physical dysfunction* (2nd ed.) (pp. 326–335). Baltimore: Williams & Wilkins.

Scott, S., Caird, F.I., & William, B.O. (1985). *Communication in Parkinson's disease.* Gaithersburg, MD: Aspen Publishers.

Someya, F., Miaki, H., Assai, H., Tachino, K., & Nara, I. (1988). Hand splint for rheumatoid arthritis patients during gait training after joint replacement in lower extremity. *Archives of Physical Medicine & Rehabilitation, 69*, 644.

Tobin, S., & Lieberman, M.A. (1976). *Last home for the aged.* San Francisco: Jossey-Bass.

Wenger, N.K. (1984). Cardiovascular status: Changes with aging. In T.F. Williams (Ed.), *Rehabilitation in the aging* (pp. 1–12). New York: Raven Press.

Williams, T.F. (1988). Introduction to rehabilitation and aging. In S.J. Brody & L.G. Pawlson (Eds.), *Aging and rehabilitation II: The state of the practice* (pp. 3–8). New York: Springer.

Zadai, C.C. (1986). Cardiopulmonary issues in the geriatric population: Implications for rehabilitation. *Topics in Geriatric Rehabilitation, 2*(1), 1–9.

Zankel, H.T. (1971). *Stroke rehabilitation: A guide to the rehabilitation of an adult patient following a stroke.* Springfield, IL: Thomas Publications.

Chapter 8

Preventing Falls in the Hospital and the Home

Jean M. Kiernat

THE INCIDENCE AND SEVERITY OF FALLS

Falls are one of the leading problems in geriatric medicine today. They are one of the five issues commonly referred to as the geriatric quintet (Cape, 1978). Falls and the other four problems—confusion, incontinence, impaired homeostasis, and iatrogenic disorders—are interrelated, and together they form a major complex of geriatric medicine.

The incidence of falls and the seriousness of their consequences are well documented. Up to 40% of the elderly living in the community are reported to fall each year, and half of these elderly persons fall repeatedly (Tinnetti, 1987). Seventy-five percent of the falls occur in the home, providing a strong mandate for occupational therapists to perform home assessments to identify the risks for falls and provide education and environmental changes to reduce these risks.

Although only 5% of falls result in a fracture, 1% of these falls result in hip fractures (Tinnetti, 1987). Over 200,000 hip fractures occur each year, and their seriousness cannot be overstated. Fifteen thousand patients with hip fractures will die while in the hospital. An equal number will expire within 6 months after hospitalization. Many will spend more than a year in a long-term care facility, and some will remain in that setting permanently. The 5-year mortality rate for hip fractures is 50%, and for persons who lie unaided more than 1 hour after the incident, the morbidity and mortality figures are even higher (Barclay, 1988).

Therapists in acute care settings must be equally concerned about falls. Being in the protective environment of a health care setting does not reduce the need for vigilance. Falls are consistently the largest category of hospital inpatient incidents (Morgan, Mathison, Rice, & Clemmer, 1985).

Hospital reports indicate that anywhere from 45% to 84% of all incidents are patient falls (American Health Care Consultants, 1985; Swartzbeck, 1983). Patient falls, therefore, are of major concern to hospitals. They are the most frequent cause of lawsuits against hospitals, although it is more usual to hear about malpractice suits, which result in much higher awards ("Patient Falls Update," 1985).

Falls may result in personal injury and increased length of stay, but even when injury does not occur, demoralization can be caused. Forty percent of the elderly report a fear of falling, and 20% of these individuals limit their activities because of this fear (Tinnetti, 1987).

Residents of long-term care facilities are even more at risk for falls, and the incidence of falls in these facilities far surpasses the incidence among the elderly living in the community. At least half of all nursing home residents will fall each year, and many will die from their falls (Nickens, 1985). The response to falls in the nursing home, and even in the acute care hospital, has frequently been to use restraints. In spite of this common response, there is evidence that restraints do not prevent falls and that their use increases agitation, incontinence, and the risk of decubitus. A decrease in strength and mobility is also experienced when movement is restricted (Catchen, 1983; Hernandez & Miller, 1986; Lamb, Miller, & Hernandez, 1987). Occupational therapists can offer a very valuable service by using their creative problem-solving skills to develop alternatives to the use of restraints.

In all settings, the incidence of falls is felt to be underreported. Unless a fall is observed or an injury occurs, chances are the fall will not be mentioned. Older persons in their own homes fear the loss of independence if they report falls to their families or physicians. The fear of institutional placement far outweighs the fear of physical injury. Those already in a health care facility fear the use of restraints, which are intended to protect them from injury but which damage their personal dignity.

Occasionally falls will happen. It is not possible to prevent all falls. Complete bedrest would stop falls, but the individual would lose 3% of his or her strength per day (Payton & Poland, 1983). The chief goal is not to limit movement but to make activity as safe as possible.

Occupational therapists employed by hospitals and long-term care settings should work with other staff to develop a strong multidisciplinary fall prevention program.

CAUSES OF FALLS

The increase in falls as people get older is related to three factors: (1) the normal changes that occur with age, (2) pathological conditions that increase in frequency with advanced age, and (3) the environment. Figure 8-1 illustrates the interrelatedness of these three factors.

Age changes and pathological conditions are the intrinsic or host factors; they constitute what has been called the liability to fall. Fifty to sixty-five percent of all

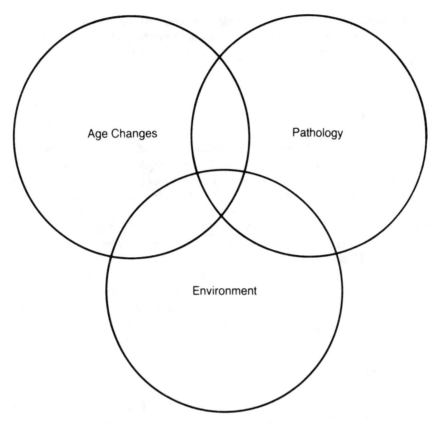

Figure 8-1 Causes of Falls

falls are attributable to these intrinsic factors, which become increasingly important in the old-old population (Rubenstein & Robbins, 1984).

Extrinsic factors (the environment) provide the opportunity to fall and are
responsible for approximately 35% to 50% of all incidents. Even when the cause
of a fall is traced to an intrinsic factor, the environment may still be implicated.
Tinnetti, Williams, and Mayewski (1986) found that 23 of 25 multiple fallers in a
long-term care setting were engaged in an activity or confronted by an obstacle that
was a potential contributor to falling.

Age Changes

Many of the changes experienced by elderly persons as they age increase the
risk of accidents. The research investigating which changes are normal and which

are due to pathology continually provides new knowledge and refutes many long held beliefs about the inevitability of decline in all functions. Some of the changes that are noted in many older people and that increase vulnerability to falls are listed in Exhibit 8-1.

Pathological Conditions

By the age of 75, most older persons have accumulated some chronic conditions that may or may not limit them functionally. However, the risk of falls increases as the number of chronic illnesses and disabilities increases. In a prospective study of patients admitted to intermediate care facilities, Tinnetti, Williams, and Mayewski (1986) found that 100% of those with seven or more chronic factors became recurrent fallers, whereas none of those with zero to three factors became fallers. Some of the disease-related factors that increase the risk of falling in older persons are noted in Exhibit 8-2.

Of course, the therapist must always keep in mind the multiplicity of factors occurring in one of these conditions. Diabetes, for example, is not only a metabolic disease but a disease in which neurological and cardiovascular complications are often evident. Diminished vision and impaired sensation are likely.

Environmental Factors

Drugs, which are among the major contributors to falls, can be considered in this category, since they are an extrinsic factor causing major intrinsic changes. Because many elderly people are treated for several chronic conditions, the likelihood of being on multiple drugs is very strong. Listed in Table 8-1 are some of the medications whose primary or secondary effects may increase the risk of falls (Lamb, Miller, & Hernandez, 1987).

Granek et al. (1987) have calculated the odds of falling for persons taking specific drugs relative to those not taking the drugs. Those on antidepressants were found to be 2.6 times more likely to fall than those not taking antidepressants. The same odds occurred in the case of sedatives and hypnotics.

The odds of falling were also calculated for persons taking two or three drugs. Very high risks were found for specific combinations. For example, persons taking a nonsteroidal anti-inflammatory drug (NSAID) plus a sedative/hypnotic were 8.3 times more likely to fall than persons not taking the combination. The odds went as high as 17.8 for a three-drug combination of diuretic, NSAID, and sedative/hypnotic or 10.5 for a combination of antidepressant, cardiac drug, and diuretic. Medications must always be a strong consideration when assessing the risk of falls.

Exhibit 8-1 Age-related Changes That Increase the Risk of Falls

Gait Changes

Decreased step height
Narrow-based waddling gait (for women)
Shorter step, wider base (for men)
Slower movement
Shuffling
Decreased ankle dorsiflexion

Postural Instability

Increase in body sway, both lateral and anterior-posterior
Decreased responsiveness of sensory receptors that alert muscles to contract when movement is
  away from center of gravity
Weakening of muscles which allows point of no return to be reached sooner

Vision Diminished

Decreased light entering the eye
Increased glare
Diminished color perception, especially blue-green perception
Increase in time required for light/dark adaptation
Increase in time required for near/far adaptation

Hearing Reduced

Reduced ability to hear high frequency sounds
Reduced tendency to notice approaching car, bicycle on sidewalk, siren, etc.

Sense of Touch Diminished

Least changeable of all the senses
Greatest change on soles of feet and palms

Increased Benign Forgetfulness

Nuisance type of short-term forgetfulness
Increased likelihood of tripping over forgotten objects

Orthostatic Hypotension

Drop of 20 mm Hg in systolic blood pressure when assuming upright position
Decrease in blood supply to brain
Lightheadedness upon standing
Decreased efficiency of baroreceptors

Degenerative Arthritis

Stiffness
Possibility of impingement of bone spurs on blood vessel and reduction of flow, especially in
  the case of cervical spondylitis

Nocturia

Decreased bladder capacity
Delay in signal to void
Increased need to void at night
Urgency to reach bathroom

Exhibit 8-2 Disease-related Factors That Increase the Risk of Falls

---

Cardiovascular Impairments

Conditions affecting cerebral oxygenation
Arrhythmias, heart blocks, congestive heart failure, and syncope
Orthostasis

Neurological Conditions

Disorders affecting movement, such as Parkinson's disease or CVA
Disorders affecting judgment, such as Alzheimer's disease or normal pressure hydrocephalus
Transient ischemic attacks

Endocrine or Metabolic Disorders

Disorders that set the stage for syncope or lightheadedness
Hypo- or hyperglycemia, anemia, dehydration, hypoxia
Hyperventilation

Psychological Disorders

Depression and anxiety
Decreased awareness of environment
Lack of mobility which leads to weakness

The Environmental Setting

In the institutional setting, the patient's room and the adjacent bathroom are where 80% to 90% of all falls occur (Iowa Hospital Association, 1982; North Star Casualty Services, 1981). Activities that patients are frequently engaged in when they fall are listed below:

- getting in or out of bed
- walking across the room with nothing to hold on to
- transferring into a wheelchair without locking the wheel locks
- reaching for an object out of reach, such as a call button, a telephone, a light switch, a urinal, or toilet paper
- leaning on an object that moves, such as a bed table
- testing skills just prior to discharge
- walking with improper footwear

At-home falls occur in a wider range of settings and activities, but the bathroom remains a high-risk location. Falls frequently occur while getting into or out of the

Table 8-1 Effects of Drugs

Drug	Action/Side Effect	Result
Sedative/hypnotics, including alcohol	Depression of the central nervous system	Decreased awareness of environment; judgment poor
Antihypertensives	Lowers blood pressure	Hypotension, including orthostatic hypotension
Diuretics Ethacrynic acid Furosemide	Decreased fluid volume Vestibulotoxicity	Hypotension Dizziness, irritability
Hypoglycemics	Lowers blood sugar	Dizziness, vertigo
Psychotropics	Orthostatic hypotension Parkinsonian-like effects	Dizziness Drop attack Gait changes Judgment changes Altered mental status

Source: From "Falls in the Elderly: Causes and Prevention" by K. Lamb, J. Miller, and M. Hernandez, 1987, *Orthopaedic Nursing, 6,* p. 46. Copyright 1987 by Orthopaedic Nursing. Reprinted by permission.

bath or shower. Slippery surfaces, loose carpet threads that can catch toes, scatter rugs that move, out-of-reach objects that invite climbing, and poorly lighted steps often account for falls and require special consideration.

Assessment of all relevant environmental settings, development of mechanisms to compensate for normal age changes, and consideration of any pathological conditions must be included in any fall prevention program.

HOSPITAL PROGRAMS TO PREVENT FALLS

Occupational therapists should work with the nursing staff to develop a comprehensive fall prevention program. A good program should include

- staff education and a system to alert staff to high-risk patients
- assessment upon admission to determine a fall risk classification for each patient
- frequent reassessment, since risk status may change
- fall prevention education for all patients
- environmental assessments
- specific interventions for high-risk patients

Staff Education

Inservice education should be developed to make staff aware of the normal age changes and the special conditions that increase the risk of falls for older persons. A system must be agreed upon to assess patients and identify those with highest risk. As an example, one hospital used the color orange to designate high-risk patients. This color was used for the identification armband, and an orange colored circle was placed on the patient's chart and callbox and on the wall above his or her bed. In addition, the nursing care plan was printed on an orange card (Fife, Solomon, & Stanton, 1984).

Assessment of Patients

A fall risk assessment, focusing on fall prevention, needs to be developed by the staff of the specific unit or by a facilitywide team. Incident reports from the previous 6–12 months can be reviewed to determine risks specific to the facility's population. An audit can be conducted for a 1- to 2-month period to collect data specific to the current period and to ask more questions than the standard incident report may generate. High-risk factors have been identified in numerous articles, and these will be helpful to consider. Spellbring, Gannon, Kleckner, and Conway (1988) identified high-risk factors and placed any patient with three or more risks in a fall precaution program. Their list of high-risk factors includes

- history of previous falls
- mental status change
- agitation or anxiety
- sensory deficits
- communication deficits
- advanced age
- mobility deficits
- weakness or debilitation
- orthostatic hypotension
- urinary alterations
- medications (diuretics, laxatives, barbiturates, tranquilizers, hypnotics, narcotics, anesthetics)

Patients should be reviewed on all shifts, since some risk factors may be present only at night or early evening or may be related only to early morning stiffness. Reassessment must be done routinely, because a patient's status may change dramatically as a result of medication changes, medical or surgical conditions, or even food and fluid restrictions prior to specific tests.

Patient Education

All patients should receive a thorough orientation to the setting and the procedures to be followed for such activities as getting out of bed and toileting. Proper transfer techniques need to be covered if a wheelchair is used, and proper use of any mobility device must be addressed. All patients can profit from instruction on rising more slowly to prevent or compensate for postural hypotension. Sitting before standing and standing before immediately walking can be modeled for the patient. The hospitalization period is an opportunity to present information that the older patient can utilize later at home.

Older people should understand that normal sleep patterns are altered with age and should learn to deal with changes without resorting to sleeping pills. Remember, sedatives and hypnotics cause orthostasis and confusion, which may result in falls. Practical approaches to enhancing sleep need to be suggested.

Relaxation programs can be offered prior to bedtime, including the use of audiotapes, videotapes, or group relaxation sessions. Van Deusen and Kiernat (1985-1986) found that well elderly persons often use their rocking chairs at home to induce sleepiness. Rocking chairs should be available in the institutional setting. Wheelchair users need not be left out, since recently the Carolina Rocker® was developed for use with a wheelchair.

Older persons should determine whether motions such as neck extension or turning the head to either side cause dizziness. Kinking of the vertebral arteries or impingement of the carotid arteries will result in insufficient blood supply to the brain. Therapists should caution patients to avoid these movements.

A safety booklet could be developed for patients and family members to read during the hospitalization. The risks already described and the reasons for specific hospital procedures and policies can be covered. Facilities with an in-house television channel might develop a fall prevention video for the patient education channel.

Environmental Considerations

The patient's room should be checked to ensure maximum safety. The bed should be in a low position to provide ease in getting in and out of bed. The call light, telephone, and TV remote control should all be within easy reach. Mobility devices used by the patient, such as a cane, walker, or wheelchair, should be easily accessible. Any furniture that the patient might lean on should be locked or nonmovable.

It is helpful if there are rails or objects to hold onto between the bed and the bathroom. Older persons use touch to get a "position fix" as they move about. Wide open spaces—spaces that provide no opportunity for holding onto or touching something along the way—are not seen as user friendly. For some patients, the walk to the bathroom should be avoided at night, in which case a commode should be placed adjacent to the bed.

High-Risk Patients

Those patients demonstrated to be high risk by the assessment will need frequent supervision. Ideally, they should be placed close to the nursing station. High-risk patients should be assisted out of bed and accompanied to the bathroom. Use of an Ambularm® or other device can signal the staff that the patient is beginning to get up and that assistance might be needed. Ambularms have been found to reduce falls by 20% to 30% and are far preferable to the use of restraints (Widder, 1985).

Specific Interventions

Exercise programs are needed to build strength and endurance. Special attention should be paid to strengthening ankle dorsiflexion, since it has been shown to be the most compromised of all lower extremity motions (Whipple, Wolfson, & Amerman, 1987). Walking groups can be used to improve balance and reduce falls. Walking one-half hour three times weekly has been shown to reduce falls for some older persons (Roberts, 1985).

Occupational therapists should provide opportunities for the discharge ready to test their performance under supervision before going home. Any risks or difficulties can be dealt with while the patients are still in the hospital environment.

PREVENTION PROGRAMS FOR THE ELDERLY AT HOME

The occupational therapist can assist the physician by doing a home assessment for the client at risk for falls. Since this will be done in the client's home, the therapist must explain carefully the reason for the visit and the physician's concerns. Permission to look through various areas of the house must be obtained from the client. During the interview, it is very important to ask the client about any history of falls. Include the following questions to elicit information that may help determine the cause of any previous falls:

- Where did you fall?
- What were you doing when you fell (getting out of bed, getting out of the bathtub, rising from a chair, standing at the sink, coming down the stairs, looking up to get something off a shelf, climbing on a chair)?
- Did you have any warning before you fell (dizziness, lightheadedness)?
- Were you taking any drugs or medications then? What are you taking now?

Balance and gait are often the most useful predictors of the risk of falls (Tinnetti, Williams, & Mayewski, 1986). The "Get Up and Go Test" (Mathias, Nayak, & Isaacs, 1986) is a very simple test that can be used in the home. It has been found to correlate well with much more involved laboratory tests for gait and balance, such as tests using the ataxiameter or the force platform. Five functions are observed and rated:

1. standing up from a chair
2. walking a short distance
3. turning around
4. returning
5. sitting down again

Clients are rated on a scale of 1 to 5, with 1 considered normal (i.e., no evidence of the person's being at risk for falling) and 5 considered severely abnormal (i.e., the person appears at risk of falling during the test). Intermediate scores of two (very slightly abnormal), three (mildly abnormal), and four (moderately abnormal) are used to document undue slowness, hesitancy, abnormal movements of the trunk or upper limbs, and staggering or stumbling. A score of three or more places the client in an at-risk category.

Women who have worn high heels for many years may have shortened Achilles tendons and may walk better with a little heel. Ideally, their gait should be tested with shoes on and off.

Imagine that the interview with the client began in the living room, as it usually does. The reason for the visit was explained and a history of falls was explored. Now the chair in which the client is seated should be evaluated for proper seat height and depth. The chair back should allow the client to sit upright without leaning back. Does the chair have arms that aid the client in rising?

A visual survey of the room should include noting the light level and other hazards to mobility. Is the lighting adequate? Is there a clear pathway for moving about? Are there any loose threads in the carpet that might present a hazard? Is the telephone near the chair the client usually uses?

When finished in the living room, the client can lead the way to the bedroom. Watch as the client rises from the chair. Are the arms used? If a walker or other equipment is used, was it positioned properly to allow easy use? Does the client forget to utilize the device?

In the bedroom, check that bed height is appropriate and that there is a light near the bed, a telephone reachable from the bed, a night light, no scatter rugs, and an uncluttered pathway. Is bedding out of the way when the bed is turned down so that the client will not trip on bed clothes during a trip to the bathroom?

The next stop is the bathroom. Items to be checked include the toilet seat height, nonslip treads in the tub or shower, a bathtub seat, a detachable shower head, and grab bars correctly placed for appropriate use. Grab bars that fit over the tub side are almost always acceptable, whereas some elderly persons will not want to damage the walls by installing wall-mounted models.

Bathroom cleanliness often indicates good vision and sufficient strength to clean as well as good cognition. Some medications may be kept in the bathroom. Names and dates of all medications, including over-the-counter medications, should be copied, and the client should be asked about any other places where medications are stored. Duplicate medications may be uncovered in the process, since some persons have been known to get a refill and continue both the old and the new prescriptions.

The client's visual ability to read the labels and manual dexterity in opening the containers needs to be checked. If the client is taking a variety of medications, which is the case with a majority of older persons, check to determine whether there are difficulties in organizing and maintaining an accurate schedule. There are a variety of medication organizers, or medisets, available commercially. These are essentially large pill boxes with many compartments in which a week's supply of medications can be organized. Arrangements may need to be made for a family member or neighbor to organize the medications if the client is forgetful.

The last stop on the home itinerary is the kitchen. The refrigerator should be checked for any additional medications and to see how much and what kind of food is stored there. This will often provide a key to the status of the client's nutrition. Poor nutrition leads to many problems, including confusion, which can contribute to falls.

If the client prepares meals, the therapist should note where items are stored. Does the client have to climb to reach any objects? Is dizziness or balance a problem in bending to reach low items? Mobile meals or attendance at a senior center where meals are served might be recommended to a client whose physical or cognitive impairments jeopardize nutrition.

Additional considerations in the home assessment are clothing and footwear. Ill-fitting clothes, such as trousers that are too large, have been implicated in some falls. Slippers, often worn at home instead of shoes, do not provide adequate stability for the foot or adequate traction on carpets.

If there are steps or stairs in the home, a handrail should be available on one side, preferably on both sides. The rail should extend beyond the last step, since this is the one most often missed in falls on stairs. A handrail can be textured at the end to provide a tactile warning that the last step has been reached. A white strip across the edge of the step will increase depth perception and allow the user to distinguish one step from the next when looking down the stairwell. Very weak individuals might be encouraged to sidestep up or down the stairs, keeping both hands on the rail, to increase safety.

For the older adult who is at risk for falls or who fears falling, a telephone emergency alert system provides a real sense of security. Children who worry about a parent who might fall and not be found are also relieved. A signaling device is worn around the neck as a pendant or on a belt clip. When the recessed button is pushed, the telephone automatically dials a predetermined number and help is summoned.

CONCLUSION

Occupational therapists can enhance the quality of life of older persons at home or in an institutional setting by developing or contributing to the development of an ongoing fall prevention program. Through environmental assessments, occupational therapists can provide recommendations to older clients and input to family physicians. Exercise programs to build strength and endurance need to be offered, and wheelchairs and other appliances need to be appropriately prescribed and utilized.

Therapists can provide creative ways to compensate for the normal changes that occur with age and that lead to the increased incidence of falls. The environment can be made safer through the use of special equipment, and research must be conducted to determine how to redesign the home to make it safer and more forgiving.

REFERENCES

American Health Care Consultants. (1985). Aggressive programs lessen frequency, severity of falls. *Hospital Risk Management, 7,* 85–96.

Barclay, A. (1988). Falls in the elderly: Is prevention possible? *Postgraduate Medicine, 83,* 241–248.

Cape, R.D.T. (1978). *Aging: Its complex management.* Hagerstown, MD: Harper & Row.

Catchen, H. (1983). Repeaters: Inpatient accidents among the hospitalized elderly. *The Gerontologist, 23,* 273–276.

Fife, D., Solomon, P., & Stanton, M. (1984). A risk/falls program: Code orange for success. *Nursing Management, 15*, 50–53.

Granek, E., Baker, S., Abbey, H., Robinson, E., Myers, A., Samkoff, J., & Klein, L. (1987). Medications and diagnoses in relation to falls in a long term care facility. *Journal of the American Geriatrics Society, 35*, 503–511.

Hernandez, M., & Miller, J. (1986, March-April). How to reduce falls. *Geriatric Nursing*, pp. 97–102.

Iowa Hospital Association. (1982). The variance reporting system looks at patient falls. *Quali-Facts, 9*, 1–5.

Lamb, K., Miller, J., & Hernandez, M. (1987). Falls in the elderly: Causes and prevention. *Orthopaedic Nursing, 6*, 45–49.

Mathias, S., Nayak, U.S.L., & Isaacs, B. (1986). Balance in elderly patients: The "Get-up and Go" Test. *Archives of Physical Medicine & Rehabilitation, 67*, 387–389.

Morgan, V., Mathison, J., Rice, J., & Clemmer, D. (1985). Hospital falls: A persistent problem. *American Journal of Public Health, 75*, 775–777.

Nickens, H. (1985). Intrinsic factors in falling among the elderly. *Archives of Internal Medicine, 145*, 1089–1093.

North Star Casualty Services. (1981). *Patient falls: North Star members* (Hospital Study). Minneapolis: Author.

Patient falls update: New approaches for reducing a perennial problem. (1985, November). *Hospital Security and Safety Management*, pp. 5–8.

Payton, O.D., & Poland, J.L. (1983). Aging process. *Physical Therapy, 63*, 41–48.

Roberts, B. (1985, December). Walking improves balance, reduces falls. *American Journal of Nursing*, p. 1397.

Rubenstein, L., & Robbins, A. (1984). Falls in the elderly: A clinical perspective. *Geriatrics, 39*, 67–78.

Spellbring, A.M., Gannon, M.E., Kleckner, T., & Conway, K. (1988). Improving safety for hospitalized elderly. *Journal of Gerontological Nursing, 14*, 31–37.

Swartzbeck, E. (1983). The problem of falls in the elderly. *Nursing Management, 14*, 34–38.

Tinnetti, M. (1987). Decreasing the risk of falling. *Clinical Report on Aging* (American Geriatrics Society), *1*, 1, 15–16.

Tinnetti, M., Williams, F., & Mayewski, R. (1986). Fall risk index for elderly patients based on number of chronic disabilities. *American Journal of Medicine, 80*, 429–434.

Van Deusen, J., & Kiernat, J. (1985-1986). An exploration of the use of the rocking chair as a means of relaxation. *Physical & Occupational Therapy in Geriatrics, 4*, 31–38.

Whipple, R., Wolfson, L., & Amerman, P. (1987). The relationship of knee and ankle weakness to falls in nursing home residents: An isokinetic study. *Journal of the American Geriatrics Society, 35*, 13–20.

Widder, B. (1985, September-October). A new device to decrease falls. *Geriatric Nursing*, pp. 287–288.

Chapter 9

Discharge Planning for the Geriatric Patient

Charlotte Campbell Maloney and Patricia K. Kasper

INTRODUCTION

"The most important and distinguishing aspect of good health care for the elderly is the switch in emphasis away from dealing with pathology and organ specific disease toward restoring the patient's resultant loss of function" (Kennie, 1983, p. 770). In teaching skills to compensate for long-term functional losses created by a disability, the occupational therapist plays a key role in assisting the elderly patient to regain lost function. Participating in discharge planning is essential to filling this role in the acute care setting.

During the discharge-planning process, the occupational therapist bridges the gap between the hospital and the community. Analyzing the activities and life style of the patient before admission, the occupational therapist breaks down the activities the patient must perform independently and teaches compensatory skills. Sometimes the therapist can merely identify the activities in preparing for the discharge. In these instances, the therapist can suggest referral to another level of care where rehabilitation services are available for developing the required skills or provide training to caregivers who will assist the patient. In other instances, treatment is initiated to teach the compensatory skills.

As a participant in the discharge-planning process, it is helpful for the therapist to view the hospitalization from a broad perspective. For most of the elderly, a hospital admission is "a phase in a career of care" rather than a discrete episode (Kane, 1988, p. 2). Recognizing this will permit the acute care therapist to view the evaluation and treatment in the context of ongoing care rather than merely treating the diagnosis.

The authors thank their coworkers—Sharon Fahrion, OTR, Kathy Temes, OTR, and Lisa Adams, RN—for their comments after review of this manuscript.

Occupational therapists are trained to address the patient's need for satisfying work (Dunleavy Taira, 1985) and, when necessary, to teach the modified method for doing a task. Whether the patient returns home or to a skilled facility, the therapist needs to assess the patient's ability to resume meaningful activity and eventually return to the preadmission roles of retiree, part-time worker, spouse, hobbyist, and so on.

Several factors influence the manner in which occupational therapy services are delivered in acute care. First is the shortened length of stay. Due to the funding constraints in the last decade, the length of hospitalization of people over 65 years of age has decreased 5.6 days since 1968 and 2.1 days since 1980 (National Center for Health Statistics, 1988, p. 109). For most older patients, this means there are fewer days to provide treatment before discharge. Thus, the focus of acute care is on assessment, followed by family teaching and recommendations, since less time may exist for the development of skills that require days of practice. This chapter describes discharge planning for patients admitted to the general medical, neurological, or surgical unit of a general hospital. The main difference between general hospital acute care and rehabilitation inpatient acute care is twofold: For the rehabilitation admission there is (1) more time to evaluate and treat the patient and (2) a more formalized team structure.

The brief length of acute care treatment often forces team members to begin forming recommendations for discharge during the initial contact with the patient. In serving the acute care patient, the occupational therapist's data often become the basis for placement and referral decisions of the team. In some cases, the shortened hospitalization period has created situations in which the occupational therapist becomes such an active participant in discharge planning that case management is shared for selected patients (Dunleavy Taira, 1985).

Another factor influencing the occupational therapist's role in discharge planning is resource availability. Programs vary widely by community. It is the responsibility of each practitioner to know the continuum of resources in the community and to provide clear information about the resources to the patient. Providing accurate information will smooth the transition to the community for the patient and significant others. If all team members provide identical information about recommended services, the patient will more likely approach the agencies with less anxiety and more confidence.

Therapists are strongly encouraged to educate themselves thoroughly before discussing resources with patients. Social service team members are often the best source for purposes of self-education. A productive second step is to contact the appropriate individuals at community agencies to clarify how best to link to their services. Many of these agencies charge for services based upon the elder's ability to pay. See Exhibit 9-1 for a list of typical community resources.

The final factor influencing discharge planning is the patient's destination. The needs of the patient will largely dictate the living arrangement after discharge. A

Exhibit 9-1 List of Community Resources

Assistance with Personal Care, Homemaking, and Respite

City or county. Referral for personal care attendants.

Church groups. Occasionally provide referral to members who provide short- or long-term assistance.

Public assistance (welfare). Funds for attendant care.

Private in-home care agencies. Provide practical nursing and attendant care, as well as skilled nursing care, on fee-for-service basis.

Home health. Provides personal care only while individual receiving other home health services.

Homemaker's service. Provides nonskilled limited personal care and light homemaking services on sliding scale or fee-for-service basis.

Meals-on-Wheels. Provides hot midday meals to the residences of those unable to prepare meals independently.

Daycare center. Limited personal care (some provide supervision of bathing and grooming).

Postdischarge Therapy

Outpatient rehabilitation centers. Free-standing and hospital-based, including Easter Seal centers.

Home health services. Free-standing and hospital-based.

Day treatment. Offers activity groups and therapy services; free-standing and hospital-based.

Private practice therapists.

Community college physical education. Adaptive classes for seniors.

Swimming programs for the physically challenged. Easter Seal centers, YMCAs, public pool facilities.

Education and Support Groups

County and state public assistance agencies. Referral to community groups.

Senior centers. Meeting place and referral.

Support groups organized by problem. American Red Cross and hospital-based groups, such as Stroke Club, Spouses' Caregivers, Alzheimer's Support, Chronic Obstructive Pulmonary Disease, Arthritis, Parkinson's Disease.

Transportation

Driver training. 65 Alive courses, driver evaluation programs in O.T. departments.

Public assistance. Funds for bus or taxi transport.

Public buses equipped with lifts.

Private van services charging fee for service.

Taxi companies. Special rates for seniors.

Volunteer programs providing car transport to medical appointments.

Other

Assistance in ramp construction or light architectural modification. Retired Senior Volunteer Program and city or county housing authority.

Leisure and social groups. City parks and recreation departments.

Medical alert services. Two types each charge monthly fee: (1) line tied to local hospital emergency room and (2) line tied to national service, which contacts local medical, fire, or police services.

patient returning to independent living may require more training or a more detailed activities of daily living (ADL) evaluation so as to verify the safety of the placement. If a patient is returning home with a spouse who will supervise the patient's practice, the spouse may require more training. If a patient is returning to a skilled nursing facility, more written documentation of recommendations may be required in order to communicate with the large number of staff involved with the patient.

ROLES OF ACUTE CARE TEAM MEMBERS

In the course of an acute care stay, various team members participate in planning care and discharge. Most settings function according to the medical model, where the team is led by the physician. As team leader, the physician carries the ultimate responsibility for all treatment and decision making. The physician establishes the medical prognosis and follows the patient after discharge.

Because the nursing staff interacts round the clock with the patient and the caregivers, the primary care nurse usually coordinates the patient's schedule. The nurse makes certain that basic personal care and all ordered treatments are provided. Education of the patient and the caregivers about the medication management program is an essential contribution of the nurse.

The social worker coordinates the team planning, provides information about community resources, and assists the family with the discharge arrangement details. The social worker or psychologist provides short-term counseling in situations where family relationships are strained. Some teams include a discharge planner, who coordinates the discharge plan by facilitating the documentation and initiating services needed after discharge. Where there is no discharge planner, the social worker often initiates referrals to community programs and places equipment orders.

The physical therapist assesses mobility, strength, and endurance, and the occupational therapist assesses ADL, cognition, and adaptive skills. Assessment results are reported to the team for the purpose of determining placement. The actual tasks performed by any team member depend upon the roles assigned in that specific setting and upon the unique needs of the patient.

EVALUATION AS A COMPONENT OF DISCHARGE PLANNING

In the acute care setting, it is impossible to separate evaluation from discharge planning; each feeds the other.

The evaluation needs to be functionally based, accurate, quickly administered, and quickly interpreted. See Chapter 6 for specific assessment tools. The therapist's professional judgment is required to interpret observations and draw conclusions from the data.

When placement is known prior to the occupational therapy evaluation, the therapist may direct the assessment toward the specific functional skills the pa-- tient will need to perform in that setting. If the discharge is to a relative's home, the evaluation will focus on the assistance that will be needed. If the patient prefers to live alone, the physician may order an ADL and/or cognitive evaluation to determine whether independent living would be safe and whether any support services will be needed. For example, if the patient would need to prepare meals independently, the therapist may decide to complete a meal preparation assessment.

The interdependence between the occupational therapy evaluation and the discharge placement is seen in other areas. Equipment needs will be determined by the evaluation, yet anticipated placement will determine the specific recommendations. The prognosis will often determine whether purchase or rental will be recommended. Similarly, the prognosis will determine whether the patient needs a written home program or referral to another level of care, such as inpatient rehabilitation, outpatient services, or home health care.

DISCHARGE PLANNING PROCESS

Because of the shortened length of stay for most patients, communication between team members is frequent and succinct. Discharge planning proceeds more smoothly when observations and conclusions are communicated clearly and concisely.

After establishing the patient's self-care, cognitive, or adaptive skill level, the occupational therapist must decide the following: (1) What will the patient need after discharge? (2) How will the patient meet the need? (3) How can the therapist facilitate that process?

Nursing home placement will require answering this set of questions. Will the patient need rehabilitation services? If so, who will provide this: a staff or contract therapist, a restorative aide, or an activity program director? What is the best method of communicating any unusual recommendations: telephone contact, a discharge summary, or an additional written report? Who is the best person to receive the recommendations and oversee their implementation?

For a patient discharged home, the therapist needs to answer these questions: (1) Will the patient benefit from additional occupational therapy or will a written home program suffice? (2) Will the patient need and receive assistance with meals, household activities, and daily living tasks? Will the caregivers require training in assisting the patient (e.g., training in how to communicate more effectively with someone who is visually impaired or hard of hearing) or require help in understanding the patient's physical abilities and limitations? Will they need written recommendations or instructions? Will the patient require commercially available and/or specially constructed equipment? Will a home assessment be needed prior to making equipment recommendations?

Some therapists find it helpful to use a checklist of the tasks to remind themselves of how to proceed once the above questions have been answered. See the sample checklist in Exhibit 9-2.

Exhibit 9-2 Discharge Checklist

SACRED HEART GENERAL HOSPITAL
OREGON REHABILITATION CENTER
DISCHARGE CHECKLIST

DISCHARGE

_____ Home Health Form, Nursing Home Form, or Outpatient Order Complete
_____ O.T. Contacted
_____ D/C Summary
_____ Functional Assessment Form
_____ Equipment
_____ List of Vendors to Patient's Family

EQUIPMENT (Initial if charged for)

1. _____
2. _____
3. _____
4. _____
5. _____

FAMILY/PATIENT EDUCATION

_____ ROM (passive, self)
_____ Use of Adaptive Equipment
_____ ADL Training
_____ Positioning
_____ Splint Schedule
_____ Lapboard
_____ Driving
_____ Safety
_____ Neglect
_____ Environmental Changes
_____ Time Management

Source: Courtesy of Sacred Heart General Hospital, Eugene, Oregon.

HOME ASSESSMENT

With the growth of home health programs in the last decade, fewer hospital-based occupational therapists perform home assessments. When the team makes a home health referral for the patient, usually the home health therapists have the responsibility of evaluating the patient's needs and ordering the equipment. The exception to this is that the acute care team will order mobility aids and toilet equipment if these are needed between the patient's discharge and the home health team evaluation. This is to avoid the expense of having the acute care therapist perform the assessment and the expense of purchasing equipment not used once the patient returns home.

Without an accurate understanding of the home environment, the therapist cannot thoroughly prepare the patient. The therapist must take into account psychosocial concerns as well as the physical layout. Both aspects will directly influence the selection of ADL methods.

The acute care therapist can gather information about the home environment in several ways. Interviewing the patient and/or family members is usually productive, especially for understanding the social factors. When a home assessment is needed, the certified assistant or the registered occupational therapist can perform an onsite evaluation. Exhibit 9-3 is a sample home assessment form.

When a home assessment is not possible, the therapist can assess the physical components by evaluating a blueprint or diagram of the home made by a family member. The diagram needs to include tub height and width, floor space for turning in the bathroom, door widths, sink heights, and measurements of both the front and rear entrances to the house.

Chapter 13 provides a description of the architectural features that need to be assessed and of methods for modifying the environment to improve the patient's function. Cost is always a major concern in making these recommendations, since the majority of older people live on fixed income (Fowles, 1988). Many communities have programs that provide low-cost assistance or volunteer labor to senior citizens who need ramp construction for their homes. Less frequently, modifications may be funded by the patient's church or by service organizations or other community groups.

THE THERAPIST'S RESPONSIBILITY IN DISCHARGE FOLLOW-UP

Establishing a follow-up plan is the last step in the discharge program. Follow-up requires communicating with all individuals concerned prior to the patient's leaving the hospital. Communication may be in written or verbal form. The

Exhibit 9-3 Sample Home Assessment Form

Name:
Doctor:
Date:

Address: _____   Diagnosis: _____

_____   Equipment: _____

General Description:

Apartment _____   Private Home _____   Other _____

No. Persons Residing _____   Relationship to Patient _____

Household Help _____   No. of Hours _____   Duties _____

No. of Floors and Rooms on Each Floor _____

Neighborhood Description: CONSIDER TERRAIN — POTENTIAL FOR OUTDOOR MOBILITY, ACCESS TO NEIGHBORS, ACCESS TO NEIGHBORHOOD SHOPS, ETC.

Transportation: CAN ONE DRIVE INTO GARAGE? IS GARAGE ATTACHED TO HOUSE? IF MUST GET OUT OF CAR IN DRIVEWAY IS IT SLOPED? NEAREST PUBLIC TRANSPORTATION?

Access to Living Area (consider entryway, ramps, elevator, steps & railing, sidewalk):

_____
_____
_____

General Household Description (consider general appearance, floor surface, laundry, width of hallways & doorways, telephone, storage area, stairs):

_____
_____
_____
_____
_____

Bedroom:
  Accessibility to:
    Bed (height, firmness) _____
    Closets _____
    Light Switch _____
    General Accessibility (pertinent dimensions, stairs, etc.) _____
    _____

continues

Exhibit 9-3 continued

Functional Abilities:
    Bed Transfers _____
    Bed Mobility _____
    Other _____
  Comments: _____
_____

Bathroom:
  Accessibility to:
    Sink (faucets, spout) _____
    Toilet _____
    Shower or Bathtub _____
    General Accessibility _____
  Equipment (grab bars, rubber mat, etc.) _____
  Turn-around Space _____
  Functional Abilities:
    Toilet Transfers _____
    Tub or Shower Transfers _____
  Comments: _____
_____
_____

Kitchen:
  Accessibility to:
    Sink _____
    Stove (range & oven, controls) _____
    Refrigerator _____
    Work Area (counter height) _____
    Storage Area _____
    General Accessibility _____
  Functional Abilities:
    Able to Transport Articles (pots & pans) _____
    Reach Stove Top and Oven _____
    Take Items from Refrigerator _____
    Reach Cabinets _____
  Comments: _____

Summary/Recommendations: LIST THOSE AREAS SET UP SUITABLY
FOR THE PATIENT AND THOSE AREAS THAT PRESENT
DIFFICULTIES.
    LIST BOTH SIMPLE AND MORE EXTENSIVE
CHANGES RECOMENDED.
    LIST WHO MAY BE ABLE TO HELP MAKE
CHANGES
    JUDGE PATIENTS OVERALL ABILITY TO FUNCTION
IN THE ENVIRONMENT AND STATE CLEARLY
_____ OTR

Source: Courtesy of Occupational Therapy Department, Pacific Presbyterian Hospital, Eugene, Oregon.

subject matter of the communication will depend upon how the team roles are delineated. Written communication may be mandated by filling out required forms or in completing an individualized home program or instructions for an attendant or caregiver. In some settings, a comprehensive, written discharge summary fills this purpose (see Exhibit 9-4). In addition to documenting the effectiveness of occupational therapy intervention, the written discharge summary helps meet third-party reimbursement requirements.

Depending upon the patient's placement, additional written documentation may be needed to ensure the follow-through of involved community agencies.

Verbal communication includes telephone conversations with the patient, significant others, team members, and community program personnel. In some settings, the occupational therapist communicates recommendations for equipment and community referral to the team's social worker or discharge planner, who in turn completes all follow-up for the entire team.

When a therapist on a team with a social worker recommends referral to a community program, mentioning the idea to the patient or family prepares them for more detailed discussion with the social worker. In this way, the "seed is sown" for the referral; the patient and family can think about the idea and prepare questions for discussion with the social worker. In other settings, the therapist will need to make telephone contact with community resource people. Examples of this include contacting equipment vendors to place orders, contacting home health therapists to provide continuity in treatment, and contacting other community programs to provide suggestions or explain special circumstances.

Consider the case of a patient who is progressing in self-care skills, has a good prognosis for return to preadmission independence in all self-care, and is returning home with a spouse who is recovering from surgery. The physician proceeds with a referral to a home health service for an OT, a PT, and a home health aide. The occupational therapist telephones the home health therapist or aide to briefly outline the methods the patient is using for major self-care activities. This provides the continuity needed in order to prevent a "back sliding" period when new personnel introduce different training approaches. This kind of telephone follow-up is also appropriate for the patient returning to a skilled nursing facility.

EQUIPMENT ORDERING

Forming appropriate recommendations for adaptive equipment will also depend upon the patient's placement. The therapist's responsibility, after determining the patient's needs, is to educate the patient and family regarding equipment options and to facilitate their participation in the decision making. Most often the role of the acute care physical therapist includes recommending mobility aids and sometimes recommending the size or height of bathroom equipment. The responsibility

Exhibit 9-4 Discharge Summary Form

Name:

Doctor:

Date:

Diagnosis:

Discharge Location:

Physical Status (compared with admission): B.P.: _____ Pulse: _____

Sensory Perceptual Status (compared with admission):*

Coordination:*

Mental Status:

Activities of Daily Living:

I = Independent   I/E = Independent with Equipment   S = Needs Supervision

A = Needs Assistance   D = Dependent

On Admit	On D/C		On Admit	On D/C		On Admit	On D/C	
		Feeding			Grooming			Dressing
		Hygiene			Bathing			Managed Assistive
		Homemaking			Communications			Devices
		Bed Mobility			Supine to Sit			Rolling
		Transfers			Bed			Toilet
		Shower			Tub			Auto
		Sitting Balance			Standing Balance			

continues

Exhibit 9-4 continued

Comments (list adaptive equipment ordered or now being used):

_____

_____

*Code: N = Normal   3 = Severely Impaired or Poor
        1 = Minimally Impaired or Good   4 = Absent
        2 = Moderately Impaired or Fair

Family Conference: _____

_____

_____

_____

Environmental Planning (home visit, adaptations, etc.): _____

_____

_____

Goals Achieved (refer to initial evaluation form): _____

_____

_____

Goals Not Achieved and Why: _____

_____

_____

_____

_____

_____

_____

Follow-up Plan: _____

_____

_____

_____

Therapist: _____ OTR

Source: Courtesy of Occupational Therapy Department, Pacific Presbyterian Hospital, Eugene, Oregon.

for recommending a wheelchair to a patient can vary. On some acute care teams, the physical therapist orders wheelchairs; on other teams, the occupational therapist does. Understanding the patient's ADL and positioning needs are essential to successful wheelchair prescription. Specific training in measurement, positioning, and the use of cushions is necessary in order to recommend the appropriate wheelchair.

The most commonly recommended equipment consists of items for independence and safety in bathing and toileting. Smaller devices for eating, personal care, and meal preparation are also frequently recommended.

Establishing a working relationship with medical supply vendors will enable appropriate delivery of equipment. The therapist and the sales representatives must communicate clearly to provide what patients need in a timely manner. It is the therapist's professional responsibility to prescribe what is needed. It is the vendors' responsibility to educate the therapist as to what is available and to arrange timely delivery and service. The therapist should provide a list of local vendors to patients and families rather than recommend a specific vendor.

LONG-TERM CARE FACILITY DISCHARGE

Because the family will follow the patient to the nursing home setting, acute care services need to include patient and family education. The occupational therapist often needs to educate family members in self-care methods and cues as well as expected long-term functional outcomes. A family member who understands and agrees with realistic rehabilitation goals is the strongest advocate in the continuum of care for the elderly. Acute care therapists need to understand the role of the long-term care facilities in the medical system. Only 5% of the elderly reside in skilled facilities, with the incidence increasing with increased age (Fowles, 1988). Nursing home placement need not be equated with an absolute end to independent functioning. Because one-third of nursing home discharges are to the community (Kane, 1988), hospital-based therapists facilitate the eventual discharge to home when they provide thorough follow-up for patients discharged to long-term care facilities.

Therapists unfamiliar with the skilled facilities in their community need to educate themselves about the staff and the services offered. Contacting a facility's therapist to learn about the facility will greatly enhance the continuity of care. For example, some facilities utilize a restorative aide rather than a registered therapist or a certified assistant to supervise the daily practice of ADL skills and to monitor exercise, feeding, and splinting programs. Other facilities expect the certified nurse assistant to provide the follow-up in rehabilitative procedures. Knowing who will be responsible for carrying out recommendations enables the acute care therapist to form more realistic recommendations.

Communicating information about adaptive equipment, the splinting schedule, and specific cues used in self-care will alleviate confusion, reduce duplication of services, and smooth the patient's transition (Dunleavy Taira, 1985). By knowing whom to communicate with at a facility, the therapist can select the best method. In some facilities, telephoning the director of nursing services is best. At other facilities, a written discharge summary addressed to the restorative aide is most effective. Therapists who know the staff at the facilities in their community will make more appropriate recommendations and communicate the recommendations more effectively.

DISCHARGE TO INDEPENDENT LIVING

ADL independence is the best predictor of discharge to home for both men and women over 65 years of age (Wachtel, Derby, & Fulton, 1984). Many of the patients who are discharged to their homes live alone (Fowles, 1988). Acute care occupational therapists often provide more direct inpatient treatment to those who are planning to return home alone and have no caregiver present.

Self-care and safety are the main focus of the discharge plan. With input from the patient and the family, the acute care therapist needs to answer many questions after the evaluation. For example, what assistance is needed? Can the patient independently dress? Toilet? Bathe? If personal care assistance is available each morning, is the patient able to put on and remove shoes to walk safely and/or perform transfers? Can the patient prepare a light meal? Reheat cooked food? Safely cut food? Safely pour hot liquids? Generally exercise good judgment? Recognize unsafe household situations? Use the telephone to request help in an emergency? Could the patient exit the home in case of fire?

Once the patient's level of ADL is established, the recommendations for community agencies are developed. The patient needing assistance in morning self-care may need a family member or an attendant to help. A homemaker service may be the ideal resource for the patient needing assistance in light household activities and shopping. If the patient is expected to regain independent ADL with practice, a referral to a home health or outpatient service is needed. Occupational, physical, or speech therapy is available for the patient who is unable to travel to an outpatient service yet is expected to regain independent living skills. Likewise, a home health aide is available for assistance with personal care and for supervision of light household activities. To provide continuity of training, specific details about the cues and the patient's compensatory methods will be needed by the homemaker or home health personnel.

DISCHARGE TO HOME WITH RELATIVE

Often when a patient is discharged home with a relative, family education and training become the focus of the discharge plan. This is especially true when the caregiver will be an elderly spouse.

Seventy-five percent of older men live with a spouse, compared with 39 percent of women (Fowles, 1988). The physical status and age of the caregiver must be considered. An elderly spouse may require a different method of transferring the patient or assisting with self-care than would a younger, physically stronger paid attendant. If multiple caregivers will assist the patient, the recommended methods may differ in order to meet the needs of the situation and promote continuity. Also, the patient or significant other may need education regarding the training of others when multiple caregivers are to be used.

Family training needs to address three areas: (1) why the person needs assistance, (2) what the goals of the recommended procedures of assistance are in the context of the patient's prognosis, and (3) how to perform the recommended procedures.

The reason the patient needs help may be obvious. However, discussing the rationale for precautions or the basis of the patient's deficit will usually result in higher motivation and greater compliance. When the caregiver understands the reasons for recommended procedures, problem solving in unexpected situations often results as well. The caregiver also needs to know what to expect over time— increased skill with repetition or declining ability due to the diagnosis.

The caregiver needs to be trained in both general and specific guidelines for recommended procedures. General concepts, such as activity analysis, can be taught. It is suggested that the patient and caregiver first be taught to break down each task into simple steps. Then they can be taught to distinguish between steps that the patient can perform and steps that require assistance. During the training, both the therapist and caregiver should complete each task with the patient.

The issue of care for the caregiver needs to be addressed. This is especially important when the caregiver is an elderly spouse who may become overwhelmed by the physical demands and the responsibility involved. Respite care can be built into the discharge plan. This can assume many forms. Attendant care can be scheduled weekly or biweekly. The occupational therapist can also educate the caregiver regarding the patient's safety while left alone, enabling the caregiver to leave the patient for specified periods. Whether the solution is hiring an attendant or leaving the patient unsupervised for specific periods, the caregiver needs to be able to meet his or her own needs.

DISCHARGE TO FOSTER CARE

In many ways, discharge to foster care is similar to discharge home with a relative. One difference is that the foster home owner may have previous experience with the patient's condition, unlike the patient's family, who are experiencing the condition for the first time. The acute care team needs to be aware of two facts. First, the owner has received basic training in care skills and usually sees him- or herself as a professional member of the medical team. Second, the owner may be providing care for several residents and may employ others to share the caregiving.

Thus, the therapist may select simpler methods to facilitate compliance by multiple caregivers. Also, written instructions, handouts, and home programs may be essential. For the patient who is cognitively and emotionally capable, the therapist may educate the patient in how to train caregivers in order to facilitate consistency among multiple caregivers.

The occupational therapist needs to ascertain tactfully what instruction or training the foster home owner may need. This can be done by asking the owner to describe what needs he or she expects to fill. If the therapist determines the owner is expecting to provide the same services required by a previous resident, sensitively delivered training may be needed. Rather than simply lecturing, an appropriate approach may be to add to the provider's expertise. For example, if a hemiplegic patient needs active-assisted range of motion and the owner discusses range of motion given to a quadriplegic resident, the therapist can emphasize the patient's need for consistency and the importance of actively moving the involved upper extremity. Written instructions for hemiplegic self-ranging would also be appropriate.

For all matters of importance, combining written and verbal instructions is recommended. For one thing, consistency is more likely among multiple caregivers when handouts with diagrams accompany the patient.

The acute care team need not provide these services in the case of a home health referral. Once the particulars are communicated to the home health personnel, they are responsible for evaluating and training the care providers.

CONCLUSION

The occupational therapist can play a significant role in discharge planning for the geriatric patient. Discharge planning takes place in a context determined by the many changes that have occurred over the past two decades, including the increased size of the elderly population, the shortened length of stay, the increased diversity of community resources, the availability of home health services, and the redefinition of geriatric health in terms of functional ability. The nature of the functional changes in many older patients results in a "career of care" through a series of hospital readmissions. Today's occupational therapy clinical specialist needs to maintain a broad perspective throughout evaluation, treatment, and discharge planning to best serve elderly patients.

REFERENCES

Dunleavy Taira, E. (1985). After treatment what? New roles for occupational therapists in the community. *Occupational Therapy in Health Care, 2*, 13–24.

Fowles, D. (1988). *A Profile of Older Americans, 1988*. Washington, DC: American Association of Retired Persons and Department of Health and Human Services, Administration on Aging.

Kane, R. (1988, October 7). New myths of aging from baby boomers to Golden Pond. Unpublished material presented at The Geriatric Patient of the 90's, Eugene, Oregon.

Kennie, D. (1983). Good health care for the aged. *Journal of The American Medical Association, 249,* 770–773.

National Center for Health Statistics. (1988). *Health: United States, 1987*. Washington, DC: Government Printing Office.

Wachtel, T., Derby, C., & Fulton, J. (1984). Predicting the outcome of hospitalization for elderly persons: Home vs. nursing home. *Southern Medical Journal, 77,* 1283–1285.

Part III

Community-Based Programs

Chapter 10

Cognitive Impairments in Older Adults

Ferol Menks Ludwig

Cognition is the process of perceiving, representing, and organizing stimuli. Components of cognition are perception, organized motor movements, imagery, memory, attention, learning, knowledge, consciousness, thinking, imagining, reasoning, generating plans and strategies, conceptualizing, classifying, relating, and symbolizing (Flavell, 1977). Allen (1985) describes a cognitive disability as a restriction in voluntary motor action that originates in the physical or chemical structures of the brain and creates observable limitations in routine task behavior. Cognitive disabilities limit the ability to perform voluntary motor actions through deficits in the mental processes that usually guide these motor actions. The ability to use and/or form sensorimotor models is impaired. The meaning of the cognitive impairment becomes apparent when one is doing an activity.

Cognitive impairments result from a variety of causes. Some are temporary and reversible and others are permanent and irreversible. Illnesses associated with fever, medications, cognitive and/or sensory deprivation, metabolic disorders, nutritional imbalances, and pseudodementia due to depression are some of the conditions that may cause a *temporary* cognitive impairment. These are remediable and their associated cognitive impairments may be *acute* and *reversible*. The reversibility of dementia is a function of the underlying pathology and the availability of timely and effective treatment. Clinical improvement depends upon the extent of damage to the brain. Dementia may be progressive, static, or remitting (American Psychiatric Association [APA], 1987). The onset and progression depend upon the underlying etiology and its effect upon the brain.

This chapter will focus on occupational therapy assessment and treatment of cognitive impairments in the elderly. Dementia and depression will be specifically discussed because of their high incidence in this population.

DEMENTIA

Incidence

According to a U.S. Office of Technology Assessment (1985) report, dementia is the most common diagnosis among nursing home residents, with prevalence estimates ranging from one-half to two-thirds of all residents. Approximately 50% of all dementias are attributed to primary degenerative dementia of the Alzheimer type (SDAT). About 18% of the dementias result from multi-infarct dementia of vascular origin. Another 18% present a mixture of these two. Disorders such as Huntington's chorea, Pick's disease, Parkinsonism, and Jakob-Creutzfeldt comprise the remaining 14% of irreversible dementias.

Progressive global impairment in short- and long-term memory, associated with impairment in abstract thinking, impaired judgment, and other disturbances of higher cortical function or personality change, is an essential characteristic of dementia. The etiology is assumed to be from an underlying causative organic factor. Dementia is diagnosed only when the loss of intellectual function is severe enough to disrupt occupational and social functioning (APA, 1987).

Primary Degenerative Dementia of the Alzheimer Type

Senile dementia, or primary degenerative dementia of the Alzheimer type (SDAT), is the most common irreversible dementia. There is no specific diagnostic test for SDAT. Diagnosis is based on clinical evidence that can be confirmed only in retrospect by postmortem examination of the brain. Acceptance of the clinical diagnosis should occur only after careful exclusion of other possible causes and symptoms.

SDAT is progressive, and signs and symptoms change over time. It has an insidious onset, with a gradual, progressive, and irreversible course that varies considerably depending on the individual. Most researchers describe an early stage, a middle stage, and an advanced stage, which terminates with death. The course of the illness is usually 1–15 years, with the average duration 7–8 years. The prognosis is worse if the onset is before age 65 (Volicer, Fabiszewski, Rheaume, & Lasch, 1988). The use of stages provides only a rough guide for planning. The disease does not progress in a sequential, routine, and stepwise progression that is the same for everyone. There is daily variability and change.

Multi-infarct Dementia

Multi-infarct dementia results from significant cerebrovascular disease and multiple strokes that occur because of repeated occlusions of small blood vessels in the brain. The onset is usually abrupt and the course fluctuates rapidly. The cognitive impairments are "patchy," depending upon which regions of the brain have been obliterated. This dementia usually involves impairments in memory, abstract thinking, judgment, impulse control, and personality. Focal neurological signs, such as limb weakness, gait abnormalities, reflex asymmetries, dysphagia, and dysarthria, are common. Generally, a single stroke causes a more circumscribed change in mental state, such as aphasia, and does not cause dementia (APA, 1987). Multi-infarct dementia may be present along with SDAT.

Symptoms of many treatable disorders may present as dementia. Correct differential diagnosis is essential. A drug reaction, dehydration, hypoglycemia, cataracts, or social isolation might produce some symptoms of dementia that can be effectively treated. To mistake these for an irreversible, progressive cognitive disorder would be tragic.

Allen's Cognitive-Developmental Frame of Reference

Claudia Allen (1985) has developed a cognitive-developmental theory and frame of reference for occupational therapists who work with the cognitive disabilities. She provides a theory of practice, propositions for testing, preliminary instrumentation, and some research studies. Allen (1985) asserts that brain impairment affects the associations made between voluntary motor actions and sensory cues.

Allen (1985) conceptualized a hierarchical ordinal scale that describes six cognitive levels. These levels are very useful to the therapist, since the new Medicare Part B guidelines have added cognitive level to the assistance code. Allen's six cognitive levels range from total assistance (Level 1) to independent of cognitive assistance (Level 6). (See Table 10-1.) Recently she has expanded these levels to allow more sensitivity to smaller degrees of change within each level. The levels are highly detailed and specific.

Assessment

Cognitive level is measured first. The therapist observes task behavior on standardized tasks. Allen (1985) has devised two standardized performance tests to assess cognitive levels: (1) the Allen Cognitive Level Test (ACL) and (2) the Lower Cognitive Level Test (LCL). She cautions that these were designed for acute psychiatric settings and that other settings might require modifications. Heying (1985) used the two tests with older persons with senile dementia and found them appropriate and useful. She reported a highly significant positive relationship between the ACL score and the caregiver's rating of performance of activities of daily living.

The ACL is a leather-lacing test that is based on the complexity of the lacing stitch that the person is able to imitate. For example, a person functioning at Level 4 is able to imitate the whip stitch and untwist the lace (see Allen, 1985, and Earhart and Allen, 1988, for specific details).

Table 10-1 Allen's Cognitive Levels

Level	Characteristics	Indicated Activity
Level 1: Automatic actions, total cognitive assistance	Automatic or habitual actions Attention to subliminal sensory cues Largely unresponsive to external cues Attention span for a few seconds Changes occur in level of arousal	Sensorimotor with tactile cueing Frequent short sessions Safe positioning by the caregiver
Level 2: Postural actions, maximum cognitive assistance	Attention to proprioceptive cues Gross body movements capture attention Not aware of effects of actions 5- to 10-minute attention span	Familiar gross motor actions
Level 3: Manual actions, moderate cognitive assistance	Attention to tactile cues and manual actions Can imitate demonstrated action Actions not connected to goal unless tactilely apparent Attention limited to what can be touched and manipulated Attention span about 30 minutes	Highly repetitive, consistent, and predictable String beads Felt eyeglass case Nonrepetitive steps need to be done by therapist or caregiver Train caregiver for home program
Level 4: Goal-directed actions, minimum cognitive assistance	Attention to visible cues one at a time Can successfully imitate clearly visible and familiar actions Attention span of 1 hour Aware of purpose of actions Understands visible cause-effect relationship Fails to explore new motor actions Follows one-step instructions Does not see safety hazards	Yard work Familiar activities Bargello pot holder Whip stitch leather project Routine and structured

continues

Table 10-1 continued

Level	Characteristics	Indicated Activity
Level 5: Exploratory actions, standby cognitive assistance	Attention to concrete related cues Trial and error problem solving Errors recognized but not anticipated Can follow series of instructions if partial familiarity exists Can plan variations in concrete ways with noticeable effects	Basketweaving Working with clay Leather tooling and carving Cooking
Level 6: Planned actions, independent of cognitive assistance	Attention to symbolic cues Covert trial and error problem solving Can follow verbal instructions without demonstration Can control impulses and anticipate consequences	Creative use of available supplies and interests Verbal discussion

The LCL was designed to help differentiate persons at Levels 1, 2, and 3. It requires the subject to try to imitate the motor action of clapping hands in specific ways.

The Routine Task History Interview was designed by Allen (1985) to provide information about the person's functional history. Please see Allen (1985) and Earhart and Allen (1988) for specific content and instructions. The interview is undergoing further research and development.

Treatment

The task must match the cognitive level in order to be successful. Tasks are selected and modified to be within the client's abilities. Earhart and Allen (1988) have developed a workbook that expands upon the original cognitive levels devised by Allen and gives more specific information regarding assessment and specific treatment techniques and tasks.

One of the essential roles of the occupational therapist is to objectively monitor degrees of functional changes that are or are not occurring. Improvement can be noted in the person's need for assistance, which differs with cognitive level and is highly dependent on the information that the person is able to process. The therapist must skillfully assess what kind of assistance will elicit better responses from the person (Allen, 1989).

Selection of program content is based upon the person's abilities and preferences. Adaptations are made to meet the cognitive level, needs, and desires of each individual, with the goal being to maximize functional abilities and promote self-esteem, dignity, autonomy, and quality of life. Unpleasant experiences should be kept to a minimum. The task environment should be designed for positive effect. Projective techniques and unstructured stimuli only serve to elicit pathology from persons who have difficulty organizing thoughts or behavior.

Past experiences, the medical condition, fatigue, stress, the environment, and the desirability of the task also affect performance. Allen (1985) states that catastrophic reactions may occur when a person encounters a task that was easily done in the past but is now too difficult.

Allen (1985) does not feel that occupational therapy per se can presently change cognitive level. Changes seen might be due to psychotropic medication or the course of the disease. She suggests *measurement* and *management* as alternatives to *improvement* as occupational therapy goals in the case of chronic cognitive disabilities.

The main goal is to recommend discharge to the least restrictive environment once the cognitive disability has stabilized. The occupational therapist specifies abilities and disabilities and their functional meaning. Compensations are made through environmental adjustments when no change in etiology, pathology, or impairment can be expected. For example, a person at Level 3 cannot recognize dangerous situations. Actions are not connected to a goal until tactilely apparent. The environment needs to be structured, with assistance provided to ensure safety. The person can learn through direct, concrete experience, but this learning is not generalized.

Realistic treatment expectations are established that capitalize on using available strengths and recognizing residual disabilities. Allen feels that developmental objectives can be harmful by supporting the proposition that treatment can overcome the incapacitating effects of chronic illness.

Allen's approach is particularly helpful in that it offers therapists and caregivers a better understanding of specific cognitive difficulties and provides guidance in recognizing and designing environmental compensations. In her current workshops, Allen presents adaptive equipment guidelines that are based upon the patient's ability to learn to use the equipment and/or the caregiver's willingness to set it up. These guidelines are written according to the amount of cognitive assistance required. For example, for Levels 1 and 2, total cognitive assistance and maximum cognitive assistance are required respectively. Toys and position cones can be used. Level 3 patients can use safe materials, such as wash mitts and built-up spoons, that utilize familiar motor actions. Working with an *S. and S. Arts and Crafts* staff member, Allen analyzed the crafts in that catalog to determine their correspondence with her cognitive levels. The 1990 *Adaptability* catalog and *WorldWide Games* have been analyzed in terms of cognitive levels as well. The continuing research and development of this assessment give it excellent potential for contributing to occupational therapy practice with cognitive impairments.

Cognitive Assessments

The global nature of cognitive dysfunction results in impairments in many areas of function. Bruce and Borg (1987) suggest the use of a broadly based assessment designed to gain information about functional abilities in a variety of task, social, and environmental situations.

Therapists need to consider the capabilities of the client, the medical diagnosis, the client's history with tasks, and the complexity of the task. Assessing the person with cognitive disabilities is more apt to produce false positives, because adults retain some familiar responses but these may not independently meet an acceptable standard of performance. Qualitative assessments are more useful than checklists with this population. Direct observation is essential. This section will discuss evaluations and assessment tools specific to occupational therapy assessment of cognitive impairments.

Sensorimotor Assessment

Bruce and Borg (1987) list specific sensory, motor, and cognitive abilities to assess while a person is doing a task (Table 10-2).

Table 10-2 Commonly Assessed Sensory, Motor, and Cognitive Tasks

Category	Task
Visual Perception	Focuses on a single stimulus Scans a visual field Identifies shapes and colors Identifies common objects, shown individually Identifies object (from photograph or in actual presentation) from a variety of perspectives Identifies objects or shapes depicted in distracting visual field Describes the purpose of objects viewed Remembers visual data
Visual Motor Synthesis	Writes familiar schemes (i.e., name) Copies simple shapes Duplicates with blocks a 2-dimensional or 3-dimensional pattern Draws a designated object without the aid of a pattern to copy
Auditory Perception	Comprehends familiar schemes (e.g., "Hello, what is your name?") Localizes where sounds are coming from Attends to one auditory stimulus and screens out irrelevant ones Comprehends complex or new auditory scheme Recalls auditory information
Auditory Motor Synthesis	Follows simple, familiar commands (e.g., waves goodbye or shakes hands) Duplicates a rhythm with a finger (or pencil); changes rhythm as therapist changes it Follows commands, less familiar schemes (e.g., touches right elbow with left hand)
Spatial Relationship Synthesis	Follows directions to go left, right, up, or down Mimics hand directions of interviewer Deals with spatial ideas (e.g., tells time, draws hands on a clock) Places objects above, below, or to the right Understands arithmetic computations
Body-Awareness Synthesis	Crosses body midline in reaching and in tasks Names body parts Indicates where body parts are in space (eyes closed) Imitates postures of interviewer sitting across from or next to the individual assessed Draws an integrated person-symbol
Vestibular-Kinesthetic Synthesis	Maintains balance (one leg and two legs, eyes open) Maintains balance (one leg and two legs, eyes closed) Maintains trunk balance when interviewer applies pressure (individual seated and standing) Walks straight line (forward and backward)

continues

Table 10-2 continued

Category	Task
Tactile Perception	Recognizes tactile qualities (cold, warm, pressure, or pain) Locates tactile stimuli applied to body Indicates specified fingers Recognizes textures (rough, smooth, or bumpy) Discriminates objects by shape and feel
Motor Synthesis	Initiates and stops movement of large muscle bodies Uses both sides of the body in purposeful movement Crosses body midline Accomplishes gross-motor purposeful movement (e.g., jumps, hops, skips, claps, catches large ball) Uses smaller muscle groups in purposeful movement (e.g., writes name or opens lock with key) Persists in motor task (e.g., keeps hand in air until therapist says to put it down)
Cognition/Attention	Maintains eye contact Attends to visual stimulus Attends to interviewer's verbal instructions Attends to conversation in a group structure
Cognition/Concentration	Sustains involvement in a task (1 minute, 10 minutes, ½ hour) Subtracts from 100 by 7s or from 30 by 3s
Cognition/Orientation To Person	Answers questions: What is your name? Your occupation? How old are you? Do you remember who I am? What I do? Who is that person (point to significant other)?
To Place	Answers questions: Where are you now? What is the name of this hospital (if not at home)?
To Time	Answers questions: What day (of the week) is it today? What is the calendar date? What is the season of the year?
Cognition/Knowledge (see also "memory" and "problem-solving" tasks)	Seriates numbers Sorts objects according to same and different Discusses simple current events Does simple math Reads (therapist begins with single words and then reads phrases and sentences) Writes Demonstrates knowledge of motor process(es), procedures, and social expectations in daily encounters
Cognition/Insight and Judgment	States why he or she is in treatment Describes strengths, limitations, and needs

continues

Table 10-2 continued

Category	Task
	Discusses family's feelings about treatment
	Describes the view others have of him or her
	Interprets proverb
	Demonstrates judgment in tasks of daily living (e.g., dresses and grooms appropriately; clothing is clean; asks for assistance from the OTR or nurse as needed; eats adequate meals)
	Uses tools appropriately (observes safety precautions)
	Follows norms of social politeness
Cognition/Memory (some common examples, illustrative only)	
Personal (and long-term)	Gives accurate personal history
	Able to describe events of last 24 hours prior to treatment (when an appropriate question)
	Can answer: What did you do last Christmas, who were you with, and where were you? (Therapist can use any significant day)
	What was for breakfast this morning?
	What did we do in therapy yesterday?
Impersonal (and short-term)	Remembers 3 unrelated items 5 minutes to ½ hour later
	Remembers content of paragraph 2–15 minutes after reading
Procedural-Motoric (long-term)	Demonstrates how to dial a phone or find a phone number
	Demonstrates how to play checkers, play badminton, or pot a plant (if this was a skill formerly in learning repertoire)
Sensory-Perceptual (short- or long-term)	Demonstrates way to hospital room (or other familiar site)
	Can find bathroom, dining room, or other landmark in the hospital or home
	Accurately recalls what is heard or seen in environment
Cognition/Problem-Solving Tasks (combines knowledge, memory, and insight in higher cognitive function)	Generates one (or more) solutions to obtaining an unknown phone number, tracing a route on a city map, reading a bus schedule, and describing how to get from one place to another
	Balances a simple checkbook ledger
	Makes change
	States what he or she would do in a medical emergency
	Constructs a 3-D box when given a piece of paper, tape, and scissors

Source: From *Frames of Reference in Psychosocial Occupational Therapy* (pp. 391–394) by M.A. Bruce & B. Borg, 1987, Thorofare, NJ: Charles B. Slack, Inc. Copyright 1987 by Charles B. Slack, Inc. Reprinted by permission.

Perception is the central nervous system function that detects a sensation, recognizes and discriminates it from other sensations, and retains it long enough for a purposeful response. These perceptions then need to be synthesized. The more complex synthesis processes are frequently impaired when there is assault to the brain. Agnosias result from the inability to comprehend sensory information. The most common agnosias are visual, tactile, and auditory (Bruce & Borg, 1987). To compensate, individuals may restrict their circle of attention, respond to the obvious message, isolate themselves from sensory stimuli, use a slow or deliberate response, or become irritable.

Purposeful activity, or an adaptive motor response, requires the ability to perceive and synthesize sensory data, utilize higher cortical function to analyze a motor problem, plan action, and execute movement. Apraxia indicates disturbances of voluntary movement at the central nervous system level. Perseveration may be another manifestation of impaired motor synthesis and may be seen in speech or in copying visual patterns. The inability to maintain a motor action might be observed. The individual may compensate by avoiding novelty, rigidly remaining with familiar schemes, responding slowly, or responding to only one aspect of a motor task (Bruce & Borg, 1987).

Cognitive Assessment

Basic to cognition are attention, concentration, orientation, knowledge, memory, judgment, insight, abstraction, and problem solving. Please refer to Table 10-2 for specific abilities that can be used to assess these areas. Inappropriate responses, avoidance of new tasks, rigidity in problem solving, frustration, denial, confabulation, or inaccuracies may indicate impairments.

Memory is likely to differ in terms of long-term, short-term, and immediate recall. Daily fluctuations occur. The person may attempt to compensate with lists, confabulation, rambling circumstantial speech, perseveration, and avoidance. A sense of continuity is lost and daily events lose much of their meaning.

Insight and judgment are also vulnerable to impairments. It is difficult to hypothesize and to anticipate consequences of actions. Thinking is concrete and problem solving is severely hampered by these losses. The individual may not be able to understand cause and effect (Volicer et al., 1988; Bruce & Borg, 1987).

Ross and Burdick (1981) present a sensory-motor-cognitive assessment that was developed by Brenda Smaga and Mildred Ross. This rates range of motion, balance, posture, general strength, proprioception, crossing the midline, finger identification, graphesthesia, stereognosis, unilateral neglect, speed, auditory figure-ground, coordination, and linguistic output and comprehension.

The Norristown State Hospital Occupational Therapy Department's (1987) Comprehensive Functional Evaluation was designed primarily for geriatric patients. It provides a standardized method of evaluating orientation, memory, gross motor coordination, sensation, fine motor movement, thinking, and perception.

Social Assessment

Cognitive impairments limit a person's ability to function successfully in a social context. Loss of judgment and insight, decreased behavioral and affective control, decreased ability to perceive verbal and nonverbal messages, and attentional difficulties may cause severe problems in relating with others.

The therapist observes the individual in a variety of settings to identify existing social skills. Behaviors that interfere with positive interactions are also observed, as is the ability to comprehend what is being said and to follow simple commands. It is important to determine in which settings the cognitively impaired person can best function.

A thorough social history is needed to establish who the primary caregivers are and who resides with the patient. An occupational history and information about premorbid life style is important in establishing data on the change in the patient's condition from former levels. Fidler's (1982) Lifestyle Performance Profile is useful if this information is not available from social services. Information about family structure and sociocultural beliefs about health and illness can help to identify supports and stressors that impact upon the person and family and can facilitate the identification of appropriate strategies and resources.

Independent Living Skills

Evaluation of independent living skills is essential to determine treatment needs, appropriate environmental settings, support services, and modifications. Please see Chapter 6 for specific assessments that may be used.

Cognitive Treatment

The correct diagnosis is essential in determining appropriate treatment interventions. The natural course of the disease is a primary consideration in formulating expectations for change. It is essential to establish realistic therapeutic expectations and to ensure that treatment takes into consideration the individual's own wishes and desires.

For SDAT there is currently no available cure to stop or reverse the progression. The treatment approach is to help the person maintain as much comfort and dignity as possible through the course of the disease (Levy, 1986). Treatment is directed at maximizing function and improving the quality of life within present abilities.

Chapter 12 presents an in-depth discussion of management approaches for the patient with dementia.

DEPRESSION

Characteristics and Incidence

Depression is a major problem among older adults. "The golden years are a time of change and adjustment, often made more difficult by the loss of psychological resiliency and the social support systems that help younger individuals to cope" (Yost, Beutler, Corbishley, & Allender, 1986, p. 1). A significant number of the elderly manifest both depression and loss of self-esteem.

The elderly experience the loss of spouse, friends, family members, physical abilities, employment, and activities. Blan and Berezin (1975) consider the core problem of depression in the elderly to be the inability to handle external losses along with perceptions of internal and external changes. This leads to a decrease in self-esteem and feelings of helplessness. The elderly fear losing control and becoming infirm and alone at death. Lewis (1971) found that 86% of the depressed elderly had some chronic health problem. Sensory losses, especially hearing and seeing, exacerbated depressive symptoms by adding to isolation and loss of control.

The death of a spouse has been found to correlate most closely with the development of depression. The symptoms of prolonged bereavement can assume all the characteristics of a major depression. Mortality rates rise from deteriorations in health status and the increased frequency of suicide. Nearly one-half of all of those who survive the loss of a mate develop a clinical level of depression that lasts several years beyond the loss (Clayton, 1979).

The incidence of depression among the elderly is felt to be underestimated, since many of the signs and symptoms of depression may look like somatic problems, may be exaggerations of normal age-related changes, may be concomitant with medical conditions, or may fail to be brought to the health care providers' attention. Frequently, the elderly do not identify their symptoms of depression, or seek medical attention for somatic symptoms. The aged have a high rate of transient, recurring symptoms of depression. These may not be pronounced enough to meet DSM-IIIR (APA, 1987) criteria for depressive disorder, but they may severely affect the person's quality of life and ability to function.

Wells et al. (1989) found in a study of 11,242 adult outpatients in three health care systems that the *physical* functioning of patients with depressive symptoms was significantly worse than that of patients with arthritis, ulcers, diabetes, or hypertension. The only medical conditions having comparable functional associations with depressive symptoms were current heart conditions. The combined effects of depressive symptoms and medical conditions were found to be additive.

Of even greater significance, because of its potential lethality, is suicide. The suicide rate is three times higher for persons over age 65 than for the general population (Chaisson-Stewart, 1985). This rate has increased 25% from 1981 to 1986 among persons over age 65 and is higher for men than women.

The severe impact that depressive symptoms and disorders have on a person's life makes it essential that depression be recognized and treated. Depressive disorders are defined by two major paradigms. One is the definition in the *Diagnostic and Statistical Manual of Mental Disorders*, third edition (APA, 1987). The other paradigm consists of the depressive symptoms that are frequently used in a wide variety of depression rating scales. (See Table 10-3 for a list of depressive signs and symptoms.)

According to Blazer (1982), depression in late life differs in many ways from that which occurs earlier in life. In the elderly, episodes are often brief but recurring, or the depression may be shallow and chronic. In both cases, depression becomes more difficult to recognize. The individual in many instances does not recognize that he or she is depressed. Somatic complaints and irritability are common. Anxiety is seen more often.

Disturbances in thought content are the most common disturbances of cognition seen in depression (Blazer, 1982). Delusions of bodily dysfunction, such as rotting insides, nonexistent odors, or nonexistent cancers, may occur. Delusions usually are mood congruent. Preoccupations and obsessions may also be seen. Compared with the thoughts of younger depressed persons, the thoughts of the elderly depressed are less often guilt provoking or self-accusing. They more commonly center on unfinished domestic tasks and physical discomfort.

Disturbances in memory and intelligence are commonly seen and may reflect psychic distress that presents as a pseudodementia. The individual may be uninterested in events going on around him or her. Retention deficits may be observed. The person may appear disoriented as a result of sensory deficits, sensory deprivation, social isolation, or lack of attention to surroundings.

Cognitive impairments associated with depression differ from those of dementia in the ways described in Table 10-4. The disorientation, apathy, memory loss, and difficulty concentrating resulting from depression are not true dementia. These symptoms will remit as the depression improves. The cognitive impairments of severe depression can lead to a misdiagnosis of dementia. Since the progression of and prognosis for these separate disorders are so dramatically different, correct differential diagnosis is essential. Depression is amenable to treatment and can be expected to remit.

Most persons with depressive disorders in late life have the initial onset after age 65. A significant minority are recurrences of unipolar or bipolar mood disorders that began earlier in life (Blazer, 1982).

Table 10-3 Depressive Signs and Symptoms

Category	Signs and Symptoms
Mood	Depressed, sad Apathetic Irritable Decreased experience of pleasure
Cognition	Pessimism Hopelessness, helplessness Delusions Racing or slowed thoughts Rumination Thinks of self as worthless Memory disturbance patchy for both recent and remote past Disorientation Decreased attention span Suicidal thoughts Feels something terrible is about to happen Indecisive
Physical Function	Insomnia or hypersomnia Increase or decrease in appetite Weight loss or gain Fatigue Decreased interest in sex Constipation Gastric distress Backache Hypochondriasis Somatic complaints
Behavior	Decreased interest and participation in usual activities Hand wringing Pacing, restlessness, agitation Psychomotor retardation Withdrawal Negative comments about self

Task Behavior

Cognitive impairments of higher cognitive processes can be observed. Problem-solving abilities decrease as a result of concrete thinking and an inability to shift lines of thought. Cognitive disturbances are more severe in psychotic depression. The difficulty in performing tasks seems to be more a difficulty in capturing and sustaining effort and attention. Depressed persons take longer to complete tasks. They devalue themselves and negatively appraise actions, abilities, and creations. They are convinced that they will fail and easily feel overwhelmed.

Table 10-4 Comparison of the Cognitive Impairments of Depression and Dementia

Depression	Dementia
Exaggerates memory loss	Conceals memory loss
Exaggerates disability	Conceals disability
Variable recent and remote memory	Poor recent memory; remote memory intact
Memory improves as depression lifts	Progressive memory deterioration
Avoids answering	Confabulates or gives near-miss answers
Rapid onset	Insidious progressive onset
Consistently depressed affect	Labile affect
Acute symptoms	Chronic symptoms
Minimal response to stimuli	Distractible
Minimizes accomplishments	Variable response
Very sensitive to specific deficits	Conceals or minimizes deficits

Somatic complaints are frequent. Slow movements, with little energy behind them, are characteristic. Poor concentration and focusing of attention create forgetfulness and disorientation. Visual-motor coordination may also be affected, and perceptual dulling may occur (Allen, 1985). The person usually has little interest in occupational therapy, is anhedonic, and receives no satisfaction from completed projects. Decision making is arduous. Depressed persons tend to ruminate, and this often distracts them from their projects. A mistake may begin a flood of depressive symptoms. They often are irritable, critical of others, and feel that they are a burden.

Activities of Daily Living

Depressed persons frequently demonstrate less involvement and effort in daily life tasks. They may withdraw from many daily activities. Grooming and hygiene are often ignored. Depressed persons complain that they do not feel like doing anything. They also have difficulty sustaining the interest, attention, and energy needed to perform activities.

Assessment

The assessments described earlier in this chapter can be helpful in providing the occupational therapist with data on cognitive functions for depressed persons as well. Accurate assessment of cognitive abilities and impairments is crucial for analyzing, selecting, and modifying activities so that they match the current and changing abilities of the individual. Cognitive behavioral symptoms of depression can be readily observed in the person's task behavior and activities of daily living, as previously discussed.

Treatment

Short-term success-oriented activities are indicated. Successful experiences increase a depressed person's performance (Hammen & Krantz, 1976) and can break the cycle of helplessness and inactivity that reinforces depression. Tasks need to be graded in a hierarchy of difficulty. As competence increases, there will be a progression from relatively short, nonresistive, simple tasks to more complex and resistive ones. With each step, the person should be reinforced by the therapist. The person will begin to recognize that he or she is able to function and can master some part of the environment.

Depressed clients tend to do best with shorter work periods and with tasks that require less energy expenditure. They are easily discouraged and require encouragement to continue. When a client is ruminating and complaining, redirection to a concrete task is more constructive. Depressed persons take longer to organize their thoughts, and adequate time needs to be alloted for this. Decisions need to be limited to choice among a few options. The therapist might say, "Would you like to paint this red or blue?" This allows the person some autonomy while helping him or her engage in decision making and exert some control. Feedback needs to be provided to help depressed persons establish realistic goals and accurately appraise their accomplishments.

In social situations, they need to be encouraged to participate in a more positive manner. By giving them small, simple, but essential tasks, they can contribute to a group or help others. An example of such a task is putting colored sugar on cookies the group is making. The results are immediately visible, and the task is an important part of making decorative cookies. The negative attitudes and isolating behaviors of depressed persons tend to alienate them from family and friends. A group situation offers opportunities for socialization, expression of altruistic needs, and reminders that others have similar or worse problems. Hatter and Nelson (1987) found that persons living in a home for the aged were more likely to participate in an activity designed to benefit others than in an activity with no altruistic purpose. Helping others increases self-esteem and motivates some to participate.

Older adults are more likely to be socially isolated due to poor health, lack of transportation, and the death of friends and loved ones. New social support networks need to be established and old ones strengthened. However, a person may not be ready to establish new relationships until he or she has adequately mourned the loss of previous ones. This mourning process may first need to be encouraged.

Suicide is a potential threat when someone is depressed. If an individual expresses suicidal ideation or intention, immediate psychiatric intervention is needed. The therapist must notify the staff and the physician verbally and document the incident.

Involvement in activities of daily living needs to be encouraged. Hygiene groups, a manicure, behavioral programs, and persuasion might be used to engage the depressed person. It is very important to meet patients at the level they are demonstrating. Do not come on too strong or overwhelm them. It is important to approach them in a calm, caring, and gently friendly manner. Actions and speech need to be slow and unrushed.

The psychiatric day treatment program described in Chapter 11 provides an effective treatment model for depressed older adults and incorporates the approaches described here.

CONCLUSION

Cognitive impairments have a global effect upon the individual, the family, and the caregivers. Some cognitive impairments are temporary and reversible, others are permanent and irreversible. Task performance and independent living skills are markedly affected. Assessment and treatment need to be comprehensive and sample many areas of function in a variety of task, social, and environmental situations. The course of the disease or disorder is a chief consideration in treatment planning in order to establish realistic treatment expectations.

In dementia the treatment is directed at maximizing function and quality of life within present abilities. This is done primarily through environmental modifications.

Acute confusion can result from a variety of causes, most of which can be treated. Cognitive impairments associated with depression are usually reversible and remit as the depression lifts. Treatment is aimed at helping the person to successfully engage in meaningful activities at appropriate levels, thereby fostering a sense of competency and control over the environment. Social networks may need to be developed, supported, and strengthened.

REFERENCES

Allen, C.K. (1985). *Occupational therapy for psychiatric diseases: Measurement and management of cognitive disability*. Boston: Little, Brown.

Allen, C.K. (1989). Treatment plans in cognitive rehabilitation. *Occupational Therapy Practice, 1*, 1–8.

American Psychiatric Association. (1987). *Diagnostic and statistical manual of mental disorders* (3rd ed.). Washington, DC: Author.

Blan, D., & Berezin, M.A. (1975). Neuroses and character disorders. In J.G. Howells (Ed.), *Modern perspectives in the psychiatry of old age*. New York: Bruner/Mazel.

Blazer, D. (1982). *Depression in late life*. St. Louis: C.V. Mosby.

Bruce, M.A., & Borg, B. (1987). *Frames of reference in occupational therapy*. Thorofare, NJ: Slack.

Chaisson-Stewart, G.M. (1985). Depression incidence: Past, present, and future. In G.M. Chaisson-Stewart (Ed.), *Depression in the elderly: An interdisciplinary approach.* New York: Wiley.

Clayton, P.J. (1979). The sequelae and nonsequelae of conjugal bereavement. *American Journal of Psychiatry, 136,* 1530–1534.

Earhart, C.A., & Allen, C.K. (1988). *Cognitive disabilities: Expanded activity analysis.* (Available from the authors, 3660 Cartwright Street, Pasadena, CA 91107.)

Fidler, G. (1982). The lifestyle performance profile: An organizing frame. In B.J. Hemphill (Ed.), *The evaluative process in psychiatric occupational therapy* (pp. 43–47). Thorofare, NJ: Slack.

Flavell, J. (1977). *Cognitive development.* Englewood Cliffs, NJ: Prentice-Hall.

Hammen, C.L., & Krantz, S. (1976). Effects of success and failure on depressive cognitions. *Journal of Abnormal Psychology, 85,* 557–586.

Hatter, J.K., & Nelson, D.L. (1987). Altruism and task participation in the elderly. *American Journal of Occupational Therapy, 41,* 379–381.

Heying, L.M. (1985). Research with subjects having senile dementia. In C.K. Allen (Ed.), *Occupational therapy for psychiatric diseases: Measurement and management of cognitive disability* (pp. 336–339). Boston: Little, Brown.

Levy, L.L. (1986). Cognitive treatment. In L.J. Davis & M. Kirkland (Eds.), *The role of occupational therapy with the elderly* (pp. 289–324). Rockville, MD: American Occupational Therapy Association.

Lewis, C.N. (1971). Reminiscing and self concept in old age. *Journal of Gerontology, 26,* 240.

Norristown State Hospital Occupational Therapy Department. (1987). *Norristown State Hospital Occupational Therapy Department Comprehensive Functional Evaluation.* (Available from Occupational Therapy Department, Norristown State Hospital, Norristown, PA 19401.)

Ross, M., & Burdick, D. (1981). *Sensory integration: A training manual for therapists and teachers for regressed, psychiatric, and geriatric patient groups.* Thorofare, NJ: Slack.

U.S. Office of Technology Assessment. (1985). *Technology and aging in America.* Pub. No. OTA-BA 264. Washington, DC: Government Printing Office.

Volicer, L., Fabiszewski, K., Rheaume, Y., & Lasch, K. (1988). *Clinical management of Alzheimer's disease.* Gaithersburg, MD: Aspen Publishers.

Wells, K.B., Stewart, A., Hays, R.D., Burnam, M.A., Rogers, W., Daniels, M., Berry, S., Greenfield, S., & Ware, J. (1989). The functioning and well-being of depressed patients: Results from the medical outcomes study. *Journal of the American Medical Association, 262,* 914–919.

Yost, E.B., Beutler, L.E., Corbishley, M.A., & Allender, J.R. (1986). *Group cognitive therapy: A treatment approach for older adults.* Elmsford, NY: Pergamon Press.

Chapter 11

Day Treatment for Behavioral Health Needs

Francesca D. Wolfe and Cindy Patrice Paulson

As the number of older persons increases in our society, the complexity of issues with which they must deal also increases. Life was simpler when those in the current geriatric population were young. Fewer people reached their seventies or eighties. When they experienced a serious illness, they succumbed more quickly, often cared for at home in familiar surroundings and with loved ones present.

Today, old age is characterized by chronic rather than acute conditions. Coping with illness and disability is often extended. While many children provide care and support to their parents, there are parents whose children live hundreds, if not thousands, of miles away. Caregiving children may be employed outside the home and have children of their own, or they may be elderly themselves and be dealing with their own health issues. It is not uncommon to see 70-year-olds caring for 90-year-old parents.

The health care system, which has extended life for many, has also increased in complexity. Skills adequate for accessing health care in earlier times may provide little help with current systems of care and reimbursement. The knowledge to deal with long-term illness or disability may be lacking.

It is easy to see that physical losses experienced by older adults are frequently accompanied by social, cultural, and psychological ramifications. Those elderly who experience emotional problems in our complex society may become isolated and withdrawn.

One kind of program that has been very helpful in breaking the downward spiral of withdrawal, depression, and isolation is the psychiatric day treatment program. This program can also provide information on physical disease processes, teach practical coping skills to those dealing with chronic conditions, and provide information about community resources and how to access the health care system effectively.

DEFINITION OF DAY TREATMENT

Day treatment should not be confused with daycare, which provides maintenance, supervision, and support for the frail elderly. Day treatment is a type of intensive outpatient psychiatric treatment, and it includes several modalities. It is often described as partial hospitalization and is reimbursed under Medicare. Day treatment programs must be hospital-based, and sessions must be at least 3 hours long to qualify for Medicare reimbursement. While socialization is an important part of treatment, Medicare does not reimburse for programs designed solely for this purpose. Typical geriatric day treatment programs include activity-oriented treatment as well as cognitive therapy and didactic sessions in a group format.

Medicare regulations require that day treatment services be prescribed by a psychiatrist and that the patient have a treatment plan that is periodically reviewed by the treatment staff and the psychiatrist (Cuyler & Galbraith, 1988). Medicare also requires that the patient's condition be treatable and that the primary diagnosis not be dementia. The patient must make progress during the course of treatment, and this must be documented in the medical record. For complete details on coverage and regulations, consult the local Medicare intermediary. Some private insurance companies will also cover day treatment, but coverage must be checked on a case-by-case basis.

THE ROLE OF OCCUPATIONAL THERAPY IN DAY TREATMENT

Occupational therapy's role in a geriatric day treatment program is to foster the development of competence in coping skills through planning for, participation in, and evaluation of purposeful goal-directed activities. These activities can include general activities, such as hobbies and arts and crafts, which can help to teach effective time usage in achieving a balance of work, rest, and leisure. More specific activities might include client assignments to research community resources and support systems. Exercise sessions can increase joint mobility and general strength and endurance. For individuals with specific deficit areas, training in activities of daily living (ADL) and instrumental activities of daily living (IADL) can be provided. Occupational therapy also helps clients (1) generalize skills learned during the therapy group and apply them to their specific circumstances and (2) gain insight into areas where additional coping skills may be needed. Group games can assist clients in clarifying their values and coping styles.

DEVELOPING A DAY TREATMENT PROGRAM

Referral sources and transportation are two critical factors to be considered when planning a new program. At least 1 month needs to be devoted to developing referral sources prior to implementation of the program. It is helpful to devise a comprehensive plan for contacting potential sources, with a specific number of contacts to occur monthly.

Families are a primary source of referrals, so it is helpful to consider what means of publicity could best alert families to the existence of a day treatment program and how it can benefit them.

Physicians can be a source of referrals, since they see many older patients, but this source requires development. Reimbursement is a question that is always raised by physicians and mental health professionals. It is helpful to advise them that day treatment is reimbursed under Medicare.

Other potential sources of referrals are case managers, aging services providers, substance abuse counselors, crisis workers, senior center staffs, ministers, adult daycare personnel, hospital staff, community and nursing home social workers, support group facilitators, and home health nurses. It is not always easy to locate appropriate clients. They tend to be isolated and withdrawn and thus not present in some of the more social settings where seniors congregate. If there is a network of aging services providers, become an active member; if there is not, consider starting one. Informal brown bag lunches once a month can be helpful in generating referrals and providing ideas for discharge plans.

Referral sources will want criteria for referrals. It is helpful to keep criteria to a minimum and somewhat nonspecific. Referred clients will need to be screened for appropriateness. It is often better to screen an inappropriate client and make recommendations for alternative treatment than to have potential clients screened out by the referring party. Potential referrers should be advised of major disqualifying factors, such as acute psychosis, longstanding mental health problems with inability to function, and severe cognitive impairment.

Home visits may be more time consuming when screening for admission, but older adults are often more comfortable meeting mental health personnel in their homes for the first time. The extra time spent in this phase will pay off in the reduction of inappropriate admissions.

Jargon and psychiatric terms should be avoided when interviewing potential clients. Elders attach a stigma to mental health treatment, and it is often best to downplay the mental health aspects of the program. Stressing that the groups help people cope with difficult transitions, such as strokes, bereavement, and retirement, is beneficial. Many clients refer to the groups as *classes*, and this is a term that is acceptable to most senior citizens.

There are several fears and misconceptions that are common among elders. It is helpful to be aware of them and consider them in marketing and screening activities. Common fears include being thought crazy, being locked up for being crazy, and being placed on addictive medications. The major misconception is that mental health treatment is a bunch of nonsense and that people should be able to get over problems by themselves.

Most mental health professionals prefer prospective clients to be motivated and have goals. Often older people will have unclear goals or no goals. It is common for them to come to treatment because a family member or doctor tells them to. Once they are in treatment, goals can be worked out with them. Prospective clients should not be screened out because they lack a clear idea of what they want or appear apathetic about the program.

ADMISSION TO THE PROGRAM

A psychosocial intake will be needed for admitted patients. The format and complexity of the intake will be dictated by local policies. The intake instrument does not need to be complex (see Exhibit 11-1).

It is helpful to have the client fill out a problem checklist (Exhibit 11-2). This gives the clinician a clearer picture of the client's concept of his or her problems. The problems that are picked can then be used in developing the client's treatment plan.

An occupational therapy assessment is also necessary when the client enters the program. A more general initial evaluation, carried out in an interview format, is the most beneficial in gleaning information about program participants. The assessment domains are included in Exhibit 11-3. If any deficits are noted that raise further questions, more detailed assessments can be given for those areas.

A psychiatric evaluation is necessary upon admission. The psychiatrist needs to be sensitive to the concerns and fears of elders. It is helpful to explain to clients that the psychiatric evaluation is necessary for Medicare reimbursement.

PROGRAMMING

The day treatment program provides experiences that promote increased feelings of mastery; stress management; management of transitions, loss, and grief; accessing of community resources; exploration of leisure skills; communication skills; identification and validation of feelings; education about the aging process, chronic illness, depression, and relapse prevention; self-esteem; a reduction in negative self-talk; and coping skills for dealing with family and significant others.

All of these areas are addressed by the occupational therapist through application of purposeful activities. Given the kind of depression that often afflicts geriatric patients, it may be easier for these patients to participate in a group project whose purpose is to produce something for others. Mobiles may be designed and created for an inpatient pediatric unit, or a group quilt may be made into a wall hanging for the day treatment area. Making something for themselves seems much more difficult and overwhelming for many participants.

Exhibit 11-1 Sample Psychosocial Intake Form

HOPE Day Treatment Program
Psychosocial Intake Assessment

Age _____ Referral Source _____

Information Provided by _____

Current Situation (living arrangements, employment, legal problems, social problems, etc.)

Presenting Problem and History of Presenting Problem

Substance Use/Abuse

Assaultive/Suicidal Ideation/Behavior

Past Psychiatric History

Medications Past and Present

Personal Development and Family History (including work/education history)

Health/Medical Conditions

Mental Status Examination (including physical description)

Leisure Activities and Interests

Significant Findings/Impressions

Goals of Therapy and Rationale for Recommended Modality of Treatment

_____   _____
          Signature and Title   Date

As progress is made and feelings of self-worth and competence increase, individual projects can be incorporated into the program. These projects can supplement activities such as games, arts and crafts, group activities (e.g., poetry or planning for a group reunion), memory and brain teaser activities, self-esteem activities (such as "warm fuzzies" or "positive attributes"), sing-alongs, lectures, research into community resources and support systems, and community outings. The types of activities incorporated are limited only by the participants' interests and the therapist's imagination.

Since investigaton of a participant's leisure interests is a part of the initial evaluation process, stated areas of interest should be focused on first. Later,

Exhibit 11-2 Problem Checklist

Please put an X in front of those problems that you would like to work on in the HOPE Day Treatment Program:

1. _____ Lonelines
2. _____ Isolation
3. _____ Lack of meaningful activities
4. _____ Depression
5. _____ Anxiety
6. _____ Grief
7. _____ Feeling overwhelmed
8. _____ Lack of knowledge about community resources
9. _____ Feeling helpless and hopeless
10. _____ Stress
11. _____ Difficulties with my family
12. _____ Worries about my health

List any other problems you would like to work on:

13. _____
14. _____
15. _____
16. _____

What would you like to change about your life?

_____
_____
_____

_____
Name

_____
Date

related areas can be incorporated to increase the base of leisure skills and promote feelings of competence and self-worth. Depression is often a factor for the elderly, so some may have difficulty identifying areas of interest. Extensive questioning about past interests, using an interest checklist to elicit information, can be helpful. A large and varied selection of activities should be available for the patient's choice.

Exhibit 11-3 Occupational Therapy Assessment Domains

1. Identifying information (name, date of birth, admission date, diagnosis, etc.)
2. Physical systems
   - Past medical history
   - ROM, strength, coordination, sensation
   - Ambulation/mobility
   - Hearing/vision
   - Precautions/restrictions
3. Cognitive systems
   - Memory, short and long term
   - Attention span
   - Task organization
   - Problem solving
4. Activities of daily living
   - Personal, self care
   - Home management skills
   - Community skills
   - Transportation
5. Psychosocial systems
   - Support systems: family and friends
   - Interaction styles
   - Coping mechanisms
6. Social and work history
   - Attitudes toward disease/disability
   - Attitudes toward aging
   - Work history
   - Retirement history
   - Relationship history
7. Leisure interests and activities
   - Past
   - Current
   - Future

AREAS OF FOCUS

The 10 major areas that geriatric day treatment programs need to address will be described briefly. Typical comments indicating problems in each area will be presented. Applicable theories and techniques will be suggested for each issue, and activity ideas will be offered.

1. Empowerment and Feelings of Mastery

There is no clearly defined role for elderly people in American society. In addition, many elderly women were socialized to be powerless. Consequently, many of the elders participating in day treatment programs will exhibit symptoms of powerlessness and may have learned that a way to get attention is to assume the patient role.

Client Comments	Theories and Techniques
"I don't like it where I live, but I have to live there. It's close to my daughter."	Learned helplessness (Seligman, 1975)
"There's nothing I can do."	Assertiveness training (Bower & Bower, 1976; Jakubowski & Lange, 1978)
"My doctor (son, wife, daughter) doesn't listen to me. I wish things were different."	

Activities

Clients write the first five things that come to mind to complete three sentences: "I have to _____," "I try to _____," and "I wish _____." The group can then discuss the feelings generated by the three sentences (e.g., "How does it feel to have to do something?"). The group then crosses out "I have to" and replaces it with "I choose to." "I try" is replaced with "I will," and "I wish" by "I want." Group discussion then centers around the difference between the feelings generated by the new sentences and the old. Discussion can also focus on the difference it makes when one takes responsibility ("I choose") rather than seeing oneself as a victim ("I have to"). If appropriate, goals can be developed for accomplishing some of the wants, or group members can be assisted in making different choices or setting different priorities.

2. Managing Transitions

Grief and loss are major issues for many older adults. Typically, elderly clients will take a fatalistic view of their losses and not be aware of the need to mourn losses other than those that occur through death. A person's losses may include his or her job, spouse, friends, home, life style, income, pets, health, and independence (e.g., loss of driver's license or physical impairment).

Client Comments	*Theories and Techniques*
"I miss my husband. He's been gone for 5 years and my life hasn't been the same."	Kubler-Ross's stages of dying (Kubler-Ross, 1969)
"I just don't have the interest in things I used to. Back home I was always busy, but now that I've moved near my sons, I don't have any pep."	Object relations theory (Blanck & Blanck, 1986)
"I had to retire. That's just the way it is. There's nothing I can do."	

Activities

Often elders take a fatalistic view of losses, especially losses such as a person's driver's license, home, or income. It may be useful to use Kubler-Ross's stages to generate a discussion of mourning. A graphic illustration of the effects of a loss can be provided by a pie chart. Each person creates a "pie" with pieces made up of various aspects of his or her life prior to the loss (work, family, church, etc.). Those areas affected by the loss are erased, illustrating that loss leaves a psychic wound. Discussion can then turn to feelings generated by the loss, ways to compensate for the loss, or ways to meet some of the needs previously met by whatever (or whoever) was lost.

3. Understanding Depression and Aging

Depressive disorders account for 51.1% of the admissions of those 65 and older to private psychiatric hospitals (Redick & Taube, 1980). "Two to 14% of elderly people who live in the community have major depression; in addition approximately 15% have at least mild depression. . . . Depression remains the most frequent reason for psychiatric hospitalization in patients over 60 years old. Over 40% of psychiatric admissions for geriatric depression are having their first episode of psychiatric illness" (Holt & Alexopoulos, 1989, p. 10). Elders however, often do not identify themselves as depressed. They frequently exhibit more of the somatic symptoms of depression than the affective ones. Many times older adults do not understand what is happening to them because of a lack of knowledge of depression. As a result, they will sometimes label themselves perjoratively as lazy.

Client Comments	*Theories and Techniques*
"I just don't have any interest in anything anymore. I don't understand it."	Beck's cognitive therapy of depression (Beck, 1979)
"I seem to have gotten lazy in my old age. I don't want to do the things I should."	Behavioral therapies
	Helmstetter's self-talk technique (Helmstetter, 1986)

Activities

The role of self-talk can be useful as a discussion topic. The group can make a list of all the things that they say to themselves when depressed. After group members run out of statements, the list is read aloud. Discussion centers on how hearing that list of statements makes the group members feel. The group then revises the statements to be more positive. When the new list is completed, it is read aloud, and the group can discuss the difference in feelings generated by the two lists. The importance of self-talk in worsening depression can also be discussed. Other areas of focus include brainstorming the symptoms of depression and correcting misconceptions, normal aspects of aging and misconceptions about aging, the use of medication in treating depression, the stigma attached to mental illness, and the difficulty others have in understanding the debilitation caused by depression. See the section on self-esteem (#10) for more on self-talk.

4. Stress Management

Stress is a subject that many elders are not knowledgeable about. They have little understanding of what it is and how it may affect them and their lives. The two aspects of stress management that apply most to the clients in day treatment are the need for balance in life and exercizing for relaxation.

Client Comments	*Theories and Techniques*
"My nerves are bad, I don't know why. I'm just nervous."	Theories about stress (Selye, 1974)
"I worry all the time."	Stress management techniques (Davis, McKay, & Eshelman, 1982)
"My stomach hurts" (or other examples of somatizaton).	

Activities

Discussions can be held about how stress affects the body, with group members suggesting various ways it does so. The physical consequences of prolonged stress and psychosomatic illnesses, the role of stress in exacerbating illness, and the balance or imbalance of work (chores) and fun in group members' lives are also good topics. Various relaxation exercises can be used with the group.

5. Dealing with the Family

Clients who come to day treatment often have longstanding conflicts with their children. These conflicts may have been apparent for a long time, or they may have been outside the client's awareness until increasing disability and dependence exacerbated them. Codependency, a concept from the addictions field, is helpful in working with elders and family conflicts. Many elders were socialized to be codependent—more aware of others' feelings, wants, and needs than their own.

Client Comments	Theories and Techniques
"I try to help my son. I know what he needs."	Codependency (Beattie, 1987; Schaef, 1986)
"My daughter doesn't understand how I feel."	Systems theory; family therapy (Satir, 1972)
"My children try to tell me how to lead my life. They act like they were my parents."	Object relations theory (especially helpful in understanding enmeshed families)

Activities

The group can be educated about codependency and its relationship to powerlessness and depression. A useful exercise involves helping group members look at the expectations that aging parents have of their children and the expectations the children may have of their parents. Often these expectations are unspoken and set older adults up to be disappointed. Reframing the reason for the children's behavior can also be useful. A statement such as "You're unhappy because you don't control the family now" can be seen as a child's explanation why the parent is no longer the vital person he or she once was. See information on the Karpman triangle in the communications section (#9).

6. Identification and Validation of Feelings

The current generation of elders were socialized to be concrete and deal with problems rather than with feelings. Thus, elders are often unaware of their own feelings or feel that they have no right to the feelings because of the situation. Anger at a spouse for being ill is a common example. It may take considerable modeling by the therapist to educate patients about their feelings and increase their ability to identify, validate, and express them.

Client Comments	Theories and Techniques
"I feel that she should not have done that" (expresses a thought, not a feeling).	Modeling and self-disclosure by therapist
"I can't be angry with my wife. It's not her fault she's ill."	Transactional analysis (James & Jongewald, 1971)

Activities

Brainstorming feelings can be helpful. A feelings game that poses situations and asks group members how they would feel can be useful. For example, "How would you feel in the following situations: (1) You're in a department store and the lights go out. (2) The person in front of you got the last one of the item you came shopping for. (3) Someone tells you that you are important to him (her)." This technique helps to identify commonalities and differences in people's reactions. It can also be useful to list and discuss possible thoughts, feelings, and actions in various situations. It may be necessary for the therapist to state how he or she would think, feel, and act to get the discussion started.

7. Learning about Community Resources

Day treatment clients may be unaware of the variety of resources available to them. They may benefit from resources for dealing with chronic illness, providing additional income, or finding jobs or volunteer work.

Client Comments	*Theories and Techniques*
"I would like to take a ceramics class but I don't know where to find one."	Exploratory behavior (Berlyne, 1950)
	Occupational behavior (Reilly, 1971)
"Being retired is driving me crazy. I don't know what to do with myself."	Adaptation (Smith, 1974)
	Competence (White, 1971)
"It's so hard not to be wanted. I wish I could be useful to someone again."	

Activities

Each group member can list what it is he or she misses most about a job (being important), a spouse (having someone to care about), a previous home (a particular social group). The members can then be assisted in locating local opportunities and resources to meet their needs. One member might be required to explore a local resource as a "pregraduation" exercise. Another member might be asked to visit a senior center close to home and report back to the group. Group discussions can center on such topics as the difficulty of going to a new place alone. Interest inventories and checklists may be useful for goal setting and discussion.

8. Leisure Skills and Having Fun

Many older adults coming to day treatment have little idea how to have fun. They have often spent their lives working or raising a family.

Client Comments	Theories and Techniques
"I have so much time on my hands that I don't know what to do with it."	Leisure inventories and checklists
"My friends do crafts to keep busy, but that never interested me."	Reminiscence
"I worked all my life. I'm just a working man."	

Activities

Reminiscence can be a useful means of getting clients to focus on leisure skills. Activities previously enjoyed in school, in early adulthood, or with one's children can be recalled. Clients can then be assisted in finding opportunities to become involved in similar activities or ones that use the same skills.

9. Communication Skills

Many of the problems older adults have with their families involve communication problems. Clients often expect that others should know how they feel or what they want. They frequently assume that they know what others want or feel as well. These assumptions can lead to major communication and family problems.

Client Comments	Theories and Techniques
"If he loved me, he'd know what I want."	Codependency
	Transactional analysis (Steiner, 1974)
"My children never call me. It would mean so much if they would call me once a week."	Assertiveness techniques (Bower & Bower, 1976)
	Role-play and modeling
"I couldn't tell him that. It would hurt him."	

Activities

Useful topics for discussion and role-playing include passive, aggressive, and assertive communication styles (the clients might write and practice assertive scripts); the difference between "you" messages and "I" messages; and what the clients' parents taught them about what is and isn't nice to say. Educating the group in the fundamentals of transactional analysis can help members see when there is crossed communication. The Karpman drama triangle (James & Jongewald, 1971) can be a useful tool for analyzing communication between group members and their families and between group members and the staff.

10. Increasing Self-Esteem

Some older adults come to day treatment with a lifetime of low self-esteem; others have developed low self-esteeem as a result of life events. Feeling unworthy and guilty are aspects of depression that contribute to a poor self-image.

Client Comments	Theories and Techniques
"I can't do anything right."	Beck's cognitive therapy of depression (1979)
"I don't think I can do it, but I'll try if you want."	
	Behavioral theories
"Why should anyone want to talk with me. I'm not very interesting."	Transactional analysis (Steiner, 1974)
	Helmstetter's self-talk technique (1986)
	Role-play and affirmations

Activities

Poker chips can be used to point out to group members how negative their conversation and thought processes are. During an activity group, the therapist hands each group member a white or red poker chip every 10 to 15 minutes with no explanation. White is used for positive comments and red for negative ones. At the end of the activity, group members can see how negative or positive their comments were. Using this exercise once can be enough to make clients who tend to be negative aware of their negativity and assist them in beginning to turn their attitude around. Group discussions can also focus on topics such as names and nicknames clients were called as children, what clients' parents said about them, and how the "parent tapes" in a person's head (transactional analysis) affect the person's feelings about him- or herself.

PROBLEMS AND CHALLENGES IN GERIATRIC TREATMENT

Participants in this type of program have been operating in their behavior patterns for many years. Expecting dramatic or extreme changes can be frustrating for the therapist and unfair to the clients. It is more realistic to plan on an increase in knowledge regarding community resources, disease processes, and methods of attaining needed health care; increased skill in coping with family members and significant others; an improvement in self-esteem; and a decrease in feelings of helplessness and hopelessness or depression.

On the whole, the older population is reluctant to enter mental health programs. Psychological sophistication is not a common characteristic of a population that grew up or were young adults during the Depression, when attitudes of personal independence and strength were valued. Seeking help for personal problems was frowned upon. Needing help in these areas implies weakness or a moral flaw. Their lack of knowledge of the health care system and how to access it poses an additional challenge.

These challenges are most successfully overcome by using nonpsychiatric language and by focusing on the desire of clients to remain independent for as long as possible. Once in treatment, clients need to be taught about the therapeutic process and how to identify and express feelings. Also, the aging process often involves physical disease components. When these are a part of the composite treatment picture, the treatment program must increase in complexity.

MANAGING CLIENT DEPENDENCY

It is not uncommon for group members to become dependent on the day treatment program to meet their needs for social contact, people to share feelings with, and a meaningful way to fill their time. This is not necessarily a problem. Clients have to become engaged with the group for the therapeutic process to work. A group member's dependence on the program and the staff may assist the staff in helping the client make a transition to other groups and to the community. As the client comes to know and trust the day treatment staff, he or she wants to please them. Consequently, the client may attend a senior center simply because the staff requested it and the client wants to please them.

A way of minimizing excessive dependence on the staff is for all staff members to assume that group members can do things unless there is proof to the contrary. Staff members should not do things for participants that the participants can do for themselves, nor should they allow other group members to assist those who can do for themselves. When in doubt, have the group member attempt the task.

A quarterly reunion is a useful way to help clients leave the group when they are dependent on it. The reunion provides reassurance to departing group members that they are still valued and may return without relapsing. Ideally, the reunion should include both current and former group members, which will provide current group members with the knowledge that there is "life after day treatment" and that others have left the group setting and done well. If the budget and the program philosophy allow, holiday observances might also include "old" group members.

It is helpful to provide departing clients with a graduation token. The HOPE (Helping Older People Emotionally) program often gives graduates a pin made of red and white poker chips as a reminder and a transitional object. HOPE also has a living quilt that includes a block from each person who has attended the program. This provides members with a sense of continuity and assures them that they will not be forgotten. HOPE graduates are told they are welcome to call the staff and let them know how they are doing; almost no one does, but it provides departing graduates with the knowledge that the staff doesn't stop caring when they walk out the door.

CONCLUSION

Older adults can benefit from psychotherapy when treatment modalities are adapted to their unique needs and life experiences. Elders do well with cognitive therapies and didactic methods of treatment. A partial hospitalization or day treatment program provides a structured and safe setting in which they can practice new skills and gain support from peers.

REFERENCES

Beattie, M. (1987). *Codependent no more*. New York: Harper & Row.

Beck, A.T. (1979). *Cognitive therapy of depression*. New York: Guilford Press.

Berlyne, D.E. (1950). Novelty and curiosity as determinants of exploratory behavior. *British Journal of Psychology, 41*, 68–80.

Blanck, R., & Blanck, G. (1986). *Beyond ego psychology: Developmental object relations*. New York: Columbia University Press.

Bower, S., & Bower, G.H. (1976). *Asserting yourself: A guide for positive change*. Reading, MA: Addison-Wesley.

Cuyler, R.N., & Galbraith, J.T. (1988). *Insurance and partial hospitalization*. Washington, DC: American Association for Partial Hospitalization.

Davis, M., McKay, M., & Eshelman, E. (1982). *The relaxation and stress reduction workbook*. Oakland, CA: Harbinger.

Helmstetter, S. (1986). *What to say when you talk to yourself* [Audiotape]. Scottsdale, AZ: Grindle Audio.

Holt, J., & Alexopoulos, G.S. (1989). Depression and the aged. In R.G. Robinson & P.V. Rabins (Eds.), *Aging and clinical practice: Depression and coexisting disease* (pp. 10–26). New York: Igaku-Shoin.

Jakubowski, P., & Lange, A.J. (1978). *The assertive option*. Champaign, IL: Research Press.

James, M., & Jongewald, D. (1971). *Born to win*. Reading, MA: Addison-Wesley.

Kubler-Ross, E. (1969). *On death and dying*. New York: MacMillan.

Redick, R., & Taube, C. (1980). Demography and mental health care of the aged. In J.E. Birren & R.B. Sloane (Eds.), *Handbook of mental health and aging* (pp. 57–71). Englewood Cliffs, NJ: Prentice-Hall.

Reilly, M. (1971). The modernization of occupational therapy. *American Journal of Occupational Therapy, 25*, 243–246.

Satir, V. (1972). *Peoplemaking*. Palo Alto, CA: Science Behavior.

Schaef, A.W. (1986). *Co-dependence: Misunderstood, mistreated*. Minneapolis: Winston.

Seligman, M.E.P. (1975). *Helplessness: On depression, development and death*. San Francisco: W.H. Freeman.

Selye, H. (1974). *Stress without distress*. New York: J.B. Lippincott.

Smith, M.B. (1974). Competence and adaptation. *American Journal of Occupational Therapy, 38,* 11–15.

Steiner, C. (1974). *Scripts people live.* New York: Bantam.

White, R.W. (1971). The urge toward competence. *American Journal of Occupational Therapy, 25,* 271–274.

Chapter 12

Treatment Approaches for Patients with Dementing Illness

Barbara Szekais

Science continues to grope its way toward explanations and cures for the variety of progressive dementing illnesses that exist. In the absence of cures, families, friends, treatment staff, institutions, and society in general must deal with day-to-day management of patients with dementia who can no longer manage for themselves. Provision of treatment services and programs for these patients and their families presents special challenges and rewards for the occupational therapist.

This chapter discusses some of the unique problems in treatment provision, and it also discusses a range of treatment and program alternatives that can be used at home, in community settings, and in institutions. The purpose is to give the therapist an overview of the wide variety of treatment options that can be utilized in daily contacts with patients, families, and caregivers. An overview, however, can give only limited information on any one treatment approach. Therefore, a resource list for further exploration is provided at the end of the chapter.

TREATMENT INTERVENTION

The selection of appropriate treatment for patients with progressive dementing illness should be based on answers to four questions: (1) Which patient functions are deficient? (2) How can the deficits be treated or managed? (3) Who can provide the services? (4) At what point will the patient need those services? In short, what, how, who or where, and when?

The first question is answered through the assessment or evaluation process. To understand the patient's dysfunction and to promote better functional status, all spheres of function should be evaluated. All problems identified may not be controllable; however, having a good overview of the patient's functioning may help to explain puzzling and seemingly unrelated behaviors and may lead to better management.

The second question (how) is always difficult to answer when the cause or causes of a disease are not known. However, various treatment and management approaches for dementing illness have developed as a result of continuing multi-disciplinary efforts, and it is to the therapist's advantage to have as wide a repertoire of treatment approaches as possible to meet the changing needs and responses of the patient. Table 12-1 lists functional areas affected and major treatment approaches used in dementing illnesses.

The third and fourth questions concern the "who and when" of treatment. Because the patient's and family's needs will change over time, the ideal situation is a continuum of care (i.e., as wide a variety of services and providers as possible for a variety of need levels). It is this continuum that allows maximization of functioning at any given point in the progression of the illness. The ideal may not be the reality, however, and actual phases of care will depend on many factors: the family's history and social support systems, the family's finances, the patient's personality, the patient's rate of decline, cultural factors, and the availability of health and social services. Part of the role of the therapist is to be aware of available services and providers and to facilitate or support the transition from one phase of care to another.

Exhibit 12-1 attempts to put all four factors together. Division of the illness's progression into "early, middle, late" is to some extent arbitrary and suggests a predictable course, which may or may not be the case. Patients will follow varying progressions. Stages may be passed through quickly or slowly or in some cases may be skipped; skill retention or loss may not be orderly or predictable. Again, the observation and assessment skills of the therapist will be important in ensuring relevant treatment.

Entry into the health care system does not necessarily follow an orderly progression, either. The occupational therapist typically enters the care sequence somewhere in the middle phase, when the family is no longer able to provide total care for the patient. In the best case scenario, the therapist becomes involved earlier; this may happen when those diagnosing the patient are also aware of services available and when the family and patient are willing and able to access the services. However, in many cases, the patient and family will not have had the benefit of services in either the early or middle phases, and the therapist sees the patient in the final stages of the illness.

TREATMENT APPROACHES

The term *treatment* may be somewhat of a misnomer, in that many dementias are not presently curable. Rather, treatment, in such cases, is essentially manage-

Table 12-1 Patient Functional Areas and Possible Treatment Approaches

Functional Areas	Treatment Approaches
Cognitive Function	Counseling (early stages) Cognitive facilitation Environmental structuring Sensorimotor therapy Relaxation Structured communication Structured activities Self-care activities Intergenerational activities
Sensory-Perceptual Function	Physical aids (glasses, hearing aids) Environmental structuring Adaptive equipment and techniques Sensorimotor therapy Adjunctive therapies Structured activities
Affective Function	Counseling (early stages) Medications Relaxation Structured activities Structured socialization Spiritual expression Exercise and movement Milieu therapy Intergenerational activities
Social Function	Counseling (early stages) Structured socialization Structured activities Milieu therapy Adjunctive therapies Intergenerational activities
Language and Communication	Structured verbal and nonverbal communication techniques Cognitive facilitation Environmental structuring Behavior modification program
Self-Care Activities	Adaptive equipment and techniques Exercise and sensorimotor therapy Environmental structuring Milieu therapy Behavior modification program
Physical Health and Sleep	Relaxation Exercise and sensorimotor therapy Structured activities Medication monitoring Environmental structuring

continues

Table 12-1 continued

Functional Areas	Treatment Approaches
Nutrition and Elimination	Adaptive equipment and techniques
	Environmental structuring
	Behavior modification program
	Medication monitoring
	Exercise and movement
Motor Function	Environmental structuring
	Adaptive equipment and techniques
	Exercise and sensorimotor therapy
	Medication monitoring

ment of the problems produced by the illness, and treatment approaches are as varied as the illnesses they address. New approaches continue to develop, and existing approaches may be refined or rejected. Major approaches are discussed here, but these are certainly not the only approaches. The therapist is encouraged to pursue further reading and investigation and to become part of the evolution of new treatment concepts.

Evaluation

The first step in provision of appropriate services is evaluation. The basic tenet of evaluation in geriatrics is that the assessment should be comprehensive, and this applies to patients with dementia as well. Typically, the first evaluation is performed by the family physician. If the physician is astute, he or she will refer the patient on for more specialized evaluation, starting the process of differential diagnosis to rule out other possible functional and/or organic reasons for the patient's problems (this is critical, as some dementias are reversible). In larger urban areas, there may be geriatric assessment services available that are designed for a comprehensive, differential, interdisciplinary approach to treatment. In smaller communities and in rural areas, the process may be less comprehensive, limiting diagnostic accuracy. The cost of specialized assessment may be another limiting factor.

The occupational therapist's evaluation will vary depending on the setting, but in general it will include physical, sensory-perceptual, cognitive, psychosocial, and activities of daily living (ADL) skills. In addition to the evaluation and to information collected by other members of the treatment team, information contributed by family, friends, neighbors, church members, and so on is also valuable. The therapist may note which evaluations have not been done and may

Exhibit 12-1 Approximate Stages in the Progression of Dementing Illnesses

Early	Middle	Late
Functional Skill Loss		
cognitive functioning		
vocational functioning		
homemaking		
leisure and recreation		
affective functioning		
		physical health
		automatic movement and physical mobility
	personal self-care	nutrition
	language and communication	elimination
	sensory-perceptual functioning	
	sleep	
	voluntary movement	
social interaction		
community mobility		

Service Providers
family, friends
health care professionals
respite care
home health
adult daycare
adult family home
institution

Treatment Approaches
counseling
cognitive facilitation
relaxation
exercise
medications
spiritual expression

sensorimotor and general movement
environmental structuring
physical health care
personal self-care
socialization
structural activities
milieu therapy
intergenerational activities
adjunctive therapies
structural communication
behavior modificaton programs
problem behavior management

advocate that they be performed if potentially helpful for patient treatment or family support.

Physical Care, Supervision, and Monitoring

Good physical care involves daily management and monitoring of the patient's physical status. Hygiene, nutrition and hydration, minor and major illnesses, sleep, sensory function, elimination and continence, and dental and foot condition all can affect mental status as well as physical health. In the early stages, the patient can self-manage or help the caretaker manage most of these functions. As the disease progresses, the patient will need increasing assistance, and the likelihood of problems being overlooked or discounted will increase also. All members of the treatment team should be aware of the importance of good physical management and should help educate the caretaker or family so they know how to provide it and understand why it is necessary.

The best overall approach is to perform care and monitoring on a regular schedule or program. This establishes a psychological climate of continuity and predictability, assists in patient learning and performance, and establishes a routine schedule around which the caretaker can plan and carry out other activities. This schedule should approximate the patient's normal routine (where possible). Ideally, the schedule would alternate active and quiet times for the patient and provide the family caretaker with some "away" time.

Performance of basic hygiene on a daily basis plays an important role in preventing minor or major health problems, provides an opportunity to use prior learning and self-care skills, and can help the patient preserve a sense of control, competence, and continuity. Checkups for vision and hearing and for preventive physical, dental, and foot care should be scheduled routinely. Checkups need not always be performed by a doctor; often a home health nurse, public health nurse, senior center nurse, community health clinic, and so on can perform these checkups. As these visits should be routine, the patient and family can make use of whatever low- or no-cost alternatives exist in their community. Short- or long-term illnesses other than the dementing illness can also be monitored in this way. Illnesses that do occur should be treated immediately; the caretaker should be instructed in how to follow the treatment prescribed and to monitor for problems.

Loss of control over elimination and eating are not usually seen until the later stages of dementing illness. Elimination and continence are best dealt with through regular bowel and bladder programs, prompt treatment of urinary tract infections, adaptive clothing and hygiene aids, regular skin checks and skin care, behavior therapy programs, and possibly medication for retention or incontinence. Eating problems are discussed later in this chapter.

Sleep disruption is a particularly difficult problem for both the patient and the caretaker. Although the easiest approach is to use medication, it is also the least desirable. Medication does not produce deep REM sleep, can become habit-forming, can produce agitation and/or night arousal instead of sedation, can produce daytime lethargy, and can negatively interact with other medications. However, medicaton is often used due to a variety of factors not always under the caretaker's or staff's control. Management must be tailored to the individual patient, but often the best management combines a number of approaches, such as accurate diagnosis and treatment of physical illness, regular hours for meals and activities, reduction of daytime napping, increased daytime activity and exercise levels, evening activities, relaxation techniques, behavior modification programs, use of natural sleep inducers (warm milk, herbal teas, etc.), a structured and safe environment, low-level sensory stimulation during evening and night, and respite to ensure the caregiver gets sufficient sleep.

Medication Monitoring

Use of medications is common in cases of dementing illness. Medications may be given, for example, for depression (in the early stages), for memory function, for motor function, for sleep disturbance, and for problem behaviors. These are given in addition to any other drugs the patient may need for other physical problems.

However, the potential for adverse reactions and interactions is high, and the patient's response must be carefully monitored by all treatment team members and caretakers. This involves knowing which drugs the patient takes, the intended results, the potential side effects, potential interactions, the physical and behavioral manifestations of adverse reactions, and who to contact when adverse effects are apparent or suspected. The occupational therapist should also be aware of differences between usual adult doses and geriatric doses. This type of information can be gained through discussion with doctors, nurses, pharmacists, psychiatrists; through reading drug-related literature; and through attendance at courses and seminars dealing with prescription medication.

Unfortunately, inadequate staffing patterns can contribute to overuse of medications. This is true whether the "staffing pattern" refers to a single caregiver at home who has no opportunity for respite or a high patient:staff ratio in an institution. Inadequate personnel is one of the most difficult problems in long-term geriatric care, and it is reflective of our society's attitudes. Until this sociocultural stance is changed, health care workers with the elderly will have to wrestle—not always successfully—with the promise and problems of medications.

Respite Care

Respite care allows the home caregiver time out and the opportunity to attend to his or her own needs. Support for the care provider is a very important and integral part of treatment in cases where the family elects to care for the patient at home. Home care is the ideal situation, but it can deplete the resources of the most determined caregiver. Respite care helps the home caretaker maintain his or her own physical and mental health.

Inside the home, respite care can be provided by other family members, friends, church members, and hired caretakers. Outside the home, adult day health and daycare centers, adult family homes, hospitals, and nursing homes may be available for short-term care and supervision. The first critical element in respite care is to make sure that the respite caregiver has enough information about the patient to be able to interact positively with the patient and to deal with actual and potential problems. The second critical element is to provide support for the primary caregiver so that he or she does not feel guilty when taking time away. Ideally, respite should be part of the daily or weekly schedule of the patient and caregiver.

Socialization

The need for the patient to stay socially active must be emphasized in both home and institutional care. Social interaction has a profound effect on cognitive and affective functioning; appropriate behaviors cannot be developed or maintained without a social milieu to give feedback, both explicitly and implicitly.

Social isolation is a common problem for both the dementia patient and the caregiver. Initially, the patient can continue at least superficial interaction without assistance, but as the patient's illness progresses, it will become necessary for home or institutional caregivers to provide and structure opportunities for social contact. Family and friends may need information or education regarding how to interact with the patient and may also need some encouragement and support. The patient may need to attend structured activities and programs designed for social interaction at a variety of levels.

Family caregivers may need support and encouragement to pursue normal social situations, as they may feel guilty about caring for themselves while the patient is struggling with a catastrophic illness. Respite care will provide family caregivers the opportunity to seek normal social interaction, which will be needed more than ever due to the stress experienced by the family as a result of the patient's illness.

Spiritual Expression

Spiritual expression is, of course, an individual matter and must reflect the patient's own life pattern. For those patients who have held religious beliefs, the opportunity for religious expression can be a great comfort and a means to deal with their present experience. This may also be true for the family or caregiver.

While the patient can still respond appropriately, attendance at religious services is perhaps the best alternative. When this is no longer possible, other opportunities exist, such as small-group worship, pastoral visits, holy book readings, and pictorial representations (e.g., books, wall hangings, and calendars). Religious music also affords an excellent opportunity, including live presentations, records, and singing. These means of religious expression can be provided in more or less intensely structured group and individual situations at home, in day programs, and in residential facilities.

Counseling

Counseling may be an appropriate intervention in the early stages of dementia. For the patient still functioning at a relatively high level and able to comprehend his or her situation, a diagnosis of Alzheimer's or other irreversible dementing illness may cause reactive depression. The patient may benefit from counseling, either by itself or in conjunction with antidepressant medication.

Counseling may take the form of formal one-to-one sessions with a trained mental health professional who has had geriatric training and experience. Counseling occurs outside of formal situations, however, and it needs to, since the patient is likely to respond better to a more spontaneous, less threatening situation. Family, friends, the religious minister, the nurse, the therapist, the aide, the chore service worker—all can and have taken the role of confidant and supporter of the patient. Trust and rapport can be very therapeutic, but their effects are often unpredictable and they should not be forced. It is wise, therefore, to assist the person having the role of counselor to be aware of the nature of the patient's illness and needs (within the limits of confidentiality) and of the responsibilities and limitations of the counselor role.

Environmental Structuring

The basic purpose of environmental structuring is to compensate for functional deficits by rearranging or changing the patient's physical environment. Environmental structuring may include something as simple as hanging a wall calendar or as complex as architecturally redesigning a facility. Effective use of this approach depends on an understanding of the patient's deficits and an analysis of how the physical environment can enhance or replace lost skills. The use of environmental adaptation can be broadened to include not only physical functioning but also sensation and perception, memory, communication, and social interaction.

For example, the home and/or institutional environment can partially compensate for sensory-perceptual loss by providing "response facilitators": large print; better lighting; high-contrast coloring for geographical contour demarcation and for stimulation; soundproofing and visual blocks to eliminate distraction; semiaccessible and controlled food preparation areas to provide familiar cooking smells, tastes, and feels; tactilely varied and safe objects that can be handled; and so on. Memory aids can be built into an environment, such as wall calendars, daily schedules, seasonal decorations, name plates, pictures of significant others and significant events, familiar furniture, favorite memorabilia, pictures or facsimiles of favorite pets (e.g., stuffed cloth animals), and favorite music. Common areas can be structured for socialization so that patients mix and face each other, and they can be furnished with items such as soft pillows, afghans, music, warm drinks and snacks (access controlled), meaningful pictures, small pets or stuffed animals, and spots for personal knickknacks or memorabilia.

The home environment is the most familiar setting to the patient, but it may need adaptation just as much as semi-institutional and institutional environments. Each type of environment will present its own advantages and limitations, and none will be ideal. But the environment must be considered, because it is always the silent partner in any treatment efforts. The environment is a passive but powerful participant in shaping behavior, and its effects should not be underestimated. In designing a treatment program, the therapist must always evaluate the environment's ability to enhance or interfere with positive outcomes.

Milieu Therapy

The social environment also needs to be structured to enhance skills or to delay loss of skills, as functional skills that have no opportunity for practice will deteriorate, needlessly hastening the general decline of the patient. Milieu therapy looks at the nonphysical environment of the patient and seeks to restructure it in order to provide opportunities to support functional behaviors. Individual environments will present specific advantages and disadvantages, but each environment can usually provide some opportunity for skill practice.

The first step is to identify the range of tasks in which patients can be involved. These tasks will address a number of skill areas, including physical, cognitive, sensory, perceptual, affective, and social functioning. The tasks are then matched with a patient's needs, skills, and interests as closely as possible. The patient is given responsibility for chosen tasks and is given assistance as necessary for successful completion of the tasks. The patient-task match will need to be reviewed regularly and adjusted to correspond to changes in the patient's condition. A milieu therapy program can be limited or quite complex, depending on the patient's needs and the resources of the caregiver or the facility.

For example, to promote task performance in the home environment, the caregiver can be trained to work with the patient in the use of self-care adaptive techniques and equipment and in menthods of cueing and assisting the patient, which is preferable to doing everything for the patient. In an adult day center setting, a patient can be part of a group that makes new members feel welcome or can participate in assembling a newsletter. In a congregate care or skilled care facility, a patient may have responsibility for doing his or her own grooming or laundry, providing plant care, changing the calendar or date board, and so on.

Cognitive Facilitation and Stimulation

Cognitive facilitation covers a number of techniques. Some of these techniques deal purely with memory function and some deal with affective problems as well, because a patient's emotional state has a strong influence on memory and on cognitive function in general.

Environmental structuring (i.e., building memory aids into the environment) has already been discussed. An important further point to mention is that this technique is perhaps the most successful in the long run. Declining memory is a hallmark of progressive dementing illness, and the patient will have less and less ability to retain or recall information. Making information a permanent part of the patient's environment gives the patient ready access to that information and helps reduce frustration and anxiety.

For higher level patients, a cognitive stimulation group or one-on-one sessions may help to ease anxiety and allow practice of intact memory skills. Rote learning is usually not appropriate; old learning will provide a more successful experience. Tasks must be adapted to the functional level of the patient and may include material that taps long-term memory, such as well-known life facts or associative material (e.g., completion of partial song lyrics, proverbs, rhymes and poems, word pairs, etc.). The tasks may involve verbal and/or written responses and may be multisensory, stimulating visual, olfactory, gustatory, auditory, and tactile memory. Other cognitive skills, such as judgment, sequencing, language and spelling, math, and abstract thinking, may also be included when appropriate.

Modified reminiscing groups present the patient with a theme for discussion or a picture or object that is pertinent to the patient's life history (e.g., farm animals, old cooking implements, old photos, older clothing fashions, baby books, etc.). This technique usually involves physical objects that patients can see, hear, handle, taste, and/or smell while listening or discussing. The patient is encouraged or helped to verbalize, share, or just enjoy silently any memories that are elicited. Such experiences can help a patient rediscover missing parts of his or her personal history and can be used for both cognitive and affective dysfunction.

Remotivation is a somewhat similar technique used for withdrawn patients with both cognitive and affective disorders (Robinson, 1970). It is done in a very small group or, initially, one on one, is highly structured and repetitive, and initially places little demand on the patient for active participation and interaction. It is short, uses a well-defined beginning and end, and involves presentation and limited discussion of a theme that reflects an aspect of reality. The therapist may use the standard format for this technique or adapt it to fit a particular patient, setting, or general treatment program. The main goal of this approach is to bring a patient out of social isolation, which can have a devastating effect on cognitive functioning.

Reality orientation is a technique for multimodal (verbal, visual, written, pictorial, musical, etc.) presentation and reinforcement of basic orientation information. This can be refined for higher level patients or made quite simple for lower level patients. Through various repetitions, the patient is reminded of basic facts about him- or herself and the immediate environment. This technique can help on a very short-term basis to reorient and to relieve anxiety, but the patient may not be able to actively retain and recall the information. Expectation that the patient will be able to do so may only frustrate both patient and therapist. It is best to use reality orientation as part of a total program of cognitive facilitation and to build information aids into the environment.

Self-Care Activities

This is an area that needs emphasis when working with the patient's caregiver, as it is very easy for the caregiver to do these tasks for the patient. It is necessary to provide (1) the rationale for activities of daily living so the caregiver will understand their importance and (2) the adaptive techniques and equipment to help the patient continue to perform them. Performance of seemingly simple grooming, bathing, and dressing tasks provides sensory stimulation, gross and fine motor coordination practice, reinforcement of old learning, reality orientation, and reinforcement of self-image. These tasks can be done with the patient one on one or sometimes in a small group. They can be performed at a very simple level, such as one-on-one grooming, or at a complex level, such as a trip to the barber shop or beauty salon.

Leisure, Recreational, and Craft Activities

Leisure, recreational, and craft activities for the patient with dementing illness can be used as treatment goals in themselves or can be used as a means to achieve other goals. It is apparent that activities must be geared to the needs, skills, and interests of the patient. The range of activities can be as broad as the range for other populations, and the activities can be performed in a variety of settings.

The therapist, however, will need to be able to adapt the activities to a very wide variety of skill levels. The therapist will need to marshal sufficient assistance if working with a group, as the patients will often need individual assistance, and the therapist will have to pay special attention to safety and judgment factors. The therapist will also need to monitor the patients for atypical or adverse reactions to the activities, because the patients will not always be able to communicate problems or control atypical responses.

Movement, Exercise, and Sensorimotor Treatment

Except with very impaired or immobilized patients, movement in its various forms provides an activity patients can participate in. However, it is very demanding for the therapist, since movement can be very stimulating. The therapist must be constantly alert for both group and individual reactions.

Simple movement can help work off excess, undirected energy that shows up as agitation or pacing behavior. Walking can be performed as an activity in itself, as in a supervised walk around the neighborhood, a park, or lake, or it can be part of more goal-oriented activity, such as a visit to a market, museum, or arboretum. Other physical activity can be generated through ADLs, such as baking, cleaning, yardwork (these activities need to be structured to fit the patient's skill level).

Exercise offers a more focused approach to movement and requires a greater ability to comprehend verbal and visual directions, to sequence, and to motor plan. Planned exercise is an excellent way to practice all of these skills and can be adapted to a variety of patients. When a patient has difficulty performing the exercises, physical prompting and assistance can be given in a nonthreatening way using "partner" exercises with staff or more alert patients. Exercise can focus on single body parts or can use adapted or simplified sports or dance patterns and situations.

Sensorimotor treatment may include automatic and spontaneous movement, planned movement, and multisensory stimulation in a one-on-one or group session. When performed in a group format, opportunities for spontaneous and structured social interaction will also be present. In this kind of session, a variety of activities can be used, and it is best to follow a standard format. The therapist may want to follow a developmental or modified developmental sequence in presenting the activities. This kind of movement activity is the most stimulating and will have to be adapted according to the patients' varying abilities to tolerate this level of stimulation.

Relaxation

Relaxation may be used specifically when anxiety and agitation are present and may also be included as part of an overall program to address other problems, such as memory loss. Standard verbal and imagery techniques may be beyond the patient's grasp. Techniques need to include more nonverbal material, such as light massage of neutral body areas (if tolerated), quiet music, tapes of soothing environmental sounds, rocking chairs, slow-paced but repetitive movements, and car or van rides. Activities will need to be adapted to fit the patient's response and attention span.

Intergenerational Activities

In this particular approach, people of other age groups are made part of the patient's life. The assumption is that mixed age group experiences will be enjoyable, will mitigate social isolation, and will provide a more normal and familiar life experience. This assumption will be valid in many cases but not in others. Again, this particular approach must fit the patient's needs, interests, and life history.

Intergenerational activities can be scheduled on a regular basis (e.g., activities involving a nearby children's daycare center) or on a one-time-only basis (e.g., when scouting or church groups perform concerts, plays, or other activities). The activities can be purely passive and observational for the patient or can be structured to include varied levels of participation. In the case of a concert, the patient may simply listen, may sing along, may help prepare and pass out refreshments, or may be a member of a patient singing group.

Intergenerational activities can be rewarding when appropriate, and to ensure they are appropriate, the therapist will need to be familiar with the patient's skill and tolerance levels. Very young children can be energetic, exuberant, fast moving—and incomprehensible to an impaired patient. A roomful of children may contain too much stimulation and interaction for a patient, and the children will not understand the situation of the patient. On the other hand, older children and adolescents will be too reticent and may be embarrassed by odd behaviors.

Adjunctive Therapies

Adjunctive therapy covers a number of less often used therapeutic approaches—less used not because they are less effective but because families and treatment facilities face budget constraints. These approaches include horticultural therapy, music therapy, dance therapy, art therapy, and pet therapy. All these various therapies have something to offer the patient, and the activities can be adapted to a variety of functional levels. The occupational therapist is well advised to investigate these adjunctive therapies and incorporate into the treatment plan any of them that might be relevant to the patient.

Behavior Analysis and Behavior Therapy

Behavior analysis and therapy offer a relevant approach to influencing behavior and have been used in a variety of situations with cognitively impaired elderly patients. The principles of behavior analysis and behavior modification offer a powerful way to maintain positive behaviors and decrease negative behaviors. These principles are at work constantly in everyone's physical and social environment. Even when rational thought and verbal communication are impaired, these principles may still be able to shape behavior.

Fundamental concepts in behavior analysis and behavior therapy include operant and respondent conditioning, positive and negative reinforcement, acquired reinforcement, reinforcement schedules, reinforcement densities, discrimination, discriminative stimuli, generalization, shaping, backward and forward chaining, and extinction. There is much more to establishing an effective behavioral program than occasional provision of a positive reinforcer; unfortunately, it is beyond the scope of this chapter to provide a full description of behavior therapy and how to use it. If the therapist or other staff members do not have special training or experience in writing and implementing behavioral programs, a behavioral psychologist may be consulted.

SPECIAL PROBLEM AREAS

Communication

Nothing highlights the essential nature of human beings as social communicators more clearly than the loss of language ability. It is more than the patient's loss; it is a loss for significant others, for the treatment staff, and for all those who come in contact with the patient. The patient's declining ability to produce and comprehend language presents progressively greater obstacles to his or her care and management. While there is yet no way to reinstate language ability, communication with the patient can be structured to facilitate the exchange of basic ideas, wants, and needs (Bartol, 1979; Porter & Rasmussen, 1979).

Here are some suggested guidelines to follow in the realm of nonverbal expression and communication: Maintain relaxed posture when with the patient and move slowly. Approach the patient from the front (preferably) or from the side, not from the back. Be aware of a need for personal space, and don't stand too close. Wear bright colors. Maintain eye contact and use facial expressions. Also use gestures. Maintain an active listening stance and listening behaviors. Touch may be used in some cases, but carefully. Use a nonpersonal kind of touch, like a handshake, or let the patient use touch first.

In verbal communication, speak slowly and clearly, using a calm voice and even tone. Speak face to face, make sure the lips are in the patient's view. Use the patient's name, and introduce yourself. Use opening and closing statements. Simplify sentences, but use adult language. Give only one instruction at a time, and repeat if necessary. Use other forms of communication to reinforce the statement (visual, tactile), but use them carefully to avoid overload. Check for understanding; watch the patient's reactions. Don't use phrases like "Don't you remember . . . ?" or "I told you before." Give choices only when there is truly a choice; don't give choices if a "no" answer is not acceptable.

In receiving the patient's response, accept the patient's statement, no matter how it comes out. Try to restate the patient's message if it is garbled, and ask if it has been correctly interpreted. Don't reject, but reassure. Don't argue. Listen for key words. A visual aid book or picture board may be helpful.

Finally, generally be aware of cultural differences. Some patients may find some of the above suggestions offensive, depending on their cultural backgrounds. Also, be aware of your own mood and emotional state, as it may well be communicated to the patient.

Nutrition

Poor eating skills and resulting inadequate nutrition are problems frequently referred to the occupational therapist. An assortment of problems may be involved. Physical and perceptual deficits, such as sensory dysfunction, dyspraxia, dysarthria, dysphagia, and poor dentition, can in themselves present formidable obstacles to good nutrition. When these problems are added to such cognitive deficits as short attention span, distractibility, poor sequencing, poor judgment, and inability to comprehend directions, the patient is at very high risk for malnutrition.

For swallowing problems, direct treatment of swallowing dysfunction, if and when appropriate, will utilize standard swallowing therapy techniques that may have to be modified on an individual basis. Invasive measures such as feeding tubes may ultimately be necessary in some cases, but in others the patient may be able to attain more functional oral-motor performance.

For self-feeding and eating behavior problems, varied approaches can be used. It is important to provide a conducive environment: quiet, homelike, separated from visual distraction, with perhaps some of the patient's personal effects or some favorite quiet music. Positioning equipment and appropriate table and chair heights will assist in improving physical function. Adaptive equipment should be utilized as necessary, such as divided plates, nonskid mats, two-handled cups, and covered cups and glasses.

When possible, the patient can be involved in selecting his or her own menu items. The patient can also be involved in general food preparation activities or in his or her own meal preparation. If the patient wears dentures, glasses, or a hearing aid, these should be used at meals. There should be continuity in the people assisting the patient to eat, and the patient should be given sufficient time to eat.

Adaptive techniques can be used, such as physical hand-over-hand assistance, reducing the number of food items or utensils presented at one time, and sequencing food item presentation. Verbal instruction should be simplified, and the instructor's manner should be calm, assuring, and accepting. Behavior modification programs can be helpful in this area.

If the patient is on a mechanical soft or puree diet, it may be possible to substitute a diet of soft but more recognizable foods, such as sandwiches with soft fillings, hard-boiled eggs, partially cooked and soft vegetables pieces, soft fruit pieces, french fries, pasta dishes, casseroles, fish, and desserts (Nangeroni & Pierce, 1983). Such food items will be visually more meaningful, more attractive, tastier, and more motivating. If the patient has difficulty manipulating utensils, many of the above items can be eaten as finger foods, allowing the patient more independence and more control.

Formal eating programs may be developed for individual patients, and these patients may be grouped into a larger eating program. If someone other than the therapist is the primary provider of mealtime assistance, education will be paramount; the eating assistant needs to understand the program in order to carry it out. In a semi-institutional or institutional setting, a larger eating program needs to be multidisciplinary and multidepartmental, with responsibility shared among different personnel, so that everyone is invested in the program's success.

Assaultive, Belligerent, or Angry Behaviors

With these difficult behaviors, it is important to have both short-term and long-term management strategies. In the short term, as the individual incident is occurring, it is necessary first to interrupt the behavior. Stay calm and reassuring, both in tone of voice and in manner, but state clear limits to the patient in short, simple sentences that deflect the patient's attention. Don't try to engage the patient in conversation or explanation or in another activity. Take the patient to a quiet place and reduce the amount of stimulation. The patient may tolerate being taken by the hand (preferably) or by the arm. It may require more than one person to lead the patient physically away from the disturbing environment; if so, both or all assistants should be firm but calm and reassuring. Someone should then stay with the patient until he or she is calm, preferably someone familiar and acceptable to the patient. Medication should be used only in extreme cases as a last resort. Those who are part of the patient's environment should be trained in these steps so that they can intervene quickly and effectively.

Understanding problem behaviors is the solution to managing or reducing them in the long run. Angry, explosive behavior is often a protective reaction to perceived threats in the patient's environment, and it is necessary to try to understand the behavior from the patient's point of view. When disruptive incidents begin to occur more frequently, it is important to look for causal factors and for patterns that can be addressed or interrupted. For example, is the patient suffering from a medical problem that he or she cannot communicate? Is the patient suffering from sensory deprivation, overstimulation, or perceptual dysfunction? Has there been a change in the physical environment or in the patient's routine? Is there something in the staff's or caretaker's nonverbal behavior? Is there something (or someone) that the patient perceives as threatening? Does the patient have fluctuating anxiety levels? Are the behavioral demands placed on the patient too high? Is the patient frustrated by his or her inability to communicate and by the resulting social isolation? Has the patient lost some vital social contact?

Management strategies for individual behaviors will depend on the causal factors involved. In addition to using specific strategies to address individual factors, it is sometimes helpful to use general strategies, including increasing verbal and nonverbal communication with the patient at times when behavior is appropriate, respecting territoriality (e.g., the patient's personal space or his or her room and belongings), maintaining a consistent physical and social environment, modifying situations as necessary (e.g., increasing or decreasing stimulation), providing a consistent routine, being aware of cultural factors and respecting them, using behavioral modificaton programs as appropriate, and providing adequate training for all involved in those programs.

Restlessness and Irritability

These behaviors are less extreme and abrupt, but also require some detective work on the part of the caregiver. They often indicate that the patient is trying to communicate some need or concern. The patient's physical condition needs to be investigated to determine whether there is a problem with vision, a foot condition, a dental condition, hunger, a fever, a headache, or some other pain or illness. The patient may simply need more physical activity and exercise. The patient's emotional state may be the cause (e.g., a loved one may not have paid a regular visit or an important anniversary may be at hand). The physical environment may need modification in some way, or the social environment may contain an irritating stimulus.

If the behavior's cause is not easily perceived or resolved, then management or change of the behavior becomes a long-term process necessitating more comprehensive intervention, such as behavioral therapy. However, it may be more fruitful to consider whether the behavior really needs to be changed; perhaps it is possible for the caregiver to accept and adapt to the behavior. Modification of staff or caretaker behavior is often just as necessary as modification and management of patient behavior.

Wandering

Wandering may have identifiable causes, such as a patient's desire to find a meaningful place or person from the past, a patient's need for security, or a patient's wish to perform previous work or roles (Snyder, Rupprecht, Pyrek, Brekhus, & Moss, 1978). Wandering may result from the need to "walk off" excess energy or anxiety, or it may be a reaction to the environment. Here also analysis of patterns and causes may assist in understanding and managing the behavior.

In cases of persistent wandering, management starts first with staff or caretaker acceptance of the behavior and with training in how to deal with it. Wandering in itself is not injurious to the patient; the problem may be more other people's perception of the behavior than the behavior itself. Second, the wandering behavior needs a physical environment that can accommodate it. The environment needs to provide (1) enough space for walking; (2) some areas that provide contact with others, even if incidental and passing; (3) familiarity; (4) some nooks and areas that provide privacy and a chance for exploration and discovery; (5) indoor and outdoor space; (6) safety; (7) orientation cues; and (8) absence of obvious restraints, such as padlocks on doors, and absence of loud, noxious alarms. Other opportunities for movement and activity should also be present, such as exercise sessions and supervised outings, recreational and "work" activities, adapted sports, relaxation sessions, or other possible activities. The environment may also contain patient-controlled opportunities for movement, such as rocking chairs.

Other Problem Behaviors

Sleep disturbance and bowel or bladder incontinence are problems that have already been discussed in previous sections. Management approaches suggested in this section may also be helpful in dealing with dysfunctional sleep and elimination. Other problem behaviors may include secretive behaviors (such as hiding one's own or others' belongings), delusions or hallucinations, inappropriate sexual behavior, and miscellaneous bizarre behaviors.

All recurrent problem behaviors need to be analyzed to see if there is some causal factor: Is it functional behavior in some way? Is it communication? If these questions are not readily answered, then it is necessary to ask if the behavior really needs to be changed or if it is possible for the caretaker to adapt to the behavior. Answers to these questions are certainly not easy to find. Investigation, analysis, observation, and treatment suggestions require the cooperation of all who are part of the patient's environment.

SPECIAL CHALLENGES FOR THE THERAPIST

The first challenge is presented by the impact of the global and progressive nature of impairment on the therapist's ability to understand and relate to the patient as a person. Therapists frequently deal with multiple handicaps, yet many patients do not experience global progressive decline and will retain some sphere of intact functioning. There is at least minimal interaction with the therapist and that interaction represents a constant and will be used as a basis for establishing communication and for forming a concept of that patient as a person.

With a patient in the later stages of dementia, the therapist may not have the luxury of such interaction. Part of the therapist's role may be to help the patient and others form and reform a concept of the patient as a person. In order to do that, the therapist will need to discover how to meet the patient at the patient's own level, a level which will change over time and cannot be taken for granted. The therapist will need to be willing to discover the patient's past identity and to integrate that identity with the present. The therapist will need to draw upon family, friends, life artifacts, and mementos—whatever may help reconstruct the patient's identity and assess and enhance the patient's present functional level.

This is perhaps the most painful loss in progressive dementing illness, the loss of the patient's identity and sense of self, the loss of the patient's life history. It is a loss for the patient, family, friends—and for treatment staff as well, as identity forms the basis for any therapeutic relationship. It requires great skill on the part of the therapist, as well as intuition, acceptance, flexibility, and compassion, to help the patient bridge the terrible gap between self and nonself.

The second challenge is to compensate for the reduced opportunity for the more usual types of positive reinforcement when working with the patient. From a short-term perspective, the usual give-and-take of verbal and nonverbal communication may be missing: the social exchanges, the eye contact, the "thank you's," the smiles, the feeling of having connected with someone. From a long-term perspective, it may not always be possible to measure progress in the usual sense, set goals in the usual way, or work toward new skill development. The therapist may have to redefine his or her own sources of personal reinforcement and outlets of positive feedback; it is incumbent upon the therapist to be clear as to what his or her sources of positive reinforcement are and to make sure that those sources are in place and functioning.

The therapist may have to redefine, for him- or herself and for others, what constitutes a valid outcome of intervention when traditional "improvement" is not a possibility. Decline, for example, does not a priori signal lack of improvement in this population. Rather, improvement is relative, with a slower rate of functional loss representing improvement in comparison to a faster rate of loss. Improvement may be seen in a family's increased coping skills and acceptance in managing a dementia victim at home or, conversely, in the willingness of a family to finally accept nursing home placement. Improvement may be seen in more frequent visits from friends and members of a patient's traditional support system.

The third challenge is for the therapist to be aware of him- or herself, to know his or her attitudes, needs, expectations, and emotional states. The therapist will be called upon for flexibility and adaptability, for empathy, for knowledge, and for support. The role of the therapist can vary widely from patient to patient, and the therapist may not be able to fall back on the comforting limits of prescribed therapeutic roles or easily available definitions and supports. When the therapist must provide more of the background for therapeutic intervention, the therapist needs to be able to depend more on him- or herself, to know just how much he or she has to give and where personal limits are.

The fourth challenge is to deal with the patient's inability to engage in full-fledged decision making. The extent to which the patient can actually make decisions depends on the severity of the illness. When possible, patient decision making should be supported, just as with any other type of patient. However, the progressive nature of the illness will necessitate the transfer of decision making to others—often to the family, often to the treatment staff. Good treatment requires the therapist to be assertive and use good judgment in making treatment decisions for the patient. It also requires working with family, friends, or caretakers, supporting them as they also assume the decision-making role. It is a difficult transition to make, but it is not good treatment to offer a false choice when no choice is available or when the patient cannot make sound judgments.

The last challenge to be discussed here arises as a result of the great variety of impairment and functional levels within each individual patient and within each group of patients. An individual patient's functioning may be quite different from one day to the next or from one month to the next. A group of patients may contain a wide variety of functional levels if the therapist does not have the luxury of sufficient staff or a sufficient number of patients to separate group members by functional level. Since much of this fluctuation cannot be anticipated completely, the therapist will need a large store of ideas and alternatives relevant to a variety of levels. In addition, the therapist will need a lot of flexibility, good humor, patience, and keenness of observation.

It is these qualities—flexibility, good humor, patience, and keenness of observation—that will help the therapist find the kind of satisfaction in working with the patients and their families that therapy at its best can offer. At times, the therapist will find the treatment suggestions offered here to be helpful. At other times, the therapist will find that discovering and sharing his or her own ideas, efforts, beliefs, and intuitions will be the most helpful and the most rewarding.

REFERENCES

Bartol, M. (1979). Non-verbal communication in patients with Alzheimer's disease. *Journal of Gerontological Nursing, 5*(2), 21–31.

Nangeroni, J.B., & Pierce, P.S. (1983). Development of a geriatric diet through behavioral observation of feeding behaviors of regressed and severely demented patients. *Journal of Nutrition for the Elderly, 3*(2), 25–40.

Porter, J., & Rasmussen, T. (1979). *Developing a working relationship.* Fort Steilacoom, WA: Western State Hospital.

Robinson, A.M. (1970). *Remotivation technique: A manual for use in nursing homes.* Washington, DC: American Psychiatric Association.

Snyder, L.H., Rupprecht, P., Pyrek, J., Brekhus, S., & Moss, T. (1978). Wandering. *The Gerontologist, 18*, 272–280.

RESOURCE LIST

Physical Care

Carstensen, L.L, & Edelstein, B.A. (Eds). (1987). *Handbook of clinical gerontology.* New York: Pergamon Press.

Foley, J.M., Cassel, C.K., Eastman, P., Fleiss, J.L., Fuld, P.A., Jarvik, L.J., Kelly, J.F., Kurland, L.T., Moossy, J., Moses, H., Obecny, J.S., & Perry, L.L. (1988). Differential diagnosis of dementing disease. *Alzheimer's Disease & Related Disorders, 2*(1), 4–15.

Gwyther, L.P. (1985). *Care of Alzheimer's patients: A manual for nursing home staff.* Washington, DC: American Health Care Association and the Alzheimer's Disease and Related Disorders Association.

Hall, G.R. (1988). Care of the patient with Alzheimer's disease living at home. *Nursing Clinics of North America, 23*(1), 31–46.

Volicer, L. (1988). *Clinical management of Alzheimer's disease.* Gaithersburg, MD: Aspen Publishers.

Family Care and Management

Mace, N.L., & Rabins, P.V. (1981). *The 36-hour day.* Baltimore: Johns Hopkins University Press.

McDowell, F.H. (Ed.). (1980). *Managing the person with intellectual loss (dementia or Alzheimer's disease) at home.* White Plains, NY: Burke Rehabilitation Center.

Powell, L.S., & Courtice, K. (1983). *Alzheimer's disease: A guide for families*. Reading, MA: Addison-Wesley.

Respite Care and Support

Aronson, M.K., & Yatzkam, E.S. (1984). Coping with Alzheimer's disease through support groups. *Aging, 347*, 3–9.

Dye, C.J., & Richards, C.C. (1980). Facilitating the transition to nursing homes. In S.S. Sargent (Ed.), *Non-traditional therapy and counseling with the elderly* (pp. 100–115). New York: Springer.

Mace, N.L., & Rabins, P. (1984). Day care and dementia. *Generations, 9*, 41–44.

Sands, D., & Suzuki, T. (1983). Adult day care for Alzheimer's patients and their families. *The Gerontologist, 23*, 21–23.

Zarit, S., Orr, N., & Zarit, J. (1985). *The hidden victims of Alzheimer's disease: Families under stress*. New York: New York University Press.

Counseling

Herr, J., & Weakland, J.H. (1979). *Counseling elders and their families*. New York: Springer.

Reifler, B., Larson, E., Teri, L., & Paulson, M. (1986). Dementia of the Alzheimer's type and depression. *Journal of the American Geriatrics Society, 34*, 855–859.

Shuttleworth, E.C., et al. (1987). Depression in patients with dementia of the Alzheimer's type. *JAMA, 79*, 733–736.

Storandt, M. (1984). *Counseling and therapy with older adults*. Boston: Little, Brown.

Socialization

Lester, P.B., & Baltes, M.M. (1978). Functional interdependence of the social environment and the behavior of the institutionalized aged. *Journal of Gerontological Nursing, 4*(2), 23–27.

Mueller, D.J., & Atlas, L. (1972). Resocialization of regressed elderly residents: A behavioral approach. *Journal of Gerontology, 27*, 390–392.

Snyder, L.H. (1978). Environmental changes for socialization. *Journal of Nursing Administration, 8*, 44–50.

Voelkl, D. (1978). A study of reality orientation and resocialization groups with confused elderly. *Journal of Gerontological Nursing, 4*(3), 13–18.

Spiritual Expression

Hendrickson, M. (Ed.). (1985). *The role of the church in aging*. New York: Haworth Press.

Vayhinger, J.M. (1980). The approach of pastoral psychology. In S.S. Sargent (Ed.), *Non-traditional therapy and counseling with the elderly* (pp. 199–213). New York: Springer.

Environmental Structuring

Batty, J. (1988, December 15). Alzheimer's center uses environment to bring life to clients. *OT Week*, pp. 16–18.

Kiernat, J.M. (1982). Environment: The hidden modality. *Physical & Occupational Therapy in Geriatrics, 2*(1), 3–12.

Liebowitz, B., Lawton, M.P., & Waldman, A. (1979). Evaluation: Designing for confused elderly people. *American Institute of Architects Journal, 68*(2), 59–61.

Skolaski-Pellitteri, T. (1983). Environmental adaptations which compensate for dementia. *Physical & Occupational Therapy in Geriatrics, 3*(1), 31–44.

Skolaski-Pellitteri, T. (1984). Environmental intervention for the demented person. *Physical & Occupational Therapy in Geriatrics, 3*(4), 55–59.

Milieu Therapy

Coons, D.G. (1978). Milieu therapy. In W. Reichel (Ed.), *Clinical aspects of aging* (pp. 115–127). Baltimore: Williams & Wilkins.

Griffin, R.M., & Mouheb, F. (1987). Work therapy as a treatment modality for the elderly patient with dementia. *Physical & Occupational Therapy in Geriatrics, 5*(4), 67–72.

Laurence, M.K., & Banks, S.I. (1978). Milieu therapy: A role for the occupational therapist consultant. *Canadian Journal of Occupational Therapy, 45*(4), 171–173.

Lester, P.B., & Baltes, M.M. (1978). Functional interdependence of the social environment and the behavior of the institutionalized aged. *Journal of Gerontological Nursing, 4*(2), 23–27.

Storandt, M. (1978). Other approaches to therapy. In M. Storandt, H.C. Siegler, & M.F. Elias (Eds.), *The clinical psychology of aging* (pp. 277–293). New York: Plenum Press.

Szekais, B. (1985). Using the milieu: Treatment-environment consistency. *The Gerontologist, 25*(1), 15–18.

Cognitive Facilitation and Stimulation

Capuano, E. (1986). Design and implementation of memory improvement classes in the adult day care setting. In P. Foster (Ed.), *Therapeutic activities with the impaired elderly* (pp. 111–116). New York: Haworth Press.

Carroll, K., & Gray, K. (1981). Memory development: An approach to the mentally impaired in the long-term care setting. *International Journal of Aging & Human Development, 13*(1), 15–35.

Holden, U.P., & Woods, R.T. (1982). *Reality orientation: Psychological approaches to the confused elderly*. Edinburgh: Churchill-Livingstone.

Hughston, G.A., & Merriam, S.B. (1982). Reminiscence: A nonformal technique for improving cognitive functioning in the aged. *International Journal of Aging & Human Development, 15*, 139–149.

Kerr, J., & Pratt, C. (1982). "Back-to-the-farm": Stimulating reminiscence and interaction among the institutionalized elderly. *Activities, Adaptation, & Aging, 3*(1), 27–35.

Zarit, S.H., & Zarit, J.M. (1982). Memory training for severe memory loss: Effects on senile dementia. *The Gerontologist, 22*, 373–377.

Activities

Goldberg, R.T. (1985). Alzheimer's disease: From benign neglect to community living. *Rehabilitation Literature, 46*(5-6), 122–132.

Killeffer, E., Bennett, R., & Gruen, G. (1984). Physical activity programs. *Physical & Occupational Therapy in Geriatrics, 3*(3), 7–35.

Killeffer, E. Bennett, R., & Gruen, G. (1984). Rehabilitation programs. *Physical & Occupational Therapy in Geriatrics, 3*(3), 37–69.

Mace, N.L. (1987). Principles of activities for persons with dementia. *Physical & Occupational Therapy in Geriatrics, 5*(3), 13–27.

Sandman, P.O., Norberg, A., Adolfsson, R., Axelsson, K., & Hedley, V. (1986). Morning care of Alzheimer's patients: A theoretical model based on direct observation. *Journal of Advanced Nursing, 11*, 369–378.

Skurla, E., Rogers, J., & Sunderland, T. (1988). Direct assessment of activities of daily living in Alzheimer's disease: A controlled study. *Journal of the American Geriatrics Society, 36*, 97–103.

Movement, Exercise, and Sensorimotor Therapy

Bower, H.M. (1967). Sensory stimulation and the treatment of senile dementia. *Medical Journal of Australia, 1*, 1113–1119.

Caplow-Lindner, E., Harpaz, L., & Samberg, S. (1979). *Therapeutic dance and movement: Expressive activities for older adults.* New York: Human Sciences Press.

Doty, R.L., Reyes, P.F., & Gregor, T. (1987). Presence of odor identification and detection deficits in Alzheimer's disease. *Brain Research Bulletin, 18*, 597–600.

Richman, L. (1969). Sensory training for geriatric patients. *American Journal of Occupational Therapy, 13*, 254–257.

Ross, M., & Burdick, D. (1981). *Sensory integration: A training manual for regressed, psychiatric, and geriatric patient groups.* New York: C.B. Slack.

Squyres, B.N. (1987). Alzheimer's disease and exercise. *Texas Medicine, 83*(1), 51–53.

Steffes, R., & Thralow, J. (1987). Visual field limitation in the patient with dementia of the Alzheimer's type. *Journal of the American Geriatrics Society, 35*, 198–204.

Miscellaneous Therapies

Damon, J., & May, R. (1986). The effects of pet facilitative therapy on patients and staff in an adult day care center. In P. Foster (Ed.), *Therapeutic activities with the impaired elderly* (pp. 117–131). New York: Haworth Press.

Gibbons, A.C. (1986). *Music in activities programming.* New York: Haworth Press.

Lindquist, B.B. (1986). They need us, we need them: A study of the benefits of intergenerational contact. In P. Foster (Ed.), *Therapeutic activities with the impaired elderly* (pp. 83–94). New York: Haworth Press.

Thralow, J.U., & Watson, C.G. (1974). Remotivation for geriatric patients: Using elementary school students. *American Journal of Occupational Therapy, 28*, 469–473.

Wiswell, R. (1980). Relaxation, exercise, and aging. In J.E. Birren & R.B. Sloan (Eds.), *Handbook of mental health and aging.* Englewood Cliffs, NJ: Prentice-Hall.

Wiswell, R. (1983). *Pets in the nursing home*. Olympia, WA: Department of Social and Health Services, Bureau of Nursing Home Affairs.

Behavior Therapy

Eisdorfer, C., Cohen, D., & Preston, C. (1981). Behavioral and psychological therapies for the older patient with cognitive impairment. In G. Cohen & N. Miller (Eds.), *Clinical aspects of Alzheimer's disease and senile dementia* (pp. 209–226). New York: Raven Press.

Gotestam, K. (1980). Behavioral and dynamic psychiatry with the elderly. In J.E. Birren & R.B. Sloan (Eds.), *Handbook of mental health and aging* (pp. 775–805). Englewood Cliffs, NJ: Prentice-Hall.

Hussian, R. (1981). *Geriatric psychology: A behavioral perspective*. New York: Van Nostrand Reinhold.

Communication

Bayles, K., & Kaszniak, A. (1987). *Communication and cognition in normal aging and dementia*. Boston: Little, Brown.

Langland, R.M., & Panicucci, C.L. (1982). Effects of touch on communication with elderly confused clients. *Journal of Gerontological Nursing, 8*(3), 152–155.

Murdoch, B.E., Chenerly, H.J., Wilks, V., & Boyle, R.S. (1987). Language disorders in dementia of the Alzheimer's type. *Brain & Language, 31*(1), 122–137.

Nicholas, M., Obler, L.K., Albert, M.L., & Helm-Estabrooks, N. (1985). Empty speech in Alzheimer's disease and fluent aphasia. *Journal of Speech & Hearing Research, 28*, 405–410.

Nutrition

DeTienne, S. (1986). Long-term care dining challenge: Adequate nutrition and maximum independence. *OT Forum, 11*(21), 17–18.

Sandman, P.O., Adolfsson, R., Nygren, C., Hallman, G., & Winblad, B. (1987). Nutritional status and dietary intake in institutionalized patients with AD and MID. *Journal of the American Geriatrics Society, 35*, 31–38.

Swartz, J. (1982). Strategies to promote diet compliance by the elderly. *Dimensions in Health Services, 59*(7), 14–15.

Problem Behaviors

Barnes, R., Veith, R., Okimoto, J., Raskind, M., & Gumbrecht, G. (1982). The efficacy of antipsychotics in behaviorally disturbed dementia patients. *American Journal of Psychiatry, 139*, 1170–1174.

Cohen-Mansfield, J. (1986). Agitated behaviors in the elderly: 2. Preliminary results in the cognitively deteriorated. *Journal of the American Geriatrics Society, 34*, 722–727.

Erkinjuntti, T., Partinen, M., Sulkava, R., Telakivi, T., Salmi, T., & Tilvis, R. (1987). Sleep apnea in multi-infarct dementia and Alzheimer's disease. *Sleep, 10*, 419–425.

Maletta, G.J. (1985). Medicaton to modify at-home behavior of Alzheimer's patients. *Geriatrics, 40*(12), 31–36.

O'Connor, M. (1987). Disturbed behavior in dementia: Psychiatric or medical problem? *Medical Journal of Australia, 147*, 481–485.

Reynolds, C.F., Hoch, C.C., Stack, J., & Campbell, D. (1988). The nature and management of sleep/wake disturbance in Alzheimer's dementia. *Psychopharmacology Bulletin, 24*(1), 43–48.

Risse, S., & Barnes, R. (1986). Pharmacological treatment of agitation associated with dementia. *Journal of the American Geriatrics Society, 34*, 368–376.

Shomaker, D. (1987). Problematic behavior and the Alzheimer's patient: Retrospection as a method of understanding and counseling. *The Gerontologist, 27*, 370.

Teri, L., Larson, E.B., & Reifler, B.V. (1988). Behavioral disturbance and dementia of the Alzheimer's type. *Journal of the American Geriatrics Society, 36*, 1–6.

General

Foster, P. (Ed.). (1986). *Therapeutic activities with the impaired elderly.* New York: Haworth Press.

Glickstein, J.K. (1988). *Therapeutic interventions in Alzheimer's disease.* Gaithersburg, MD: Aspen Publishers.

Lawton, M.P. (1980). Psychosocial and environmental approaches to the care of the senile dementia patient. In J.O. Cole & J.E. Barret (Eds.), *Psychopathology in the aged* (pp. 265–278). New York: Raven Press.

McDonald, K.C. (1985-1986). Occupational therapy approaches to treatment of dementia patients. *Physical & Occupational Therapy in Geriatrics, 4*(2), 61–72.

Olin, D. (1985). Assessing and assisting the person with dementia: An occupational behavior perspective. *Physical & Occupational Therapy in Geriatrics, 3*(4), 25–32.

Rogers, J.C. (1986). Occupational therapy services for Alzheimer's disease and related disorders. *American Journal of Occupational Therapy, 40*, 822–824.

Taira, E. (Ed.). (1986). *Therapeutic interventions for the person with dementia.* New York: Haworth Press.

Toseland, R.W. (1984). Alzheimer's disease and related disorders: Assessment and intervention. *Health & Social Work, 9*, 212–226.

Chapter 13

Home Care Programs

Cindy Patrice Paulson

In recent years, home health care services have increased in proportion to the cost of caring for those with a long-term illness or disability (Jackson, 1984). In 1983, when diagnostic-related groups (DRGs) were instituted and hospitals began discharging patients according to the new regulations, older patients often left the hospital more ill than previously. Many continued to require home nursing and therapy after discharge.

Most home health care patients referred to occupational therapy have more than one treatable diagnosis. The average number of treatments or visits provided is 7.25, and that number increases with neurological conditions (Mac Rae, 1984). Neurological conditions not only affect physical capacity to perform functional tasks. They can also influence cognitive and perceptual skills and thus impinge on task performance. Occupational therapy can effectively address all of these areas. In one study, 79% of the patients receiving occupational therapy services were able to remain safely in the home, either independently or with assistance (Mac Rae, 1984).

As medical science and technology continue to expand the base of knowledge, a greater number of illnesses will be more effectively treated and lives will continue to be prolonged, often with long-term residual effects. With the turn of the 21st century, the baby boomers will begin to enter the geriatric population and will experience the maladies of aging, straining an already stressed health care system.

For all these reasons and because home care can be much more cost-effective than institutional care, home care is expected to grow rapidly. Occupational therapists must orient physicians and other home health care professionals to the benefits of their services, since ADL training may be significant in preventing institutionalization or self-care dependency (Mac Rae, 1984).

CHALLENGES AND PRACTICE IN HOME HEALTH

The practice of home health occupational therapy differs in several respects from occupational therapy in more traditional settings (e.g., hospitals, rehabilitation centers, outpatient clinics, and nursing homes). Most importantly, the therapist is not on his or her own "turf," as in a clinical setting. The therapist is a guest in the client's home and must be careful to acknowledge the client's control of the environment and the program. Because of the change in setting, the "basic" equipment, which is often taken for granted, is missing. The therapist is left to his or her own devices and must use ingenuity to adapt materials borrowed from the home setting. That is one of the many reasons home health care can be an exciting challenge. Here in the patient's own familiar environment, the therapist can see how well clinically taught adaptation skills have been generalized. Here the therapist can focus on true functional level and actual independence.

Occupational therapy home health evaluation and treatment include the patient's biomechanical status, medication management, environmental barriers, cultural values regarding aging, disease and disability, and family dynamics. Reilly's (1962, 1971) *Occupational Behavior* provides a helpful frame of reference, because it allows the gathering and integration of information from a variety of disciplines.

Most occupational therapy services will be provided to a home patient through a home health agency. Although it is not absolutely necessary, it is advisable that a new graduate have a year or two of experience in a hospital or rehabilitation setting before working in home health. In this area of practice, therapists are virtually in the field on their own. Not only is there no onsite supervisor, but there are often no other therapists to answer questions or help problem solve. Private practice therapists can provide services to home health patients, but they will need a Medicare provider number and knowledge of billing and reimbursement procedures. Additionally, there is a maximum billing ceiling of $750 per year per patient set for individual therapists (Somers, 1990; U.S. Department of Health and Human Services, 1987).

If a therapist does not have a secretary or other office help, it is helpful to have a phone answering machine or answering service to take referrals while in the field. When a referral is received, it is important to contact the patient or family to set up an evaluation appointment as soon as possible. In fact, many agencies have time limits for this initial contact. If the home health client has received OT services in another setting, these records should be available. For continuity of care and treatment, it can be very helpful to speak with the therapist who previously treated the patient. To create an atmosphere of trust with the patient and family, it is best to be on time for regularly scheduled appointments. It may also be helpful to contact the patient or family between visits to monitor any areas of concern.

Although the initial evaluation visit may easily last an hour or more, visits usually last 45 minutes. However, recording or documentation time is included in the total time for the visit. In some cases, time spent talking with the patient's physician or other team members on a topic that relates directly to the treatment visit or plan is allowed. This will be discussed further in the section on Medicare reimbursement. It may be helpful to put together an assessment kit of equipment and supplies to assist in evaluation and treatment. Include such items as a goniometer, a dynamometer, a blood pressure cuff and stethoscope, a homemade stereognosis kit, a measuring tape, clothespins for pinch, theraputty and theraband of various grades, cones, nuts and bolts of various sizes, a rolling pin, a sponge and wash cloth for supination and pronation, ADL aids (e.g., elastic shoelaces, Velcro, a buttonhook, a long-handled shoehorn, a dressing stick or reacher), a plate guard, a rocker spoon, foam tubing for building up utensil handles, masking or duct tape and foam rubber, scissors, and a tool box for wheelchair repairs (American Occupational Therapy Association [AOTA], 1987b).

It's also helpful to have examples of commonly recommended adaptive equipment and assistive devices. Hospital and equipment vendors often loan items such as bath benches. If an item is not Medicare reimbursable, the patient and family must be informed that they must pay for the item themselves, unless supplemental insurance covers the cost. If they are financially unable to pay, the therapist can provide the names of local agencies or organizations for the disabled that might be able to provide assistance. Older adults can always put the item on their birthday or Christmas "wish" list.

The team approach to rehabilitation is as important in the home as it is in the clinical setting. Yet because of the nature of home health, it can be more difficult for the team to meet together formally. Telephone conversations at least weekly with other team members or with the team coordinator are recommended. Sometimes it is helpful to make a joint visit with one of the other therapists or the nurse involved in the case (AOTA, 1987b; Trossman, 1984).

If the therapist is fortunate enough to have a COTA to assist with treatment, joint visits should be scheduled biweekly or every four to six treatments. The patient's performance and progress can be observed firsthand and the treatment plan updated accordingly. A home health aide is frequently assigned to help the patient and family in the home. Once trained in the treatment program and the rehabilitation process, the aide can contribute substantially to the success of the OT program. Under periodic supervision by the therapist, the aide can carry out restorative activities to promote client independence or perform functional tasks.

On occasion, the therapist may be asked to treat a patient whose behavior is found to be inappropriate or threatening. Making joint visits with another therapist or the nurse may resolve the problem. If joint visits are not possible, the supervisor should be notified immediately. No one should work in a situation that is dangerous or threatening.

MEDICARE GUIDELINES AND REIMBURSEMENT

There are two types of Medicare coverage. Part A covers hospital inpatient, skilled nursing facility, home health, and hospice care. Part B is a supplemental medical insurance program that covers hospital outpatient, physician, home health, comprehensive outpatient rehabilitation facility (CORF) treatment, and other professional services. There is no limit to the number of home health visits and no requirement for previous hospitalization (Somers, 1990).

To qualify for Medicare A benefits for home health, a patient must be homebound, under a physician's care, and in need of skilled nursing or physical or speech therapy on an intermittent basis (Table 13-1). A patient is homebound if there is a functional limitation due to an illness or injury that restricts the ability to leave the home or if leaving the home requires great and taxing effort. Absences from the home are therefore infrequent or only for short periods of time, preventing the individual from receiving treatment outside the home (U.S. Department of Health, Education and Welfare, 1972). Occupational therapists in private practice may also provide services to patients at home under Medicare Part B coverage. To qualify for reimbursement, the patient must be under a physician's care, and services must be furnished under a plan of treatment that is reviewed and signed by the physician every 30 days. There are three primary differences in this coverage. The patient does not need to be homebound; the patient does not need to be seen by a specialist in nursing, physical therapy, or speech; and there is a $750 maximum

Table 13-1 Qualifications for O.T. Services in Home Health

Medicare Part A	*Medicare Part B*
Patient is under the care of a physician.	Patient is under the care of a physician.
There must be a written plan of treatment signed by the physician.	There must be a written plan of treatment signed by the physician.
Plan of treatment reviewed and recertified every 30 days by physician.	Plan of treatment reviewed and recertified every 30 days by physician.
Patient must need skilled nursing, PT, or ST services.	Patient need not be seen by another discipline.
Patient must be "homebound."	Patient need not be homebound.
OT services, if established during nursing, PT, or ST treatment, can continue after other services are no longer provided.	OT services separate from other services.
No billing ceiling.	$750 yearly maximum for OTs in private practice.
Services must be provided by an OTR or COTA under supervision of an OTR.	Services must be provided by an OTR or COTA under supervision of an OTR.
Treatment must be reasonable and necessary for significant practical improvement in function in a reasonable time.	Treatment must be reasonable and necessary for significant practical improvement in function in a reasonable time.
OT may design and monitor maintenance and restorative programs but can't conduct these programs.	OT may design and monitor maintenance and restorative programs but can't conduct these programs.

billing ceiling for services provided within one calendar year (Somers, 1990; U.S. Department of Health and Human Services, 1987).

Under current Medicare A regulations for home health agencies, occupational therapy is not considered a "skilled" or qualifying service. Nursing, physical therapy, or speech therapy is needed before an agency's OTR may treat the patient. Once the patient has met the criteria, the occupational therapist may continue to treat the patient even though other services are discontinued. However, when occupational therapy is the only service provided through the agency, occupational therapy charges may be closely scrutinized. Therefore, it's important for occupational therapy to begin early in the patient's program. When a qualifying service provides only one or two visits so that continuing occupational therapy services can be provided, reimbursement may be denied.

Home health services, including occupational therapy, are also covered under Medicaid for some groups of low-income persons or under innovative "waiver" programs. These services (part-time nursing, home health aid, and medical supplies and equipment) are required for any person entitled to skilled nursing facility or skilled rehabilitation services. In addition, physical therapy, occupational therapy, speech therapy, and audiology are optional services which may be covered by Medicaid Programs (Somers, 1990).

Recently Medicare coverage has broadened so as to encompass not only diagnostic-related services but also therapy designed to improve the patient's condition, even without a severe disability (Pini, 1990).

DOCUMENTATION

Documentation of each visit is required, and use of descriptive terminology is particularly important for reimbursement. For example, "continue self-range of motion" may not be reimbursable, but bilateral upper extremity activities constitute a neurodevelopmental treatment modality to decrease neglect of the affected side, increase proprioceptive input, and decrease flexion synergy and hand spasticity, and they should be documented as such (Trossman, 1984).

Progress notes need to emphasize progress in functional activities or precursor skills that relate to function. Often the occupational therapist will treat the same patients as the physical therapist, and the treatments may seem to overlap. This will not be a problem for Medicare reimbursement if the occupational therapy plan and treatment emphasize functional exercises and if purposeful activities are performed to promote independence or improved function in daily living tasks. The physical therapist will focus on increasing strength and endurance (AOTA, 1987a). Occupational therapy notes shouldn't sound like physical therapy notes; emphasize improvement in functional activity and/or mobility for functional task performance. If the use of physical therapy modalities such as electrical stimulation or hot packs is mentioned, reimbursement can be denied. However, if these modalities improve the patient's performance in occupational therapy activities or tasks, the physical therapist can instruct the patient and family in their application and advise that they be used just prior to the occupational therapist's arrival.

Occupational therapy may also appear to overlap with speech therapy in the treatment of dysphagia, cognitive disorders, or perceptual deficits. However, each discipline has its own unique approach and emphasis in dealing with different functions, so reimbursement need not be an issue (AOTA, 1987a). For example, the occupational therapist can address cognitive or perceptual deficits in order to increase functional task performance or can focus on the swallowing process in order to increase self-feeding skills.

Payment is denied when documentation doesn't indicate that skilled care was given or when no progress is indicated (Eppler-Colvin & Tanbe-Levine, 1984). Therapy is covered when there is a reasonable expectation at the time of the evaluation that improvement can occur. When it becomes apparent that further progress will be minimal or nil, therapy will no longer be reimbursed. However, the therapist may design a maintenance program and check on the patient's status periodically, for example, one or two times a month (De Paoli & Zenk-Jones, 1984).

Occupational therapy services may include prevocational evaluation and treatment. However, Medicare will not cover prevocational and vocational evaluation and training if they are related only to a patient's specific employment, job setting, or work skills. Certain assessments, such as assessments of sitting and standing tolerance for performance of self-care or home care tasks, can be covered if they relate to functional independence. They will not be reimbursed if they are related solely to performance of a specific job or in a given job setting (U.S. Department of Health and Human Services, 1987).

Progress is documented in monthly summaries by comparing current performance to that of the previous month or the initial evaluation. Words such as *maintain, plateau,* and *slight increase* should be avoided. Describe any teaching or instruction given and report that the patient demonstrated the skill or task being taught. If exercise of specific muscles or groups is described, relate the exercise to practical task performance. For example, increased strength of forearm supinators will allow the patient to operate household appliances such as the stove, oven, microwave, or washing machine, leading to greater independence (De Paoli & Zenk-Jones, 1984).

While Medicare does not reimburse directly for calls to the physician, other professionals, or the patient or family, it is possible to keep track of the time spent and include it on a regular treatment visit charge. The purpose and outcome of a conversation must be documented to show it was related to the treatment plan (AOTA, 1987a).

ASSESSMENT

The initial evaluation should include some assessment of functional mobility, balance, transfers, ambulation, upper extremity range of motion, strength and coordination, deformity, synergy, pain or edema, sensory and perceptual performance, writing, activities of daily living, eating and home skills, past work history and leisure interests, activity and endurance levels, time use and structuring, medication management, architectural barriers, and the need for any equipment to increase safety or independence in functional activities. Any precautions or contraindications to treatment should be noted. If there are significant deficits, they can be evaluated in greater depth in later treatment sessions (AOTA, 1987b; Mac Rae, 1984).

During the evaluation process, it is important that the therapist have the patient actually perform the task rather than accept a verbal report by the patient or family. They may describe the patient as being independent when in fact some assistance is being given. Conversely, assistance may be given when the task could be performed more independently with minor modifications or assistive devices. Remember that one of the primary goals is to assess and teach functional safety in the home. How to obtain help in an emergency should be covered in the initial visit if it has not been taught by another team member. (This is one way Medicare's requirement that some teaching occur on the first visit can be met.) Exit routes from the house should also be identified.

It is helpful to use the same evaluations and terminology for patients with similar disabilities. Reviewers will become more familiar with the results and can better determine the validity of the treatment program and each patient's progress in therapy.

The evaluation form used by the Visiting Nurse Association (VNA) of California has been included in Exhibit 13-1. This four-page form was chosen because the first two pages include information required by Medicare that can be transferred directly to the Medicare 485 and 486 forms for documentation by the home health agency. Sections for medication management and assessment of architectural barriers will need to be added.

When the occupational therapist receives a referral from the agency, some basic information about the patient should be included. This may be given over the phone, but it is usually provided on a referral form. Information covering the first three questions on the VNA form, plus the patient's address and phone number, should be given. Additional information may also be provided, and it can be transferred to the appropriate line on the evaluation form. The first two pages of the VNA form are for general information and are fairly self-explanatory. However, a few words of explanation may be helpful. For item 10a, be sure to state homebound status reasons that are acceptable according to Medicare definition (e.g., "patient confined to bed" or "patient unable to ambulate more than 15 feet without severe dyspnea or cardiac arrhythmia"). In item 10b, "prior level of function" refers to the patient's physical status and social living situation prior to the most recent illness. For example, the therapist might document "Patient lived with his wife in their own home and was independent in all self-care, social, and transportation activities." If the outcome of treatment (item 16) is in question so that "good" cannot be justified, the therapist might state "fair for goals given." If the prognosis is poor for the goals given, the goals need to be downgraded and simplified.

Discharge plans (item 17) may consist of (1) a long-term goal if the patient's homebound status is not expected to change or (2) referral to outpatient rehabilitation if the patient is expected to progress beyond homebound status.

Item 20 offers the opportunity to report the skilled care provided. This provides the justification for billable visits. The third and fourth pages contain occupational therapy assessment items.

If nursing services are not being provided to the patient, it's important for the occupational therapist to assess the patient's medication management and status. Since the taking of medications is part of the patient's everyday life, it becomes an important component of activities of daily living or self-care skills. The therapist should ask the patient and family where medications are kept—and keep asking until all locations have been determined. Information regarding medications should be carefully written down, including the names of all medications being taken (prescription and over-the-counter medicines), the prescribing physicians, and dosages. Often patients take drugs prescribed by more than one physician and may be at risk for drug misuse or noncompliance. It's important that the patient and family understand how the medicines interact with each other, with alcohol, and with various foods. It may be necessary for the therapist to set up a schedule or mechanism to ensure the correct taking of medications. This might include use of a mediset, color-coded schedules, or checklists or flow sheets (Hasselkus and Bauwens, 1982). Although the nurse must be the one to actually dispense medications and may therefore have to be called in to do the actual setup if the patient and family are unable, the therapist can determine the functional performance needs and design the most appropriate program based on knowledge of the patient and family.

Once the evaluation is completed and the treatment plan formulated, written instructions should be provided for the patient and family and the home health aid or the COTA if they will be involved in treatment. Go over the program to make sure they understand and are performing the activities correctly and safely. Include any precautions or contraindications regarding treatment.

If the therapist reviews the referral information or makes an initial visit and determines that the referral is inappropriate, the occupational therapy supervisor should be notified. Usually a call to the physician explaining the situation will

Exhibit 13-1 Evaluation Form

☐ RN ASSESSMENT   ☐ PT   ☐ OT   ☐ ST   **EVALUATION**

1. a. PATIENT NAME _____ b. Eval Date _____ c. SOC Date _____
   d. Cert. Period from _____ to _____ e. Acct # _____ f. Fee Basis _____
   g. Dist./C.T./Spec _____ h. Case Manager _____ Medi Cal VC # _____
2. a. DOB _____ b. M ___ F ___ c. Hosp/SNF Date _____
3. a. PRINCIPAL DX   1. _____ ONSET DATE _____ ICD _____
   b. SURGERY(les)   • _____ DATE _____ ICD _____
       RELATED TO CARE   • _____ DATE _____ ICD _____
   c. OTHER DIAGNOSIS ☐ _____ DATE _____ ICD _____
       PERT. TO PLAN ☐ _____ DATE _____ ICD _____
       OF TREATMENT ☐ _____ DATE _____ ICD _____
       (Prioritize) ☐ _____ DATE _____ ICD _____
       ☐ _____ DATE _____ ICD _____

4. DME ☐ N/A ☐ PRESENT _____
   Ordered/Rec. _____
   Med. Supplies ☐ N/A _____
   S.C.A.Aids (830) _____

5. SAFETY MEASURES/INSTRUCTION GIVEN _____

6. NUTRITIONAL REQUIREMENTS _____

7. a. FUNCTIONAL LIMITATIONS   b. ACTIVITIES PERMITTED

a. FUNCTIONAL LIMITATIONS			b. ACTIVITIES PERMITTED	
☐ Amputation	☐ Paralysis	☐ Legally Blind	☐ Complete Bedrest	☐ Partial Weight Bearing
☐ Bowel/Bladder	☐ Endurance	☐ Dyspnea With	☐ Bedrest BRP	☐ Crutches
(incontinence)	☐ Ambulation	Minimal Exertion	☐ Up as Tolerated	☐ Cane
☐ Contracture	☐ Speech	☐ ADL's	☐ Transfer Bed/Chair	☐ Wheelchair
☐ Hearing		☐ Pain	☐ Exercises Prescribed	☐ Walker
☐ Other _____			☐ Other _____	
(specify)			(specify)	

8. MENTAL STATUS: ☐ ORIENTED   ☐ FORGETFUL   ☐ DISORIENTED   ☐ AGITATED
             ☐ COMATOSE   ☐ DEPRESSED   ☐ LETHARGIC   ☐ OTHER _____
                                                    (specify)

9. MEDICAL PROGNOSIS: ☐ POOR   ☐ GUARDED   ☐ FAIR   ☐ GOOD   ☐ EXCELLENT

10a. HOMEBOUND DUE TO (Describe related architectural barriers) _____

10b. PRIOR LEVEL OF FUNCTION _____

11. FAMILY/CULTURAL/ENVIRONMENTAL SUPPORT SYSTEMS   LIVES WITH: Alone   Spouse   Relative   Friend
    MARITAL STATUS: S   M   W   Sep   D   LIVES IN: House   Apt.   Upstairs   Ground Level   Mobile Home
    SOCIAL PROBLEMS: None or Describe: _____
    LANGUAGE SPOKEN: English Other _____ READS/WRITES: English Other _____
    COMMENTS _____
    UNUSUAL HOME/SOCIAL PROBLEMS/CAREGIVER STATUS _____

12. PT. LEAVES HOME ON A ROUTINE BASIS? ☐ Yes ☐ No   Frequency _____ Reason _____

Exhibit 13-1 continued

13. MEDICAL HX. RELEVANT TO REFERRAL _____

14. PROBLEMS Clinical/Social
[ ] _____
[ ] _____
[ ] _____
[ ] _____
[ ] _____
[ ] _____
[ ] _____
[ ] _____

15. GOALS
[ ] _____
[ ] _____
[ ] _____
[ ] _____
[ ] _____
[ ] _____
[ ] _____
[ ] _____

16. REHAB POTENTIAL FOR STATED GOALS IS (describe) _____

17. DISCHARGE PLANS _____

18. OVERALL FREQUENCY _____ OVERALL FREQUENCY

TREATMENT PLAN
[ ] CODE _____ _____ FREQ _____ [ ]
[ ] CODE _____ _____ FREQ _____ [ ]
[ ] CODE _____ _____ FREQ _____ [ ]
[ ] CODE _____ _____ FREQ _____ [ ]
[ ] CODE _____ _____ FREQ _____ [ ]
[ ] CODE _____ _____ FREQ _____ [ ]
[ ] CODE _____ _____ FREQ _____ [ ]
[ ] CODE _____ _____ FREQ _____ [ ]

19. HHA ORDERS   CODE/FREQUENCY _____
Referral Completed For: RN   PT   OT   ST   MSW   HHA   None _____   _____ Refused
(specify discipline)

20. SKILLED CARE GIVEN _____

21. PLAN FOR NEXT VISIT _____

22. TC to MD _____ Date: _____ Time: _____ LEFT MESSAGE WITH _____
VERIFICATION OF POT [ ]

SIGN/TITLE/DATE _____ SUP. SIGN/DATE _____

continues

Exhibit 13-1 continued

FUNCTIONAL STATUS CODE: I=Independent-safe alone; NF=Not Functional, S=Supervised-someone should be in same room; SB=Someone in reaching distance if assist is necessary; MIN=Minimum Assistance-needs cueing and/or hands on physical assist which supplies up to 25% of effort; MOD=Moderate Assistance-needs hands on assist which supplies 25 to 75% of effort; MAX=Maximum Assistance-needs hands on assist which supplies 75% of effort or whenever more than 1 person assist is required; U=Unable, NT=Not Tested.

	I	NF	S	SB	MIN	MOD	MAX	U	NT	COMMENTS/EQUIPMENT
FEEDING: Reported/Observed										
Manages liquids										
Manages solid food										
Appetite (specify) _____										
Diet (specify) _____										
GROOMING/HYGIENE: Reported/Observed										
Cleans teeth/dentures										
Shaves										
Washes face										
Combs hair										
Manages nail care										
BATHING: Reported/Observed										
Previous method (specify) _____										
Current method (specify) _____										
Transfers										
DRESSING: Reported/Observed										
Upper body										
Lower body										
Fastenings										
Slings/splints/braces (specify) _____										
TOILETING: Reported/Observed										
Bowel status _____										
Bladder status _____										
Manages clothes										
Hygiene										
Transfers										
HOME ACTIVITIES: Reported/Observed										
Meal preparation										
Household chores										
Financial management										
Leisure activities (specify) _____										

ENDURANCE FOR ACTIVITIES _____

_____

MOBILITY

Transfers _____ in _____ out of bed   COMMENTS _____

Rolling (R)_____ (L)_____   _____

Supine ↔ sit _____   _____

Ambulation _____   _____

Balance-sitting _____   _____

Balance-standing _____   _____

Exhibit 13-1 continued

PHYSICAL ASSESSMENT

ROM _____

_____

_____ SUBLUXATION _____

STRENGTH _____

_____

TONE _____

Hand Dominance	(R)_____	(L)_____	Palmar Pinch	(R)_____	(L)_____
Gross Grasp	(R)_____	(L)_____	Lateral Pinch	(R)_____	(L)_____

COORDINATION ☐ IMPAIRED ☐ INTACT   MEMORY ☐ IMPAIRED ☐ INTACT

DESCRIBE _____   DESCRIBE _____

PAIN YES NO DESCRIBE _____   JUDGMENT/SAFETY ☐ IMPAIRED ☐ INTAC:

_____   DESCRIBE _____

EDEMA/LOCATION _____

SENSATION	PERCEPTION	BULBAR FUNCTION
☐ IMPAIRED ☐ INTACT	☐ IMPAIRED ☐ INTACT	☐ IMPAIRED ☐ INTACT
Sharp/dull _____	Neglect _____	Tongue Movements _____
Touch _____	Denial _____	Swallowing Sequence _____
Temperature _____	R/L discrimination _____	Chewing _____
Proprioception _____	Figure/ground _____	Reflexes _____
Stereognosis _____	Form constancy _____	Drooling _____
Localization _____	Position in space _____	Cough _____
Extreme sensitivity _____	Apraxia _____	Food Pocketing _____
Numbness _____	Agnosia _____	Facial Droop _____
Comments _____	Spatial relations _____	Eyelid Closure _____
_____	Comments _____	Sensation _____
_____	_____	Comments _____
_____		

VISION	COMMUNICATION
Functional _____ Hemianopsia _____	Language spoken _____
Tracking _____ Scanning _____	Expressive Language _____
Surgeries _____	Receptive Language _____
Corrective Lenses _____ Comments _____	Hearing _____
_____	Telephone use _____
_____	Reading _____
_____	Writing _____
_____	Comments _____

Source: Courtesy of the Visiting Nurse Association, Sacramento Valley Division, Sacramento, California.

suffice. The agency may have its own utilization or peer review committee to deal with these situations.

ARCHITECTURAL BARRIERS

Patients who spend hours in treatment each day in a rehabilitation setting are often discharged home as independent in self-care and home care skills. But when they arrive home, they can't get in and out of the house because of the steps or go through the narrow doors in a wheelchair. A home full of architectural barriers can be an additional handicap at best and a prison at worst, requiring services or assistance that might not be needed otherwise. The long-term expense of these services can be justification for the one-time expense of architectural modifications. Some European nations have taken the lead in meeting the needs of their disabled citizens by providing accessible housing and support services for independent living. Others require government offices to assess homes of the disabled and provide financial assistance for needed structural alterations. Our own country provides only minimal housing and support services for the disabled. Until more resources are available, patients' homes need to be assessed for barriers and modifications (Hale, 1979).

As the result of a 1980 pilot program, Project Open House found that an average outlay of $1,000 for architectural modifications made the difference between an individual being able to stay in the home and having to return to a hospital or nursing home—at costs of up to $128,000. Of course, prices have increased since 1980, so the difference in potential expense is even greater (Eppler-Colvin & Tanbe-Levine, 1984).

It is vitally important to realize that altering a family's living space is not merely a structural issue. It has emotional, social, and physical components as well, and any recommended changes must be acceptable to the patient and family.

Several evaluation forms are available for assessing the home. For examples, write (1) Project Open House, United Cerebral Palsy Housing Services, 105 Madison Avenue, New York, NY 10016, or (2) Estelle Newman, OTR CRC, Senior Vocational Rehabilitation Counselor, OVR-NYS Office Building, Veterans Highway, Haupage, NY 11788. AOTA's *Accessibility and Architectural Modifications* is also an excellent reference source for information.

Areas for Assessment and Modification

Entrance

If there are stairs or steps, a 1:12 ratio (12 inches of ramp length for each inch of rise) must be provided if the patient is to be independent in wheelchair mobility.

For the elderly, this ratio might be even greater. If the patient must be assisted, a 1:4 ratio ramp is sufficient (Hale, 1979). At the top of the ramp, there must be a sufficient flat area in which to maneuver and turn the chair. Three feet of open area is needed if the door opens inward, and 5 feet is needed if the door opens outward. The ramp should be a minimum of 30 inches wide to allow for steering (36 inches is better). It should have a nonskid surface and be fireproof. In severe weather areas, it is best enclosed. When traveling on the ramp, the individual should go up facing forward and down facing backward to avoid being spilled from the chair. If space is insufficient for a ramp, a wheelchair lift or elevator can be installed (Hale, 1979).

Doors

The minimum doorway width is 30 inches, with 36 inches preferred. If the doorway is only slightly too narrow, adapted hinges can be installed to provide an additional inch. If the opening is still too narrow, the door and framing can be removed and a curtain hung to provide visual privacy. As a last resort, the doorway can be enlarged. Sometimes a sliding closet-type door can be installed if the room is very small, or a bifold door may provide additional space in which to maneuver the chair. Door knobs can be adapted with levers on the knob if purchasing new hardware is not cost-effective (Hale, 1979).

Stairs

If the individual's residence is more than one story, a first-floor room can be used for the bedroom. If this is not possible or desirable, a wheelchair lift can be installed, although the expense is great (Hale, 1979).

Flooring

Smooth, clutter-free floors are easiest to negotiate. Carpet makes self-propulsion of a wheelchair very difficult. The longer the carpet fibers, the harder the work. Uneven surfaces, clutter, and throw rugs can be dangerous to the ambulatory patient (Hale, 1979).

Lighting and Electrical Outlets

Most light switches are not reachable from a wheelchair. Inexpensive assistive devices can be purchased to make them accessible. Electrical outlets ideally should be reachable without having to stoop from a standing or seated position. The outlets should be grounded and the electricity should be sufficient to carry the load of appliances in the house. Remote controls for televisions and stereos are a great help to the disabled (Hale, 1979).

Furniture

Rearrangement of furniture may be helpful in improving mobility. If chairs, sofas, and beds are so low that standing up from a seated position is difficult or impossible, blocks with a depression in the center or a rim around the edge for safety can be placed under furniture legs. Footstools can be used for a footrest if raising the piece of furniture means the individual's feet are not able to touch the ground when seated (Hale, 1979).

General Storage

Frequently used items should be easily and safely accessible. Kitchen, bath, and bedroom storage may have to be rearranged to ensure comfortable reachability from standing and sitting positions. Reachers to extend the patient's reach can also be used (Hale, 1979).

Bedroom

A hospital bed may be needed for positioning the patient. If the patient is a hemiplegic, the bed should be placed so that exit and entry can be accomplished using the strong, nonaffected side. Sometimes a trapeze, siderails, or a flexible ladder that fastens to the foot of the bedframe is needed to increase independence in bed mobility. The position of the bed must be modified for some patients with cardiac or pulmonary problems. The head of a regular bed can be raised with the use of wooden wedges that rest on the box springs or against the headboard, with pillows piled against it (Hale, 1979).

Bathroom

Grab bars can be installed around the toilet for safety. Permanent bars that attach to the wall should be installed by a contractor for safety reasons. Special considerations may have to be made in older homes. One type of bar rests on the floor, and one style anchors to the toilet. A bedside commode with the bucket removed can be placed over the toilet to add height. If the bedside commode needs to be weighted for safety, sand or buckshot can be poured into removable-leg-types before the legs are replaced. Raised toilet seats can be removable if other family members use the same bathroom. Other seat types anchor to the toilet for more security.

In the shower or bathtub, grab bars must be installed for safety. Drilling holes in a fiberglass tub or shower stall can cause the fiberglass to crack or shatter. Temporary grab bars that screw onto the tub edge can be installed. Water faucet handles can be changed to the lever type, and detachable handheld shower heads can increase independence in bathing. Nonskid surfaces should be applied in showers and tubs. A shower chair or transfer bath bench can prevent falls while bathing. If the bathroom has a tub-shower combination with sliding glass doors, the doors can be removed and a shower curtain installed to increase safety. A small ramp can be built over the shower lip for safer shower entry and exit. The patient should be cautioned never to use towel bars or a wall-hung sink as a grab bar. Long-handled bath sponges and bath mitts can increase independence in bathing. Most of the items discussed are not Medicare reimbursable. There are some private insurance companies that will pay for equipment if it is required for safety or independence. A physician's prescription is necessary. If this is not an option, community agencies such as the Multiple Sclerosis Society, Arthritis Foundation, or Easter Seal Society may be able to loan or provide equipment (AOTA, 1987b).

Kitchen

The doors and threshold or toe plate can be removed from the sink cabinet to allow wheelchair access. Pipes under the sink can be insulated to prevent burns or injury. A plastic dishpan can be turned upside down in the sink to provide a higher work surface for someone in a wheelchair. Tilted mirrors above the stove and sink help a seated person see the work area. Pullout shelves can be added to cabinets for easier access. Stoves with front controls make it possible for the wheelchair user to cook. Long-handled reachers can be used to adjust knobs mounted at the back of the stove. Care should be taken to keep dangling clothing or skin away from the burners. If the patient is ambulatory but endurance is poor, a high stool placed near work centers can be a real energy saver. An apron with large pockets, wheelchair bags, or a wheeled cart can also save many trips. Sitting at a table to do tasks previously performed while standing is helpful. Energy conservation techniques are very important for homebound patients. If a lower work height is needed, a drawer can be pulled out and a breadboard or other flat surface placed on top. To stabilize bowls or plates, dycem or a damp tea towel can be placed underneath. Durable medical equipment companies often carry a variety of assistive devices and adaptive equipment for the kitchen and bath. The patient's home, however, may be a treasure trove of items that can be used or adapted without the expense of purchasing new ones (AOTA, 1987b; Hale, 1979).

Medicare covers "durable medical equipment," which it defines as items that can withstand repeated use, are primarily for a medical purpose, and are not useful in the absence of an illness or injury. If equipment is to be supplied through the home health agency, a 20% coinsurance payment will be required. A physician's prescription, including diagnosis, prognosis, the reason for need, and the estimated length of time the item will be needed, is required for Medicare coverage. If the period of need is indefinite, reevaluation is done after 6 months. Below is a list of equipment the occupational therapist might determine to be useful for the patient's safety or increased independence. The status of Medicare coverage is given for each item (AOTA, 1987a, 1987b):

- Bedrails: covered if the patient is bed confined, is disoriented, or has vertigo or a neurological disorder such as convulsions or seizures.
- Hospital bed: covered if the patient is bed confined and positioning is needed but is not possible in a regular bed.
- Bedside commode: covered if the patient is confined to bed or room.
- Grab bars: not covered; considered a "self-help" device.
- Hoyer lift: covered if movement is needed to improve the patient's condition or prevent a deterioration of the condition.
- Splints: covered if they are required to improve or restore function.
- Raised toilet seat: not covered; considered a "convenience" item.
- Trapeze: covered if the patient is bed confined and needs it for bed mobility.

If the patient received a wheelchair while in the hospital, the fit may need to be adjusted or the prescription may need to be modified. The seat should be 2 inches wider than the patient. Solid seats improve position and decrease fatigue, but they may cause pressure sores. A variety of seat inserts, such as foam, Roho, or Jay cushions, are available if skin breakdown is a concern. Detachable and adjustable desk or wrap-around (full-length or desk) arms are recommended for transfer safety (Hale, 1979). An acrylic, see-through lap tray may also be helpful. Swing-away, detachable foot rests are also recommended, and heel straps may be useful. The back of the chair should come to the patient's scapulae, unless the patient has excellent trunk control and sitting balance and can use a sport or lightweight chair. If the patient is to be wheelchair mobile and use the feet to help propel the chair, a lower hemi-chair is needed (AOTA, 1987b).

Medicare will cover the cost of a wheelchair if it prevents the patient from being bed or chair confined. Power chairs are covered if the patient is unable to operate a standard wheelchair manually (AOTA, 1987a, 1987b).

If payment for equipment or services is denied, the local Medicare intermediary should be contacted to request the reasons for denial. If the reasons are unrelated to Medicare law, the *OT Medicare Guidelines* can be taken to a meeting with the intermediary and used to point out areas of compliance. If reimbursement continues to be denied, the Government and Legal Affairs Division of AOTA can be contacted (AOTA, 1987a).

TREATMENT PLANNING: PATIENT AND FAMILY

Returning home allows a patient to feel partially back in control of his or her life. It is very important that the therapist discover the stated needs and goals of the patient and primary caregiver or family. A major focus of home health care occupational therapy is to help the patient restructure previous activities to allow for maximal independence. In the home setting, family members and significant others are intimately involved in the treatment process. Ongoing family dynamics are affected by the patient's change of status and must be considered in the therapy process. Attitudes toward illness and disability play a vital role in the rehabilitation process and in defining the treatment program.

Goals and values are greatly influenced by the culture in which we are raised. If the patient belongs to a different cultural group or subgroup than the therapist, an understanding of that culture's view of health and illness and the roles of disabled men and women would be invaluable for appropriate treatment planning. Discussion of this area is beyond the scope of this chapter, but the reader is referred back to Chapter 2.

It is essential to involve the family in treatment planning and training. The therapist may visit only one to three days per week, but the family is there every day and will be working with the patient on a daily basis. The family must understand the rationale for the treatment program and be able to carry it out (AOTA, 1987b; Mac Rae, 1984). Written and verbal instructions should be given early and reviewed periodically. The family and the patient need to be aware of the patient's progress and potential. Even though the patient may have received therapy in a variety of settings, there may be little understanding of the extent or consequences of the disability, including the fact that the patient may not fully recover. This is a delicate topic and should be broached with great tact and sensitivity. The patient and family should not be left devoid of hope for improvement or of desire to learn alternative or adaptive means of task performance. Some doors of functional activity and involvement may close, but others may open to offer new avenues of interest, exploration, and growth. The therapist can be a guide through that unexplored territory (AOTA, 1987b).

RESPITE CARE

When a family member becomes ill or disabled, family dynamics and patterns of interpersonal relationships are upset. If the family places a high value on self-sufficiency, they may shift roles to fill the void left by the ill member and refuse outside help from a home health aide or other assistant. Teaching such techniques as energy conservation for home care tasks and joint protection to the patient can be helpful to the patient's partner or caregiver (Hale, 1979; Mac Rae, 1984).

In 1972, a national survey indicated that families provide 80% of the support system for the ill elderly (U.S. Department of Health, Education and Welfare, 1972). Another study found that in 65% of the cases in which the frail or ill elderly were hospitalized, there were three contributing factors: (1) a decrease in the self-care skills of the older person, (2) physical and mental difficulty experienced by the family in providing care, and (3) a decrease in the family's financial resources (Eggert, Granger, Morris, & Pendleton, 1977). The frail ill or elderly are institutionalized when they have no family support or when financial resources have been exhausted (Lindsey & Hughes, 1981).

Families can become quickly overwhelmed by the amount of care, involvement, and supervision needed, and they can develop feelings of anger and social isolation. As time goes on, holidays and vacations are given up by the caregivers (Hasselkus & Brown, 1983).

Factors that are poorly tolerated by family caregivers in caring for the ill elderly include (1) sleep disturbances, (2) fecal incontinence, (3) the need for assistance in toileting and transfers, (4) the lack of safety judgment, and (5) the potential for falls. Conversely, urinary incontinence and difficulty with dressing, personal hygiene, ambulation, and stair use were more tolerable to families (Sanford, 1975). Black and Sinnot (1979) demonstrated that the majority of abused elderly require assistance with self-care skills. The tasks of caring for a disabled family member and assuming the responsibility for the tasks that person once performed can become overwhelming to the partner or family. They need periodic respite or relief from the caregiving tasks.

If no other family members or friends are able to provide this on a periodic basis, other options should be considered. Respite sitters can be provided by county and private agencies. Respite care may also be provided in some hospital or nursing home settings for a brief period to give the caregiver a vacation (Hasselkus & Brown, 1983). This has the benefit of allowing medical follow-up and monitoring. Daycare several days a week may be considered for relief on a regular basis.

DISCHARGE PLANNING

The discharge process can be difficult for a patient and family who feel ongoing treatment is needed. On the first visit, the therapist can begin educating them about the differences between therapy in acute and rehabilitation settings and home care and can provide a simple explanation of Medicare coverage for home-care services. By discussing treatment goals during the initial evaluation, the way can be paved for discharge planning early on (Mac Rae, 1984). The therapeutic plan can include exploration of community services such as stroke clubs, public transportation, or daycare for the elderly, remembering that the patient's homebound status must be taken into consideration. If upon discharge the patient no longer qualifies as homebound, referral can be made to an outpatient clinic or rehabilitation setting (assuming further treatment is needed).

CONCLUSION

In providing occupational therapy services in the home health setting, few of the "props" from more traditional treatment settings are available to the occupational therapist. The home environment provides a unique challenge for therapists to think in new and creative ways—to rely on their head and their hands. In addition to the typical assessment of the patient's biomechanical status, family dynamics and sociological and cultural factors must be considered in planning the treatment program and modifying the environment.

Practical suggestions were provided regarding evaluation, treatment, documentation, and provision of equipment as they relate to third-party, especially Medicare, reimbursement. The importance of establishing a team approach in this unique treatment environment was emphasized. Finally, options for respite care for caregivers of the ill or disabled were explored.

Although working in home care is not for every occupational therapist, providing therapy services in this nontraditional setting offers creative opportunities and presents exciting challenges not often afforded in an institutional setting.

REFERENCES

American Occupational Therapy Association. (1987a). *Occupational therapy Medicare handbook.* Rockville, MD: Author.

American Occupational Therapy Association. (1987b). *Guidelines for occupational therapy services in home health.* Rockville, MD: Author.

Black, M.R., & Sinnot, J.D. (Eds.). (1979). *The battered elder syndrome: An exploratory study.* College Park, MD: University of Maryland Center on Aging.

De Paoli, T.A.L., & Zenk-Jones, P. (1984). Medicare reimbursement in home care. *American Journal of Occupational Therapy, 38,* 739–742.

Eggert, G.M, Granger, C.V., Morris, R., & Pendleton, S.F. (1977). Caring for the patient with long term disability. *Geriatrics, 32,* 102–114.

Eppler-Colvin, M., & Tanbe-Levine, K. (1984). Eliminating barriers to the disabled. *American Journal of Occupational Therapy, 38,* 748–753.

Hale, G. (Ed.). (1979). *The sourcebook for the disabled: An illustrated guide to easier and more independent living for physically disabled people, their families and friends.* Philadelphia: W.B. Saunders.

Hasselkus, B.R., & Bauwens, S.F. (1982). Occupational therapy and pharmacy: Adapting drug regimens for older people. *Gerontology Special Interest Section Newsletter* (American Occupational Therapy Association), *5,* 1–2.

Hasselkus, B.R, & Brown, M. (1983). Respite care for the community elderly. *American Journal of Occupational Therapy, 37,* 83–88.

Jackson, B.N. (1984). Home health care and the elderly in the 1980's. *American Journal of Occupational Therapy, 38,* 717–720.

Lindsey, A.M., & Hughes, E.M. (1981). Social support and alternatives to institutionalization for the at-risk elderly. *Journal of the American Geriatric Society, 29,* 308–315.

Mac Rae, A. (1984). Occupational therapy in a Medicare approved home health agency. *American Journal of Occupational Therapy, 38,* 721–725.

Pini, R. (1990). NAHC conference providers forum for home care practitioners. *OT Week* (American Occupational Therapy Association), *4,* 9, 16.

Reilly, M. (1962). Occupational therapy can be one of the greatest ideas of twentieth century medicine. *American Journal of Occupational Therapy, 26,* 1–9.

Reilly, M. (1971). The modernization of occupational therapy. *American Journal of Occupational Therapy, 25,* 243–246.

Sanford, J.R.A. (1975). Tolerance and debility in elderly dependents by supporters at home: Its significance for hospital practice. *British Medical Journal, 3,* 471–473.

Somers, F. (1990). O.T. home health services: Who pays? *OT Week* (American Occupational Therapy Association), *4,* 6–7.

Trossman, P.B. (1984). Administrative and professional issues for the occupational therapist in home health care. *American Journal of Occupational Therapy, 38,* 726–733.

U.S. Department of Health, Education and Welfare. (1972). *Home care for persons 55 and over.* Pub. No. HSM 72-1062. Washington, DC: Author.

U.S. Department of Health and Human Services. (1987). *Medicare carriers manual: Part 3. Claims process.* HCFA Pub. No. 14-3. Washington, DC: Author.

Chapter 14

Adult Daycare Programs

Lory P. Osorio

Adult daycare may be one of the most useful community resources available to occupational therapists who treat the growing number of older adults in our population.

Bob, 63, came to adult daycare after months in an acute care hospital recovering from a cerebral hemorrhage and subsequent inpatient rehabilitation at a regional facility. He could ambulate short distances with a short leg brace and quad cane and could dress, eat, and toilet independently; however, expressive aphasia limited his speech to a few words and his right arm was nonfunctional. Mary, his wife, had been optimistic that he could stay home alone while she continued to work. However, an incident when Bob failed to react to a kitchen smoke alarm convinced Mary that his judgment would not support 10 hours at home alone every day. A series of home companions left them both frustrated as a result of absenteeism (which interrupted Mary's work), the frequent need to orient new workers sent by the agency, and the lack of stimulation in Bob's day. When Bob's endurance declined from days spent in front of the television, Mary looked for another option. A coworker suggested adult daycare, and Bob was enrolled within a week. Mary said she felt their lives were finally getting back to normal when they both left the house together each morning, Mary to her job, which had been the stabilizing force in her life during Bob's illness and rehabilitation, and Bob to the daycare center, where he quickly regained his waning physical abilities and made dramatic progress in speech in the stimulating daycare environment.

Marie had struggled with anxiety all of her adult life. Now in her early seventies, she spent most days in bed, was unable to go out alone due to anxiety about "falling," and made no contribution to maintaining the home she shared with her working middle-aged daughter. After years of living with an incapacitated mother, her adult children had no expectation that Marie could lead a productive life. A change in physicians brought Marie to adult daycare. Facing yet another psychiatric hospitalization, the physician sent Marie and her daughter to visit an adult daycare center instead. To emphasize the seriousness of his recommendation the physician gave Marie a prescription that read "adult daycare 5 days/week; please send me progress reports." Reluctantly, Marie agreed to give daycare a try. She spent more of her first weeks at the center "resting" than involved in activity. Gradually the busy and interesting milieu of the center had more appeal than resting alone in an isolated room. Working closely with the center's occupational therapist, Marie learned to use purposeful activities and stress management techniques to help control her anxiety.

Hazel, a hospital social worker, brought her 84-year-old father to live with her after he was diagnosed as having Alzheimer's disease. Initially he stayed home alone while she worked, performing simple household chores and working in the yard. As his illness progressed, he began calling Hazel many times each day at work, worried about where she was and when she would be home. Struggling with guilt stemming from the paradox of "abandoning" her own father for a career aiding others, Hazel looked for help through the local chapter of the Alzheimer's Association. Following the suggestion of a helpline volunteer, Hazel learned that adult daycare met both her father's and her own needs. Hazel goes to work knowing her father is in a safe environment where he will receive the support, care, and companionship he needs. With the center's own social worker, she co-leads the monthly family support group.

NATIONAL DEFINITION

The National Institute on Adult Daycare (NIAD) defines adult daycare as

> a community-based group program designed to meet the needs of functionally impaired adults through an individual plan of care. It is a structured, comprehensive program that provides a variety of health, social and related support services in a protective setting during any part of a day but less than 24-hour care. . . . adult daycare assists its participants to remain in the community, enabling families and other caregivers to continue caring for an impaired member at home. (1984, p. 20)

Adult daycare programs are known by a variety of names, including *adult daycare, adult day health care, adult care, senior daycare, day health care, medical daycare, day hospital, social daycare, day treatment,* and *adult day center.* All programs have in common the element of serving frail or impaired adults who attend on a planned basis, both to receive needed services and to benefit from opportunities for fun, friendship, acceptance, new experiences, and improved quality of life. Adult daycare utilization reduces participant and caregiver isolation and provides a positive means of maintaining the older person in the family structure and community.

HISTORY AND PHILOSOPHY: ROOTS IN OCCUPATIONAL THERAPY

Adult daycare in the United States grew out of the day hospital movement developed in England in 1950 (O'Brien, 1982). Daycare as a preventive and health maintenance service for older adults was a logical development, given the success of day hospitals operated for psychiatric patients in the Soviet Union beginning in 1942 (Padula, 1983). The Soviet experience demonstrated that some patients benefitted more from day programs combined with living at home than from inpatient treatment (Webb, 1989). Adult daycare was introduced in the United States in the late 1960s with the opening of a center in North Carolina directed by an occupational therapist (Padula, 1983). Given the preference of many older adults for community rather than institutional care and the consistent finding that quality of life is higher for community-living elderly than those in institutions (Billings, 1982), adult daycare has significant appeal to elders, family members, and professionals. Adult daycare in the United States started as a grassroots effort on the community level. It was not until the late 1970s that the momentum increased and centers were more available. By 1978, 300 adult daycare centers were known to exist (U.S. Department of Health, Education and Welfare, 1980). By 1986, approximately 1,200 centers were in operation (On Lok Senior Health Services, 1987), and more than 44,000 families were estimated to be using the service (Webb, 1989). Most centers are located in urban and surburban areas; however, one-quarter are located in rural areas (Conrad, Hughes, Campione, & Goldberg, 1987).

The first English geriatric day programs were located in hospital occupational therapy departments and were designed to prevent or reduce inpatient hospitalizations. Staffing of the English geriatric daycare programs was multidisciplinary. However, the leadership of occupational therapists and their early influence on the philosophy of adult daycare is apparent even today. Comparison of the values underlying the practice of occupational therapy and the philosophy of adult daycare shows striking parallels. Yerxa (1983) described occupational therapy as concerned with the essential humanity of the individual and the quality of the individual's life in spite of disability. Productivity, self-directness, active participation, and faith in the patient's potential are all valued. An integrated view of the patient acknowledges the value of play and leisure and the importance of supporting the healthy aspects of the person so he or she can act on the environment rather than be determined by it. Based on a philosophy that closely parallels the values underlying occupational therapy, adult daycare

- approaches each person as a unique individual with strengths and weaknesses yet with a potential for growth and development
- assumes a holistic approach to the individual, recognizing the interrelationship among the physical, social, emotional, and environmental aspects of well-being
- promotes positive attitudes and a positive self-image, restoring, maintaining, and stimulating capacities for independence while providing supports for functional limitations (NIAD, 1984, p. 5)

MODELS OF CARE

Any discussion of adult daycare soon focuses at the issue of models of care. Robins (1975), Weiler and Rathbone-McCuan (1978), Padula (1983) and O'Brien (1982) all attempted to describe the diversity that is characteristic of the adult daycare service by developing models of care. Early efforts to develop a systematic method of classifying adult daycare programs are understandable, given the wide variety of programs operating under the adult daycare umbrella. Kelley and Webb (1989) suggest that this diversity between centers is unique in the long-term care field and that the diversity contributes significantly to the success of adult daycare in meeting the varied and changing needs of individual participants and communities. Diversity in location, sponsorship, staffing, services provided, eligibility criteria, and other characteristics are largely the result of the grassroots evolution of adult daycare and the impact of the dominant funding source on a center's purpose and programs.

Although the issue of models of care is less visible now than a decade ago, some adult daycare centers may continue to describe themselves or be perceived by others as based on a particular model. Some centers may be identified as "social model" centers, meaning they provide supportive social and recreational services to a group of elders who have stable health conditions but who may be "at risk" due to social isolation, lack of family support, physical frailty, or other similar characteristics. Services are primarily social and recreational, although screening or episodic health monitoring may be available. Prevention is a primary goal of social model programs. Other centers may claim to be based on the "health model" or "medical model," suggesting that they serve participants with unstable health and specific functional impairments. Such centers generally offer onsite nursing care, one or more therapies on a consult or contract basis, medical social work, therapeutic recreation, and adapted social or recreational activities. Maintenance of function and, in some cases, restoration of function are the goals of these centers. "Restorative model" centers are more acute in orientation, serving those with rehabilitation potential who need shorter term nursing, occupational therapy, physical therapy, or speech therapy. These restorative programs may be classified as day hospitals or day treatment centers and are usually located in hospitals, rehabilitation centers, and skilled nursing facilities or as separate programs in medical model centers. Their goal is short-term treatment and timely discharge, frequently to a medical model center, where the participant can receive longer term maintenance and episodic restorative services.

Although in theory "classical" types of centers or models of care can be identified, it is probably more useful for the occupational therapist (and other professionals) to conceptualize the universe of adult daycare centers as a continuum from social to restorative. Although few centers correspond exactly to any detailed description of a particular model center, all can be placed on a social-restorative continuum to facilitate appropriate referrals.

The primary purpose of any discussion of models of care or other attempts to classify centers is to maximize the match between the needs of the participant and the services offered by the adult daycare center. In cities where there are several adult daycare centers, the family or referral source may be able to choose among centers to select one offering the array of services most appropriate for the participant's current and future needs. The growing number of specialized centers (e.g., dementia, geropsychiatric, young adult physically disabled centers) offer even more specialized programs for urban residents. In smaller communities, choice of providers may be limited; however, a varied case mix within each center may be more likely. Suburban and rural centers usually must serve a very diverse group of participants to maintain an adequate census and remain viable. Like other centers, they are experienced at developing individual care plans based on the participant's functional abilities and needs rather than the diagnosis. Some participants may be served with a plan of care that is essentially social in nature, and others, who are more impaired, may receive medical or restorative services in addition. However, care must be taken to avoid serving a participant with significant health problems and functional limitations in a center that provides only social model services unless supplementary care is available to meet health and functional needs. Similarly, an isolated and frail but otherwise independent elder would probably be better served in a social model center than in a medical-oriented program.

In addition to facilitating an appropriate match between participant needs and service options, there is a second obvious reason for continued attention to models of care. In adult daycare, as in other industries, funding or reimbursement is clearly dependent on the underlying program philosophy and the services provided. Centers in states where social services block grant (SSBG) funding is the dominant funding source for adult daycare have historically been more social in orientation. Von Behren (1988) found that SSBG-funded centers are less likely to provide professional services and predominantly serve people who are less impaired and are able to live alone. Centers that qualify for Medicaid reimbursement are more likely to offer the professional services (e.g., nursing, occupational therapy, physical therapy, speech therapy, and professional social services) associated with the medical model and to serve more impaired participants, such as those who are incontinent or in need of constant supervision.

POPULATION SERVED

Adult daycare is unique among long-term care services in that it provides individualized care in a group or congregate setting. Unlike home care or residential care for the impaired elderly, adult daycare emphasizes the "therapeutic community" of participants and staff working together in small groups to achieve individual goals. Therefore, the abilities and needs of each participant are critical within the context of the group program. Decisions about admission to adult daycare and continuation of services must take into account not only the needs and skills of the individual participant but also their role in and impact on the daycare milieu. Von Behren (1986) found that most centers make these decisions on a case-by-case basis, considering such issues as specific care needs, degree of impairment, case mix, and census.

Adult daycare clients are commonly called *participants,* a term that reflects the activity orientation and purposefulness characteristic of adult daycare programs.

Most adult daycare participants have multiple chronic illnesses and specific functional impairment. Participants commonly come to adult daycare on referral from an acute care hospital, a rehabilitation center, the family physician, or a community social service agency. Participants vary in their ability to safely spend periods of time alone, a measure of independence frequently involved in decisions about adult daycare admissions and the level and type of daycare provided.

- Mrs. J. is diabetic and has arthritis and congestive heart failure. She lives alone in a large senior housing development, where she feels isolated and lonely. She comes to the daycare center twice a week for socialization and health monitoring. Staff help her access other services as needed. The center staff and participants are her extended family.
- Mr. L. lives with his widowed daughter. He has Parkinson's disease and depression and has had two heart attacks in the past 3 years. His unsteady gait and complex medication regime make it unsafe for him to be alone for more than an hour. He comes to daycare 5 days a week while his daughter works. A lifelong worrier, he not only needs the physical and health support but emotionally he feels safer with professional help readily available.
- Mrs. M. has late stage Alzheimer's and is aphasic, apraxic, and incontinent if not on a voiding schedule. She wanders and is disoriented to time, person,

and place. She requires constant supervision now, although when she enrolled in the center 5 years ago, she was independent in bathrooming, oriented to person and place, had only sporadic problems with word finding, but became behaviorally disruptive over changes in her routine. She spends a full 10 hours at the center every weekday. Her husband's goal is to minimize the length of time she spends in residential care. The staff support his goal. Their daily plan of care has evolved over the years from one emphasizing maintenance of function and self-esteem to one that meets basic physiologic and safety needs. Mrs. M. is very comfortable in the daycare center, responding positively to the familiar staff and environment.

Functional characteristics of adult daycare participants were recently identified through a study involving 847 centers (Von Behren, 1986). Cognitive impairment requiring supervision (45.4%) or constant supervision (19.8%) was the most common characteristic. Mobility limitations were also prevalent in the centers studied, with 17.3% of participants reliant on a cane or walker and 12.4% unable to transfer from a wheelchair without assistance. Clients who were behaviorally disruptive (7.6%) or developmentally disabled (10.1%) were also served. In spite of specific programs to manage incontinence (toileting reminders, continence training programs), 7.8% remained incontinent and required changing during the attendance day.

Demographically, the typical adult daycare participant has been described as a 72.9-year-old white female who lives with one or more family members and has a monthly income of $478 (Von Behren, 1986). However, 32% of adult daycare participants are men, 22.5% are nonwhite, and many live alone in the community (18.8%) or in a congregate setting (12.3%), such as senior housing. The oldest participant served in the 847 centers responding to the survey was 110.

Subsequent analysis (Von Behren, 1988) of center and participant characteristics suggests the following:

- Centers that serve "heavy care" participants (incontinent, needing constant supervision, wheelchairbound, etc.) are more likely to be willing to serve other difficult participants.
- In the adult daycare population, there is a negative relationship between (1) incontinence and the need for constant supervision and (2) living alone.
- There is a positive correlation between the availability of professional staff and the acceptance of wheelchairbound and incontinent participants.

SERVICES PROVIDED

There is a necessary relationship between participant characteristics and services provided to meet their needs. Specific services provided in the adult daycare setting can be divided into three categories (Von Behren, 1988):

1. basic—meals, transportation, recreation, and personal care (dressing, grooming, and toileting)
2. professional—nursing, social services, occupational therapy, and physical therapy
3. medical—physical assessment and treatment, dentistry, podiatry, and psychiatry

Center staff usually provide basic services. Professional services may be contracted or be provided by center staff. Medical services are usually contracted. However, they are more frequently available in medical or restorative model centers. These types of daycare centers are likely to be located in a hospital rehabilitation center or skilled nursing facility, where medical care is provided onsite.

The average adult daycare center provides 6.87 services. Of the 13 services identified in the basic, professional, and medical categories, basic services are provided in all but a few centers. Almost 95% of the centers also provide professional services, and about half the centers provide one or more medical services (Von Behren, 1988).

Adult daycare services are designed to meet goals articulated by the National Institute on Adult Daycare (1984):

- to promote the individual's maximum level of independence
- to maintain the individual's present level of functioning as long as possible, preventing or delaying further deterioration
- to restore and rehabilitate the individual to his or her highest possible level of functioning
- to provide support, respite, and education for families and other caregivers
- to foster socialization and peer interaction
- to serve as an integral part of the community service network and the long-term care continuum

A service plan is developed for each participant. The plan identifies the participant's specific needs, goals specific to each need, activities that will be used to achieve the goals, and the responsible staff members.

Service plans may be developed by supervisory staff or at multidisciplinary team meetings. Periodic review and updating is an important part of the care-planning process. In states where adult daycare centers are licensed or certified, there may be specific standards for initiation of the plan, the plan content or format, and the frequency of review and revision.

Adult daycare services are delivered in a manner that is both structured and flexible. For the participant, therapeutic activities generally form the structure for each (Exhibit 14-1). The emphasis is on creating a home-away-from-home that is both relaxing and reassuring and provides just the right stimulation. The daily routine offers predictability for those who need it, and yet there is enough flexibility to allow participants to engage in activities according to their needs and abilities. Professional and personal care services are integrated into the schedule based on individual needs.

OCCUPATIONAL THERAPY

Occupational therapists and certified occupational therapy assistants have varied and significant roles in adult daycare, particularly in restorative and maintenance programs. Providing direct services may be the most common role for occupational therapists in adult daycare. The traditional referral, screening, assessment, planning, treatment, reassessment, discharge process employed in most occupational therapy settings is appropriate in adult daycare and is well defined (AOTA, 1986b). Direct services may be provided by staff or on a contract basis. The emphasis is on cognitive, sensorimotor, and psychosocial skills as they affect self-care, work, and leisure. Daycare participant and family caregiver goals and expectations are critical to the treatment process, given the shared caregiving of the family and the daycare staff. The occupational therapy plan also may involve creating a supportive and therapeutic environment in the daycare center and modifying the home environment to enhance performance.

Indirect service roles may offer even greater challenges. The occupational therapist may serve as administrator, board member, consultant, researcher, or educator, roles that have the potential to define the scope and content of the program. As *administrator* of an adult daycare center or network of centers, the occupational therapist is responsible for all aspects of program management, including program development and supervision, financial management, supervision of the multidisciplinary team, coordination of services with other professionals and agencies, marketing, public relations, and licensing. These positions can offer challenges beyond those available in most department head positions, since the adult daycare director, in the majority of these facilities, is responsible for overall management of the corporation, not just the daycare program.

Every nonprofit adult daycare center has a board of directors that is legally responsible for the center. As a *board member,* an occupational therapist can play a role in setting policy and monitoring the business and programmatic aspects of the agency. Board members are volunteers, so it is ideal to combine this role with paid employment in other occupational therapy settings. For-profit and public centers usually have advisory boards, which have less legal authority but which offer many of the same opportunities for involvement in program development and evaluation.

Exhibit 14-1 A Typical Adult Daycare Day

7:30 AM	Center opens. Four working caregivers and participants are waiting. Coffee, newspaper, quiet music begin the day.
7:45 AM	Mrs. S. (Alzheimer's) arrives and goes directly to ladies' bathroom with aide. Husband never successful with bathroom attempts in AM. Mr. T. arrives and has a bowl of cereal and juice. Son overslept and must get to work.
8:30 AM	Twelve participants have arrived and a staff member begins current events group. First van arrives with 6 more participants. Two bring in refills of medications for RN.
9:30 AM	All 30 participants are at the center. Exercise groups start (3 groups, based on functional abilities). One incorporates reminiscing, another current events for late arrivals. Music, scarves, rhythm instruments are used. Nurse gives early AM meds and checks Mr. J.'s blood glucose. (Still over 300, so she calls MD about increasing medications.) Mr. M. paces in the hall with an aide, worried about where his wife is.
10:15 AM	Snack is served (fruit with yogurt topping). OTR orients aide to transfer skills of new post-CVA participant.
10:30 AM	Small group games begin (animal dominoes, indoor bowling, simple card games, etc.). Social worker meets with Mrs. V., who is depressed about the progression of her Parkinson's disease. Nurse checks weights and blood pressures of several participants with CHF. Mr. L. and Mr. K. work on a volunteer project stuffing envelopes for a Red Cross mailing.
11:30 AM	Several participants go for a walk with aides and recreation staff. Mrs. C. lies down for a short rest before lunch. Nurse begins prelunch medications.
12:00 NOON	Lunch is served. Half get special diets. OTR evaluates self-feeding skills of new participants (apraxic man with Alzheimer's and woman poststroke) and later incorporates findings into care plans.
1:30 PM	Relaxation group begins, led by OTR and attended by several participants with physical disabilities, depression, anxiety. RT CTRS leads balloon volley ball with Alzheimer's participants. Social worker meets with small group of caregivers about nursing home placement decision. Mr. B. becomes agitated and tries to leave, saying he has an appointment. Aide provides one-on-one supervision until his wife arrives at 3:30.
3:00 PM	Vans arrive to take 12 people with nonworking caregivers home. Others enjoy individual crafts, music; staff member reads aloud. Mrs. D. takes a nap (son not due until 5:15 PM).
4:00 PM	Afternoon snack (cheese and crackers—both low sodium—and apple juice).
4:30 PM	Individual activities continue as working caregivers arrive. Nurse talks to Mr. J. about wife's blood pressure and need for return MD appointment. OTR asks Mrs. S. to sign release of information so she can contact hospital OTR who treated her husband.
5:00 PM	Six participants remain, along with two staff members, who engage group in discussion about upcoming holiday.
5:25 PM	Last participant goes home with son and daughter-in-law.

Source: Stuart Circle Center, Inc., 1990. Richmond, Virginia.

Consultant roles vary from traditional case consultation, a critical role in centers with no occupational therapy staff, to program consultation, where the occupational therapist is involved in defining programs, evaluating and resolving problems, and carrying out special projects. The occupational therapist may serve as a consultant to the board, director, or staff on a long-term or time-limited basis.

Research opportunities are abundant in adult daycare, particularly for the occupational therapist interested in evaluating outcomes of care. Although few centers have a research budget, the growing interest in adult daycare should create opportunities for privately funded research projects.

Educator roles vary from fieldwork education supervisor to inservice, health, and community educator. Centers without occupational therapists would benefit from inservice education on topics such as environmental modification, adaptation of activities, and the impact of activity on health. Health education programs and support groups directed at participants and caregivers can stress various aspects of health behavior, coping, and caregiving skills. Community education activities involve developing public awareness of the potential and needs of older adults and the services available to them and their families.

Occupational therapy roles in adult daycare are varied and challenging. However, the extent to which occupational therapy services are actually being provided in adult daycare centers is difficult to determine. In Von Behren's (1986) survey of 847 centers, 22% reported that staff provided occupational therapy, 28% provided occupational therapy on a contract basis, and 37% arranged referrals for those needing occupational therapy. Given the distribution of adult daycare centers, it seems unlikely that a staff occupational therapist in an adult daycare center works in more than one center. If 22% of the 847 centers have staff-provided occupational therapy services, approximately 186 occupational therapists should be working in adult daycare. However, the *1986 Member Data Survey* published by American Occupational Therapy Association (AOTA) (1986a) identified only 21 occupational therapists who reported working in a daycare program with those 65 and older. There are at least three possible explanations for the discrepancy between the data:

1. Some adult daycare centers that report providing occupational therapy may not employ qualified occupational therapy personnel. ''Occupational therapy'' may have been interpreted as a generic term rather than as referring to a professional service.
2. Occupational therapists responding to the AOTA survey may work in adult daycare at a higher rate than they reported. Some may be part-time staff or consultants who identify more with their primary place of employment (hospital, rehabilitation facility) than with the adult daycare program.
3. Occupational therapy personnel working in adult daycare may not have responded to the member data survey.

Regardless of whether the adult daycare survey data or the AOTA data are correct, there appears to be tremendous potential for development of occupational therapy services in the adult daycare setting.

STAFFING

Staff are the critical element of a successful adult daycare center, since the "personality" of a center is largely determined by the staff philosophy, attitudes, and skills. Although most centers have a multidisciplinary staff of professionals, the critical staff characteristics are more likely to be personal rather than disciplinary. Flexibility is probably the essential characteristic required for all staff, considering the diversity of participants served, the interdisciplinary nature of many daycare activities, the reliance on the team approach, and the financial constraints found in many centers. Adult daycare centers work best when there is an easy sharing of the many generic caregiving tasks inherent in providing a safe, stimulating day for 20–30 impaired elders. The typical adult daycare center serves approximately 20 participants a day and maintains an active caseload twice that size (Von Behren, 1986). Individual staff members who insist on a division of labor along disciplinary lines can be detrimental to the overall operation of the program. A hierarchical, departmentalized staff structure is inappropriate in the adult daycare milieu. Mutual respect and constant collaboration among the professional staff and between professionals and paraprofessionals are essential. Other important staff characteristics include a positive attitude about aging, enthusiasm, common sense, a sense of humor, and patience. In adult daycare, participant progress is usually measured over weeks and months and gains may be small. In some cases, the goal is maintenance of function, not restoration. Therefore, therapists accustomed to the fast-paced acute care or rehabilitation environment will have to "down shift" to appreciate the low-tech, activity-based milieu consistent with the functional skills, needs, interests, and experimental learning style of most impaired elders.

REFERRALS

Occupational therapists who work with older adults have an important role to play in referring patients to adult daycare. Although self-referral may occur with some frequency in the case of social model programs, it is more common for potential consumers to access adult daycare on the recommendation of other care providers, such as physicians, therapists, social service agencies, health agencies, and hospitals. Family, friends, and word of mouth are also common sources of referral, perhaps reflecting growing consumer awareness of the adult daycare option and a high level of community satisfaction with the service.

Occupational therapists in a variety of settings should routinely screen their older adult patients for the appropriateness of adult daycare referral.

Although many geriatric patients discharged from *acute care* are appropriately referred to home health services, many of these patients could also be appropriately cared for in adult daycare. Given growing restrictions on the duration of home health care and the relatively episodic or part-time nature of home health visits, some patients may be better served over the long run by a comprehensive adult daycare center that can meet health, personal care, socialization, and family respite needs at low cost. Similarly, patients being discharged from home health care should be screened for adult daycare referral to maintain functional levels and meet continuing health needs.

Geropsychiatry patients often benefit significantly from inpatient evaluation and treatment. However, without intensive outpatient follow-up, many soon return to a daily home routine that offers insufficient structure, contains low levels of physical and cognitive stimulation and activity, leads to noncompliance with medication regimes, and generates growing levels of patient-caregiver stress. Serial hospitalizations or nursing home placement are common outcomes. Many adult daycare centers report successful long-term interventions with geropsychiatric patients who are referred directly to adult daycare from inpatient hospitalizations. Although family caregivers and patients may press for some "time off" between the hospitalization and initiation of adult daycare services, the most successful interventions usually involve starting the psychogeriatric patient at the adult daycare center even before hospital discharge by using a series of day passes. This strategy increases the likelihood of long-term compliance with the mental health staff's recommendation for adult daycare, assists the family caregivers with daycare intake, provides an interval for medication adjustment, and allows close communication between mental health and adult daycare staff, which facilitates the development of a long-term plan of care.

Specialty inpatient and outpatient *geriatric assessment programs* are increasingly called upon to assess and plan care for high-risk elders, most of whom have multiple diagnoses and significant functional limitations. Occupational therapists serving on these assessment teams are frequently involved in decisions about whether to recommend residential care (intermediate or skilled nursing homes, continuing care retirement communities, adult board and care homes), in-home care services (home health, live-in companions, home-delivered meals), and community-based care services (adult daycare). The comprehensive and flexible nature of adult daycare makes it a logical choice for those who have adequate family and community support and do not need 24-hour nursing care. The adult daycare plan of care can be tailored to the changing needs of the participant, and the medical conditions can be monitored for further follow-up.

Rehabilitation units, outpatient rehab programs, and *day hospitals* serve many patients who would benefit from adult daycare. Although the patient may reach his or her maximum functional level in the rehabilitation setting, the larger goal of maintaining function in the future requires careful attention. Discharged from the active rehabilitation setting, the older person may experience diminished expectations about performance and the maintenance of therapeutic routines. Ambulation, self-care, and communication skills may be compromised if family members think it is less stressful or more loving to "do for" the person. In this case, including adult daycare in the discharge plan can prevent regression. Other rehabilitation patients may make progress but at a rate too slow to justify continuation of therapy. Long-term goals must be compromised due to reimbursement limitations and the demand on staff to serve those who can progress at a more reasonable pace. The older adult with multiple medical problems may not have the physical or cognitive endurance to meet established treatment timetables. However, a restorative or medical model adult daycare center could afford the patient a slower paced, yet appropriately challenging program that would not have the pressures of a timebound program.

FUNDING AND FEES

The ways in which adult daycare centers are financed and the resources available for adult daycare consumers to pay for their daycare vary from state to state and center to center. In Von Behren's (1986) survey, 579 centers reported on their major source of funding. Medicaid (48.6%) and participant fees (34%) were found to be the main funding sources in terms of total dollars. However, collectively centers reported a total of 15 possible sources of income, including

- Title III of the Older Americans Act
- foundations
- donations and fund-raising
- mental health funds
- Medicare
- Social Services Block Grants (SSBGs)
- county or city government
- state funds
- other federal funds
- Community Development Block Grants (CDBGs)
- private insurance

- United Way
- other

In addition to cash income, most centers also depend to varying degrees on in-kind contributions of specialized and/or paraprofessional personnel, space, meals, equipment, and supplies. The high rate of in-kind support received by centers, an average of $4 per day per participant (Von Behren, 1986), may be a reflection of the continuing grassroots investment of local groups and individuals in the adult daycare movement. Since the overwhelming majority of centers (74%) are private, nonprofit agencies, in-kind support may be more available to them than to the 10% operated by for-profit entities.

The net effect for consumers of multiple funding sources and a high level of in-kind support is the availability of a reasonably priced long-term care service. In fact, 20% of adult daycare centers report having no fee or asking for donations only (Von Behren, 1986). Sliding fee scales or other income-based fee structures are in place in many centers. The average charge in centers with a fixed fee is $22.18 per day (Von Behren, 1986).

For the referring occupational therapist, there is little evidence to suggest that participant fees are a pervasive barrier to adult daycare utilization. Sliding fee scales and other methods of subsidy; Medicaid reimbursement, now available in many states; SSBG and CDBG funding; and several other funding sources are all targeted at the financial needs of lower and middle income applicants. Since 34% of centers already report participant fees as their leading source of income, it appears that participants with higher incomes can and do pay for adult daycare out of pocket. Many upper income families have realized that the comprehensive skilled care available in an adult daycare center is generally much less expensive than paraprofessional-level in-home care (e.g., home companions or aides) or residential care. For those who must pay for services out of pocket, utilization of adult daycare can result in considerable savings.

LICENSING AND CERTIFICATION

Thirty-four states have a mechanism in place or in the process of being put in place for licensing adult daycare centers (Zawadski & Von Behren, 1990). Licensure is a common requirement of funding and reimbursement sources, and it also provides a level of reassurance to participants, caregivers, and other professionals that a center meets certain standards. State licensing standards address such issues as ratio of space to number served, accessibility, staffing, services provided, arrangements for meals and snacks, documentation, staff continuing education, and many other aspects of center operations. Life safety and health code enforcement may be incorporated into the licensing standards or may be handled separately by local or state health and fire officials. Announced and unannounced licensing inspections are used to verify compliance with established standards.

Certification is also an established option for centers in 42 states (Zawadski & Von Behren, 1990). Certification may be an independent process separate from licensing. In other states certification may be an added credential for an already licensed center. Certification may qualify a center to receive reimbursement from a particular source (e.g., Medicaid) or serve a specific population (e.g., mentally retarded adults).

Although no national licensure or other method of credentialing is currently in place, the National Institute on Adult Daycare, a unit of the National Council on the Aging, publishes national standards that are available to centers who desire additional guidance in providing quality adult daycare. The national standards contain separate additional standards for care of participants with dementia. Profiles are also included that address adult daycare in rural areas and in adult daycare homes. Less detailed than the dementia standards, there are also profiles for serving six other special populations: (1) those with rehabilitation needs, (2) the head injured, (3) mental health clients, (4) the mentally retarded or developmentally disabled, (5) those with AIDS, and (6) those with sensory impairment (NIAD, 1990a). A companion self-assessment workbook provides a protocol for applying the standards to center operations for program evaluation activities (NIAD, 1990b).

THE FUTURE

The future need for adult daycare appears significant, as indicated by the following facts:

- Growing numbers of older adults in the population are living to an advanced old age, many with significant functional impairments that tax family caregivers and increase the risk of institutionalization. The need for adult daycare and other long-term care services will grow as the baby boom ages.
- Policymakers and service planners have a growing awareness that long-term care means more than nursing home care; community care options will move to the forefront as a result of economic restraints, continuing concerns about quality care, and increasing consumer sophistication about service options.
- The congregate nature and activity emphasis of adult daycare provide the added socialization benefit critical to most older adults' mental health, a benefit not available through home-based services. Growing knowledge of

the impact of activity on health status will add to the credibility of adult daycare as a preventive and restorative service.

- For those who are not bedridden, providing services in a group setting is more cost-effective than one-on-one home care and has the systemwide benefit of sharing increasingly scarce health professionals among a group of older adults. Staff travel time and associated costs are eliminated.

- The cost-effectiveness of adult daycare extends beyond its impact on the direct costs of care. The extended hours of care available at most centers support caregiver employment, thereby maintaining the financial integrity of caregiver households and contributing to the tax base.

- Although initially wary, most adult daycare participants are very positive about the service because it allows them to continue living at home while offering them a life away from home—friendships, meaningful activity, physical and emotional support, stimulation and variety, and a reassuring and familiar routine.

REFERENCES

American Occupational Therapy Association. (1986a). *1986 member data survey*. Rockville, MD: Author.

American Occupational Therapy Association. (1986b). Roles and functions of occupational therapy in adult day-care. *American Journal of Occupational Therapy, 40*, 817–821.

Billings, G. (1982). Alternatives to nursing home care: An update. *Aging, 2*, 325–326.

Conrad, K.J., Hughes, S.L., Campione, P.F., & Goldberg, R.S. (1987). Shedding new light on adult daycare. *Perspective on Aging, 16*,(6), 18–21.

Kelley, W., & Webb, L. (1989). The development of adult daycare in America. In L. Cooke (Ed.), *Planning and managing adult daycare* (pp. 9–17). Owings Mills, MD: National Health Publishing.

National Institute on Adult Daycare. (1984). *Standards for adult daycare*. Washington, DC: Author.

National Institute on Adult Daycare. (1990a). *Standards and guidelines for adult daycare*. Washington, DC: Author.

National Institute on Adult Daycare. (1990b). *Standards and guidelines for adult daycare: Self-assessment workbook*. Washington, DC: Author.

O'Brien, C. (1982). *Adult daycare: A practical guide*. Monterey, CA: Jones-Bartlett Publishing.

On Lok Senior Health Services. (1987). *Directory of adult daycare in America*. Washington, DC: National Council on the Aging.

Padula, H. (1983). *Developing adult daycare: An approach to maintaining independence for impaired older persons*. Washington, DC: National Council on the Aging.

Robins, E. (1975). *Operational research in geriatric daycare in the United States*. Paper presented at the 10th International Congress on Gerontology in Israel.

U.S. Department of Health, Education and Welfare. (1980). *Directory of adult daycare centers*. Washington, DC: Health Care Financing Administration.

Von Behren, R. (1986). *Adult daycare in America: Summary of a national survey*. Washington, DC: National Council on the Aging.

Von Behren, R. (1988). *Adult daycare: A program of services for the functionally impaired*. Washington, DC: National Council on the Aging.

Webb, L. (1989). *Planning and managing adult daycare: Pathways to success*. Owings Mills, MD: National Health Publishing.

Weiler, P.G., & Rathbone-McCuan, E. (1978). *Adult daycare: Community work with the elderly*. New York: Springer.

Yerxa, E.J. (1983). Audacious values: The energy source for occupational therapy practice. In G. Kielhofner (Ed.), *Health through occupation: Theory and practice in occcupational therapy* (pp. 149–162). Philadelphia: F.A. Davis.

Zawadski, R., & Von Behren, R. (1990). *National Adult Day Census 89: A descriptive report* [unpublished manuscript]. Prepared under Health Care Financing Contract #589-0024.

Part IV

Special Issues for Long-Term Care

Chapter 15

Providing Consultation to the Long-Term Care Facility

Richelle N. Cunninghis

THE ROLE OF THE OCCUPATIONAL THERAPY CONSULTANT

Consulting can be a challenging and exciting role for many occupational therapists. However, it differs in some respects from other types of practice, and certainly from other models presented in this text. Consultation may not be for everyone.

The relationship that a consultant has with the facility, personnel, and residents is not as intimate, permanent, or, in many cases, as satisfying as that experienced by the direct service provider. By definition, a consultant is an outsider who works part-time in a particular setting, has no responsibility for implementing change, and is not privy to many of the dynamics of the facility. But, consultants may also have opportunities that full-time staff do not have—opportunities to see the larger picture, to identify strengths and weaknesses, to bring a fresh perspective to ongoing situations, and to have an impact on the total system of patient care. It is important to be aware of these differences and one's own needs before going into consultation.

Occupational therapists are well qualified to serve as consultants to long-term care facilities, and they can provide many services in that capacity. This chapter deals primarily with activity consultation, but it is important to remember that other models also exist. Consultants may be asked to perform several functions, including

- providing direct treatment on a referral basis
- advising on long-range planning
- assessing the environment (e.g., identifying architectural barriers, designing space and furniture, and providing input on additions and modifications)

- serving as a resource person for such things as adaptive equipment design and purchase, interpretation of regulations, form construction and implementation, and interrelated roles of other departments in rehabilitation programs
- counseling families on rehabilitation techniques that could be used for the client at home
- providing information on the identification and use of community resources
- helping to prepare residents for discharge by leisure counseling and/or teaching the daily living skills necessary to promote effective functioning
- serving as a general resource person, such as an information collector and provider or a liaison with other agencies and health care professionals
- conducting inservice and other types of educational activities

Although an occupational therapist may serve many roles in a facility, that does not mean that there is an active treatment program in place. Even in situations where the same person may do restorative occupational therapy as well as provide consultation to the activity program, clear differences remain between the two programs. Although they are both dependent on good assessment information and often use similar activities as their prime modality, the similarities end there. The purpose, duration, process, scope of services, and education and preparation of personnel are all quite different. Table 15-1, based on Rogers' (1983) comparison of occupational therapy and activity programs, illustrates these differences.

THE CONSULTATION PROCESS

Consultation involves a unique relationship. Many attempts have been made to define exactly what it is, but few are entirely successful, because each consultation is so different. A consultant may be defined as someone who, by virtue of personal knowledge or experience, gives professional advice and provides guidance so that others may do their jobs more effectively (Cunninghis, 1985). The consultant is usually an outsider to the organization and its system and can only advise. The consultee and organization remain free to accept or reject any suggestions that may be offered.

Another way of describing consultation is that it is a combination of teaching and administration. However, the teaching differs from other educational processes in that, again, (1) the consultee is free to reject the "teaching" of the consultant, (2) the communication between consultant and consultee should go almost equally in both directions, and (3) if the relationship is truly effective, they should both learn during the process.

Table 15-1 Comparison of Occupational Therapy and Activity Programs

Variable	Occupational Therapy	Activity Programming
Education of provider	Registered, licensed	Varied
Use of assessment information	To identify treatment goals and therapeutic interventions	To identify needs, interests, and levels of involvement
Purpose	Problem-specific skill building, remediation	Health maintenance, retention of abilities, self-actualization
Modalities	Variety of therapeutic procedures	Leisure, recreation, work-related, housekeeping, and ADL activities
Length of involvement	Completion of treatment plan	Length of stay in facility
Choice of activity	Can be based on identified interests but is determined by treatment plan	Based on identified needs, interests, current abilities and desires, variety, and balance
Choice of client	Referrals or patients likely to improve	All residents in facility

Source: Data from "Roles and Functions of O.T. in Long-Term Care: O.T. and Activities Programs" by J.C. Rogers, 1983, *American Journal of Occupational Therapy, 37*, pp. 807–810. Published 1983 by American Occupational Therapy Association.

Livingston and O'Sullivan (1971) defined an "effective consultative process" as one that "is on-going and dynamic, the results of which will be measurable and also observable. Consultation is both an art and a science. The art of consultation is a blending of knowledge and experience and applying these talents to help produce a solution to the problem or outline a course of action to be taken" (p. vii).

Consultants often view themselves as "agents of change or facilitators" (Miller, 1978, p. 380). They need to have an understanding of the health care providers' needs and to demonstrate that they can be of assistance in making the best use of existing resources and pointing out ways to maximize opportunities (Nackel, Jacoby, & Shellenbarger, 1986, p. 2, 23). Consultants, in order to be prepared for these roles, must possess a variety of skills and background knowledge, including the basic skills common to dealing with people and groups, such as the ability to remain objective and task-oriented and to listen and communicate effectively.

Some of the necessary skills are more specific to the consultant role, such as being able to explain what that role is, giving effective feedback, dealing with resistance, identifying problems, and identifying possible solutions (Hausser, Pecorella, & Wissler, 1977). Consultants must also possess a good sense of timing, salesmanship, flexibility, and, perhaps most importantly, the ability to recognize the normal self-interest of the consultees and their potential for growth.

Consultants need to establish credibility and understand the structure and goals of the organization. They also need to realize that consultation does not take place in a vacuum. The particular department that a consultant is involved with is part of a larger social system that the consultant must constantly consider. First, the consultant must question why he or she is there, who requested a consultant, why was the consultant the one selected, and under whose authority does he or she operate? It is a good idea to try to identify who are the real power people in the facility and how they might impact the department and the ongoing consultative relationship.

Finally, consultants must be able to maintain sanction, that is, permission to continue to operate. A consultant has a legitimate sphere of operation, and once this is overstepped, the consultant's mission is no longer viable. This concept is clearly tied to the concept of the consultant's role within the social system. Although other problems may be identified and other personnel may request help, it is important that the consultant remembers his or her primary role and the legitimate scope of the sanction. It is not the consultant's place to carry out programs, diagnose or criticize other departments, or indicate in any way that he or she might be better able to do the consultee's job (Leopold, 1966). These areas often require great sensitivity and restraint on the part of consultants but can lead to serious problems if ignored.

Activity consultants need to understand and interpret all regulations that impact activity programming. They must have a thorough knowledge of the type of clients they are likely to encounter and the physical, mental, medical, environmental, and social conditions that must be considered in program design and participation. They must understand the basic philosophy of activity programming and be able to assess and determine the effectiveness of the current program in meeting individual and collective needs.

Activity consultants should be familiar with activities and programs that can be used successfully with these groups and be able to determine the suitability of activities for individual residents (Cunninghis, 1984).

ACTIVITY PROGRAMMING IN LONG-TERM CARE

The primary concern of nursing home personnel has traditionally been to provide custodial care. In most cases, it was thought that their responsibility had been met if residents were fed and sheltered and received medical treatment as needed. In long-term care facilities (or nursing facilities, which is now the common designation), this has slowly begun to change, and more and more emphasis is being put on the quality of life. Ideally, a complete care program is designed to promote maximum health and to make use of the remaining skills that the residents possess (Incani, Seward, & Sigler, 1975). The facility staff should recognize each resident as a unique individual with basic interrelated human needs (Hagen, 1967). These needs may vary in intensity and means of expression, but they are not essentially different from those of all people in every stage of life.

The physical needs encompass exercise and activity within the individual's tolerance as well as independence in the skills of self-care and daily living. The primary psychological needs, as with everyone, are to be loved and needed. Accompanying these is a need for self-esteem, which is often heightened by institutionalization and the many losses that may have been sustained prior to admission. Additionally, individuals may feel threatened and require help in adjusting to their age, physical condition, and impending death and in maintaining maximum mental functioning. Companionship, group identity, new experiences, and feeling useful to others are some of the identifiable social needs of nursing home residents.

In most facilities, the activity program is the primary means of meeting many of these needs. Unlike most programs or departments, it is not concerned with treatments or other aspects of physical care but is free to concentrate on the quality of life within the facility. In fact, in the original training guide for activity coordinators (U.S. Department of Health, Education and Welfare, 1972), it was stated that "the goal of resident activities is to create and support an enriched environment for quality living which relates to the individual's life style, capabilities, and indigenous community. Adequate activities programming decreases the need for treatments and maintains people at higher levels of function than is possible with a 'treatment-oriented' approach" (p. 12).

There are several different definitions that are used for activity programming, and in many cases the facilities and activity personnel themselves are not entirely sure of what their role should be. In its broadest sense, *activity* encompasses all things a resident does during waking hours that are not treatment. This definition at least does not limit the scope of activities to what used to be called the BBC (Bible, bingo, and crafts), but it does little to define the role of the activity department and its personnel. A much more comprehensive definition is as follows:

> "Activities programming" is understood to mean the provision of exercise for the individual's physical, mental, and social abilities when the environment does not encourage such exercise naturally. The purpose is to prevent and cope with isolation, dependency, helplessness, institutionalization, apathy, lowered sensory input, atrophy, etc. By adequate "activities programming" we mean the involvement of all residents in the facility in some activities in which they are individually interested, and which meet their physical, competitive, mental, and social needs daily, including Saturday and Sunday. . . . The adequacy is determined by the documented interests of the individuals served,

their physical, mental, and social needs, and how well these individual interests and needs are matched by activities provided. Staffing, numbers of activities offered or "busyness" of the staff and residents are not necessarily an indication of adequacy. (U.S. Department of Health, Education and Welfare, 1972, p. 12).

Although this too is a general definition, it does include several important considerations. Perhaps the most important is the emphasis upon the resident. Any effective program should start with determining the needs and interests of the individual and channeling them into an activity plan that will be satisfying. It is not always easy to identify these factors, nor to use them to devise a program that the resident will want to participate in and get satisfaction from. But discovering them is both the necessary place to start and the key to continued effectiveness (American Health Care Association, 1972). Furthermore, it is essential that activities be integrated into the daily life of each resident and not be thought of as a separate entity that has no relation to the rest of care. Activity, as indicated by the definition above, does not have to be planned or supervised by activity personnel to be effective or to qualify and be documented as such. Visiting, letter writing, television watching, and reading are just a few examples of possible activities.

REGULATIONS AND REQUIREMENTS FOR ACTIVITY PROGRAMS

In most states, several different agencies may monitor nursing facilities. If a facility accepts Medicaid patients, then it is subject to Medicaid regulations and, in some cases, surveys. The regulations vary from state to state but usually focus on the Medicaid patients and their care. Because the program is jointly funded by federal and state governments, each jurisdiction has the right to determine what it will fund and to design the mechanisms for monitoring and enforcement.

Individual state regulations are tied in to the federal standards, but states may have additional requirements of their own. State inspection teams usually have the authority to approve a nursing facility's license to operate. Each state is also the representative of the federal government for Medicare recipients. In most cases, the state will survey a sample of the entire resident population, including Medicare, Medicaid, and private pay residents. These two functions may be done in one survey or by two separate teams.

The Joint Commission on Accreditation of Healthcare Organizations (Joint Commission) is a voluntary program that is accrediting an increasing number of nursing facilities and sets standards for those that choose to be monitored by the commission. Addressed in its guidelines are four basic areas for activity programs: staffing, provision of services, participation in the team care plan development and implementation, and quality assurance. All of these focus on meeting the individual needs, abilities, and interests of the residents and "the quality and appropriateness" of the services offered (Joint Commission, 1986).

Additionally, some facilities admit patients through the Veterans Administration and therefore need to meet its requirements as well. And all facilities are also subject to local and county regulations, mainly fire and safety codes. If the facility is part of a group or corporation that has its own standards and/or quality assurance program guidelines, then they too must be followed.

The provision of quality care is the main focus of all regulations written for nursing facilities. In fact, the new requirements for long-term care facilities that went into effect on August 1, 1989, state that "a facility must care for its residents in a manner and in an environment that promotes maintenance or enhancement of each resident's quality of life" (U.S. Department of Health and Human Services [DHHS], 1989, p. 5363).

Specified under this requirement are the rights of dignity, participation in resident and family groups, participation in other activities (including "social, religious, and community activities that do not interfere with the rights of other residents in the facility"), accommodation of needs, social services, and "a safe, clean, comfortable and homelike environment" (DHHS, 1989, pp. 5363–5364).

The activity requirements stipulate that "the facility must provide for an ongoing program of activities appropriate to residents' needs and interests designed to promote opportunities for engaging in normal pursuits, including religious opportunities of their choice . . . [and designate] a member of the facility's staff as responsible for the activities program, who, if not a qualified patient activities coordinator, functions with frequent regularly scheduled consultation from a person so qualified" (DHHS, 1989, p. 5330).

The specific qualifications for the activity coordinator are spelled out, as is the role of activity personnel in the total resident care plan. Assessment must include functional capacity and activity potential. It was recommended by many who responded to the initial version of these regulations that three types of activities— supportive, maintenance, and empowerment activities—be added to the requirements. Although the suggestion was rejected, these classifications will be included in the interpretive guidelines for the surveyors (DHHS, 1989, pp. 5330–5331).

A consultant to an activity program must be familiar with all the agencies and regulations that impact that facility. As regulations differ for each area and each location, the best strategy is to contact the state department of health and the local Medicaid office and to ask the administrator about other relevant regulations. In cases where there are variations in requirements, the rule of thumb is that the most stringent take precedence. Also, the higher the authority, the more important it is that its guidelines be followed. Thus, federal government regulations will usually prevail if there is a direct conflict.

ACTIVITY PROGRAM CONSULTING

As with activity programs themselves, the consulting process has to start with assessment. It is necessary to know who the residents are in terms of age, gender, prevailing illnesses and disabilities, predominant ethnic and socioeconomic backgrounds, and numbers of long-term versus short-term admissions.

It is also important to know about facility schedules, spaces available, attitudes and needs of other departments, and what is currently being done in the activity department, including how personnel are used and what activities are offered.

There are many methods for gathering the necessary data, including interviewing staff, families, and residents; auditing charts; monitoring activities; and walking through the facility and observing. However the information is garnered, it is essential that sufficient time be allowed to get to know the strengths and weaknesses of the key people, provide reassurance, and listen to the concerns of others (the ability to listen is often the most important skill for the consultant to possess) (Katcher, 1969). Many consultants go in with their own agendas and don't really meet the needs of the facility or consultees. In a recent interview in a publication for activity personnel, this author was asked to comment on the statement that "activity professionals have been voicing dissatisfaction with their O.T. consultants, saying they are offering ROM, feeding programs and adaptive equipment when what they really want and need is help with programs, documentation and practical advice" (*Activity Professionals Quarterly*, 1989). Although, as was indicated in the answer, much of the blame for this problem belongs to consultees, it is an important pitfall to avoid.

Most consultants develop a tool for the purpose of gaining information and assessing those with whom they will be working. Completing this form often provides much useful information on which to base future planning. A typical assessment form is presented in Exhibit 15-1.

After the assessment process is completed, the consultant should be prepared to report on present conditions and problems identified, set goals, outline services that he or she may be able to provide, and indicate appropriate time frames (Katcher, 1969). In many cases, this is when the consulting contract is negotiated and the scope of services determined. The administration is, of course, free to accept or reject all or some of the recommendations. The consultant is equally free to decide whether any change can be effected and whether the conditions are consistent with his or her own professional standards (Miller, 1971).

Although the services provided may vary widely from facility to facility, any or all of the following might be among those included:

- assisting in developing a philosophy of and policies and procedures for activity programming

Exhibit 15–1 Sample Assessment Form

PROGRAM EVALUATION

Facility name _____

Address _____

Telephone _____

Administrator _____

Other personnel who impact on activity department _____
_____

Number of residents _____

Medicare _____ Medicaid _____ VA _____ JCAHO _____

Activity director _____

　Length of service _____

　Prior experience _____

　Education _____

　Organization memberships _____

　Working hours _____

　Other responsibilities _____

Assistant(s) _____

　Length of service _____

　Prior experience _____

　Education _____

　Working hours _____

　Other responsibilities _____

Does the activity department have copies of:

　Facility organization chart _____

　Accurate job descriptions _____

　State and federal regulations _____

　　Understand requirements _____

　Accurate department policies and procedures _____

　QA plan for dealing with problems _____

Are ongoing records kept of:

　Budget _____ Department input _____

　Long-range department goals and plans _____

　Minutes of meetings attended _____

　Activity breakdowns and descriptions _____

　Resources utilized/available _____

Do procedures exist for:

　Completing calendars at required times _____

　Posting calendar _____

　Other means of notifying residents of events _____

　Communicating activity schedules and needs to other departments _____

　Notifying residents of changes in location or condition _____

　Activities orientation for all new employees _____

　Monthly reports:

　　Content adequacy _____

　　Procedure for distribution _____

　　Report feedback _____

---

continues

Exhibit 15–1 continued

Does the activity department participate in:
  Care conferences _____ How often _____
  Staff meetings _____ How often _____
  Utilization review _____ How often _____
  Discharge planning _____ How often _____
  Department head meetings _____ How often _____
  Inservices _____ Present _____ Attend _____
  QA team _____
  Surveys _____ Deficiencies _____
  Recommendations/changes _____
Do other departments:
  Help with transportation _____
  Help with programs _____
  Have awareness of scheduled activities _____
  Try to avoid schedule conflicts _____
  Communicate useful information _____
  Cooperate with requests _____
  Understand mandate of activity program _____
Does the activity program:
  Base activities on identified needs _____
  Base activities on interests of individual residents _____
  Change as resident population changes _____
  Include individual activities _____ Goals set _____
    Activities for the frail/bedside _____
    Activities for the cognitively impaired _____
    Small group activities _____
    Clubs and committees _____
    Resident council _____ How often _____
      Member selection _____
      Staff attendance _____
      Follow-up of suggestions _____
    Large group activities _____
    Outdoor activities _____
  Provide transportation for outside trips _____
  Offer weekend activities _____ PM _____
  Provide materials for residents' use _____
Are staff:
  Meeting number requirements _____
  Utilized effectively _____
  Assigned individual responsibilities _____
  Using good time management techniques _____
  Familiar with group dynamics _____
  Effective as group leaders _____
  Knowledgeable about resident population _____
  Knowledgeable about individual residents _____
  Tuned in to their needs/goals _____
  On good terms with other departments _____

continues

Exhibit 15–1 continued

Is there dedicated space available for:
Programming ———————————————————————————————
Equipment and supplies ————————————————————————
Are other areas used ——————————— Outdoor areas ——————
Adequate storage ———————————————————————————
Is there an active volunteer program ——————————————————
Recruited ——————————————————————————————
Oriented ———————————————————————————————
Supervised —————————————————————————————
Recognized —————————————————————————————
Retained ———————————————————————————————
Records kept ————————————————————————————
Resident documentation:
Effective forms ————————————— Sufficient space ——————
Ask right questions ——————————————————————————
Completed on time ————————————— Initial assessment ————
Updates ————————————————————————————————
Copies kept ——————————————— Where ————————————
Levels of participation indicated ————————————————————
Include physician's permission ——————————————————————
How obtained ———————————————————————————
Is behavior described or labeled ————————————————————
Do goals address identified problems ——————————————————
Needs/interests ———————————————————————————
Are goals specific/measurable/observable ——————————————
Do goals have reasonable time frames ——————————————————
Does resident participate in goal setting ————————————————
Are needs/interests translated into activities ——————————————
Is activities plan part of total care plan —————————————————
Do updates include progress toward goal ————————————————
Is there continuity in notes ——————————————————————
Are there discharge plans ———————————————————————
Are there discharge summaries —————————————————————

Conclusions:

- increasing residents' involvement in setting their own goals and choosing activities in which they want to participate
- interpreting and promoting to the rest of the staff the role of the activity program and its relationship to total resident care
- helping the activity staff to define and defend its appropriate turf
- advising on appropriate activity areas, staffing, storage, equipment, and supplies based on the assessment of the resident population and available resources
- providing input on the selection and maintenance of forms and documentation procedures that meet necessary requirements and help facilitate evaluation of the program's effectiveness
- helping in the development and implementation of effective individual resident care plans
- advising on scheduling and efficient use of time by personnel
- identifying available resources and how they might be utilized
- suggesting new activities to broaden the scope of the program and to meet identified needs and interests of the current residents
- developing criteria for appropriate volunteer roles and developing policies and programs related to recruitment, training, and supervision
- assessing residents with special problems and helping to identify appropriate goals and ways to achieve them
- advising on enhancement of group dynamics, resident involvement, and leadership skills
- determining activity adaptations required as a result of individual interests, abilities, and needs
- training personnel in new techniques and approaches
- keeping activity personnel apprised of changes in regulations and requirements, educational programs, publications, impending legislation, or anything that impacts on their professional development and provision of services

CONSULTATION METHODS

The way that a consultant operates depends very much on his or her own personal style and preferences and the services that are being provided. Each visit may be different or may follow a preset pattern. After the assessment and evaluation stage is concluded, subsequent sessions may include discussion and problem solving, chart audits, the observing of activities in progress, or the conducting of activities, demonstrations, inservice training, or other educational tasks. It is also possible to give the consultees assignments, such as writing care plans for certain residents or keeping track of how their time is spent, and then to evaluate the results together (Cunninghis, 1985).

One method often used is to critique how personnel conduct an activity. Much useful information can be given and received in these sessions. Although critiques can be used as part of the assessment process, they are generally more effective when the consulting relationship has progressed to the point where the group leader does not feel overwhelmed and threatened by criticism. Exhibit 15-2 indicates some of the areas that the consultant might evaluate.

ETHICAL AND PROFESSIONAL CONSIDERATIONS

Although consultants may not deal directly with residents, there are a number of decisions they may be called upon to make that may impact directly on resident

---

Exhibit 15-2 Group Leader Evaluation

	Yes	No
Does the leader meet/greet/seat all residents?		
Is the leader prepared?		
Are work areas/surfaces cleared?		
Is knowledge of individual goals demonstrated?		
Is the activity geared to identified needs/interests?		
Is the purpose of the activity being met?		
Does the time length seem appropriate?		
Does the group size seem appropriate?		
Is there a "Plan B" if needed?		
Does the title describe the program?		
Is the activity the same as the one posted?		
Is the leader comfortable handling the group?		
Are volunteers utilized effectively?		
Is there group socialization/interaction?		
Are residents listened to/providing input?		
Are directions clearly given?		
Is there a pleasant atmosphere/environment?		
—Free of noise?		
—Free of distractions?		
—Free of glare?		
—Appropriate for activity?		

Source: © Geriatric Educational Consultants, 1989, Willingboro, New Jersey.

care. One task is to define who exactly the client is. If serious problems exist in a facility, do consultants owe their loyalty to the administration, the staff with whom they are directly involved, the residents, or the regulatory agents who might be interested in their findings? A related issue is confidentiality: To whom do consultants report their findings and under what conditions? And if they do encounter poor conditions of care, do they leave or stay and try to effect change?

Other issues involve fee setting. What is considered effective working time? Should rates be based on experience or realism? Competition with other health care providers, setting and keeping of appointments, territoriality, and determining the appropriate time and method of termination are other items to be considered.

Consultation requires prior knowledge and experience, a great deal of preparation, and an ability to work independently. As stated at the beginning of this chapter, providing consultation to long-term care facilities may not be for everyone, but those who choose to do it are likely to find it is an exciting professional experience.

REFERENCES

Activity Professionals' Quarterly, 1(2), May 1989. (P.O. Box 633, Charlton, MA 01504)

American Health Care Association. (1972). *Activities coordinator's guide.* Washington, DC: Author.

Cunninghis, R.N. (1984). *A professional guide for activity coordinators.* Willingboro, NJ: Geriatric Educational Consultants.

Cunninghis, R.N. (1985). Working with an activities consultant. *Activities, Adaptation, & Aging, 7*(2), 123.

Hagen, M.P. (1967). Nursing home residents: A challenge to the occupational therapist, *American Journal of Occupational Therapy, 21,* 151.

Hausser, D.L., Pecorella, P.A., & Wissler, A.L. (1977). *Survey-guided development II: A manual for consultants.* LaJolla, CA: University Associates.

Incani, A.G., Seward, B.L., & Sigler, J.E. (1975). *Coordinated activity programs for the aged: A how-to-do-it manual.* Chicago: American Hospital Association.

Joint Commission on Accreditation of Hospitals. (1986). *LTC/86: Long term care standards manual.* Chicago: Author.

Katcher, A. (1969). On becoming a consultant to an extended care facility. In *Project for consultants to extended care facilities* (pp. 1–18). Los Angeles, CA: Atkins-Katcher Associates. (Guide draft)

Leopold, Robert L. (1966). *The techniques of consultation: Some thoughts for the occupational therapist.* Paper presented at the Consultancy Workshop, Eastern Pennsylvania Occupational Therapy Association, Norristown.

Livingston, F.M., & O'Sullivan, N.B. (1971). *Occupational therapy in the skilled nursing facility: An overview.* Pomona, CA: Southern California Occupational Therapy Consultants Group.

Miller, D.B. (1978). Reflections concerning an activity consultant by a nursing home administrator. *American Journal of Occupational Therapy, 32,* 375–380.

Miller, P. (1971). Development of the consultant occupational therapist: The key to obtaining the job and successful implementation. In C. Satterly, E. Goodman, & W. Lipson (Eds.), *Report of an institute: The occupational therapist consultant in nursing homes* (pp. 32–47). Metropolitan New York District, New York Occupational Therapy Association.

Nackel, J.G., Jacoby, T.J., & Shellenbarger, M.T. (1986). *Working with health care consultants.* Chicago: American Hospital Publishing.

Rogers, J.C. (1983, March). Roles and functions of occupational therapy in long-term care. *Occupational Therapy Newspaper*, pp. 8–9.

U.S. Department of Health, Education and Welfare. (1972). *Planner's and instructor's guide for activities coordinators continuing education programs.* Washington, DC: Author.

U.S. Department of Health and Human Services. (1989, February 2). U.S. Department of Health and Human Services proposed regulations Medicare and Medicaid: Requirements for long term care facilities. *Federal Register, 54*(21), 5330–5331, 5363–5364.

Chapter 16

Community Building as a Basis for Activity Programs

Jean M. Kiernat

One of the consistently overwhelming feelings experienced when spending time in a long-term care facility is the awareness of a lack of togetherness. Each resident seems so alone, yet all share a common fate as inhabitants of the same geographic space during the same perilous journey in time. Old age, frailty, and dependence in a number of spheres are commonalities shared by all, commonalities that bring them to this central place.

Common concerns are frequently heard from individual residents regarding the lack of control over their own lives: loss of independence; the limitations in choice, decision making, and privacy; and the lack of meaning and purpose (Spaulding, 1985). Residents, who have so much in common with one another, do not appear to give or receive support from each other. They do not seem to lean on one another and gain strength through fellowship. There is no feeling of community among this group.

Residents interviewed 6 to 12 months after their admission to a nursing home report they do not perceive themselves as belonging to the environment. They feel like outsiders and find it very difficult to become socialized into the new environment (Melanson & Meagher, 1986).

Kastenbaum (1972) has described these residents as permanent captives in a sick role. In earlier life and in other settings, these same individuals could accept that they needed temporary assistance, knowing that the tables would turn and they would be able to reciprocate by helping others. Now in the institution each becomes the "One-Who-Is-To-Be-Helped. And tomorrow will be very much like today" (Kastenbaum, 1972, p. 367). Older institutionalized persons are expected to receive but never give, to follow but never lead. The staff, on the other hand, are similarly locked into their role as givers and helpers.

INTERPERSONAL RELATIONSHIPS

The quality of life in nursing care facilities is intimately related to the quality of the interpersonal relationships that exist (Institute of Medicine, 1986). In general, relationships between individuals involve one of two types of bonds. The first of these, the sibling bond, involves a similarity between two persons and a reciprocity that implies some measure of equality. It may be expressed thus: "I have some things to offer and some needs to fill" (Hochschild, 1978, p. 64).

The second type of bond is found in the parent-child relationship. It does not involve reciprocity or similarity. There are few similar needs, resources, or experiences. "I depend on you more than you depend on me" characterizes this type of bond (Hochschild, 1978, p. 64).

Institutions tend to foster relationships of the parent-child type. All services are provided to the patient or resident, who cannot reciprocate. These strong parent-child bonds may actually overwhelm any potential sibling solidarity, according to Hochschild. For example, even if each resident has a roommate, each has a nonreciprocal relationship with the staff rather than a sibling or peer relationship with each other. Miller and Beer (1977) found that many times nursing home residents did not know the full name of their roommates, nor did they know if those roommates had spouses.

Sibling bonds (or peer relationships) are very delicate, but the two conditions required for their formation are clearly present in the aged population—rapid social change and more age stratification (Hochschild, 1978). The other age group in which these two conditions are present is the teenage population, and sibling bonds are certainly evident in their activities! It would seem that an admirable goal for an activity program would be to increase the bonds between residents and improve their relationships by encouraging specific types of activity.

ACTIVITY PROGRAMS

Occupational therapists who serve as consultants to long-term care facilities often provide advice and technical assistance regarding activity programming. The general expectation of activity programs is that social activities will bring people together and provide opportunities to have interesting, stimulating interactions with other residents.

In actual practice, what one often sees are many older individuals in a group setting engaged in solitary activity. Each person is observing the entertainment offered, attending the sing-along, or working on some type of craft project, but social interaction tends to be between the staff and each resident.

The harder the staff work to direct these social activities, the more they defeat their own purpose. Professionals acting as activity experts further strengthen the parent-child bond. Bowker (1982) believes that programmed social interaction may be a misleading concept, since it is possible to organize programs so rigidly that no reduction in the formal institutional milieu occurs. He found that unprogrammed social interaction was usually more important in the lives of residents than highly programmed social interaction under the direction of recreational therapists and social workers. What better example of rigidly programmed activities than the reality orientation and remotivation classes offered universally!

Activities and programs can be offered simply to keep residents busy, or they can be planned in meaningful ways to maximize resident involvement and interaction. In a series of studies conducted in a geriatric hospital, Kastenbaum (1972) offered daily gatherings for small groups of residents who were not socially active, although many could have been. The activity was much like a happy hour or cocktail party, with beer, wine, fruit juice, and cheese available. No format was planned, no special program was offered. People came together over food and drink in a normal type of setting.

Dramatic results occurred, with patients spontaneously forming themselves into groups for the first time since entering the hospital. They stepped outside the patient role and functioned as adult peers who enjoyed one another's company. Less was done to and for the patients and more was done with them, as staff joined in this mutually gratifying experience.

Through activities, it is possible to facilitate resident self-determination and foster the development of peer relationships. This can best be accomplished by helping residents create their own personal environment to meet their own needs rather than controlling and modifying the environment for them (Bayne, 1971).

Hochschild (1978) describes how near strangers in a senior housing project unexpectedly became a community in such a manner. "There wasn't nothin' before we got the coffee machine. I mean we didn't share nothin' before Mrs. Bitford's daughter brought over the machine and we sort of had our first occasion, you might say" (p. 38).

This community had its start with six people brought together by a coffeemaker. Others saw them and joined in. There was no planned, step-by-step approach intended to develop a full range of activities. Yet 6 months later there was a beehive of activity, including a service club, a bowling club, Bible study, a morning workshop, a washtub band, and fund-raiser activities.

OLD PEOPLE AND NEW COMMUNITIES

New social worlds do develop among strangers in new locations. Anthropologists have found that the conditions that promote community formation among the old are the same as those that have operated in communities ranging from urban squatters to utopian experimenters. "What is intriguing about old age communities is not how different the old people are, but how much they act like everyone else given the opportunity'' (Keith, 1982, p. 11).

Keith-Ross (1977) has identified three major themes that appear consistently in developed communities:

1. *Territory*. Individuals live in the same space with clearly marked boundaries.
2. *"We-feeling."* There is a sense of shared fate, and there are common needs, interests, and problems and a group distinctiveness.
3. *Social organization*. There are patterned social contacts, mutual expectations, and common beliefs.

The greater the extent to which these themes are present, the greater the degree to which community will be felt and experienced.

Atchley (1980) refers to these same components in his description of a community as a group of people who share their location in space, interact with one another, depend upon one another to fill their needs, and share an identity with the place where they live.

While living with elders in a French retirement residence, Keith-Ross studied the way in which these elements develop to form community (1977), much like anthropologists have studied primitive cultures to determine their customs, mores, and social organization. Factors promoting community tend to fall into two groups: those present from the beginning, called *background factors*, and those that develop over time, called *emergent factors*.

Background Factors

The first background factor is homogeneity. The greater the social and cultural homogeneity of the group, the more likely the group is to have a ''we-feeling.'' How the residents perceive the alternatives to living in the facility also affects their level of attachment to the community. A perception that there are few alternatives, because of health or financial needs, can lead a resident to feel that his or her personal destiny is tied to others in the group. Since nursing care facilities are frequently viewed by older persons as residences of last resort, one could expect them to score high on this factor. And in fact all the residents in Melanson and Meagher's (1986) study relocated because they felt they had no choice.

When there has been an irreversible investment or a giving up of individual property, attachment to the new community usually develops. Utopian and religious communities often required members to give up individual property to minimize material differences among members and stimulate greater commitment to the community. Many nursing home residents have sold their homes (an irreversible act) and have had to give up many personal possessions because of the spatial limitations imposed upon them in the new setting.

The size of the collective unit also makes a difference, with small groups developing faster. Most residences for the elderly are relatively small. In addition, weaker kinships and lessened social ties with the outside world tend to direct the individual toward the new collective.

Emergent Factors

Whereas background factors can only be documented as to their presence or absence, emergent factors develop over time. Since they emerge gradually, there is the potential to influence their development and encourage the formation of a community. The emergent factors that must be considered are discussed below:

1. *Communal Work—Work for the Good of the Whole*. Communal, unpaid work promotes feelings of connectedness and belonging. Work carries a special value for older persons. Being productive is highly desirable. Hochschild (1978) defines older people as "workers without work" (p. xiii). Even when members of her group died, they continued to be evaluated according to their work ("She was such a good worker," p. 39).
2. *Participation in Communitywide Events and Decision Making*. The strength of the "we-feeling" is related to the quantity and quality of the total group contacts. The more community members participate, the more they value group solidarity. The more they share in decision making, the stronger their attachment to the community becomes. The communal dining experience, which brings residents together in the dining room at least once and usually several times each day, cannot be overestimated as a communitywide event.
3. *Shared Contacts*. There should be a wide range of social contacts which residents share with one another. Contacts should vary to include interactions between two residents, small, intimate groups, and larger groups of different sizes. Activities should take place in a variety of areas including the resident's own personal space. Contacts should range from spontaneous encounters to planned events. The more types of activities residents share among themselves, the more likely it is that their contacts will become the basis of a distinct social organization. The strength of the we-feeling is promoted in proportion to the time members spend in contact with one another.
4. *Interdependence and Reciprocity*. This is a critical factor in all communities. The more residents see themselves as interdependent, the more likely they are to have a sense of shared fate. Interdependence brings people together to satisfy their needs better than they could acting alone. Examples

of reciprocity include helping in cases of sickness and in emergencies, offering solace and concern, and exchanging items such as cups of coffee, meals, and plant cuttings. According to Hochschild (1978), the refrigerator in the senior housing apartments she studied often told the story—homemade jam from one friend, homemade butter from another, cornbread baked by a woman who had a large family and loved to bake.

5. *Shared Symbols.* Over time the group will develop shared responses that are symbols of their life together and represent their common experiences. The longest-term resident of the facility, the "worst" resident, the chairperson of the resident council—all of these represent experiences shared by the group and are liable to evoke similar emotional responses.

It is important to note that status held inside the facility differs from status based on the past or recognized on the outside. In fact, residents vigorously oppose any emphasis of differences derived from the past. Hochschild (1978) found intense opposition to publishing a Who's Who containing brief biographies of residents. It was expected to be a stimulus to community development, but it was viewed as a threat. Status and prestige are determined primarily by participation and leadership in activities in the new community.

A final aspect of shared symbols is the presence of rituals or "our way" of doing things. A custom may not be apparent until one has the misfortune of violating it!

6. *The Perception of Threat.* In the outside world, frailty and a limited income can limit participation and put a person at risk. Fear of threats in the outside world can lead to a perception of the inside community as a safe haven where it is still possible to be involved, be popular, and have some influence. The outside world is always present in the facility in the attitudes of the staff, who often present the conflicting values of the outside community.

USING ACTIVITIES TO FOSTER COMMUNITY DEVELOPMENT

Human behavior can be viewed as an adjustment to social stressors. Intervention can be directed either toward helping the person adjust to the situation at hand or toward changing the social situation so it is less stressful (Anderson & Carter, 1978). One of the ways stress can be lessened is through the provision of social support.

Social support is a protective mechanism that can lessen the effects of life stress. Studies have documented that it protects people in crisis from a wide variety of pathological states. It has been known to reduce the amount of medication required, accelerate recovery, and improve compliance with medical regimens (Cobb, 1976).

Social support is not ensured just by having a number of associates, friends, or even family. "Support comes when people's engagement with one another extends to a level of involvement and concern, not when they merely touch at the surface of each other's lives" (Perlin, Lieberman, Menaghan, & Mullan, 1981, p. 340).

Activities can serve as a powerful medium to foster the development of the "we-feeling" that is a prerequisite for the formation of community. Through activities, bonds of friendship can be formed and a community of mutual aid and interpersonal support can be nurtured.

This will not be effected by planning more and more activities for the residents to do but by setting the stage for residents to create a new community through their own efforts. This is far more challenging than simply scheduling activities. It means taking those factors that we have identified as important for community development and using them as the goals of the activity program.

The emergent factors that promote community can be the basis for the activity program. Suggestions for each emergent factor are listed below, but the reader should bear in mind that the potential is limitless and the final decision to accept or reject any activity must rest in the hands and minds of the emerging community.

1. Communal Work
   - Make a quilt and raffle it off to purchase something for the community.
   - Develop an herb garden for use by the facility's kitchen.
   - Make flower arrangements for dining room table centerpieces (some mortuaries will provide used flowers, which can be rearranged and recycled).
   - Refinish old toys and donate to needy children.
   - Adopt a needy family at Christmas and provide homemade gifts.
   - Build birdhouses and install outside the windows of bedfast residents.
   - Knit or sew items for the homeless.
   - Make banners or collages to vary the environment.
2. Communitywide Events
   - Utilize the potential of the communal dining room by welcoming newcomers, announcing new events, and publicizing accomplishments of members.
   - Sponsor a float and enter it in the local town's parade (this has actually been done by at least one facility).
   - Plan a Hawaiian luau, with residents making leis, choosing food, decorating, and so on.
   - Develop a facility choir or band that performs routinely for all residents.

- Present a Las Vegas night, with residents preparing the activities.
- Celebrate holidays, election days, and special events, with residents making the decisions.

3. Shared Contacts
   - Encourage spontaneous visits by residents by having table games and cards visibly available in day rooms and congregating spots.
   - Help a resident to serve tea to friends in his or her room.
   - Group people with similar interests together so they can form their own poker group, bridge club, or other kind of club.
   - Arrange a happy hour before dinner.

4. Interdependence and Reciprocity
   - A sighted resident might read to a blind resident, who returns the favor by caring for the reader's plants or performing some other service.
   - A good sewer could mend garments for other residents, who then, for example, might push her wheelchair so she could take "walks" outside.
   - The homemaker's club could make jellies and jams to share with the group.
   - A newcomers club might be formed to accompany the new residents to activities and to introduce them around. Newcomers could serve on the next committee to help others.
   - Garden club members might start cuttings for new plants and deliver to other residents.
   - A sunshine club could be created to visit the sick and send flowers.

5. Shared Symbols
   - Use dinner as an opportunity to announce awards, such as the winner of the facility's senior Olympics.
   - Have an awards banquet for the outgoing chairpersons of various committees.
   - Hold a memorial service for a resident who died so that all might share in the passing of a group member.
   - Establish a Book of Friends for a recently deceased member. Each resident writes something in the book about that individual. The book can be presented to the family.

Religion advances a sense of belonging. It continues meaningful symbols from the past and can create new rituals specific to the long-term care setting (Seicol, 1989).

6. Perception of Outside Threat

- Encourage reminiscing about the good old days to enhance the feeling of a shared past.
- Create a Bible study group to provide solace and comfort.
- Develop small support groups so that members can provide comfort to one another.

The focus on community building as a basis for activities is founded upon the assumption that old people can and do develop new lives in new places. The therapist using this approach exhibits a belief in older people's ability to make decisions, provide support for others, and enrich their own lives through engagement in meaningful shared experiences with others.

Sandra Howell (1983) issued a warning that is worth heeding, a warning especially appropriate for new members of a long-term care facility:

> If . . . my society or proximate environment, including their built aspects, changes rapidly and I am not a participant in the change decisions, I must surely lose or have great difficulty placing myself in space, time, and society. I will likely survive such disruptions, but the required adjustments may have major intra-psychic costs—I fear the disintegration of myself. (p. 105)

We must not allow the disintegration of any self. We must encourage residents to make decisions about their lives. We must help them to become a part of a new community from which they will then derive aid and support.

> Only when current practice is changed from a task-oriented to a person-centered system, and when a sense of community for all who live and work in the nursing home is fostered will the spirits of residents and caregivers be nurtured and strengthened (Williams, 1990, p. 28).

REFERENCES

Anderson, R., & Carter, I. (1978). *Human behavior in the social environment: A social systems approach* (2nd ed.). New York: Aldine.

Atchley, R.C. (1980). *The social forces in later life: An introduction to the social sciences.* Belmont, CA: Wadsworth.

Bayne, J.R.D. (1971). Environmental modification for the older person. *The Gerontologist, 11,* 314–317.

Bowker, L. (1982). *Humanizing institutions for the aged.* Lexington, MA: D.C. Heath.

Cobb, S. (1976). Social support as a moderator of life stress. *Psychosomatic Medicine, 38,* 300–314.

Hochschild, A. (1978). *The unexpected community: Portrait of an old age subculture* (rev. ed.). Berkeley and Los Angeles: University of California Press.

Howell, S.C. (1983). The meaning of place in old age. In G.D. Rowles & R.J. Ohta (Eds.), *Aging and milieu: Environmental perspectives on growing old*. New York: Academic Press.

Institute of Medicine (1986). *Improving the quality of care in nursing homes*. Washington, DC: National Academy Press.

Kastenbaum, R. (1972). Beer, wine and mutual gratification. In D.P. Kent, R. Kastenbaum, & S. Sherwood (Eds.), *Research, planning and action for the elderly* (pp. 365–394). New York: Behavior Publications.

Keith, J. (1982). *Old people as people: Social and cultural influences on aging and old age*. Boston: Little, Brown.

Keith-Ross, J. (1977). *Old people, new lives: Community creation in a retirement residence*. Chicago: University of Chicago Press.

Melanson, P.M., & Meagher, D. (1986). Living in a long-term care institution. *Gerontion, 1*, 26–30.

Miller, D.B., & Beer, S. (1977). Patterns of friendship among patients in a nursing home setting. *The Gerontologist, 17*, 269–275.

Perlin, L., Lieberman, M., Menaghan, E., & Mullan, J. (1981). The stress process. *Journal of Health and Social Behavior, 22*, 337–356.

Seicol, S. (1989, August-September). The aging spirit: Religion can provide a key ingredient for "created communities." *The Aging Connection, 10*, 13.

Spaulding, J. (1985). *A consumer perspective on quality care: The residents' point of view*. Washington, DC: Citizens' Coalition for Nursing Home Reform.

Williams, C.C. (1990). Long-term care and the human spirit. *Generations, 14*(4), 25–28.

Chapter 17

Specialized Restorative Programs

Cynthia F. Epstein

Maintaining the older person's ability to participate in functional activities is a core goal for the long-term care team. Developing specialized restorative programs to support this must be a core goal for occupational therapy. Therefore, a long-term care rehabilitation service delivery model should be created that gives equal emphasis to direct patient treatment and to the maintenance and continued growth of skills through specialized restorative programming.

The concept of specialized restorative programs carried out by trained facility teams was developed to support the goal of patient independence in activities of daily living (ADL) and related skills. The long-term care industry and its regulators have now recognized that skilled therapeutic intervention provided directly to the patient must be supported by more global programs to ensure successful outcomes (Institute of Medicine, 1986). These restorative programs, designed and monitored by the therapist, are then implemented by a trained team. Key team members who focus on ADL include the nurse and nursing assistant.

We must recognize that helping the patient regain function is not the province of one discipline or team segment. Too often, goals achieved in therapy are only functional in the therapy setting. Within a facility setting, critical elements for the successful integration of therapy gains include specialized restorative programs that can be carried out by the patient and support staff on a daily basis. Rehabilitation goals are usually specific, measured, and time limited. The older person's ability to regain and sustain ADL independence often requires service beyond this. The creation of a restorative focus within the facility team is therefore of the utmost importance. For example, the Resident Assessment Profile (RAP) for ADL, which is part of the federal uniform resident assessment system designed for nursing facilities (Morris et al., 1990), clearly identifies the need for restorative programs when patients meet specific criteria. These restorative programs are designed by the therapist in concert with the team. The therapist becomes a consultant to the team to ensure effective follow through. This approach allows the patient to continue integrating and developing skills that were initiated during the direct treatment service component. Assurance of the program's effectiveness is accomplished through the monitoring process performed by the consultant therapist.

Occupational therapy's unique perspective, incorporating functional performance, purposeful activity, and environmental needs, makes this discipline the logical source for development and coordination of many restorative programs. Occupational therapists' versatility and their ability to understand and integrate aspects of other team member roles have, at times, resulted in role confusion. As the developers and coordinators of specialized restorative programs to maintain resident independence, this liability becomes an asset. By drawing upon knowledge of the facility, the staff, and the patient population needs and combining this knowledge with occupational therapy theory and practice, meaningful programs can be developed and integrated into daily routines with the support of all concerned.

Important areas of focus for occupational therapy restorative programs include daily living skills (i.e., dressing, grooming, eating, cooking, and leisure activities), positioning, mobility, exercise, and range of motion. In areas where there are concerns shared with other departments, programs may be developed cooperatively.

Multiple issues must be considered in order to achieve successful restorative programs. Access to funding, levels of patient and facility need, adequate and knowledgeable staff, and interdisciplinary team motivation are but a few.

FUNDING

Legislation promulgated through the Omnibus Budget Reconciliation Act of 1987 (OBRA) emphasized the importance of quality care issues in long-term care. Rehabilitation is identified as one of the key components in this plan. Integration of rehabilitation-generated programs into patient care plans and the monitoring of such programs through a quality assurance mechanism are recognized as important aspects of resident care plans (American Occupational Therapy Association, 1989). Funding for rehabilitation services must therefore be considered for both direct treatment of acute conditions and the development of restorative programs to maintain and facilitate continuation of gains achieved through therapeutic intervention. In addition, OBRA recognized that restorative programs were needed not only by people who recently suffered acute episodes but also by residents whose chronicity puts them at risk of continuous decline (Morris et al., 1990). Occupational therapy's increased involvement in restorative programming should thus be supported as administrators receive increased funding for these services.

POPULATION CHARACTERISTICS AND NEEDS

Residents

The demographics of elderly persons requiring long-term care indicate that we are increasingly challenged to serve an older and sicker, predominantly female population in which the average age is beyond 85 (Hing & Sekscenski, 1987). In addition to this older and sicker group, developmentally disabled elders are now surfacing with multiple decompensation problems (Brody & Ruff, 1986; Haines, 1988), as are older psychiatric patients who have been marginally maintained in the community since deinstitutionalization went into effect. It is estimated that as many as 75% of long-term care patients have mental impairments (Larsen, Lo, & Williams, 1986). Among these, nearly one-half have a diagnosis of Alzheimer's disease (Frazier, Lebowitz, & Silver, 1986).

This population is characterized by multiple chronic illnesses, including cognitive, emotional, and behavioral impairments. They are at high risk for injury, acute illness, and debilitative changes in homeostasis. Henschke (1983) identified an interrelated complex of clinical problems unique to the care of the very old. These are falling and the related issue of mobility, confusion and its length of duration, incontinence, impaired homeostasis, and iatrogenic disorders that may arise due to the increasing number and high dosages of drugs prescribed for the institutionalized elderly. These factors must be considered as plans for restorative programming begin to be developed in a given setting.

Within the long-term care setting, dysfunction will be a key determinant of restorative programming needs. Levenson (1987) suggested using four major dependency categories to help establish program levels that can address individual needs. The categories are independent, independence threatened, independence delegated, and dependent. These categories can be further defined from an ADL perspective. In terms of the amount of support needed to perform ADL tasks, independent would require no staff assistance, independence threatened would require setup only, independence delegated would require moderate one-person assistance, and dependent would require total assistance by one or more persons. Residents requiring restorative programs would fall in the latter three categories. Use of these categories can then be helpful in planning programs.

All restorative programming should be consistent with the goal identified by most elderly, whether in the community or an institution: to be as independent as possible and to maintain a sense of self and self-esteem.

Staff

Primary responsibility for carrying out restorative programs falls to nursing aides on the units. The average facility's nursing staff includes 15% registered nurses, 14% licensed practical nurses, and 71% nurse aides (Institute of Medicine, 1986). In most facilities, the aide staff has a high rate of turnover. Minorities make up a large proportion of the aide staff. Given poor pay levels and a high degree of physical work, those seeking this type of position usually have minimal education and erratic work histories (Hersch, 1988; Waxman, Carver, & Berkenstock, 1984). Their nursing supervisors, professional and technical, have usually had less training than nursing counterparts in acute care (American Nurses' Association, 1981).

Until recently, aide staff were given minimal training before taking their place as caregivers. National standards now require they have a minimum of 75 hours of in-house education prior to assuming responsibilities on a unit. In many states, this requirement has been expanded to 100 or more hours. This extended educational program provides a unique opportunity to the occupational therapist and nurse educator to develop a training curriculum for aides that emphasizes the importance of carry-over through restorative programs.

In order to successfully incorporate the concepts of restorative programming into this learning experience, the curriculum must address the issue of staff attitudes along with physical care issues. Positive attitudes create an environment that encourages sharing, caring, and teamwork (Tellis-Nayak & Tellis-Nayak, 1989). Such an environment is critical for the successful development of restorative programs.

TEAMWORK

Restorative programming requires commitment from the facility team. Through the efforts of an interdisciplinary team, specific programs can be coordinated using a systems approach (Nystrom & Evans, 1986). The level of participation and the size of the team are variable. In most instances, preliminary planning involves a larger team with representation from all departments identified in the plan. As the program evolves, a core team representing the major players on the team takes primary responsibility.

Teams work best when they share common goals. The goals of restorative programming are of concern to all. They include

- providing appropriate and meaningful resident care
- preventing resident deterioration
- maintaining resident gains achieved in therapy
- encouraging resident independence
- ensuring consistency in program delivery
- using staff cost-effectively

Using these areas of commonality, a written plan can be developed and a system for implementation and ongoing care can be created.

Team Members

The planning team should include a resident representative. Having a resident representative is particularly important when considering a program for independent residents. During planning phases, this representative can help the team understand important resident issues related to the program in question. For example, in planning assigned seating for the more independent residents in a dining program, social interaction and relationships are issues for which resident input is vital.

Nursing is represented in a majority of programs, and generally nurses are members of the core team. Realistic procedures for staffing and scheduling at all levels cannot take place without their perspective. Most importantly, they can provide input regarding the multiple needs of residents who are independence delegated and dependent. Nursing commitment will be a major factor in the program's success.

Ideally, nursing will establish restorative nurse and nursing aide positions on the core team. These staff members eventually will assume coordinating roles for specific programs when it is not feasible or appropriate for these roles to remain the responsibility of the occupational therapy department.

A majority of specialized restorative programs are initiated through rehabilitation services. Occupational therapy, physical therapy, and speech therapy are therefore very involved in the team process, and usually one of these disciplines takes the lead. The programs identified in this chapter have been developed under the aegis of occupational therapy.

Resident care services, including activities, social services, and dietary services, and such support services as housekeeping and maintenance are involved in the planning team. Some may be very involved in a particular core team, such as dietary services in a mealtime program or maintenance in a wheelchair program.

Administration may not be directly represented on the team but must be kept informed regarding plans, issues, and progress. Each program's rationale must address areas that are of concern to the facility administrator, medical director, and director of nursing. Restorative programs will help the facility meet survey standards and prevent deficiencies and loss of funding. From an administrative point of view, the programs developed must be congruent with the goals of the facility.

Core Team

Utilizing the perspective and expertise of the total team will help develop programs that are acceptable and workable. For each particular program, a core team will be identified (Harnish & Schmidt, 1988). For instance, a wheelchair management program core team may consist of representatives from occupational therapy, nursing, housekeeping, and maintenance, whereas an active exercise program might involve occupational therapy, physical therapy, activities, and nursing. The core team must keep communication lines open to the larger team as the work progresses.

COORDINATION

Program coordination must be delegated to one discipline or department. Ideally, the programs initiated by occupational therapy should be coordinated by it. With their expertise in analysis, understanding of occupational performance, knowledge of adaptive techniques, skill in group dynamics, understanding of behavior, and awareness of the importance of human and nonhuman environments, occupational therapy personnel can energize the team and ensure each program's timely and effective integration into the system.

Within the department, the level of personnel assuming the coordinator role for a program may vary depending on the stage of program development and on staff experience levels. As the program matures and participants are secure regarding implementation, an experienced aide trained by occupational therapy may be able to assume the position of coordinator. In the wheelchair program previously mentioned, an occupational therapy–restorative nursing aide assumed this position. Appointing a coordinator who has shared the experiences of frontline staff and has also been trained by the occupational therapy department provides caregivers on the nursing units with a peer mentor and a realistic support system.

In facilities where occupational therapy is provided on a consultative or very part-time basis, another discipline should assume the coordinating role. Preferably a member of the nursing department who is identified with nursing restorative programs will be available. Occupational therapy would then work closely with the coordinator.

STARTING SPECIALIZED RESTORATIVE PROGRAMS

New program development requires a short-term but substantial time commitment from team members. This investment will enable staff to deal with unforeseen problems and provide the necessary support to line staff involved. As the program becomes integrated into the daily care plan, the need to devote substantial time diminishes.

The concept of restorative programming—programming designed to maintain and help continue gains achieved in therapy or prevent further deterioration—is familiar to most nursing and rehabilitation team members. Floor ambulation, passive range of motion, and specialized dining are programs commonly found in long-term care settings (Heim & Stoeckel, 1985; Lundine & O'Sullivan, 1978; Maloney, 1976; O'Sullivan, 1990). Although these programs may be listed as routine, in many instances the services are much less than routine.

Consistency in program application requires staff and resident commitment. Getting aide staff to become invested in a given program first requires commitment from team leaders such as the administrator, director of nursing, and charge nurses. Without ongoing support from the top, the program will falter and grind to a halt. With it, the needed time and funding for inservice education, program development, environmental adaptations, pilot programming, and team building will be allocated.

Inservice Education

Inservice must be directed toward everyone involved in the program. For instance, a mealtime program that is targeted at independence delegated and dependent residents must have an extensive inservice module for staff, residents, and volunteers, including family members who often assist at mealtime. Focal training areas for this program would include proper positioning principles and techniques, special feeding concerns and approaches, adaptive feeding equipment, and environmental awareness. The residents and families must understand and support possible changes that may occur in scheduling, seating assignments, and diet consistency. Educating the consumer and consumer advocate along with facility personnel is a way of acknowledging the importance of their participation in the program (Hasselkus, 1986).

Learning and applying new information can be threatening and stressful to staff who have limited time and education. Therefore, it is critical to have extensive support, patience, and positive reinforcement from the program coordinator and inservice staff (Grayson, 1982). Helping the staff, the family, and volunteers view the dependent eater not as a "feeder" but rather as an individual who has the potential to take an active role in self-feeding will be an important aspect of the training for this program (O'Sullivan, 1990). Changing caregiver attitudes and behaviors so that resident independence rather than dependence is fostered (Sperbeck & Whitbourne, 1981) must be one focus of the training program.

Program Development through Occupational Therapy

Residents identified as appropriate candidates for a restorative program—a dining program, for example—will have received direct occupational therapy services for eating and feeding problems prior to program placement. During this intervention, specific approaches and needed adaptations will have been identified in preparation for referral to the maintenance program.

The process consisting of problem identification, referral to occupational therapy for evaluation, treatment if needed, development of an individualized maintenance plan, and then occupational therapy referral to a specialized restorative program can lead to the successful maintenance of therapy gains. The expertise and planning skills of the therapist can help provide staff with a specific process to follow for each resident. Knowing that the plan has been carefully designed and tried allows staff to comfortably pick up the procedure.

Environmental Issues

Much has been written in occupational therapy literature regarding the importance of the environment for improving functional performance. Kiernat (1987) stresses the importance of providing nursing home residents with opportunities for control in their environment. Offering residents choices and opportunities for decision making as part of the restorative program will therefore be a major consideration. Levine and Merrill (1987) emphasize the need to assess human and nonhuman environmental components that influence behavior and interact to form the psychosocial environment.

Many of the institutionalized elderly who become dependent are responding to staff control of their daily life skills and the negative factors present in the physical environment. Imagine walking into a dayroom where dependent residents are being fed. The TV is blaring, a partially finished cigarette is still smoking in an ashtray, window blinds are open, and sunlight glares throughout the room. The aides involved in feeding are talking to each other while rapidly spooning purée into the mouths of their assigned residents. The environmental press (Lawton, 1980) in this setting causes residents to retreat from the mealtime process and lose the desire to eat. Restorative programs that are successful will address environmental issues as an integral part of planning and daily routine.

As noted previously, helping staff understand these issues must be done during the preliminary phase of the program. Simple but critical environmental changes can be easily incorporated into the overall plan. Some changes can make the difference between dependence and independence. For instance, as part of the daily living skills program, residents experiencing difficulty in bed transfers might be evaluated. The relationship between the height of the bed and the height of the resident is often the problem. Removing the bed casters and/or replacing the mattress with one that is less thick might be all that is needed. Programmatically, providing the proper bed height must be a part of the care plan. Should the resident move to another room or leave the facility, this environmental adaptation will again need to be considered.

Pilot Programs

It must be understood that new programs do not become an integral part of facility procedure overnight. A key to establishing restorative programs with a team approach is to start with one nursing unit. Ideally, this pilot unit will have staff that value the program's concept and are motivated to make it work.

By starting the program on a unit with a positive environment, success is more readily obtained. Achieving a positive outcome here will tend to spread the program to the other floors. For instance, when occupational therapy introduced a passive range of motion program on one unit, the very debilitated residents began showing improved tolerance for remaining out of bed, and their awareness of the environment improved. Aides were so pleased with their success that they began selling the program to staff on other floors, despite the fact that just a few months before they had been tentative and unsure of their ability to perform the ranging.

A pilot program allows the team to test their premise without committing the entire facility. Unforeseen problems arising in this phase can be quickly addressed. At times, the solution to a problem found early in the program can serve as a springboard to more effective and appropriate procedures. This occurred in the pilot phase of a wheelchair management program (Epstein, 1981).

In this pilot program, all wheelchairs on the pilot unit had finally been individualized and assigned. To ensure correct daily assignment, each chair had the resident's name and room number written on a piece of tape placed across the back of the chair. Soon after, float staff who had not been inserviced regarding the new program were assigned to the floor. Suddenly, the pieces of tape that had been carefully placed disappeared. In some cases, they reappeared on other chairs that had the same color upholstery but not the same equipment configuration. In researching the problem, it became evident that aides were in a hurry and took chairs close at hand to use for their residents, disregarding the labels. To cover errors, they then found the right chairs and switched the labels.

Obviously a new procedure was needed. The new procedure utilized a double labeling system using labels that could be attached more permanently at two different sites on the chair. This allowed the program coordinator to identify quickly the correct equipment user when the main tag was missing. In addition, a module on the importance of providing the assigned wheelchair and positioning equipment was added to inservice orientation for all staff, including floats. Thus, an improved and more effective procedure was developed in response to what initially appeared as a catastrophic program derailment.

Team Building

The implementation phase of a new program creates an environment for sharing the highs and lows of risk taking, for creative brainstorming, and for problem solving as a team. Team members become more aware of each other's roles and learn to appreciate the complexities of assigned jobs, the environmental demands associated with their tasks, and the need to clarify roles and expectations (Maguire, 1985).

The critical maturation period for each interdisciplinary team takes place during the implementation stage. This bonding, particularly for core team members, facilitates their ability to be flexible and mutually supportive as the program expands. Role blurring, so often an area of concern, becomes more common. The core team, achieving a high degree of comfort, then performs in a transdisciplinary rather than interdisciplinary mode (Nystrom & Evans, 1986).

MAINTAINING SPECIALIZED RESTORATIVE PROGRAMS

Using the pilot experience as a guide, programs can be gradually expanded to other parts of the facility. The complexity of a given program and the number of disciplines involved will guide the length of time needed to phase it in. Once it is in place, the importance of maintaining specific procedures and ensuring the appropriateness of the program for specific sites and patients must be addressed.

Quality assurance monitors should be developed for each program. These help staff maintain set standards while concurrently helping the coordinator assess the status of the program and its participants.

Policies and Procedures

The policies and procedures developed for each program clearly identify team responsibilities. They are placed in each participating department's manual and form the core of the system.

In a wheelchair management program created for a large facility, broad policy and procedure statements were distributed to occupational therapy, administration, nursing, maintenance, inservice, and housekeeping. The individual departments then supplemented these with more detailed procedures involving their personnel. Housekeeping, for example, described the role of housekeeping personnel in the routine cleaning of all wheelchairs. Its policy also delineated the specific interface needed with nursing to ensure that positioners and adaptations requiring special handling when cleaned were not left on a chair scheduled for routine cleaning.

Utilizing the policy and procedure format as a communication tool and role delineation mechanism reinforces team member participation and accountability. Having contributed to policy development and agreed to a final format, team members are familiar with each discipline's role and aware of the important part each department plays in the program.

Coordination

The coordinator must understand the system and be attuned to its needs in relationship to the program demands. This very sensitive position requires an individual who enjoys working with others; has good communication and organizational abilities; and can be flexible, creative, and supportive.

For example, a mealtime program geared to the independence threatened or independence delegated level may require adaptive eating or feeding equipment and approaches. Carrying out numerous individualized plans at mealtime can be extremely stressful for line staff as well as volunteers and family. The stress level escalates when the equipment outlined in the individualized plan fails to appear at mealtime. Nursing blames dietary, dietary blames purchasing, and purchasing blames occupational therapy!

Enter the coordinator. Several mealtimes later, the required equipment is back in place. So is a new procedure. Adaptive equipment used at mealtime is listed on the diet card. Each unit has a supplemental list for all assigned equipment. At the end of mealtime, all used equipment is placed in one special bin and accounted for. The case of the missing equipment is closed.

Patience, caring, intuition, and understanding of the system help the occupational therapy coordinator to carry out the tasks at hand. Adding to the complexity of this job is the issue of quality assurance. Here the coordinator works closely with the therapist monitoring the patient's performance and with staff members performing the daily routine.

Quality Assurance

Establishing a maintenance program to help patients continue to perform meaningful activities after discharge from therapy is the first step on a continuum. Periodic reassessment must be built in to ensure the appropriateness of the plan. This is one role for quality assurance.

Quality assurance is the linchpin that can secure the program's place within the system. It is identified as an expected component of care by federal, state, and private regulatory agencies. Using program monitors appropriately will help keep the system on track and will identify new and potential problem areas before they escalate out of control (Ostrow & Joe, 1987).

Monitors can be developed to measure performance outcomes for the resident, environment, and overall program. In addition to the therapist, a variety of staff members can be involved in quality assurance. Each department on the team can develop a monitor for its assignment. The coordinator may look at the overall functioning of the program, whereas the therapist will assess the resident's performance and relationship to the environment. In each case, reasonable standards must be set.

PROGRAM ISSUES AND OUTCOMES

Specialized restorative programs can take a variety of forms in the long-term care setting. Realistic constraints shaping program choice include available staff, money and space, nursing and administrative priorities, and the experience level of the therapist.

A general rule of thumb is to perform a needs assessment when program needs have not been clearly defined. In most cases, nursing and administrative staff have already identified important issues. An occupational therapy needs assessment will often point up additional issues that underlie those identified by the facility. When these underlying issues can be incorporated into the program requested, congruence is achieved.

For instance, suppose occupational therapy is asked to develop a dining program geared to all levels. Through an occupational therapy needs assessment, it becomes clear that the first priority should be a positioning program, as a significant number of residents require seating modifications in the environments they use throughout the day. This facility has recently been cited for lack of appropriate mealtime interventions, and the staff and administration are therefore strongly in favor of a mealtime program. Occupational therapy needs to support the facility with respect to this issue.

A dining program can, and must, incorporate principles of positioning (Harnish & Schmidt, 1988; Perket, 1986). The program plan will therefore incorporate major inservice education regarding positioning, and funding will be requested to provide adaptive equipment needed at mealtime. This will include special eating equipment and positioning equipment that must be in place for successful mealtime participation.

Each facility will have unique issues and needs that must be taken into consideration in program development. Given the increasing number of independence delegated and dependent individuals residing in long-term care, occupational therapy must work to develop programs that can maintain those at higher levels and prevent further deterioration or reverse the downward spiral for those more involved (Epstein & Sadownick, 1989).

Gaines (1986) dramatically points out the potential for reversing the downward spiral toward dependence in eating. Using a systems approach in a 120-bed facility, an interdisciplinary feeding training program was coordinated by occupational therapy. Before the program was initiated, 6 of the 80 residents targeted for intervention were classified as independent eaters. A year and a half later, 40 of the 80 were independent.

Similarly, through the development of a wheelchair program, the frustrating and time-consuming problem of wheelchair shortages and inappropriately positioned residents can be addressed (Epstein, 1980). The structure of the program will ensure that the staff understand the rationale and procedure for proper application of individualized positioners when placing residents in their seating systems. Residents who are more independent will understand why they cannot take their wheelchairs into the shower to clean and why they need to have their chairs periodically safety checked. Families will be more involved and supportive regarding the purchase of specialized wheelchairs for their relatives when other funding sources are unavailable (Epstein & Sadownick, 1989).

Another important area of concern for occupational therapy is daily living skills. Dependence in dressing and related daily living tasks tends to be fostered when staff do not have a structured program to encourage patient independence.

Ehrman (1983) discusses a daily care program designed to promote patient independence. As residents were being prepared to exit the occupational therapy treatment program, a structured plan was developed for carry-over through the specialized restorative program. Focusing on extensive inservice and a simple, clear information sheet containing each resident's performance level and need for assistance, the program was able to maintain and expand daily living skills. The occupational therapy coordinator reinforced carry-over through an accountability monitor. This daily documentation of resident performance was then incorporated into the ongoing data base for program evaluation.

Group activity programs directed toward confused or regressed residents have been a mainstay of long-term care occupational therapy. Sensory retraining, multisensory stimulation, and active exercise are but a few of the more familiar services (Hames-Hahn & Llorens, 1988; Orloff, 1984; Richman, 1969). These programs can be extended beyond the confines of occupational therapy. Within the restorative nursing component, aide-level staff who are comfortable with group activities and formats can be identified. These aides will need a longer and stronger support system and closer consultation. However, bringing the activity format into the nursing unit through the caregivers allows for a change in daily routine for both residents and staff. It also encourages both to work together in a more nonjudgmental setting, thus supporting a more independent role for the residents.

CONCLUSION

Occupational therapy's specialized restorative programs create a bridge between therapy gains and the residents' individualized plans of care. It allows therapists to expand their sphere of influence, advocating for this programming in a productive and meaningful manner. These important programs support the maintenance of functional independence for the institutionalized elderly, who are threatened by increasing levels of dependency.

Assuming the role of coordinator, trainer, or consultant, the occupational therapist facilitates the development of these special programs using a systems approach. Working closely with each core team and the restorative nursing staff, the therapist helps to initiate, maintain, and monitor the progress of programs.

As institutions acquire increasingly large numbers of older and sicker residents, the need for these programs becomes more critical. Caregivers, supervisors, and administrators within facilities are seeking innovative methods to maintain and prevent rapid deterioration in their targeted population. Specialized restorative programs created with the guidance of occupational therapists can make a substantial contribution toward meeting this goal.

REFERENCES

American Nurses' Association. (1981). *Facts about nursing, 1980–1981*. New York: American Journal of Nursing Company.

American Occupational Therapy Association. (1989). *Occupational therapy news: Federal report*. Rockville, MD: Author.

Brody, S.J., & Ruff, G.E. (Eds.). (1986). *Aging and rehabilitation: Advances in the state of the art* (pp. xiv–xv). New York: Springer.

Ehrman, L.S. (1983). Working with non-professionals to promote independence. *AOTA Gerontology Special Interest Section Newsletter, 6*(4), 1–2.

Epstein, C.F. (1980). Wheelchair management: Developing a system for long term care. *Journal of Long Term Care Administration, 8*(2), 1–12.

Epstein, C.F. (1981). *Wheelchair management guidelines*. Somerville, NJ: Occupational Therapy Consultants.

Epstein, C.F., & Sadownick, P. (1989). Specialized seating for the institutionalized elderly: Prescription, fabrication, funding. In *Technology Review '89* (pp. 13–16). Rockville, MD: American Occupational Therapy Association.

Frazier, S.H., Lebowitz, B.D., & Silver, L.B. (1986). Aging, mental health and rehabilitation. In S.J. Brody & G.E. Ruff (Eds.), *Aging and rehabilitation: Advances in the state of the art* (pp. 19–26). New York: Springer.

Gaines, B.J. (1986). Systems theory and feeding programs: Application in a mental retardation institute. In F.S. Cromwell (Ed.), *Occupational therapy for people with eating dysfunctions* (pp. 101–115). New York: Haworth.

Grayson, W. (1982). The occupational therapist and in-service education in nursing homes: A focus on Canada. *AOTA Gerontology Special Interest Section Newsletter, 5*(3), 1–2.

Haines, E. (1988). A programming model for aging persons with developmental disabilities. *AOTA Gerontology Special Interest Section Newsletter, 11*(1), 7–8.

Hames-Hahn, C.S., & Llorens, L.A. (1988). Impact of a multisensory occupational therapy program on components of self-feeding behavior in the elderly. In E.D. Taira (Ed.), *Promoting quality long term care for older persons* (pp. 63–86). New York: Haworth.

Harnish, S.K., & Schmidt, O.K. (1988). Developing and implementing an inter-disciplinary feeding training program within a large institution: The manager's planning responsibility. In F.S. Cromwell (Ed.), *The occupational therapy manager's survival handbook* (pp. 153–174). New York: Haworth.

Hasselkus, B.R. (1986). Patient education. In L. Davis & M. Kirkland (Eds.), *The role of occupational therapy with the elderly* (pp. 367–372). Rockville, MD: American Occupational Therapy Association.

Heim, M., & Stoeckel, L. (1985). *Maintenance Ambulation Program: An instructional manual for the nursing home.* Jericho, NY: MAP-JHMCB Center.

Henschke, P.J. (1983). Diagnoses: Overview. In R. Cape & R. Coe (Eds.), *Fundamentals of Geriatric Medicine* (pp. 103–108). New York: Raven Press.

Hersch, G. (1988). A nursing home in-service program: Characteristics and experiences. *Physical and Occupational Therapy in Geriatrics, 6*(3-4), 99–110.

Hing, E., & Seksenski, E. (1987). Use of health care-nursing home care. In *Health statistics on older persons—United States, 1986* (pp. 71–72). Hyattsville, MD: National Center for Health Statistics.

Institute of Medicine. (1986). *Improving quality of care in nursing homes.* Washington, DC: National Academy Press.

Kiernat, J.M. (1987). Promoting independence and autonomy through environmental approaches. *Topics in Geriatric Rehabilitation, 3*(1), 1–6.

Larson, E.B., Lo, B., Williams, N.E. (1986). Evaluation and care of elderly patients with dementia. *Journal of General Internal Medicine, 1,* 116–126.

Lawton, M.P. (1980). *Environment and aging.* Monterey, CA: Brooks/Cole.

Levenson, S.A. (1987). Innovations in nursing home care. *Generations, 12*(1), 74–79.

Levine, R.E., & Merrill, S.C. (1987). Psychosocial aspects of the environment. *Topics in Geriatric Rehabilitation, 3*(1), 27–33.

Lundine, P, & O'Sullivan, N. (1978). The role of the consultant in restorative care programming. In F.M. Livingston & N. O'Sullivan (Eds.), *Occupational therapy consultancy in the skilled nursing facility: An overview* (pp. 54–98). Pomona, CA: Southern California Occupational Therapy Consultants Group.

Maguire, G.H. (1985). The team approach in action. In G.H. Maguire (Ed.), *Care of the elderly: A health team approach* (pp. 221–225). Boston: Little Brown.

Maloney, C.C. (1976). The occupational therapist on a geriatric rehabilitation team. *American Journal of Occupational Therapy, 30,* 300–304.

Morris, J.N., Hawes, C., Fries, B.E., Phillips, C.D., Mor, V., Katz, S., Murphy, K., Drugovick, M.L., & Friedlob, A.S. (1990). Designing the national resident assessment instrument for nursing homes. *The Gerontologist, 30,* 293–307.

Nystrom, E.P., & Evans, L.S. (1986). The interdisciplinary team approach. In L. Davis & M. Kirkland (Eds.), *The role of occupational therapy with the elderly* (pp. 351–357). Rockville, MD: American Occupational Therapy Association.

Orloff, S.N. (1984). Sensory based evaluation and treatment for the psycho-geriatric patient. *AOTA Gerontology Special Interest Section Newsletter, 7*(2), 1–2.

Ostrow, P.C., & Joe, B.E. (1987). Quality assurance in geriatric occupational therapy. *AOTA Gerontology Special Interest Section Newsletter, 10*(1), 6.

O'Sullivan, N. (Ed.). (1990). *Dysphagia care: Team approach with acute and long term patients*. Los Angeles: Cottage Square.

Perket, S. (1986). The role of occupational therapy in planning dining programs in institutions for the frail elderly. In F.S. Cromwell (Ed.), *Occupational therapy for people with eating dysfunctions* (pp. 39–48). New York: Haworth.

Richman, L. (1969). Sensory training in the treatment of geriatric patients. *American Journal of Occupational Therapy, 23*, 253–257.

Sperbeck, D.J., & Whitbourne, S.K. (1981). Dependency in the institutional setting: A behavioral training program for geriatric staff. *The Gerontologist, 21*, 268–275.

Tellis-Nayak, V., & Tellis-Nayak, M. (1989). Quality of care and the burden of two cultures: When the world of the nurse's aide enters the world of the nursing home. *The Gerontologist, 29*, 307–313.

Waxman, H.M., Carver, E.A., & Berkenstock, G. (1984). Job turnover and job satisfaction among nursing home aides. *The Gerontologist, 24*, 503–509.

Chapter 18

Development of a Volunteer Program

Charlene L. Ager and Nancy Luttropp

This chapter addresses issues that arise in developing a volunteer program in a nursing home; the principles and stages of program development also pertain to the use of volunteers in homes or alternative care facilities. Elderly persons are used as a primary resource for recruitment and training because they can serve as successful role models and they understand and respond to others of their age. As a result, they are increasingly in demand as volunteers.

Two beliefs pervade this chapter: (1) The decision to start a volunteer program should not be made lightly. Although a volunteer program can be of considerable value to an agency, to occupational therapy, to residents, and to the volunteers themselves, it is not without cost to the organization—in terms of time, energy, space, personnel, and possibly dollars. (2) Occupational therapists should be alert to all opportunities for engaging residents of the institution in volunteer activities; they are entitled to the therapeutic benefits of useful work. (See Ager, 1987, for an in-depth discussion of the therapeutic benefits of volunteer and advocacy activities.)

This chapter is divided into the following sections: demographics of the elderly volunteer population, identifying a need, developing job descriptions, recruiting, screening, training, placement, problems, and rewards and benefits.

DEMOGRAPHICS OF THE ELDERLY VOLUNTEER POPULATION

Older persons constitute a vast untapped resource (Harris, 1981). These trained and experienced individuals "possess a range of skills and talents [and years of experience] never before found in an older population" (Sheppard, 1981, p. 39). They are motivated, believe in helping, and have a strong, healthy work ethic (American Association of Retired Persons [AARP], 1983). Harris reported in 1975 that 4.5 million Americans aged 65 and older worked as volunteers; 2.1 million others said they were interested in volunteering. The percentage of elderly Americans who actively engage in volunteer activities has remained at about 23% during the past 15 years, and the percentage who are interested in volunteering has fluctuated little from the 10% recorded in 1974 (Harris, 1981). It is important to remember, however, that the total elderly population has increased during that period of time and that the percentages do not reflect the increase in numbers of older volunteers.

The changing demographics of the elderly who volunteer are interesting to examine. The greatest increase in volunteerism has occurred among men (4% increase); the percentage of older women who volunteer has remained relatively constant. "Evidently, the continuing trend toward more working women, both young and old, is having a real effect on the traditional male-female balance of volunteer workers" (Harris, 1981, p. 29). The 65- to 74-year-old cohort is the most likely elderly group to take on volunteer responsibilities; this is true for both males and females (Van Wert, 1989).

Despite increasing numbers of people volunteering, the need for volunteers today is more critical than ever. The steady growth in the numbers of elderly, especially the old-old, has created a mushrooming need for social services; at the same time, the deficit-reduction action of Gramm-Rudman has curtailed public resources, needed services, social welfare monies, and programs for the elderly (AARP, 1983; Morrow-Howell & Ozawa, 1987; Opsata, 1986). In addition, the traditional volunteer pool of mothers at home with young school-age children now find themselves juggling work and children. Demands for older volunteers "to help fill the gap" are being heard in all social agencies. If occupational therapy is to get its fair share of the volunteer market to help carry out programs in nursing homes, alternative care facilities, and so on, now is the time to discover the how-tos of developing successful volunteer programs.

IDENTIFYING A NEED

The American Association of Retired Persons (1983) advises organizations and agencies to clearly identify their problems and needs and decide if a volunteer program is *the* answer. If it is, these questions must be answered: How many volunteers are needed and what skills should they have? Is there support for the program? Who will make the commitment to sponsor it? Acceptance of staff members, especially those who will work most closely with volunteers, must be ensured. "Setting program goals and realistically assessing community [institution or home] support are tasks that must be undertaken before volunteers can or should be mobilized" (p. 5). Occupational therapists also need to clarify their own philosophies regarding the appropriate use of volunteers. With what aspect of the program can volunteers assist? How much responsibility can realistically and comfortably be delegated? How much time can be allocated for training, and what kinds of training should be scheduled?

Organizations should question whether they are ready to fully utilize the volunteers' potential. Seguin and McConney (1982) recommend that the following conditions be present:

1. Volunteers must be able and permitted to help accomplish the central mission of the organization and contribute to its productivity.
2. The structure of the organization must permit innovation and tolerate differences. For instance, policies for volunteers must be different from those for paid workers, and volunteers must do work that does not compete with or duplicate tasks performed by paid staff. Cooperation between paid staff and volunteers can occur only when this structure exists.
3. The organization must be willing to allocate resources for older volunteers. Among other things, this may include financial support for a competent full-time volunteer coordinator who has a role in the central structure of the organization; support staff, such as a secretary; reimbursement of out-of-pocket expenses; and physical space and equipment, as needed.
4. The organization must provide opportunities for stimulating relationships with the "regulars" in the organization; "real work" that can be accomplished given the time, talents, and energies of the older volunteers; recognition of the value of volunteers; continued utilization of services and resources throughout the organization; and positive identification of volunteers with the organization.
5. The attitude of the organization toward older persons and volunteers must be shown to be positive.

In the process of identifying the need for volunteers, it should be kept in mind that the more volunteers there are, the more paid staff are needed to manage them. "How these staff members are to be paid remains a critical question for the success of [many] volunteer programs" (Van Wert, 1989, p. 17).

JOB DESCRIPTIONS

The importance of having a job description that clearly outlines the ongoing duties and expectations of each volunteer cannot be overemphasized (AARP, 1983). What will volunteers do? How many hours per week or month will they work? What is the duration of the obligation? (A 3- to 6-month "contract" that can be renewed, depending on mutual needs, is usually seen as reasonable.) To whom are the volunteers responsible? Are there any costs to the volunteers? What are the qualifications for each job? What skills are required to do it?

The kinds of jobs that can be done by volunteers in conjunction with occupational therapy programs will depend in large part on the occupational therapist's philosophy about using volunteers, the policies of the organization, and the type of program, and the type of resident. Examples described in the literature include planning and conducting group games; assisting in personal care, such as dressing, feeding, or giving manicures; transporting clients; teaching craft and recreation skills, such as art or needlework (Leitner & Leitner, 1985); visiting on a one-on-one basis; reading to residents; hosting an event; doing clerical work; preparing craft projects; taking residents on a field trip; providing respite to caregivers (Van Wert, 1989); showing films or slides; giving lectures (Windchime Court, 1983); and conducting a gardening group. Persons with physical impairments may contribute by doing telephone work, operating a computer, tutoring, peer counseling, teaching basic reading and math skills, and performing clerical duties, to name but a few possible jobs (Kouri, 1989).

As job descriptions are formulated, occupational therapists should recognize that each job has inherent sensorimotor, cognitive, and psychosocial components as well as a setting in which the work is done. (Work settings may be private or quite public in nature.) Some jobs require great commitment in terms of time and energy, level of responsibility, and supervision of other persons. Other jobs are more routine and require a lower level of skill, emotional involvement, and responsibility. (See Appendix 18-A for examples of job descriptions.)

Perhaps the most critical and pressing task is the selection of a volunteer coordinator. (The position of volunteer coordinator may be a paid or volunteer position.) Other volunteers will report to the coordinator, who is responsible to a high-level authority within the organization (AARP, 1983). The volunteer coordinator provides continuity for the volunteers and a point of contact for agency staff to request volunteers and to provide feedback on services that have been provided. "The coordinator serves as a bridge, advocate, interpreter, trouble shooter, colleague, leader, mediator, and lender of vision" (Seguin & McConney, 1982, p. 12).

The Older Adults Sharing Important Skills (OASIS) project (Franklin & Smith, 1986) confirmed the importance of having a key staff person in the facility serve as a source of appropriate client referral, guidance and information, and volunteer support and recognition. This person must have a clear understanding of clients' needs and of volunteers' skills, interests, and training to ensure appropriate referrals and effective channeling of volunteers' energy.

RECRUITING

Recruitment occurs after the identification of talents needed and the development of clearly defined expectations in the form of a job description. Leitner and

Leitner (1985) suggest the following resources for recruitment of volunteers: (1) professors and students in local universities and community colleges (contact departments of recreation and leisure studies, gerontology, community services, occupational therapy, and human development as well as fraternal organizations); (2) local high schools; (3) local churches; and (4) service groups such as the Lions, Elks, or Masons. Retired teachers associations or other professional groups, the American Red Cross, the United Way, men's and women's clubs, the Junior League, and senior centers are other resources for volunteers. Community organizations and local businesses can also contribute to a volunteer program. The police and fire departments, the local humane society, ministers, dance studios, florists, clothing stores, and beauty supply stores can enhance activity programs through lectures, demonstrations, classes, and so on. (See Appendix 18-B for names and addresses of formal agencies that attract older volunteers.)

People who are already volunteers are effective recruiters of others and should be involved in shaping and implementing the volunteer program (AARP, 1983; Sheppard, 1981). Although advertising may be indicated, perhaps the "largest single reason people volunteer is because someone asks them." Clear, specific requests to individuals are most effective. Asking "Can you spend an hour with Mrs. Jones once a week?" seems to be much more successful than saying "Will you become a volunteer?" (Van Wert, 1989). Frequently, older adults become acquainted with the residents while visiting a loved one in the nursing home and decide to volunteer. Those needing care themselves constitute another valuable recruitment resource for volunteers. People who are frail can "give back" in a variety of ways. Van Wert (1989) tells of a woman who knits afghans for the needy, of a blind diabetic man who talks regularly by phone to a young man recently blinded, and of others who answer phones, collate newsletters, and tape stories for the blind.

SCREENING

Screening is the process of matching volunteers, based on their attitudes, interests, skills, and needs, with the job or jobs identified as important to the organization. The same criteria should be used for selecting volunteers as would be used for hiring a paid worker.

An application form provides basic information about an applicant and serves as an initial screening tool. (See Appendix 18-C for an example of an application form.) An interview with the applicant should follow. As you talk with the applicant, ask yourself whether he or she has the time, interest, motivation, skills, values, and personality attributes to fill the position. Will the applicant be able to support the goals of the program and fit in with paid staff, other volunteers, and potential consumers (AARP, 1983)? "The mental health of the applicant; level of interpersonal skills; . . . motivation and willingness to learn; lack of personal impediments (health, time, transportation); and receptivity to program goals and methods'' will be important determinants of a successful volunteer (Gatz, Hileman, & Amaral, 1984, p. 352).

The screening process should also help to identify what the volunteer expects from the volunteer experience. In interviews held in conjunction with the OASIS project, learning (acquiring new skills, new information, ways of dealing with people, etc.) and serving (doing something of value for other people) were the themes most commonly cited. Reinforcement of previously learned skills was also mentioned (Franklin & Smith, 1986).

Potential volunteers may have difficulty recognizing how their past experiences interface with the needs of the organization. They may not know what they can do or what they want to do, and they may feel they have few skills with which to serve residents. In such cases, the occupational therapist (or the volunteer coordinator) will need to guide the process of identifying skills and preferences. Listing the tasks done by an applicant in his or her various roles—that is, as paid employee, family member, homemaker, or neighbor—is one way to ascertain skills. For instance, if an applicant has driven children to school year after year, he or she is skilled in driving or chauffeuring. Reflecting on favorite hobbies and special interests may help identify other skills (AARP, 1985). Myers and Andersen's (1984) adaptation of Bolles' (1978) scale of transferable skills is an excellent tool for this clarification process. Although Bolles' scale was developed to identify career interests, it is highly recommended for helping volunteers inventory their personal skills and interests.

TRAINING

Training of volunteers can take many forms. Initial orientation to the facility and its residents is done on a fairly routine basis in most organizations; ongoing training, it seems, is less common. The training program can be divided into three components: (1) initial orientation, (2) general education about aging, and (3) occupational-therapy-related topics. Suggestions are extensive and probably reflect "ideal" rather than typical circumstances.

The *initial orientation* introduces the volunteer to the organization. It should include a tour of the facility (smoking areas, restrooms, parking areas, storage places for personal items, work area, location of fire alarms) and introductions to the staff. The policies, standards, and mission of the agency should be reviewed and explained. This will entail discussion of the goals of the organization, the chain of command, the dress code and name code, the policy regarding phone calls, sign-in/sign-out procedures, visiting hours, the policy regarding accepting gifts from residents, volunteer rights (Appendix 18-D) and responsibilities

(Appendix 18-E), benefits, and reimbursement and insurance issues, to name but a few topics (Windchime Court, 1983).

Reinforcement of job-related information and volunteer duties should occur during the initial orientation. Volunteers deserve to know the agency's expectations regarding the work they are to perform, such as the time the job is to be done, the procedures to be followed, and the quality of work expected.

Aspects of confidentiality, such as policies and procedures regarding confidences shared by residents, should also be discussed early in the training period. Volunteers should be trained and supervised to ensure that standards of confidentiality are maintained in the organization. Access to confidential files should be on a need-to-know basis, just as it is for paid staff (AARP, 1983).

The characteristics of the residents and the implications of these demographics for services and therapy are also pertinent topics. Data about age, marital status, income level, ethnic and religious backgrounds, physical abilities and impairments, and typical family support systems would be pertinent (Leitner & Leitner, 1985). Volunteers who will be involved in activity programs will want to know about participation patterns and numbers, types of activities, reasons for not attending, the turnover rate, and favorite leisure pastimes (Leitner & Leitner, 1985).

General education about the process of aging should be part of the ongoing training of all volunteers who interact with the client population. Whether volunteers are involved in serving meals, transporting residents, "visiting," showing slides, or playing the piano for a sing-along, they need information about the impact of aging on psychological, sociological, and biological functions as well as information about the individual nature of the changes that occur. While education related to pathology in old age would be of interest to volunteers (e.g., typical disease processes, mental health problems such as depression and disorientation, medications, and Medicare and Medicaid), it is probably more important for them to gain a phenomenological appreciation of what being in a nursing home is all about. Recommended topics for discussion include aspects of loss in old age and the importance of finding new activities, roles, and people to reestablish one's sense of self; effective ways to communicate (especially important in the case of persons who have visual, auditory, or cognitive problems); how to help by focusing on strengths and "enabling" people as opposed to discounting their abilities and "taking over"; and hints for motivating. Dickey (1986) provides some insight into the problem of motivation when she reminds us that "most of us are afraid of failure. So are the residents. If you asked me to come to the activity room for a game, chances are I would refuse. Perhaps it's a game that I don't know how to play. I don't want to be the only one who doesn't know how. I don't want to make a fool of myself" (p. 80).

Education and training in the philosophy and techniques of occupational therapy will play a big part in producing effective occupational therapy volunteers. In addition to the above-mentioned topics, volunteers need to understand the importance of activity in meeting individual needs for recognition, achievement, intellectual stimulation, and socialization and in maintaining neuromotor, cognitive, and social skills. They should be aware of the impact of ethnic, racial, and religious background on needs and interests (Leitner & Leitner, 1985). Activities provide residents with something to look forward to and something they can talk about—other than their illnesses and troubles (Leitner & Leitner, 1985).

Volunteers should have access to personal and treatment information about the clients with whom they work, but only on a need-to-know basis. They should also have a basic understanding of the goals and methods of therapy. What is the resident expected to gain from occupational therapy? And why is it an appropriate activity?

There is some indication that occupational therapy volunteers trained at the paraprofessional level might better serve the needs of the client population of a nursing home. The number of activities and techniques occupational therapists use with the elderly can be overwhelming, and volunteers who are well-versed in recreational games, exercises and sports, arts and crafts, and creative and performing arts (music, art, drama, poetry) would be quite valuable. Paraprofessionals could be engaged in learning other therapeutic activities used with elderly, such as self-care, oral history, life review, reality orientation, and reminiscence. The how-to's of teaching activities to maximize a person's ability to perform is another area in which occupational therapy paraprofessionals might be trained.

Paraprofessionals in the OASIS project (Franklin & Smith, 1986) were trained to deliver low-cost effective mental health services in an attempt to counteract funding problems associated with Medicare and Medicaid reimbursement. They participated in 6 hours of training for 5 consecutive weeks in addition to monthly inservices. Aging, communication skills (active listening, open-ended questioning, and interviewing), therapeutic techniques used with the elderly, and mental health issues were the focus of the educational program. Gatz, Hileman, and Amaral (1984) reported that paraprofessional training usually includes both didactic and experiential approaches and that content typically includes listening and communications skills, problem solving, referral protocols, and recordkeeping. Training can vary from 30 to 150 hours; weekly individual and group supervision is not unusual.

Specific attainable goals and deadlines should be set for volunteer training. Involving volunteer personnel to train other volunteers is recommended whenever possible (AARP, 1983).

JOB PLACEMENT

Volunteers should be involved in their own placement if possible. In most cases, the job will be determined after the interview, and training will be provided for the job given. A probationary period should be set, during which time a volunteer can decide whether the job seems suitable. This also gives the occupational therapist time to evaluate the appropriateness of the placement (AARP, 1983).

During the placement period, it is important to provide consistency in work hours, tasks, and sites. Volunteers need a consistent contact person to deal with problems, changes in schedules, or questions. Continuity can be reinforced by keeping in close contact through regularly scheduled meetings to discuss problems and concerns and to identify additional training, education, and motivational needs (Leitner & Leitner, 1985). Evaluations should be done frequently. Remember that volunteers have many other options and that a job is not a lifetime contract. One method that seems to help retain volunteers is to keep a file that lists hobbies, skills, and interests. If a volunteer seems to be losing interest in his or her assignment, consult the file and offer this individual a new job that will add variety to the volunteer experience (S. Henderson, personal communication, February 17, 1989).

One of the most important tasks of the placement stage of volunteer program development is to differentiate professional and volunteer responsibilities. Although volunteers can provide many helpful services and can learn to monitor residents and notify professionals when necessary, they cannot and should not be expected to replace trained professionals (Morrow-Howell & Ozawa, 1987). It is the professionally trained occupational therapist's job to identify individual needs and interests, to plan programs, and to adapt activities to meet the broad spectrum of physical, intellectual, social, spiritual, and creative needs of individual residents. Occupational therapists are also responsible for analyzing the symbolic, physical, mental, social, and environmental aspects of activities; for determining the appropriate instructional techniques for a particular person or activity; and for documenting the delivery of occupational therapy services (Cunninghis, 1985).

Volunteers stay in their jobs because they are comfortable and feel they are doing important work and contributing to the organization. They may also see opportunities for self-growth and for learning new skills. The organization should support these feelings by demonstrating respect for their talents, time, and opinions on an ongoing basis.

Some volunteers like to have their own individual projects to work on when they have free time at the center. This is a special opportunity for them to be creative. The occupational therapist could, for instance, assign a volunteer the task of planning a special event such as a field trip, which would involve making phone calls to arrange transportation and advertising and to check out accessibility and costs. Other suggestions for special projects include writing a journal with a particular resident; researching a specific area of interest and presenting results at an inservice for staff and other volunteers; creating and taking responsibility for upkeep of a weekly or monthly bulletin board; or collecting information from residents, staff, and volunteers for a monthly newsletter (Leitner & Leitner,

1985). Volunteers associated with the Andrus Project (Seguin & McConney, 1982) initiated educational activities to increase their understanding of the aging process, publications on aging, a speaker's corps to fill requests from community groups for guest speakers, a leadership development project, and various research projects.

The range of jobs performed by nursing home resident volunteers is also extremely wide. In addition to providing services such as visiting, helping in the library, and transporting other residents to the dayroom, resident volunteers can participate in community-related volunteer tasks. Stevens Square Nursing Home in Minneapolis (Rustad, 1984) engaged its residents in a Residents-in-Service Volunteer Program that resulted in saving Medicaid $98,000 for one year. A small general store serving the needs of residents and staff was established; it was managed by a resident who assumed responsibility for ordering, banking, and scheduling other workers. Assisting with receptionist duties on a weekend and relief basis, publishing a newsletter, running a boutique with "second-time-around clothing," and reading to the blind were other ways residents provided genuinely useful service. Recently, the organization added an infant daycare center, registering 16 babies 6 weeks to 15 months old. "While the center has its own staff, Stevens Square residents are free to rock, cuddle, and walk the babies" (Rustad, 1984, p. 8).

INSURANCE AND LEGALITIES

As "gratuitous employees," volunteers have the right to work in a reasonably safe environment within the limits of a job description. Although it is unlikely that liability situations will occur when volunteers are properly trained and supervised, comprehensive general liability insurance should be in force to protect both the agency and its volunteers against negligence claims and legal defense costs. Such a policy would also protect the organization if a volunteer sues for personal injury suffered while volunteering. The cost for this kind of insurance is usually quite low, and it can be extended to cover volunteers' automobile and personal liabilities for as little as $5 per volunteer per year (AARP, 1983, 1985). (Contact the Volunteers Insurance Service Association, 4200 Wisconsin Avenue, N.W., Washington, DC 20016 for details.)

The Retired Senior Volunteer Program (RSVP) of Larimer County provides enrolled volunteers with supplemental accident, personal liability, and automobile insurance without cost (*Retired Senior*, 1988). As a general rule, potential volunteers should ascertain areas in which they may be held liable and contact their insurance agents to ensure that there are no gaps in coverage. In some instances, personal insurance may need to be increased. Volunteers who use their own cars to transport residents should be especially vigilant in checking their coverage (AARP, 1985).

Federal Standard 81H is a legal standard that applies to nursing home residents who wish to volunteer. It states that residents may not be *required* to perform services for the facility. However, a physician's order may be obtained that allows residents to participate in ongoing voluntary duties and/or perform services usually done by an employee of the organization (e.g., clearing tables, folding laundry). Residents who are enrolled as RSVP volunteers also need a physician's order to participate even though they are covered by RSVP insurance (S. Henderson, personal communication, February 17, 1989).

PROBLEMS

Problems related to staff expectations, volunteer expectations, communication, and task performance may well occur in the process of developing a volunteer program. Staff are advised not to overwhelm or intimidate volunteers with the seriousness of the tasks they assign and to keep expectations realistic (Morrow-Howell & Ozawa, 1987).

Faulkner (1975) reported that volunteers may reject some duties in favor of doing others; in particular, her volunteers preferred to assist the staff in organizing activities where their roles were most similar to that of staff and where they felt safer, had more visibility, and got more recognition. This points out the importance of knowing volunteers' needs and concerns and using this information to make assignments (Gatz, Hileman, & Amaral, 1984).

How much training is right and what makes an elderly paraprofessional a good helper? "We do know that informal helpers naturally do some things just like professionals would do, but they also do other things that trainers would discourage, such as giving advice, changing the topic, telling the person to count his or her blessings, or presenting alternatives rather than having the helpee come up with them" (Cowan, 1982, cited in Gatz, Hileman, & Amaral, 1984, p. 353). "Doing for" instead of "doing with" can erect barriers and discount potential abilities. Staff members associated with the OASIS project felt that the level of volunteer involvement with clients was too superficial; volunteers failed to deal with emotional issues, attempting instead "to make people happy" (Franklin & Smith, 1986, p. 18). One might question whether staff had unrealistic expectations.

OASIS project volunteers themselves admitted discomfort in dealing with all ranges of emotion, and they tended to avoid interactions with residents who expressed hopelessness and despair as well as anger. Volunteers also felt frustrated when working with clients who showed no progress, because there was no tangible evidence of any benefits associated with their efforts. The death of a client was identified as another difficulty; volunteers who had become close to clients quite naturally felt a sense of loss (Franklin & Smith, 1986). The comments by volunteers indicate the importance of maintaining close contact with them in order to support and process ongoing experiences. They also point to the value of holding small-group sessions in order to share feelings and concerns.

REWARDS AND BENEFITS

What benefits do volunteers bring to the organization? Most basically, they augment the work force. Volunteers in occupational therapy can do much to help carry out individual treatment programs and to help plan, organize, and conduct small-group activities. Elderly volunteers are especially effective in working with elderly residents "insofar as [they] are willing to invest more time and energy, to adopt a more active role as a client advocate, and to present themselves as role models, successfully coping with later life transitions" (Gatz, Hileman, & Amaral, 1984, p. 353).

The dollar value of time contributed by volunteers of all ages in the United States has been estimated at more than $65 billion a year, which is about twice as much as individuals donate to their favorite charities in actual dollars (AARP, 1983). In 1986, the average RSVP volunteer gave more than 18 hours of service to the community each month, and in Larimer County alone RSVP volunteers gave more than 172,000 hours of community service, the equivalent of 83 full-time employees (*Retired Senior*, 1988).

Older volunteers consistently have impressive attendance records and low attrition rates. Van Wert (1989) claimed that the attrition rate in his program over a 3-year period was 3%; volunteers who dropped out of the program did so because of personal reasons, such as a move out of the area, an illness, or family problems.

And what benefits accrue to the volunteers themselves? Participants acknowledge that rewards come in both tangible and intangible forms. Sponsoring agencies frequently honor volunteers with pins, plaques, and special dinners. Gatherings such as fish fries, recognition days, and memorial services are a popular way of making volunteers feel "connected" (Van Wert, 1989). Phone calls, notes, and birthday cards may be used to let the volunteers know they are appreciated and supported.

Reimbursement of out-of-pocket expenses and various benefits, such as lunch for those who work a full day, transportation (if not accessible in the community), parking, security, and liability insurance, are other tangible rewards that may be offered (AARP, 1983). RSVP volunteers who use a personal vehicle to go to and from an assigned station may be reimbursed at the rate of $.20 per mile up to a limit of $12.00 per month (*Retired Senior*, 1988). The IRS also allows some deductions associated with costs for volunteering. Since rules change from time to time, and since each rule may not be applicable to every volunteer situation, the agency should seek expert advice about allowable deductions for its volunteer staff and share this information with volunteers.

Opsata (1986) claims that most volunteers feel that the intangible rewards of volunteering more than compensate them for the efforts they expend. Such benefits include having an identity in a socially valued role (Seguin & McConney, 1982), doing meaningful work that confers status and self-esteem (Gatz, Hileman, & Amaral, 1984), helping others by sharing their skills (Sheppard, 1981), having opportunities for personal growth and development within an organization (AARP, 1983), changing and enriching their lives, finding new friends, remaining productive, discovering unknown skills, and feeling needed and useful (Van Wert, 1989). "Meaningful tasks provide for the volunteer a means for accomplishment, recognition, interest, challenge, and growth" (Seguin & McConney, 1982, p. 13). Volunteers can generate "ways of relating to one another and to their work that releases person power and potential" (Van Wert, 1989, p. 7). In becoming a network of friends and an extended family, they can establish norms for cooperation, innovation, and some risk taking (Seguin & McConney, 1982). Indeed, the socialization aspect of the volunteer experience may well be the most potent reward.

In conclusion, it is clear that a volunteer program can be a mutually beneficial endeavor that has the potential to enhance an occupational therapy program and enrich the lives of residents and the lives of the volunteers as well. Occupational therapists are encouraged to examine their current programs to determine what needs can be met through a volunteer force and then to take the steps outlined in this chapter to develop a volunteer program.

REFERENCES

Ager, C.L. (1987). Therapeutic aspects of volunteer and advocacy activities. *Physical & Occupational Therapy in Geriatrics, 5*(2), 3–11.

American Association of Retired Persons. (1983). *Older volunteers: A valuable resource.* Pub. No. PF3289. Washington, DC: Author. (For information, write American Association of Retired Persons, Program Department, 1909 K Street, NW, Washington, DC 20049.)

American Association of Retired Persons. (1985). *To serve, not to be served.* Pub. No. PF3304. Washington, DC: Author. (For information, write American Association of Retired Persons, Program Department, 1909 K Street, NW, Washington, DC 20049.)

Bolles, R.N. (1978). *The three boxes of life and how to get out of them.* Berkeley, CA: Ten Speed Press.

Cunninghis, R.N. (1985). Working with an activities consultant. *Activities, Adaptation & Aging, 7*(2), 123–130.

Dickey, H. (1986). What is an activity professional? *Activities, Adaptation & Aging, 9*(1), 79–83.

Faulkner, A.O. (1975). The black aged as good neighbors: An experiment in volunteer services. *The Gerontologist, 15*, 554–559.

Franklin, B., & Smith, B.K. (1986). *OASIS for the old*. Austin, TX: Texas University, Austin-Hogg Foundation for Mental Health. (For information write Austin-Hogg Foundation for Mental Health, Publications Division, P.O. Box 7998, Austin, TX 78713-7988.)

Gatz, M., Hileman, C., & Amaral, P. (1984). Older adult paraprofessionals: Working with and in behalf of older adults. *Journal of Community Psychology, 12*, 347–358.

Harris, L. (1975). *The myth and reality of aging in America*. Washington, DC: National Council on the Aging.

Harris, L. (1981). *America in the eighties: America in transition*. Washington, DC: National Council on the Aging.

Kouri, M. (1989, March). Volunteering: Knocking on opportunity's door. *Senior Edition USA/Colorado*, p. 7.

Leitner, M.J., & Leitner, S.F. (1985). *Leisure in later life: Activities, adaptation and aging*. New York: Haworth Press.

Morrow-Howell, N., & Ozawa, M.N. (1987). Helping network: Seniors to seniors. *The Gerontologist, 27*, 17–20.

Myers, A., & Andersen, C.P. (1984). *Success after sixty*. New York: Summit Books.

Opsata, M. (1986, July). Get up, get out, volunteer! *50 Plus*, pp. 58–62.

Retired Senior Volunteer Program of Larimer County. (1988). (Available from Larimer County Senior Employment Services, 145 East Mountain, Fort Collins, CO 80521)

Rustad, R. (1984). Stevens Square Wholistic Wellness Program. Unpublished manuscript. (Available from Rachel Rustad, 101 East 32nd Street, Minneapolis, MN 55408)

Seguin, M.W., & McConney, P.F. (1982). *Older volunteers: Bridge builders in the workplace*. Paper presented at the 28th Annual Meeting of the Western Gerontological Society, San Diego, CA, February 27 to March 3.

Sheppard, N.A. (1981). Older Americans: An untapped resource. *VocEd, 56*(2), 39–42.

Van Wert, J. (1989). *Interfaith volunteer caregivers: A special report*. Princeton, NJ: Robert Wood Johnson Foundation. (Available from the Robert Wood Johnson Foundation, P.O. Box 2316, Princeton, NJ 08543-2316)

Windchime Court. (1983). Unpublished material. (Available from Windchime Court, 811 East Myrtle, Fort Collins, CO 80524)

Appendix 18-A

Volunteer Job Descriptions

Job Title:	GROUP ACTIVITY LEADER
Summary:	Share your special skills in _____ or interests in _____ with residents.
Skills Required:	Sensitivity to the needs of the elderly with disabilities.
	Organizational skills (able to work well with small groups and on a one-to-one basis).
	Patience with elderly individuals.
	Cooperation with staff members.
Duties:	Talk with the Occupational Therapist about your group activity ideas and arrange date and time.
	Some group activity suggestions:

- discuss current events
- poetry reading
- creative writing
- group discussions
- sewing circles
- sing-alongs
- music appreciation
- music recitals
- slide shows

	Assist in helping residents to and from the activity.
	Keep a resident participation record.
Time Commitment:	This can be a one-time activity or an ongoing commitment. Duration of activity 30 to 60 minutes per group.
Supervision:	Provided by Occupational Therapist.

Job Title:	CRAFT COORDINATOR
Summary:	To provide and supervise a biweekly crafts program that includes a variety of projects.
Skills Required:	Knowledge of craft projects and how they may be adapted for elderly individuals.
	Leadership skills.
	Sensitivity to the needs of the elderly.
	Patience and creativity.
Duties:	Plan a bimonthly craft program and coordinate with the Occupational Therapist.
	Organize supplies needed from the supply closet at the facility, or purchase with money available from the activity budget. (Confirm expenses with OT prior to purchase.)
	Prepare, set up, and conduct craft sessions.
	Assist residents to and from craft sessions.
	Clean up.
	Keep weekly resident participation record.
	Supervise volunteers who assist you and record their hours.
Time Commitment:	Twice a month for 2 hours plus any shopping required; minimum 4-month commitment.
Supervision:	Trial period of 1 month (meet with OT after 1 month to evaluate program).

Source: Courtesy of Windchime Court, Fort Collins, Colorado.

Appendix 18-B

Recruitment Suggestions

1. **American Council to Improve Our Neighborhood (ACTION).** ACTION is a federal agency that sponsors the Senior Companions program and the Retired Senior Volunteer Program (RSVP).

   a. The Senior Companions program matches elderly volunteers who have limited incomes with the homebound elderly. Assistance with shopping, transportation to medical appointments, or friendship is provided. An hourly stipend is awarded to offset expenses. More than 5,000 seniors are currently active companions (telephone: 1-800-424-8867) (Opsata, 1986).

   b. RSVP has over 375,000 volunteers in community agencies in all 50 states. Choices of service are almost unlimited. Many RSVP volunteers are engaged in home visitation, transportation, and nursing home work (telephone: 1-800-424-8867) (Opsata, 1986).

2. **Local industries.** Businesses are often a good source of volunteers. In Philadelphia, Scott Paper has a SERVE (Scott Employee Retiree Volunteer Effort) program, which uses a computer to match willing volunteers with needy agencies. Levi Strauss, Dow Chemical, and Honeywell have similar programs (Opsata, 1986).

3. **Volunteer Clearinghouses.** Some 350 centralized volunteer clearinghouses or voluntary action centers maintain a current list of voluntary opportunities—and often candidates for filling them—and help match volunteers with needs. For more information about such centers or for guides to starting one in your community, write VOLUNTEER: The National Center for Citizen Involvement, Suite 500, 1111 North 19th Street, Arlington, VA 22209 (AARP, 1985).

4. **Area Agencies on Aging (AAA).** These regional government agencies often have information about voluntary programs involving older men and women. If you are looking for older volunteers, look in the white pages to find the telephone number of the agency nearest you (AARP, 1985).

5. **American Association of Retired Persons (AARP).** With more than 15 million members, AARP is a wellspring of volunteers and volunteer opportunities. The AARP Volunteer Talent Bank identifies potential volunteers nationwide for referral to appropriate organizations with specific volunteer needs. For more information, contact the Volunteer Bank, 1909 K Street, NW, Washington, DC 20049. For information on AARP chapters, contact the area office that serves your location (AARP, 1985).
6. **Governor's Office for Voluntary Service.** Many states have a governor's office for volunteer groups and organizations. Such offices can provide technical assistance and referral in many instances. Some also keep registers of volunteer trainers, speakers, and other leaders in the volunteer community. These offices are listed under state government services and are sometimes located in state capitals. You can obtain the number of the Governor's Office for Voluntary Service for your state from your operator (AARP, 1985).

Appendix 18-C

Volunteer Application

1. Name _____ Telephone _____
   Address _____
2. Referred by _____
3. Birth date (month/day) _____
4. How often would you like to volunteer? (circle preference)
   Twice weekly   Weekly   Every two weeks
   Other _____
5. Time preference: (circle preference)
   Morning   Afternoon   Evening
6. Length of time you wish to serve: (circle preference)
   1 hour   2 hours   3 hours
7. Day(s) of the week preferred _____
8. How long do you anticipate your volunteer commitment will last?
   3 months   6 months   1 year   Indefinite
9. Can you provide transportation for residents? _____
10. What special skills would you like to share with our residents (e.g., foreign languages, needlecraft, hobbies, work or volunteer experience)?
    _____
    _____
    _____
11. What clubs or organizations do you belong to? _____
    _____
12. Check the activities below that interest you.
    ____ Show slides
    ____ Show films
    ____ Write letters
    ____ Help with games
    ____ Teach painting

_____ Teach watercolors/oils
_____ Teach gardening
_____ Teach flower arranging
_____ Provide instrumental talent
_____ Provide vocal talent
_____ Help with parties (refreshments, decorations, etc.)
_____ Take residents for walks, rides, tours, or picnics
    _____ with staff help
    _____ without staff help
_____ Take residents to church
    _____ with staff help
    _____ without staff help
_____ Help to prepare for special days (Christmas, birthdays, Halloween, etc.)
_____ Distribute magazines and books
_____ Play records
_____ Read to residents
_____ Help with group sings
_____ Provide scrap material for crafts
_____ Assist residents with craft projects
_____ Make patterns for craft projects
_____ Work with residents on a facility newsletter
_____ Work with residents in a flower/vegetable garden
_____ Assist residents with personal care
_____ Recruit other volunteers
_____ Contact community persons for assistance with program or donation of supplies
_____ Help residents with writing exercises
_____ Be a friendly visitor
_____ Supply activity coordinator with new ideas
_____ Coordinate people for book reviews, current events, group discussions regarding antiques, travel, movies, etc.
_____ Other _____

13. Why do you want to volunteer to work?
_____
_____
_____

14. Please list two people who would provide a character reference for you.

OFFICE USE

Interviewed by _____
Date of interview _____
Date of orientation _____
Assignment and date _____

Source: Courtesy of Windchime Court, Fort Collins, Colorado.

Appendix 18-D

Volunteer Bill of Rights

- The Right to be treated as a co-worker—not just free help.
- The Right to a suitable assignment—with consideration for personal preference, temperament, life experience, education and employment background.
- The Right to know as much about the organization as possible—its policies, people, and programs.
- The Right to training for the job and continuing education on the job—including training for greater responsibility.
- The Right to sound guidance and direction.
- The Right to a place to work—an orderly, designated place that is conducive to work and worthy of the job to be done.
- The Right to promotion and a variety of experiences—through advancement or transfer, or through special assignments.
- The Right to be heard—to feel free to make suggestions, to have a part in planning.
- The Right to recognition—in the form of promotion and awards, through day-to-day expressions of appreciation and by being treated as a bona fide co-worker.

Source: Copyright 1990, American Association of Retired Persons. Reprinted by permission.

Volunteer Responsibilities

Responsibilities

A volunteer who accepts assignment assumes these responsibilities:

- To consider the volunteer assignment as a serious commitment.
- To be present at times agreed to, follow the job description and accept the supervisor's assigned volunteer tasks.
- To inform the volunteer's supervisor whenever the volunteer is unable to perform the assigned volunteer tasks.
- To offer suggestions and provide feedback to the volunteer's supervisor, including informing the supervisor of any problems encountered in performing the assigned volunteer tasks.
- To attend training provided when necessary to perform assigned volunteer tasks.
- To observe the same rules and policies of the organization to which the volunteer is assigned as the organization's paid staff.
- To give the volunteer's supervisor adequate notice before terminating volunteer services and be honest about reasons for leaving.

Source: Courtesy of Retired Senior Volunteer Program of Larimer County, Fort Collins, Colorado.

Chapter 19

Occupational Therapy with the Terminally Ill

Barbara Thompson

A BRIEF HISTORY OF DEATH

Historically, death has had many faces, each shaped by the myths, existing institutional structures, and the social character of the dominant culture of the time. Ivan Illich in *Medical Nemesis* (1976) and Fritjof Capra in *The Turning Point* (1982), among others, have discussed death within this context, tracing the origins of our contemporary view of death. Such an evolutionary perspective is helpful in appreciating our cultural conditioning relative to death and how this conditioning affects both our personal and professional practices.

In the 4th century A.D., Christianity became the official religion of the Roman Empire. From the 4th century to the early 14th century, delirious crowds, church prohibitions notwithstanding, danced on the tombs of their ancestral dead in cemeteries and Christian churches. Poems and songs, as well as the more familiar woodcuts, record this tradition of ''dancing with the dead'' as an occasion to celebrate life (Illich, 1976).

By the end of the 14th century, the dance of death became more introspective. Death was taken inward and the dance partner, rather than being a dead ancestor, became a mirror image of oneself. One's own mortality was embraced in the dance, with death becoming an integral part of human life (Illich, 1976).

By the late 15th century, death was no longer just a mirror image. It had become a separate entity represented in the form of a skeleton that exacted its due from each individual at an appointed time. Death, holding the hourglass, was seen as a final and certain interruption in a time-measured existence (Illich, 1976).

I would like to express my deep appreciation for the generous conceptual and editorial assistance given to me by David De Noble, MS, OTR, and Daniel Gabriels, MD. Their capable help in preparing this chapter made the process all the more rewarding for me.

This view continued into the 16th century, with death perceived as a force of nature, an inevitable encounter at the end of life. Practices were designed to assist people in dignifying this final and personal life event. Manuals were published on the art of dying, and medical folk practices proliferated. During the 15th and 16th centuries, the involvement of a doctor in a death was limited to providing comfort and working in concert with what was considered to be a natural process (Illich, 1976).

During the latter part of the 16th century and throughout the 17th century, the ideas of Copernicus, Kepler, Galileo, and Bacon began to reshape the vision of death and the role of medicine. Francis Bacon, who advanced the empirical method of science in England, viewed nature as a force to be controlled and placed in the service of humankind. Bacon was the first to assign doctors the three tasks of preserving health, curing disease, and prolonging life, with the latter being the most important task. A century and a half later, the ill began to look to doctors to intercede with death on their behalf. Death was no longer the sole custodian of the hourglass (Capra, 1982; Illich, 1976).

This changing world view became fully developed through the work of Descartes and Newton, whose thinking has profoundly shaped the course of Western civilization. Capra (1982) notes that "the influence of the Cartesian paradigm on medical thought resulted in the so called biomedical model, which constitutes the conceptual foundation of modern scientific medicine" (p. 123).

Basic characteristics of this prevailing contemporary medical model include (1) a belief in the duality of body and mind; (2) a view that all aspects of living organisms can be understood by reducing them to physical and chemical interactions among the smallest constituents; (3) a definition of diseases as "well-defined entities that involve structural changes at the cellular level and have unique causal roots" (Capra, 1982, p. 150); (4) a shift in attention from patients to pathology; (5) a transformation from the Medieval "houses of mercy" to modern centers for diagnosis, treatment, and research (p. 130); (6) a shift in authority from patient to doctor as the protector of health; and (7) a belief in the certainty of science that holds the art of healing in suspicion and values specialization, technology, and the hard sciences.

Death is now seen in the form of various diseases identified by medical science, which then accepts the responsibility of opposing death. Having been alienated, death is next identified as the greatest enemy, propelling an unsatisfiable search for a technological defense. In turn, preoccupation with this ever-expanding arsenal perpetuates the image of death as enemy and other.

Thus the spectacular and positive achievements of modern medical science may have limited our understanding of the relationship we have with death. Within the context of the Western medical model, death no longer has dignity as a natural event. The art and craft of dying are no longer practiced, patients no longer preside at their own deaths, and death is removed from the everyday sphere of home and family as well as individual cultural or spiritual values (Capra, 1982; Illich, 1976).

HOSPICE: AN ALTERNATIVE PROGRAM OF CARE

Hospice [həs pis] house of rest, 'home' .XIX. – (O)F. hospice – L. hospitium hospitality, lodging, f. hospit-, hospes HOST (*Oxford Dictionary of English Etymology,* 1966)

In the literature, *hospice* refers both to a place or environment and to the nature of the relationship between guest and host (Saunders, 1986).

Records of ancient hospices date to the 4th century A.D. As way stations for pilgrims and travelers and as charitable Christian institutions for the sick and dying, hospices proliferated in Medieval Europe. Hospices subsequently disappeared and did not reappear until the 19th century. A number of hospices, all with religious affiliations, were then founded to care for the dying (Saunders, 1986).

The hospice movement of the 20th century developed in response to the unmet needs of patients dying in traditional medical environments. Through her work as a nurse and social worker in England, Dame Cicely Saunders recognized the necessity to develop an alternative program of care for persons with advanced illness for whom there was no hope of a cure. With this intention, Dame Saunders became a physician and subsequently opened St. Christopher's Hospice in 1969. Based in a London suburb, St. Christopher's gained an international reputation and became the model for hospice programs in the Western world (Thompson & Wurth, 1988).

In 1971, St. Luke's Hospice opened in Sheffield, England, under the direction of Professor Eric Wilkes. Whereas St. Christopher's Hospice offered only inpatient care, St. Luke's offered inpatient, home care, and day treatment services. The first Canadian hospice opened in 1973 at the Royal Victoria Hospital in Montreal under the medical direction of Dr. Balfour Mount. Connecticut Hospice, in New Haven, became the first hospice in the United States, opening a home care program in 1974 and an inpatient facility in 1980 (Thompson & Wurth, 1988).

By the late 1970s, there were over 200 U.S. hospice programs, with many variations in scope of services and organizational model. Explosive growth in the type and number of hospices led concerned providers to recognize the need for principles of hospice care and standards for developing programs. This crucial consensus was achieved by the National Hospice Organization (NHO) soon after its first annual conference in 1978 (Thompson & Wurth, 1988).

In 1981, the NHO issued the following statement on the philosophy of hospice:

Dying is a normal process, whether or not resulting from disease. Hospice exists neither to hasten nor to postpone death. Rather, hospice exists to affirm life by providing support and care for those in the last phases of incurable disease so that they can live as fully and comfortably as possible. Hospice promotes the formation of caring communities that are sensitive to the needs of patients and families at this time in their lives so that they may be free to obtain the degree of mental and spiritual preparation for death that is satisfactory to them. (p. 3)

The NHO (1981) also recognized the following as basic tenets and characteristics of a hospice program:

1. Pain and other symptoms of incurable disease can be controlled. When cure is no longer possible and patients experience curative efforts as unduly burdensome, palliative care is the most appropriate form of care.
2. Hospice care is respectful of all patient and family belief systems and commits its resources to meeting the personal, moral, philosophical, and religious needs of patients and their families.
3. The patient and family are the unit of care, although hospice programs do seek to identify, mobilize, and supervise other care providers if family members are not available.
4. Inpatient care and/or home care are provided according to patient and family needs.
5. Bereavement care is provided to hospice families following the patient's death.
6. Hospice care is provided under the direction of a physician by an interdisciplinary team that includes trained and supervised volunteers.
7. Each hospice is responsible for administering its own program in compliance with NHO standards and applicable health care laws and regulations.
8. Structured and informal means for staff support, along with ongoing education and training programs, are imperative.

With the surge in the hospice movement during the 1970s, Congress mandated the Health Care Financing Administration (HCFA) to study hospice and its potential impact on the Medicare and Medicaid programs. This study ultimately showed that hospice was a cost-effective means of caring for the terminally ill, and 1982 legislation provided hospice benefits to Medicare beneficiaries. These regulations established beneficiary requirements, reimbursement standards and procedures, the required scope of services, and the conditions for a program to become Medicare certified. Additional legislation, approved in 1986, allocated federal funds for an optional state Medicaid hospice benefit. Individual states could thereby choose to amend their Medicaid plans to provide beneficiaries with coverage for hospice care (Thompson & Wurth, 1988). In 1990, Congress passed legislation extending the coverage provided to eligible Medicare and Medicaid beneficiaries (Selinske, 1991).

To receive hospice care under Medicare, an individual must be entitled to Part A of Medicare and have a physician certify a prognosis of approximately 6 months or less. Eligible beneficiaries then transfer their coverage from traditional Medicare to the Medicare hospice benefit. Under the Medicare hospice benefit, care must be provided by a Medicare-certified hospice program. According to a 1989 survey conducted by the NHO, there were 996 Medicare-certified hospice programs in the U.S., and approximately 150 programs pursuing hospice Medicare certification (NHO, personal communication with Margaret Duncan, April 2, 1991).

A combination of factors can delay development of Medicare-certified hospice programs. These factors include federal and state requirements for certification, certificate of need laws, inadequate reimbursement levels, survey procedures, a community's geography and population density, and the particular constellation of community resources. Although an increasing number of programs have opted for certification, many others have chosen to postpone certification or to provide hospicelike services to terminally ill patients and their families through other arrangements. Hospicelike programs, although varying in organization, usually rely on a small staff in combination with well-trained and coordinated volunteers to provide support to patients and families and consultation to other agencies or personnel providing medical care. Since hospicelike programs have no recognized authority, they must rely on their ability to collaborate and negotiate with traditional providers of medical services to ensure provision of quality care that is consistent with hospice philosophy and standards. With hospicelike programs, medical care can be difficult to arrange due to restrictions inherent in the traditional Medicare system.

OCCUPATIONAL THERAPY: BASIC VALUES AND TENETS

The basic values of occupational therapy are rooted in the "moral treatment" movement of the 1800s. The founders of occupational therapy, as advocates of the moral treatment approach, recognized and stressed the individual's need for participation in a balanced program of activity and his or her right to a supportive environment as basic conditions underlying health and, therefore, any successful treatment approach. The importance of human occupation became a central tenet of the emerging profession (Kielhofner & Burke, 1983).

The increasing authority of 20th-century medicine stimulated criticism of occupational therapy practice in the 1950s and 1960s, especially criticism that it lacked scientific credibility. In response to this criticism, practitioners gradually narrowed their perspective to more closely coincide with that of the medical model (Kielhofner & Burke, 1983). In the practice of occupational therapy, as in the practice of medicine, the reductionism of Cartesian philosophy and the biomedical model has been responsible for significant advances, but there has been inattention to, if not active avoidance of, the "existential" concerns that arise in connection with serious illness. By adhering carefully to the tenets of the Cartesian-based biomedical model, occupational therapy has narrowed its scope of thinking on illness and health, the role of the occupational therapist, and the patient's experience of meaning through activity.

One of the existential issues that finds no comfortable place in Cartesian medicine is the nature of our relationship to death. In fact, this is the ultimate existential issue, but since death is considered the enemy of modern medicine, the issue is avoided. The potential meanings of illness and human suffering are not addressed, and the concept of dying well therefore remains necessarily unintelligible (Barrett, 1958; Capra, 1982).

We need to understand the process of dying as a continuation of a developmental process.

> The fact is that death is inevitable. We will all die. . . . Death is as much a part of human existence, of human growth and development, as being born. It is one of the few things in life we can count on, that we can be assured will occur. Death is not an enemy to be conquered or a prison to be escaped. It is an integral part of our lives. . . . It sets a limit on our time in this life, urging us on to do something productive with that time as long as it is ours to use. (Braga & Braga, 1975, p. x)

The view of life as a developmental process is consistent with the work of Ayres, Llorens, and Mosey in occupational therapy and with the work of Erikson, Gesell, and Piaget outside the field of occupational therapy. Erikson (1982), while not necessarily speaking of dying, does speak of old age as a developmental stage with its own particular task. That task involves the integration of all that has come before into some unified whole. Failure in that task results in despair. Erikson characterizes this integration as a "sense of coherence and wholeness" (p. 65). This sense of coherence is at risk for the terminally ill individual who faces loss of physical and mental self as well as loss of relatedness to others.

The final task in the living and dying process can be viewed as the discovery of personal meaning, which supports an experience of integration and wholeness. As occupational therapists, we can help to "widen and broaden the visual field of the patient so that the whole spectrum of meaning and values becomes conscious and visible to him" (Frankl, 1962, p. 110). Frankl states that individuals can discover meaning in life in three ways: "(1) by doing a deed, (2) by experiencing a value . . . and (3) by suffering" (p. 111).

The recognition of humanistic values, which is indispensable for occupational therapists who work with terminally ill patients and their families, encompasses the following: (1) a focus on wellness as a state of being rather than just the absence of disease; (2) a belief in the functional unity of body and mind; (3) a view that people live in dynamic relationship with cultural, social, personal, and physical systems; (4) a recognition that the occupational therapist also exists in dynamic relationship with those systems; (5) an appreciation of the centrality of the subjective perceptions of the individual regarding the quality of his or her own life; (6) placement of the patient in a position of authority (based on the recognition that each individual can influence his or her own health and sense of well-being); and (7) a belief in the healing role of the therapeutic relationship and the value of compassion.

THE OCCUPATIONAL THERAPY PROCESS

Understanding the Diagnosis

To be effective, the occupational therapist needs a thorough working knowledge of the specific disease process and its implications for dysfunction and distress. Review of a patient's medical record can yield valuable information on the diagnosis, history of treatment, current treatment regime, prognosis, and involvement of other professions (Pedretti, 1985). In addition, it is essential to utilize whatever formal and informal mechanisms are available for communication with other professionals and nonprofessional caregivers.

A thorough understanding of the disease process and the patient's medical and personal history will help the therapist answer questions from the patient and family that arise during occupational therapy sessions. It is also important to understand the meaning a certain diagnosis may have for a particular person.

A 70-year-old gentleman with advanced amyotrophic lateral sclerosis (ALS) was admitted to the general hospital for control of his symptoms and was referred to occupational therapy for relaxation training and activities of daily living (ADL) assessment. A review of the chart showed that the patient had been diagnosed 9 months earlier, had experienced rapid progression of symptoms, and had requested that a copy of his living will be placed in the medical chart. The physician noted that the patient's prognosis, based on pulmonary function studies, was less than 6 months. According to a nurse's note, the wife had described the patient as being "very anxious at home" and "afraid to do anything." The nurses stated that the patient experienced great anxiety and associated periods of breathing difficulty. During the initial interview with the patient, the occupational therapist asked the patient what he understood about ALS. The patient responded, "I know it's a fatal disease." Later in the conversation he added, "I spend most of my day fantasizing about my death." When asked to describe these fantasies, the patient responded, "I'm afraid of choking and suffocating to death."

The patient's conceptions and fears regarding his diagnosis were intimately related to his level of occupational performance and his capacity to enjoy his life. Addressing the meaning that ALS had for the patient allowed the occupational therapist, in concert with other team members, to develop an effective program of care.

Awareness of the Environment

Physical Considerations

In the evaluation process, it is important to consider the physical environment, whether the patient is at home or in an institutional setting. In the hospital, areas of concern might include (1) positioning and the patient's comfort level in bed or in a lounge chair; (2) the patient's ability to operate bed controls and the call button; (3) the placement of objects in the room for convenience, general comfort, and safety; and (4) the patient's equipment needs.

Mr. L.'s illness resulted in a bilateral hip disarticulation and episodes of internal hemorrhaging, which necessitated hospitalization on a medical floor. His medical condition was very unstable, which interfered with plans for alternative placement. Mr. L. knew that his prognosis was guarded at best. He was described by staff as very depressed, and a psychiatric consult was being considered. An occupational therapy evaluation was requested.

A Clinitron bed, utilized to prevent skin breakdown and provide optimal comfort, did not allow Mr. L. to be easily moved outside of his room. The addition of an overhead trapeze did permit Mr. L. to reposition himself, but he was otherwise physically confined to the narrow world of his bed. Mr. L.'s room was cluttered with medical paraphernalia and a few personal items, all of which were inaccessible to him. A photograph of his granddaughter seemed the only remnant of Mr. L.'s life before he entered the hospital. Mr. L. said his days were structured according to meals, medical treatments, and a few select television programs. He said that he had at one time been instructed in active range of motion (AROM) exercises but that he did them irregularly now, adding "What's the point?" The initial interview revealed that Mr. L. had run a small business and, in his leisure time, had been a gardener and an enthusiastic modelmaker. Though divorced from his wife and partially estranged from his children, he maintained a strong bond of affection with his granddaughter.

In discussing goals for the occupational therapy program, Mr. L. expressed strong interest in reorganizing his physical environment for increased accessibility and aesthetic appeal. Additionally, he stated that he would very much enjoy resumption of his modelmaking. It was suggested to him that he consider making something for his granddaughter.

With some initial reservation on the part of the hospital staff, a philodendron plant was wrapped around the trapeze in a way that would not interfere with its use. Mr. L. had complained of "staring at the metal bar" and, given his interest in plants, the addition of the philodendron seemed fitting. Eventually, other staff and visitors added an assortment of photographs and small items to the trapeze, the whole suggestive of a tropical garden.

Under Mr. L.'s direction, shelving was added to the room to reduce the clutter and make space for his project. Personal items were arranged for accessibility from the bed.

Mr. L. decided to assemble a large, intricate dollhouse kit for his granddaughter. After fashioning an elaborate system of numbered boxes to store the dollhouse components, he spent most of his available time organizing and assembling the kit. Modification of the physical environment became an important part of Mr. L.'s program, and it became his business to supervise the changes.

During his remaining 6 weeks of life, Mr. L. was able to reclaim part of a past that had been lost to him, improve the quality of his present life, and leave a legacy for his granddaughter. He died before he was able to complete the dollhouse, but he left directions that enabled another interested patient and a volunteer to finish the project.

The occupational therapist can provide invaluable assistance in evaluating the patient and family's home environment, either in anticipation of discharge from the hospital or to assist the patient in comfortably and safely remaining at home. As always, the therapist needs to be aware of personal, familial, and cultural values when recommending changes and to consider funding sources if equipment is proposed.

Areas of assistance might include (1) educating caregivers in safe ways to move and care for the patient; (2) providing equipment, such as an elevated toilet seat, grab bars, adapted phone system, or electric recliner, to enhance functional independence; (3) rearranging furniture to increase safety, improve comfort, or remove barriers (e.g., moving the patient's bed from an isolated bedroom to a more central room in the house to increase opportunities for interactions with the family); (4) installing a ramp or railings at the entrance of the house; and (5) providing information on wheelchair-accessible transportation in the community. There are ample resources in the occupational therapy literature on methods of assessing the home environment, ways to remove barriers to independence, and the use of equipment to enhance functional performance (Pedretti, 1985; Trombly, 1983).

In work with the terminally ill, therapists should make goals achievable within the short term and relevant to a longer term picture, which may include continual changes in functional ability.

Social and Cultural Considerations

A person's social and cultural history will influence how he or she will perceive, act, and perform in the world (Barris, Kielhofner, Levine, & Neville, 1985).

Mrs. R. was a 64-year-old Frenchwoman with advanced breast cancer who was admitted to a hospice inpatient unit for terminal care. Mrs. R. was an animated and interesting conversationalist who seemed particularly to enjoy speaking about her experiences as a resistance fighter in France during World War II. After the war, she had immigrated to the United States, where she later met and married her husband. The marriage only lasted a few years, and then Mrs. R. left her husband to live on her own. For many years she was employed as a state worker in a position of responsibility. Although she lived alone, she attracted and cultivated an extensive network of friends and work associates.

Her occupational therapy goals focused on increasing her independence in self-care activities, the completion of her memoirs, and the organization of her will and distribution of her personal belongings among her friends. Adapted equipment enabled Mrs. R. to achieve a level of self-care that she found satisfying.

At most times Mrs. R. was accompanied by an entourage of friends and associates. Curiously, however, there always seemed to be some sort of interpersonal conflict in process, either between a friend and Mrs. R. or between one friend and another. The occupational therapist was drawn into an increasingly intricate and divisive web of intrigue, as one friend after another called her aside to enlist her support. In spite of increasing levels of tension between Mrs. R. and her friends and the occupational therapist's apparent inability to serve as a mediator, Mrs. R. appeared unperturbed as she proceeded with her memoirs and the organization of her estate. One day, as Mrs. R. again proudly recounted her experiences with the French underground, it became apparent to the occupational therapist that Mrs. R.'s current interpersonal pattern closely paralleled her stories of the resistance. The occupational therapist then wondered if her vision for Mrs. R. might be inconsistent with Mrs. R.'s character and personal history. When this concern was verbalized by the therapist, Mrs. R.'s facial expression slowly changed to one of wry amusement. After a moment, Mrs. R. quietly nodded and then continued to work on her memoirs.

In the end Mrs. R. died quite peacefully with a few close friends by her side. Her will excited further tensions among some of her friends and afforded amusement for others. In her living and dying, Mrs. R. was consistent and taught the occupational therapist a valuable lesson.

Attention to Occupational Behavior

In working with the terminally ill, it is essential that assessments of occupational behavior address the patient's experience of meaning through activity while drawing upon the more technical accounts of occupational therapy theory and practice. Kielhofner (1983) notes that "the meaningfulness of activities" is uniquely determined by each person according to the person's accumulated repertoire of experience in a particular environment or system and that "persons achieve meaning in their lives by performing those occupations which have come to bear a certain significance or importance" (p. 19).

When illness disrupts occupational performance and the person experiences a concomitant loss of meaning, occupational therapy can assist by helping the person adapt to changes in occupational performance and restore a meaningful balance of activities (American Occupational Therapy Association [AOTA], 1986).

The use of ritual can provide important benefits to patients and families. Kielhofner (1983) supports the use of ritual in occupational therapy practice as a way to affirm a person's membership in a larger group and as a context for viewing personal experience, including suffering, as part of the greater human condition. In his view, "allowing patients to create their own celebration and ritual is an important consideration in allowing patients to find meaning" (p. 305).

Mr. B. was an 82-year-old man of German descent who suffered from advanced small cell lung cancer and had been admitted to a hospice home care program for terminal care. Mr. B.'s wife had died a few years earlier, and he had recently moved to the home of his daughter and son-in-law, both of whom worked during the week.

At the time of the initial occupational therapy home visit, Mr. B. appeared to be very depressed. He stated that he spent most of his day lying on the couch and that he did "not want to be a burden on his family." Mr. B. said that he had very much enjoyed his profession as a tailor and the outings to a senior citizen center that he and his wife had made prior to her death.

Although Mr. B. expressed little interest in attending the hospice daycare center, he did agree to do so on a trial basis. In daycare, Mr. B. found a reliable system of physical and emotional support. He was introduced to a volunteer of German descent, and an occupational therapist worked with him on a consistent basis in both home and daycare settings.

It became apparent that Mr. B. was grieving the multiple losses of his German homeland and heritage, his wife, his occupational role, his independent living status, his health, and his home. In collaboration with Mr. B. and other staff, the occupational therapist planned a pair of rituals to help Mr. B. externalize his grief and celebrate his life and heritage.

The first ritual took the form of a memorial and celebratory service for Mr. B.'s wife. Preparing for this provided Mr. B. with an occasion to reflect on his marriage, his children, his own and his family's aging process, his wife's death, and his present illness. Once the ceremony was designed, Mr. B. invited his family, his friends, and other daycare participants to join him in celebrating the memory of his wife. By embracing his losses and affirming his grief, Mr. B. was able to more fully embrace and affirm his life.

Several weeks later, Mr. B. and the occupational therapist planned a German feast day for the daycare center. Complete with a traditional German meal and music and photographs from his homeland, this reclamation of Mr. B.'s heritage provided him with an important context for personal renewal and the experience of an interconnected past and present, in both outer and inner worlds.

THE PROFESSIONAL IN AN UNCERTAIN ENVIRONMENT

A sound and varied professional grounding is especially important in work with the terminally ill, since the occupational therapist must continuously adapt programs to meet changing patient and family needs. Professional competence allows the occupational therapist to respond more spontaneously and flexibly to the unpredictable nature of this work (AOTA, 1987).

Another sphere of uncertainty is the particular role that the occupational therapist will have in relationship to other participating staff. A degree of role blurring inevitably occurs among the disciplines, and this needs to be permitted (AOTA, 1987). Flanigan (1982) states that in order "to serve the best interests of the patients who are striving for meaning in a limited life, we [occupational therapists] must be able to sidestep the defined limits of our traditional roles and cooperate in providing hospice care" (p. 276).

If we, as occupational therapists, are to nurture the "whole spectrum of meaning and values" (Frankl, 1962, p. 111), we must be open to ambiguity and, aided by a sense of humor, approach Death as the Great Teacher. If we are to bring our professional skills and our open-hearted selves to the service of patients and their families, we must learn to listen to our inner selves and to others.

> A good traveler has no fixed plans
> and is not intent upon arriving.
> A good artist lets his intuition
> lead him wherever it wants.
> A good scientist has freed himself
> of concepts
> and keeps his mind open to what is.
> (Lao Tzu, *Tao Te Ching*, 6th century B.C.)

REFERENCES

American Occupational Therapy Association. (1986). Occupational therapy and hospice [Hospice Task Force position paper]. *American Journal of Occupational Therapy, 40,* 839–840.

American Occupational Therapy Association. (1987). *Guidelines for occupational therapy services in hospice.* Rockville, MD: American Occupational Therapy Association.

Barrett, W. (1958). *Irrational man.* Garden City, NY: Doubleday.

Barris, R., Kielhofner, G., Levine, R.E., & Neville, A.M. (1985). Occupation as interaction with the environment. In G. Kielhofner (Ed.), *A model of human occupation: Theory and application* (pp. 42–62). Baltimore, MD: Williams & Wilkins.

Braga, J.L., & Braga, L.D. (1975). Forward. In E. Kubler-Ross, *Death, the final stage of growth* (pp. x–xiii). Englewood Cliffs, NJ: Prentice-Hall.

Capra, F. (1982). *Turning point.* New York: Simon & Schuster.

Erikson, E. (1982). *The life cycle completed.* New York: W.W. Norton.

Flanigan, K. (1982). The art of the possible: Occupational therapy in terminal care. *British Journal of Occupational Therapy, 45,* 274–276.

Frankl, V. (1962). *Man's search for meaning.* New York: Simon & Schuster.

Illich, I. (1976). *Medical nemesis.* New York: Random House.

Kielhofner, G. (1983). The art of occupational therapy. In G. Kielhofner (Ed.), *Health through occupation: Theory and practice in occupational therapy* (pp. 295–308). Philadelphia: F.A. Davis.

Kielhofner, G., & Burke, J.P. (1983). The evolution of knowledge and practice in occupational therapy: Past, present and future. In G. Kielhofner (Ed.), *Health through occupation: Theory and practice in occupational therapy* (pp. 3–54). Philadelphia: F.A. Davis.

Lao Tzu. (1988). *A new English version: Tao te ching* (S. Mitchell, Trans.). New York: Harper & Row.

National Hospice Organization. (1981). *Standards of a hospice program of care.* Alexandria, VA: Author.

Owens, C.T. (Ed.). (1966). *Oxford dictionary of English etymology.* Oxford: Clarendon Press.

Pedretti, L.W. (Ed.). (1985). *Occupational therapy: Practice skills for physical dysfunction.* St. Louis: C.V. Mosby.

Saunders, C. (1986). The modern hospice. In F.S. Wald (Ed.), *In quest of the spiritual component of care for the terminally ill: Proceedings of a colloquium* (pp. 39–48). New Haven, CT: Yale University School of Nursing.

Selinske, C. (1991). The fourth hospice benefit period. *New York State Hospital Association Newsletter,* March 16.

Thompson, B., & Wurth, M.A. (1988). The hospice movement. In K.N. Tigges & W.M. Marcil (Eds.), *Terminal and life-threatening illness: An occupational behavior perspective* (pp. 19–40). Thorofare, NJ: Slack.

Trombly, C.A. (Ed.). (1983). *Occupational therapy for physical dysfunction* (2nd ed.). Baltimore: Williams & Wilkins.

Chapter 20

Ethical Dilemmas and the Older Adult

Jeffrey L. Crabtree

Occupational therapists in gerontology face a unique twofold challenge: First, to understand the ethical implications of caring for older adults with chronic illness, and second, to discover ways of influencing public policy to ensure access to and appropriate levels of occupational therapy services in an aging society. This challenge results from the convergence of three powerful factors: (1) the daunting growth in both the number and proportion of the population aged 65 and over; (2) the positive correlation of chronic illnesses and increasing age, which rises to remarkably high levels in those 65 years and over (Jennings, Callahan, & Caplan, 1988); and (3) the correlation of advanced age and the physical or mental conditions that can have a severe impact on an older adult's competency (Caplan, 1985).

ETHICAL DILEMMAS IN GERIATRIC CARE

Biomedical ethicists have traditionally explored the physician's conduct in relationship to the patient. Little attention has been given to the family's or therapist's conduct. However, times have changed. As stated above, the unrelenting growth of the older population and the positive correlation of age with chronic disabilities that limit the individual's ability to behave independently place relatives of dependent older adults, occupational therapists, and other nonphysician health professionals squarely in the middle of a cluster of bioethical issues.

Occupational therapists face a wide range of choices in dealing with older patients and their families professionally. What turns some of these choices into ethical dilemmas is the existence of strong and equal moral support for two or more choices simultaneously. In an ethical dilemma, no matter which decision is made, one's actions will be desirable in some respects and undesirable in others (Beauchamp & Childress, 1983).

338

Ethical Principles

The study of ethics includes a number of principles that need to be discussed in order to better understand the ethical dilemmas faced by occupational therapists. First, the principle of *autonomy* defines the person as able to deliberate about available options and decisions, make a choice, and follow through with an action (Beauchamp & Childress, 1983).

The autonomous older adult, according to this principle, has the capability of gathering and comprehending information critical to sound decision making. This principle presumes the individual to be competent. The competent older adult, then, can either voluntarily consent to certain medical or social interventions or identify a representative or proxy to make these decisions.

Ethical dilemmas associated with this principle often involve the right to know the outcomes of treatment and right to refuse treatment (American Occupational Therapy Association [AOTA], 1988). For example, how much does the occupational therapist tell a dying patient about his disease when his wife does not want him to know he is dying? When an older adult becomes unable to drive safely, how does the occupational therapist protect that individual's autonomy and also protect society from an unsafe driver?

The principle of *beneficence* and the reciprocal principle of *nonmaleficence* require health professionals to contribute to the health and welfare of those they treat and to refrain from doing harm. A dilemma occurs when the health care professional's view of what is beneficial or harmful to the older patient is in conflict with the patient's view. In such circumstances, the patient may have one opinion, the family a different opinion, and the occupational therapist a third opinion. The term *paternalism* applies to those situations when the health care professional or the family override the wishes or decisions of the patient.

Cost-benefit analysis of programs and services is a way of comparing, for example, (1) the costs and benefits of providing community-based rehabilitation services and those of providing institutionalized services, or (2) the costs and benefits of occupational therapy services that help keep an older adult in the home and the costs and benefits of a life of institutionalization.

The principle of *justice* is associated with the notions of desert and fairness. If an older person, for example, deserves to be informed of available treatment options, then justice has been done when that person is informed (Beauchamp & Childress, 1983). Two-tiered health care systems in which occupational therapy services are available only to those who can pay for them are considered to be unjust by many. We tend to consider public policies to be fair and just when services are fairly distributed and when individuals receive deserved and needed services.

Understanding and applying these principles when providing occupational therapy services to older patients can help the therapist make decisions that are fair and equitable.

Factors that Challenge the Autonomy of Older Adults

While the dramatic aging of our population may well present the single most important challenge to the future of our society (Baker, 1988), aging alone does not challenge older patients' autonomy or create special ethical dilemmas for occupational therapists and other health care professionals.

The challenges come from factors associated with chronic care needs that have been found to be highly correlated with growing old. As Scanlon (1988) indicates, of the population 65–69 years of age, 13% need some kind of long-term care. Even more significant, of the population 85 years of age and over, 55% require some form of assistance.

There are three forces that can compromise older adults' ability to make reasonable and informed choices about their health care and thus lose some degree of autonomy: (1) the inability to perform activities such as activities of daily living, (2) the environment, and (3) society's response to older adults. Occupational therapists need to understand the relationship between these forces and older adults' autonomy if they are to make just decisions regarding the access of older adults to needed care, the level and scope of services to be offered, and the maintenance of older adults' autonomy and dignity.

Performance deficits resulting from chronic diseases, traumas, or other causes do not automatically put older adults at risk of losing their autonomy. We have all known fiercely autonomous and competent individuals who are physically challenged.

However, when mental and physical deficits begin to stack up to the point of forcing an individual to change the way daily activities must be done, the individual's self-confidence may become undermined. When dependence upon others preempts the individual's ability to choose when and how bathing or dressing are accomplished, the individual may feel a loss of control over his or her life. When, as a result of the individual's disabilities, others expect less, the individual may lose his or her sense of purpose and meaning in life. As Snow and Rogers (1985) expressed it, "These losses . . . raise issues of rights and responsibilities for the continuation of self-determining behavior" (p. 354).

Environment can play a critical role in bolstering the older adult's autonomy and in threatening it. According to Kiernat (1985), the consequences of a frail adult's physical and social environment may play a significant role in determining his or her level of independence.

The sick and frail elderly living in nursing homes, for example, often do not have the opportunity to dress or feed themselves. These activities are performed for them often because the baths or feedings need to be accomplished by a certain hour. To allow older adults to bathe or dress themselves may take too long. Furthermore, these individuals are often excluded from making decisions about their own health care simply because their efforts to make such decisions are ignored (Caplan, 1985).

The home, an environment that for decades may have been a safe and secure harbor that fostered an individual's competence and autonomy, can become a dangerous environment to a frail elder. The combination of undone repairs and intrinsic physical dangers (e.g., a bathtub or dark staircase), together with old habits of doing daily activities, may create an environment that now threatens the individual's competence and autonomy.

As an older adult's need for long-term care increases, so does the risk of losing autonomy. A significant contributor to this risk is society's response to the demographic imperative. As Scanlon (1988) put it, "Perhaps one of the most critical elements that will shape the future long-term care system will be the choices made regarding the socially acceptable or desired level of service and access" (p. 14).

Decisions made by Congress influence, if not reflect, what is socially acceptable or desired in our society. Several bills introduced in the 101st Congress provided long-term care services for the frail and dependent elderly in nursing homes. Virtually all of these bills defined eligibility for these services in terms of activity of daily living (ADL) deficits coupled with certain levels of cognitive impairment. Should one of these bills become law, it will establish, in effect, acceptable standards of access and levels of service.

Examples of society's reaction to increased demands for health care services are legion. Currently the federal government is working to identify and support private financing that can assist the rapidly growing population of older persons in paying for long-term care (Burke, 1988). Congress will likely establish a physician fee schedule for Medicare designed to limit the rapidly rising volume of physician services (Ginsburg, 1989). If such a fee schedule helps to limit the amount of services provided by physicians, the same sort of schedule could be applied to rehabilitation professionals such as occupational therapists. Arizona and Idaho officials are evaluating the effectiveness of state tax incentives for informal family caregivers (Hendrickson, 1988). Favorable findings could prompt other states to look for ways of offering financial support to family caregivers and redefine what institutional and noninstitutional services are acceptable and desired.

CURRENT BIOETHICAL THINKING

Over the past 2 decades, a body of bioethical thinking has developed that, according to Jennings, Callahan, and Caplan (1988), has become ingrained in health care delivery through such institutions as the courts, government regulating bodies, hospitals, and other health care facilities. Furthermore, they claim that this recent body of bioethical thinking, which they call "the autonomy paradigm" (p. 8), is becoming the framework health care professionals, ethicists, and policymakers will use to make health care policy decisions in the future.

The autonomy paradigm, as we will discover, is most relevant in the case of individuals who receive treatment for acute illnesses. It is not well suited for understanding the distinctly different chronic care issues, many of which are only indirectly related to health, involved in the treatment of the elderly. Yet in order to consider the ethical dilemmas that may arise when providing services to older adults, it is useful to discuss this body of ethical thinking.

The Autonomy Paradigm

According to Jennings, Callahan, and Caplan (1988), three interrelated concepts form the foundation of most contemporary bioethical thinking and constitute the autonomy paradigm. This paradigm includes the medical model of illness, the contractual model of medical care, and a way of thinking about an individual as unique and autonomous.

The medical model of illness assumes medicine's ability to successfully isolate the cause of an acute illness and cure the patient or compensate for any residual loss from the illness. This model is reductionist, since it attempts to reduce a disease to its most basic elements and relationships in order to understand and influence it (Kielhofner & Burke, 1983).

The contractual model of health care casts the provider in the role of an authority on health. The patient, a rational individual interested in personal well-being, voluntarily submits to the authority of the health care practitioner in order to regain health. The transient nature of acute illness and the brief abrogation of autonomy make collaboration with the health care professional on a short-term basis acceptable. Both partners in this situation have the shared goal of curing the disease and restoring the patient to health.

The third component of the autonomy paradigm assumes that the individual's interests and autonomy precede the need for medical help and are independent of the process of receiving that medical intervention. In other words, the individual is first and foremost an autonomous individual who, because of enlightened self-interest, chooses to utilize medical services when needed.

The Autonomy Paradigm Applied to Acute Care and Chronic Care

As stated earlier, the autonomy paradigm is poorly suited to provide a framework for making occupational therapy decisions regarding older adults whose chronic dependence on others is neither caused by a single organism nor temporary in nature and often encompasses housing, transportation, and many other non-medical problems.

A new way of framing ethical issues in long-term care is needed because of several remarkable differences between acute and chronic care. First, any older dependent adult, in order to find meaning and purpose in life and to maintain autonomy, needs to function as independently as possible in spite of chronic deficits. As long as these deficits are thought to be medical problems and the health care professional takes the role of an authority, the older patient is at risk of losing autonomy.

The older adult's functional status and sense of worth and purpose are not usually threatened as a result of an acute illness. The patient with an acute illness will recover within a reasonable period and will no longer require the services of health care professionals. By comparison, a long-term illness may necessitate medical and social intervention for decades and pose ongoing challenges to the patient's autonomy.

The level of family involvement in acute care tends to be minimal. For example, suppose a daughter transports her mother to the physician's office, talks to the physician about her mother's progress, and then takes her mother to the pharmacy. Although the daughter is being helpful and is staying informed, she is not an integral part of the care of her mother. In the case of an older adult with chronic disabilities, the family provides support at virtually all levels of care—from wound care to financial assistance to emotional support. In addition, the family will likely perform many of the dependent elder's ADLs and instrumental ADLs (e.g., shopping and banking) and make life and death decisions for the older family member.

Finally, health care and social service providers must recognize that older adults have the potential for personal growth and development throughout life (Rogers & Snow, 1985). By recognizing and supporting this human potential for growth and achievement at all stages of life, they can accept each older adult as a complete person who, despite chronic deficits, is a dynamic and productive member of society.

The long-term nature of the individual's deficit, the high degree of family involvement in care and services, the need for the older adult to be as functionally independent as possible to maintain a sense of self-worth, and the need to support human potential for growth and development throughout the entire life cycle demand a new way of thinking about the care of the frail and dependent elderly. (See Table 20-1 for a summary of the differences between acute and chronic care.)

TOWARD AN ETHICAL FRAMEWORK FOR CHRONIC CARE

The next phase in the evolution of bioethical thinking could be termed the *partnership model*. In this model, the dependent older adult and the family join in

Table 20-1 Comparison of Acute and Chronic Care

Acute Care	Chronic Care
By definition, the illness or deficits are time limited.	By definition, the illness or deficits are ongoing.
The provider emphasizes the diagnosis and the etiology of the illness (reductionistic).	The provider emphasizes the individual's adaptation and functioning despite the illness (holistic).
The services tend to use high technology.	The services tend to be high touch.
The provider views the older adult as a patient (in the paternalistic model) or as fiercely autonomous (in the autonomy paradigm).	The provider views the older adult and the family as partners in the caring and decision-making process.
A military metaphor is apt: The patient marshals resources to battle the illness.	A statesmanship metaphor is apt: The patient negotiates and makes compromises in order to find meaning in life despite the illness.
The provider places only modest demands on the family.	The provider places a demand on the family to participate thoroughly in ongoing care.
There is a narrow range of services, and the focus is on the illness.	There is a broad range of services, including medical and social services, and support is provided in areas such as housing, transportation, and employment.

an autonomous partnership that participates in the care and decision-making process.

The Partnership Model

An ethical framework that properly describes chronic care of older adults and helps to guide the decisions of occupational therapists and other health care professionals will address four critical issues: (1) the need of older adults to maintain autonomy in spite of deficits; (2) the temporal nature of chronic illnesses; (3) the inextricable involvement of family members in the care of older adults, including decision making; and (4) the potential for personal growth and development possessed by older adults throughout the final stages of life.

Furthermore, this framework should be broad enough in scope to encompass transportation, environment, housing, and other nonmedical issues that often attend the chronic illnesses of the aged.

The partnership model borrows from business law the concept of a legal association of two or more persons. A partnership in the business sense is an association of partners that makes each member "coprincipal and a general agent for . . . transacting partnership business" (Franscona et al., 1981, p. 679). A partnership, in this new ethical context, is not a master-servant or authority-patient relationship but a relationship that makes each member a coauthority and coequal in the caring and health care decision-making process.

As described in business law, each partner is an agent of the partnership and has both express and implied authority to act on behalf of the partnership. The partners "agree that one is to act on behalf of the other, subject to the other's control" (Franscona et al., 1981, p. 213).

The partnership model borrows the notion of agency in order to empower both the older adult and the family, which for purposes of this discussion can include individuals who are not kin to the older adult but have a significant relationship with that individual. Caplan (1985) said of the importance of such a relationship, "If health care providers make a sustained effort to involve family members early on in discussions with elderly patients about their care, then family members will be in a better position to act, not as surrogate decision-makers, but as what might be termed 'proxy amplifiers' " (p. 14).

In the partnership model, the older adult, as an agent of the partnership, may or may not be legally competent and may or may not be able to express the desire to be healthy and free of disease. Certainly, if the older adult is competent, he or she will want to exercise autonomy and actively exercise control regarding care decisions. If the older adult is incompetent and incapable of making important decisions about health care, the family, which is an agent of this partnership, must make those decisions.

Here is where the partnership model of ethics departs from the business partnership analogy. When one agent in the business partnership is incompetent, the partnership may be dissolved. But it is precisely at the point when the older adult becomes incapable of maintaining control or making necessary care decisions that the ethical partnership model is needed the most. It is at this point the family can step in and advocate for the older adult's needs.

The family, as an agent of the partnership, is a potential ally of the older adult. The family, more than any other partner, can be counted on to be supportive, to make reasonable decisions, and most of all, to carry out the wishes of the older adult when he or she is unable to act.

An example of the way this role can be formalized is California's durable power of attorney for health care, which is a legal document that an older adult can use to appoint a family member (or friend) to make health care decisions on his or her behalf in prescribed circumstances. The appointed family member can make all decisions about the older adult's health care and is subject only to the limitations specified in the document or imposed by law (Kato & Feder, 1988).

In this model, the occupational therapist (or any other health care provider) is considered to have expertise in certain areas of health care and certain social services but is not considered to be the single authority to whom the older adult or family should come with all medical or social problems. Each provider is essentially a third party with which, as in the autonomy paradigm, the autonomous partnership contracts for needed health care services.

The Role of Occupational Therapy in the Partnership Model

Further exploration of the partnership model requires an examination of the occupational therapist's role in supporting the rights of the older adult, in supporting the family's ability to become a fair and effective partner, and in helping to create just long-term care public policies.

Supporting the Older Adult as Partner

Occupational therapy is well suited to help the chronically dependent become as independent as possible in the least restrictive environment available. Johnson and Kielhofner (1983) emphasize the special contribution occupational therapy can make to the chronically dependent:

> Occupational therapists can be active in helping the client or patient and their families (*sic*) maintain a balanced level of activity, including work, play, rest, and leisure. Therapists assist persons to organize their daily activities, schedules, and routines to maintain physical and emotional endurance and strength while providing meaning and satisfaction and a continuing sense of competence and contribution to family, neighborhood, and other relevant social systems. (p. 190)

Successful occupational therapy treatment generally supports an older adult's autonomy. Occupational therapists need to ensure a successful outcome, however, by considering such ethical issues as beneficence, justice, and the patient's autonomy when developing treatment plans and assessing the effectiveness and quality of occupational therapy programs.

Supporting the Family as Partner

In addition to the direct services offered the older adult, the occupational therapist should facilitate the family members' use of their valuable experience and expertise in caregiving. For example, while treating the older adult, whether in the clinic, the home, or a daycare center, the therapist should include family members in the therapy and decision making. This allows joint identification of the potential limits of the older adult's autonomy, helps the family members feel they belong to a true partnership, and validates the expertise they have acquired in helping care for the older adult. Furthermore, it develops a climate of trust and helps the older adult and family members gain respect for and an understanding of each other (Jennings, Callahan, & Caplan, 1988).

The occupational therapist, in this model, must facilitate the family's acceptance of proxy consent for a dependent adult who is unable to make decisions. The family is most likely able to accurately infer what decisions the older adult would have made (Dworkin, 1988). By taking on the role of proxy consent, the family may be able to reflect the elder's authentic desires rather than be party to the denial of his or her autonomy and authority (Caplan, 1985).

It is widely recognized that about three-quarters of all older adults requiring long-term care live in the community. These individuals are able to live in the community primarily because of the untrained and unpaid assistance of family and friends. Given the chronic nature of the frail individual's needs, caregivers are faced with years of daily caregiving. It is unlikely that many of these caregivers come in contact with occupational therapists, yet the profession has much to offer them.

Although family caregivers are able to cite benefits of caregiving, there are many stresses as well. Sources of stress include the limitations placed on a caregiver's personal life, the competing demands from family and employment, and emotional and physical demands placed on the caregiver. The combination of these stressors "creates various levels of emotional, physical, financial and familial strain for informal caregivers" (Select Committee on Aging, 1987, p. 30).

Occupational therapists must discover ways to provide services to informal family caregivers. Perhaps an informal caregiver's sense of occupational achievement and competency has a bearing on the quality of the care provided the frail family member. Furthermore, there may be a correlation between the sense of occupational achievement and competency and the degree to which the caregiver strives to uphold the autonomy of the aged adult.

Health care partnerships need to be formally explored. Through research into these relationships, occupational therapists will better understand the clinical and ethical implications of having families care for frail older adults.

Toward Just and Fair Public Policies

In addition to providing direct services to older adults and support to families, occupational therapists have another important role: influencing the development of just and fair long-term care public policies.

The home health benefit established by the Medicare program defines an individual's access to services and the amount of services that will be offered. For some years prior to 1981, occupational therapy was not covered under the Medicare program. In 1981, Congress modified the program to include occupational therapy services when the beneficiary qualifies for home health services based on the need for physical therapy, speech therapy, or skilled nursing services (Scott, 1988). Occupational therapy is not what is called a qualifying service for home health benefits.

When public policies exclude or limit occupational therapy services, occupational therapists lose the opportunity to provide services to the older adults who need them. Just and fair public policies that value occupational therapy's contribution to the care of the frail and dependent elderly might be likened to tickets sold for a dance. If you don't have one, you can't dance.

Making a difference in public policy will require vision and concerted effort on the part of the profession. Individual therapists' efforts, especially at the clinical level and without support of other therapists, will have little impact.

A careful examination of the profession's strengths and weaknesses measured against the demographic imperative of increasing numbers of elderly could lead therapists to conclude that the practice of gerontic occupational therapy is at "the very heart of our profession—the balance of work and play and self-care and the interaction of these elements with the health of the person" (Hasselkus & Kiernat, 1989, p. 79). It is with that sense of purpose and conviction that occupational therapists must enter into the public dialogue and discover ways to influence public policy.

Hasselkus and Kiernat (1989) further assert that occupational therapists have a leadership role to play in the care of the aging but point out that if they are to accept this role they will need to be proactive rather than reactive in all dimensions of their practice. This must include producing and sharing research that is relevant to health care for older adults.

The public policy–making process has many points of entry. Individual therapists can provide Congressional delegates with thorough and well-reasoned arguments in favor of targeted legislation. Medical schools can generate significant research in the area of geriatrics and offer a greater number of opportunities for students to become effective practitioners in the field of gerontology. The American Occupational Therapy Association can capitalize on opportunities to place occupational therapists on national committees dealing with public policy, and it can also support members of Congress who are active in the struggle to provide comprehensive health and human services to older Americans.

No matter how they exercise their leadership, occupational therapists, by actively participating in the public policy dialogue, can help respond to Illich's (1977) warning that "once a society is so organized that medicine can transform people into patients because they are unborn, newborn, menopausal, or at some other 'age of risk,' the population inevitably loses some of its autonomy to its healers" (p. 72).

CONCLUSION

The continued increase in the number and proportion of older adults in our society poses serious challenges to the occupational therapy profession and its practitioners. These challenges include the need to understand the ethical implications of providing chronic care to the older adults in our society and the need to influence public policy to ensure access to and appropriate levels of needed occupational therapy services.

Current bioethical thinking tends to view the patient as someone who is autonomous and who temporarily submits him- or herself, out of enlightened self-interest, to the authority of health care experts. The short-term nature of acute illness, the emphasis on high technology, and a reductionist approach to acute care make this paradigm applicable to the active, healthy older adult. However, it falls short of providing a guide for occupational therapists caring for chronically dependent elders.

The positive correlation between advancing age and the need for chronic care places older adults at risk of losing their autonomy. The partnership model, an ethical framework that places the family and the frail or dependent older adult in a partnership, seems to have utility for understanding the ethical issues of chronic care. This model is based on the belief that human development is possible throughout the entire life cycle. It recognizes the critical role of the family in caring for the older adult and identifies the role of the occupational therapist and other health care providers as basically supportive.

Occupational therapists also have a role in developing fair and equitable public policies. For example, more research is needed to understand the relationship between occupational competence and the effectiveness of family caregivers in caring for dependent family members and upholding their autonomy. The combination of meaningful research and active participation in public policy dialogue will allow the profession to help ensure that older adults receive the chronic care they deserve.

In an era when the demand for chronic care is increasing and the resources to provide that care are not keeping pace, an ethical framework such as the partnership model may help occupational therapists and other care providers make daily decisions that help to promote the dignity and autonomy of older adults.

REFERENCES

American Occupational Therapy Association. (1988). *Occupational therapy code of ethics*. Rockville, MD: Author.

Baker, G.T. (1988). Aging and the aged in America: Introduction. In Select Committee on Aging, House of Representatives, and Special Committee on Aging, U.S. Senate, *Legislative agenda for an aging society: 1988 and beyond* (pp. 13–17). Washington, DC: Government Printing Office.

Beauchamp, T.L., & Childress, J.F. (1983). *Principles of biomedical ethics* (2nd ed.). New York: Oxford University Press.

Burke, T.R. (1988). Long-term care: The public role and private initiatives. *Health Care Financing Review* (Annual Supplement), pp. 1–5.

Caplan, A.L. (1985). Let wisdom find a way: The concept of competency in the care of the elderly. *Generations, 10*, 10–14.

Dworkin, G. (1988). *The theory and practice of autonomy.* New York: Cambridge University Press.

Franscona, J.L., Conry, E.J., Ferrera, G.R., Lantry, T.L., Shaw, B.M., Siedel, G.J., III, Spiro, G.W., & Wolfe, A.D. (1981). *Business law.* Dubuque, IA: W.C. Brown.

Ginsburg, P.B. (1989). Physician payment policy in the 101st Congress. *Health Affairs, 8*, 5–20.

Hasselkus, B.R., & Kiernat, J.M. (1989). Nationally speaking: Not by age alone: Gerontology as a specialty in occupational therapy. *American Journal of Occupational Therapy, 43*, 77–79.

Hendrickson, M.C. (1988). State tax incentives for persons giving informal care to the elderly. *Health Care Financing Review* (Annual Supplement), pp. 123–128.

Illich, I. (1977). *Medical nemesis: The expropriation of health.* New York: Bantam Books.

Jennings, B., Callahan, D., & Caplan, A.L. (1988). *Ethical challenges of chronic illness.* Briarcliff Manor, NY: Hastings Center.

Johnson, J., & Kielhofner, G. (1983). Occupational therapy in the health care system of the future. In G. Kielhofner (Ed.), *Health through occupation: Theory and practice in occupational therapy* (pp. 179–195). Philadelphia: F.A. Davis.

Kato & Feder (Law Firm). (1988). *What you should know about durable power of attorney for health care.* Unpublished manuscript.

Kielhofner, G., & Burke, J.P. (1983). The evolution of knowledge and practice in occupational therapy: Past, present, and future. In G. Kielhofner (Ed.), *Health through occupation: Theory and practice in occupational therapy* (pp. 3–54). Philadelphia: F.A. Davis.

Kiernat, J.M. (1985). Environmental aspects affecting health. In G.H. Maguire (Ed.), *Care of the elderly: A health team approach* (pp. 41–51). Boston: Little, Brown.

Rogers, J.C., & Snow, T.L. (1985). Later adulthood. In G. Kielhofner (Ed.), *A model of human occupation: Theory and application* (pp. 123–133). Baltimore: Williams & Wilkins.

Scanlon, W.J. (1988). A perspective on long-term care for the elderly. *Health Care Financing Review* (Annual Supplement), pp. 7–15.

Scott, S.J. (Ed.). (1988). *Payment for occupational therapy services.* Rockville, MD: American Occupational Therapy Association.

Select Committee on Aging, U.S. House of Representatives. (1987). *Exploding the myths: Caregiving in America.* Comm. Pub. No. 99–611. Washington, DC: Government Printing Office.

Snow, T.L., & Rogers, J.C. (1985). Dysfunctional older adults. In G. Kielhofner (Ed.), *A model of human occupation: Theory and application* (pp. 352–370). Baltimore: Williams & Wilkins.

Index

A

F